Praise for *Bridging Worlds*

"Fishkin's book is a fascinating and completely original study of one of the most difficult to understand figures in medieval Jewish thought and literature, and in fact the scholarship on him is mostly split between scholars of literature, philosophy, and exegesis. Fishkin's book is the first attempt to bring these different worlds together. What emerges is a singular figure whose philosophy and biblical exegesis informs his literature and whose literature serves to spread and develop ideas found throughout the Maimonidean tradition. In other words, Immanuel not only innovates in the way he adapts vernacular literary forms to Hebrew but he is also original in the way he uses poetry and literature to teach, popularize, and reflect on philosophical ideas and debates."

—James Theodore Robinson, Caroline E. Haskell Professor, University of Chicago Divinity School and the University of Chicago

"For centuries, Immanuel of Rome has been pigeonholed as merely a comic, sensual poet, but that narrow image of him has been built on a selective reading of his literary production. With *Bridging Worlds*, Fishkin offers an important corrective by examining his oeuvre more fully."

—Fabian Alfie, professor of Italian, University of Arizona

"This book is the first attempt to produce a holistic reading of the oeuvre of Immanuel of Rome, most famously the stunning and sometimes ribald poetry and prose of his *Maḥbarot*, but also the thousands of surviving manuscript pages of biblical exegesis as well as a number of short works. By reading across these genres, especially by probing the tantalizing cross-references through which Immanuel bridged his literary and philosophical-exegetical works, Fishkin has produced a work that fully situates Immanuel in an intellectual world informed by Iberian Hebrew literature, Maimonidean and Scholastic thought, Latin rhetoric, and Italian vernacular literature."

—Jonathan Decter, Edmond J. Safra Professor of Sephardic studies, Brandeis University

"Fishkin's *Bridging Worlds* is definitely worth the long wait for a book dedicated to Immanuel of Rome. Brilliantly written, groundbreaking in its insights, this consequential book provides a poignant display of the art of the fourteenth-century master of Hebrew erudition and literature, providing a significant contribution to fill the lacuna left by Hebraists."

—Tovi Bibring, professor, Bar-Ilan University

"*Bridging Worlds* is the first major study in years—and the first ever in English—of Immanuel of Rome, the fourteenth-century author of one of the most popular works of premodern Hebrew fiction, the *Maḥbarot* ('Compositions'). It is the first study in any language to draw extensively on Immanuel's Bible commentaries, which were much admired in their time, but which have attracted little attention in modern scholarship and largely remain unpublished. Focusing on a chapter of the *Maḥbarot* with the Dantesque title of 'A Tale of Heaven and Hell,' Fishkin illuminates the *Maḥbarot* from the commentaries and the commentaries from the *Maḥbarot* and shows how Immanuel's charming, sometimes even salacious fiction relates to the philosophical traditions of Maimonides and of Christian scholasticism. *Bridging Worlds* shows Immanuel to be not merely an entertainer but a serious intellectual representative of his time."

—Raymond P. Scheindlin, professor emeritus of medieval Hebrew literature, Jewish Theological Seminary of America

Bridging Worlds

BRIDGING WORLDS

Poetry and Philosophy in the Works of Immanuel of Rome

Dana W. Fishkin

Wayne State University Press
Detroit

© 2023 by Wayne State University Press, Detroit, Michigan 48201. All rights reserved. No part of this book may be reproduced without formal permission.

ISBN 9780814350355 (paperback)
ISBN 9780814350362 (hardcover)
ISBN 9780814350379 (e-book)

Library of Congress Control Number: 2023930082

On cover: Detail from *Maḥberot Immanuel*, manuscript page, Immanuel of Rome. Image courtesy of the Ministry of Culture—Complesso Monumentale della Pilotta, Palatina Library, Parma, Italy.

Grateful acknowledgment is made to the Leonard and Harriette Simons Endowed Family Fund for the generous support of the publication of this volume.

האיגוד העולמי למדעי היהדות ע"ר
WORLD UNION OF JEWISH STUDIES R.A.

Publication of this book was supported by a grant from the World Union of Jewish Studies.

Wayne State University Press rests on Waawiyaataanong, also referred to as Detroit, the ancestral and contemporary homeland of the Three Fires Confederacy. These sovereign lands were granted by the Ojibwe, Odawa, Potawatomi, and Wyandot Nations, in 1807, through the Treaty of Detroit. Wayne State University Press affirms Indigenous sovereignty and honors all tribes with a connection to Detroit. With our Native neighbors, the press works to advance educational equity and promote a better future for the earth and all people.

Wayne State University Press
Leonard N. Simons Building
4809 Woodward Avenue
Detroit, Michigan 48201-1309

Visit us online at wsupress.wayne.edu.

For Yudi

כי עזה כמות אהבה קשה כשאול קנאה

For love is as fierce as death,
Passion is mighty as *She'ol*

—Song of Songs 8:6

CONTENTS

Acknowledgments **ix**

Introduction: Assembling the Corpus **1**

Part I: The Historical and Intellectual Contexts

1. Of Fallacy and Fraud: Immanuel's "Biography" **21**
2. Between the Eagle and the Lion **39**
3. *Shalom* and *Shelemut* (Peace and Perfection): Immanuel on the Ethical Life **59**

Part II: *Maḥberet Ha-Tofet V'Ha-Eden*

4. Navigating the Afterlife **85**
5. The World of the Body **103**
6. The World of the Mind **129**

Conclusion: What Is an Author? **155**

Appendix: English Translation of *Maḥberet Ha-Tofet V'Ha-Eden* **163**

Notes **209**

Bibliography **247**

Index **265**

ACKNOWLEDGMENTS

A man once told me that writing a book is like giving birth to a baby. While there are analogies to be drawn between the two processes, my experience has been such that producing a book has proved itself far more challenging than having babies. Recognizing that both authorship and parenthood take some skill and a lot more luck, I want to acknowledge the villages that have helped me do both these things over the past several years.

My teachers and mentors have been supportive in unimaginable ways. At NYU, professors Brigitte Bedos-Rezak, Robert Chazan, John Freccero, Alfred Ivry, and Penelope Johnson introduced me to new ways of seeing the medieval period. My earliest exploration of Immanuel's works was in a class taught by Brigitte Bedos-Rezak, while John Freccero guided me through Dante's *Inferno*. Fellow PhD students, and now friends, Flora Cassen, Yechiel Schur, Josh Teplitsky, and Katja Vehlow, continue to provide much-needed camaraderie and support.

My study of Immanuel's poetry, however, changed forever after an enriching week at the Shalom Spiegel Institute of Medieval Hebrew poetry under the leadership of Professor Raymond Scheindlin. Since that fateful week, Ray has crucially supported my work on Immanuel in myriad ways, and this project is a direct result of his patient guidance and masterful pedagogy. Granting me the opportunity to create a Spiegel seminar entirely devoted to Immanuel, Ray facilitated some of the most fruitful scholarly interactions I have ever experienced. Whenever I read Hebrew poetry, Ray's voice will forever be the one in my head. That Immanuel seminar also introduced me to Jim Robinson, another generous and thoughtful individual who continues to serve as a patient guide to the world of medieval philosophy and Jewish thought. The intensity of this writing process has, at times, left me with feelings of despair similar to those expressed by Immanuel's literary character in *Maḥberet Ha-Tofet V'Ha-Eden*. In those moments Jim has been a veritable Daniel, a reassuring and helpful mentor who continually reminds me of Immanuel's importance in the world of medieval Jewish thought. Other seminar participants, including Rachel B. Katz and Isabelle Levy, have since become trusted colleagues and good friends. I thank my codirector, Jonathan Decter, for his hard work and partnership.

Numerous colleagues have offered invaluable advice, and I am especially grateful to Benjamin Gampel and Ephraim Kanarfogel for their candid insights and constant encouragement. A silver lining of the pandemic, my Zoom study sessions with Lucy Pick and Rachel Katz have given me tremendous support throughout the final stages of this book. I am so grateful to the leadership at Touro University, President Alan Kadish, and to Deans Michael Shmidman and Marian Stoltz-Loike, who always provide encouragement and support for my scholarship. Research for this book was funded by a presidential research grant from Touro, for which I am grateful. My colleagues Zvi Kaplan, Yael Krumbein, Susan Weissman, and Matt Zarnowiecki have always been available to offer answers, advice, and support.

If writing a book is akin to giving birth, I could not have asked for a better trio of doulas than Rachel Furst, Marc Herman, and Maud Kozodoy. Their patience and generosity have truly helped *Bridging Worlds* come into being. I treasure our meetings and look forward to celebrating your forthcoming books with you. A special thank you to Gillian Steinberg for her patient encouragement and constant presence. Thank you to Alexander Trotter for the index. Publication of this book was supported by a grant from the World Union of Jewish Studies, and I am grateful to the nominating committee for their vote of confidence. It has been a pleasure to work with the team at Wayne State University Press, and I am grateful to Marie Sweetman, Carrie Teefey, Mindy Brown, Kelsey Giffin, and Emily Gauronskas for all their hard work and dedication.

This book's title reflects actions that, in my estimation, Immanuel of Rome engages in to produce his own work, *Maḥberot Immanuel*. On further reflection, however, I realize that the title *Bridging Worlds* aptly fits my own life as well. This book has been written in "scholarly spaces" like libraries and archives as much as in "life spaces" like amusement parks, sports games, and birthday parties. I am indebted to the helpers who so lovingly continue to care for my children: Zehavit Milikowski, Nadia Moses, Emy Estevez, and Lesly Diaz. My children have grown up with a textual sibling that demands much of their mother's attention and devotion. As I attempt to bridge worlds, I am forever indebted to my family for all the love, encouragement, and support extended to me throughout these years. A heartfelt thank you to my Fishkin crew: Rachel Fishkin and Izzy Garti, Yosi and Lisa, Tami and Jeff, Aviva and Nochi, Shoshana and Daniel, Orlee and Ashi, Menachem and Elizabeth, and Libby and Nathaniel. Merav and Mike, Tamara and Jason, and Gilad and Olivia, you have been my personal cheerleading squad. Thank you to my parents, Barry and Shula Wenig, for always believing in me. Without my children, Reuven, Sydney, Coby, Gabriel, and Liam, I would have spent my days immersed solely in matters of hell and heaven. Thank you for pulling me out of there occasionally to remind me of the truly important things in life. I dedicate this book to my partner, Yudi, who in a heartbeat would traverse hell and heaven for me and our family.

A note about Immanuel's title and chapter titles is in order to prevent confusion over variant spellings. When Iberian Jewish authors translated the Arabic literary *maqama* form, they coined a new Hebrew term, "*Maḥberet*" (Composition), for it. Yet, medieval authors use the term *Maḥberet* rather loosely, often referring to individual chapters within a work or to an entire work itself. Since the plural form of *Maḥberet* is "*Maḥbarot*," this book uses the capitalized version to refer to Immanuel's complete anthology and to distinguish it from individual chapters (*maḥberet*) or several chapters (*maḥbarot*). As the centerpiece of this book, the final chapter of Immanuel's anthology is distinguished with a capitalized title as *Maḥberet Ha-Tofet V'Ha-Eden*. To make matters more confusing, however, the anthology has also been characterized as Immanuel's anthology and this is called *Maḥberot Immanuel*. The alternate spelling reflects a grammatical change that occurs in Hebrew when one noun containing a particular vowel is modified by another noun.

INTRODUCTION

Assembling the Corpus

Rabbi Joseph Karo (1488–1575), author of the most influential early modern compendium of Jewish law, was no fan of secular literature. His 1565 *Shulḥan Arukh* ("The Set Table") rules that books of parables and historical chronicles should be avoided, certainly on the holy Sabbath and during the week as well. But of all the forbidden books, Karo names but one, what he dubs "Immanuel's book," better known as *Maḥberot Immanuel* ("Immanuel's Compositions").[1] This lengthy compilation of love poetry and fanciful tales by the fourteenth-century Italian Jew Immanuel of Rome remained popular enough to attract Karo's ire some two hundred years after its author's death. And Karo's ban, as many book bans do, failed: *Maḥberot Immanuel* continued to attract attention well into the nineteenth and twentieth centuries.[2] Most popular of all is the closing chapter of this work, a guided tour of heaven and hell that gained Immanuel the moniker "the Jewish Dante." However, Karo's ban in certain ways did succeed, helping shape the image of Immanuel and of *Maḥberot Immanuel* as "secular" poetry that should be judged primarily for its literary and entertainment value. But a holistic reading of Immanuel's corpus—far larger than just these poems—underscores just how inaccurate his reputation is. When one reads the whole of Immanuel's writings, it becomes clear that even his next-worldly tour is, in fact, a complex moral tale, one that imparts the values of a fourteenth-century Jewish intellectual in new and exciting ways.

In addition to his *Maḥberot Immanuel*, a varied anthology that includes so much more than erotic verse, Immanuel of Rome wrote numerous biblical commentaries, works of Hebrew grammar, and collections of homilies. When one adds in his Italian poems, mostly sonnets, Immanuel emerges as one of the most diverse late medieval Jewish intellectuals. Yet Immanuel has never merited serious consideration as a multidimensional thinker who consciously crafted parallels and intertextual links between his poetry and his biblical commentaries. This book advocates for a complete reading of Immanuel's entire oeuvre. In so doing it offers more than just a long-awaited corrective to Immanuel's intellectual biography. Through a new reading of Immanuel's celestial tour, *Maḥberet Ha-Tofet V'Ha-Eden* ("A Tale of Hell and Eden"), it uncovers a didactic morality tale, an accessible narrative that disseminates philosophical ideas about ethics, sin, and immortality in the guise of fictional, but realistic, characters and plot details. This mixture of poetry and prose establishes Immanuel's literary persona as an authoritative messenger, a man who is divinely appointed to encourage the multitudes to repent and attain perfection. The *Maḥberet*'s ethical imperative can be understood only in the world that created it, the spiritually vibrant late medieval Italian peninsula. While *Bridging Worlds* focuses on one chapter of Immanuel's poetic anthology, this case study offers varied and rich insights into Immanuel's authorial motives as he engaged with the dynamic intellectual culture of the fourteenth century broadly and with Christian penitential movements and ideas about the afterlife in the late medieval Italian ambience specifically.

An unintended effect of the *Shulḥan Arukh*'s ban, arguably, has been the preservation and commemoration of a work that might otherwise have been consigned to the dustbin of history. While *Maḥberot Immanuel* is a unique work in the annals of Jewish literature, one that offers a window into the culture of medieval Italian Jews, it might be regarded as a limited and very local source from a peripheral medieval Jewish community, preserved only by the lure of a prohibition. *Bridging Worlds*, however, demonstrates that *Maḥberot Immanuel* is anything but a limited and local text. Jews of course inhabited the Italian peninsula since antiquity, with a long history of composing literary texts—both liturgical and secular—in Hebrew. In many ways *Maḥberot Immanuel* represents another link in the chain of that tradition, with unique inflections of its particular historical moment. Synergies between *Maḥberot Immanuel* and the Hebrew poetry of Iberia on the one hand and *Maḥberet Ha-Tofet V'Ha-Eden* and Dante Alighieri's (1265–1321) *Divine Comedy* on the other reveal the ways in which ideas and conventions traveled around the Jewish communities of western Europe. This collection also illuminates the complexity of minority identity in the Italian peninsula, as Jews and Christians express shared values and overlapped approaches to universal questions. At a time when western European Jewish communities experienced antagonism and opposition, *Maḥberot Immanuel* reminds us that Jews and Christians could still dialogue, in person and in writing. *Bridging Worlds* maintains that this case study has larger implications for our understanding of cross-cultural and interreligious exchange in the late medieval period.

Maḥberot Immanuel

Let us then dive into the world that produced *Maḥberot Immanuel*. The "Compositions of Immanuel" consists of twenty-eight chapters in rhymed prose interspersed with verse poetry, modeled on the Arabic *maqama* genre.[3] Originating in the Near East, *maqamat* were widely known for their fictive quality, although some authors embellished the tales with famous personae and contemporary characters.[4] The *maḥberet* (pl. *maḥbarot*), a prosimetrical composition that mixed rhymed prose and metered verse, developed by Andalusian Hebrew authors, flourished in twelfth-century Iberia.[5] Works like Judah Al-Harizi's *Sefer Taḥkemoni*, Jacob ben Eleazar's *Sefer Ha-Meshalim*, and Solomon Ibn Saqbel's *Neum Asher Ben Yehudah* experimented with popular Arabic literary *maqama* form, with its characteristic features that included stock characters (a pair of roving interlocutors), a travel narrative, and a didactic flavor.[6] While the genre likely entertained audiences with its witty content, Hebrew *maḥbarot* were studded with biblical allusions, puns, and extratextual references, a technique known as *shibuts*, to showcase an author's erudition in traditional Jewish texts.[7]

Maḥberot Immanuel is rich and varied, as the roguish pair—Immanuel and his patron (*Ha-Sar*, The Nobleman)—embark on endless adventures. Not all the experiences and musings are humorous or provocative, and Immanuel often reflects on somber topics like the soul, the human condition, the cruelty of fate, and the trap of materialism. Philosophical jargon is peppered throughout the narrative prose and rhymed poems, which call God "the First Cause," mention the cosmic spheres and intelligences, and allude to a conjunction between the human rational intellect and the agent intellect, considered the lowest of the cosmic intelligences and the source of universal truth. Both Immanuel's *Maḥbarot* and his biblical commentaries display the fundamental influence of the Aristotelian philosophical tradition as shaped by Hellenistic and Arabic interpreters and synthesized with the Neoplatonic philosophy emergent from Christian Scholastic circles in the Italian peninsula. In short, his writings reflect the multifaceted intellectual currents of his day.

The conceit of Immanuel's book lies in his concern for his own reputation, particularly as he recounts that other poets had claimed his work as their own or attributed inferior poetry to him, leading Immanuel to fear that his brand had been tainted. The drama is resolved by a generous patrician who suggests that Immanuel anthologize his poems, writing connective prose about two traveling interlocutors to remold the poetry and prose into a literary unit, like Al-Harizi's *Sefer Taḥkemoni*.[8] This patrician's generosity extends well beyond his purported financial contribution: He becomes Immanuel's narrative wingman, known only by the epithet "*Ha-Sar*" (the nobleman). The two consistent characters, Immanuel and the nobleman, maintain a tenuous relationship throughout the tales of the first twenty-seven *maḥbarot* as they challenge each other, laugh together, and quarrel over women. By the final chapter, *Maḥberet Ha-Tofet V'Ha-Eden*, the *Sar* character disappears, leaving Immanuel to traverse the paths of hell and heaven alone. Broken and weeping, Immanuel's character is relieved to find an angelic guide named Daniel.

The Guide Figure

In addition to the abrupt change of setting from terrestrial Italy to the otherworldly realms, the replacement of the unnamed *Sar* with a well-known prophetic guide in *Maḥberet Ha-Tofet V'Ha-Eden* signals a boundary between the previous *maḥbarot* and the final chapter. The figure of the celestial guide is a common motif in both Jewish and non-Jewish literature, and Immanuel engages multiple traditions when choosing the character of Daniel as the divine proxy motivating his journey. Yet it is rare to find guide characters in earlier Jewish literature besides the traditional rabbinic figure of Rabbi Joshua ben Levi (ca. 3rd c. CE) or Elijah, the prophet.[9] Against convention, Immanuel must have chosen the character of Daniel for a specific purpose, which has drawn scholars from different disciplinary approaches into fierce debate.[10] Some view Daniel's character as an ode to Immanuel's Italian muse since "Daniel" is phonetically reminiscent of "Dante" in Hebrew; others go to great lengths to identify a historical Daniel who was important to Immanuel.[11] The link between Immanuel and Dante, and the impetus to extract historical or biographical information from *Maḥberot Immanuel*, reflect dominant scholarly approaches to the study of Immanuel and his works. One of this book's interventions is to utilize Immanuel's philosophically inflected commentaries, rather than relying on readings of Dante or Immanuel's biography, as a key to his poetry, particularly since Immanuel's biblical allusions consistently enrich the fictive narrative and bolster his authority as a narrator, especially in *Maḥberet Ha-Tofet V'Ha-Eden*.

When analyzing the celestial guide, for example, no earlier, positivistic studies have considered the significance of the biblical book of Daniel, which contains the only scriptural reference to any form of afterlife or the role of the biblical Daniel as a seer within the Maimonidean tradition. Daniel's visions, which Immanuel mines for both imagery and language, add a prophetic aspect and otherworldly realism to his journey tale, exemplified by the initial exchange between Immanuel's literary persona and his guide, Daniel. At the outset of *Maḥberet Ha-Tofet V'Ha-Eden*, Immanuel begs his guide to satisfy him "from the streams of your Edenic delight," a citation from Psalm 36, which contrasts God's merciful treatment of his creations with the pettiness of evil men tempted by transgression. Immanuel interprets this psalm as an affirmation of God's involvement in the world, which stands in direct contrast to the misdirected notion that God's power extends only until the sphere of the moon, precluding divine involvement in sublunar human affairs. Citing this psalm, Immanuel argues that divine involvement in the world is evident through God's physical nourishment of both humans and beasts, and the spiritual sustenance extended to man by divine emanation. Immanuel interprets Psalms 36:9 ("they feast on the rich fare of your house . . . you let them drink from the streams of your delight") as proof that God provides spiritual rewards for man's rational intellect after death via cosmic emanation of the agent intellect. Immanuel's injection of philosophically pregnant verses from his allegorical reading of Psalm 36 into his literary journey signals a methodology that embeds complex philosophical ideas into a more accessible literary narrative. The appreciation of Immanuel's intertextual technique enriches readers' understanding of this *maḥberet*, transforming it from an aesthetic delight into a didactic morality tale; an accessible narrative to disseminate philosophical ideas about ethics, sin, and immortality in an entertaining and engaging otherworldly tour. A general principle might be extracted from this small example: Immanuel's important intertextual practice is easily overlooked without more knowledge about his exegetical corpus.

Philosophical Exegesis

While Immanuel is best known as a poet with tendencies for sarcasm, irreverence, humor, and even the burlesque, his philosophically oriented biblical commentaries—which significantly outweigh his poetry in their breadth and length—leave a different impression. The opinion of one eighteenth-century rabbi, Hayyim Joseph David Azulai (1724–1806), that the book of Proverbs should be studied only with Immanuel's commentary, indicates that Immanuel's exegesis was known and even celebrated.[12] Immanuel's commentaries on wisdom literature—Proverbs and Song of Songs—were his most popular exegetical writings; commentaries on Job, Psalms, Lamentations, Ruth, Esther, and parts of the Pentateuch and Ecclesiastes each exist in a single copy.[13]

Immanuel's commentaries must be read in light of a longer Jewish tradition. In the wake of Maimonides' *The Guide of the Perplexed*, thirteenth-century Provence witnessed the birth of a new exegetical genre, the philosophical commentary.[14] As opposed to the freestanding philosophical treatise, this type of work presents a philosophical program attached to the biblical text, infusing the verses, characters, and words of the Bible with speculative significance.[15] The symbolism identified by Maimonides and extrapolated by his diverse Provençal, Iberian, and Italian followers invests traditional terminology with philosophical import, fostering what has been called a "Maimonidean allegorical lexicon" as well as sustained commentaries on complete biblical books.[16] Like other post-Maimonidean scholars who explicated biblical books to reveal an esoteric layer of meaning related to philosophic and scientific concepts, Immanuel refracts biblical images and narratives through philosophical and scientific lenses, advancing the deepest secrets of the universe as encoded in the stories and verses of the Bible. Where Immanuel's lengthy biblical commentaries reveal his mastery of rationalistic philosophy, language, and semiotics, those resonances appear frequently in his *Maḥbarot* as well.

The belief that the Bible contains an esoteric core of truths accessible only to trained initiates (i.e., truths consistent with medieval philosophy and science) indirectly served medieval Jewish rationalists as a mechanism with which to validate philosophical or scientific theories. This belief also assumes a multidimensional audience, including those who read scripture literally. Like Maimonides and his followers, Immanuel perceives the biblical text as simultaneously targeting different audiences. In the introduction to his commentary on Proverbs he explains, "The literal story and the core of all these parables are yielding. The literal details aid in the improvement of the popular collective and the core aids those who comprehend them to gain the truth of their matters."[17] To this end Immanuel's commentaries offer multiple readings of scripture, ranging from the literal and grammatical to philosophical allegory, and including citation of the Aramaic Targum in his commentaries on the Pentateuch.

Immanuel frequently cites an exemplar of his exegetical methodology, attempting to demonstrate the paradigm of multiple modes of reading and exegesis through the verse about the four rivers emergent from Eden (Genesis 2:10). He explains:

> He [i.e., God] disclosed the locations of the aforementioned rivers for a reason, since the entire Genesis narrative reflects matters as they simply are, as well as their wondrous secrets that cannot be imagined. In order that a person should not say that the matter of creation did not happen, as is plainly stated, but rather it is an allegory of esoteric matters, Scripture recalled the names of the rivers and their locations. For they are famous and rivers well-known to all. Even though the narrative of the Garden of Eden and the rivers that flow from it allude to esoteric matters, nevertheless the details are as they simply appear. There is a Garden of Eden on Earth and those rivers flow from there, and yet they are also an allegory for divine matters as we will mention.[18]

This interpretation of the four rivers encapsulates Immanuel's exegetical method, allowing multiple truths to coexist depending on the mode of interpretation deployed. He does not doubt that the four rivers named in Genesis exist in the physical world, but a symbolic reading of the rivers reveals esoteric truths while preserving the integrity of the literal verse. Immanuel cites the number four as an allusion to the material elements whose admixture forms all matter in the universe.[19] The rivers, realistically present in nature but also symbolizing the four elements when read allegorically, serve Immanuel as a potent image. This methodological comment is especially important in light of Immanuel's historical context, as Jews waged debates over the value and utility of allegorical readings of the Bible.[20] An antirationalist camp expressed anxieties that allegorical readings of biblical characters and events would make Jews doubt the veracity of the entire biblical narrative. An avowed Maimonidean, Immanuel could not reject allegorical readings altogether, but his comment about the four rivers implicitly addresses that critique by affirming both the literal and allegorical legitimacy of any verse.[21] This methodological statement is so important to Immanuel that he repeats it verbatim in most of his commentaries, using it as a shorthand term to refer to this type of reading.[22]

On each biblical book, Immanuel offers a puzzling array of citations from other authors, a bricolage of attributed and unattributed sources reworked to appear as Immanuel's original words, which led the nineteenth-century German scholars Leopold Zunz (1794–1886) and Moritz Steinschneider (1816–1907) to pronounce Immanuel's commentaries unoriginal and unworthy.[23] Immanuel's commentaries are characterized by their fundamental reliance on Maimonides and a second commentator, often Samuel Ibn Tibbon (ca. 1150–ca. 1230s) or his son Moses (1195–1274), whose writings Immanuel embellishes with his own creative additions and scriptural interpretations.[24] Modern scholars justify Immanuel's "plagiaristic" practices as medieval rhetorical conventions, which define terms like "originality" and "citation" in vastly different ways from modern ones.[25] They may point to his familiarity with scholastic writing modes that reflect different compositional functions. Or, rather, they assert that Immanuel's creativity lies in his editorial hand, weaving disparate texts together and seamlessly blending them into his own insights. Whether Immanuel consciously deploys different modes is unclear, but his omnivorous appetite for texts of all kinds results in wide-scale and creative plagiarism as well as repeated use and recycling of his own words.

Other Nonpoetic Works

In addition to poetry and biblical commentary, Immanuel also wrote grammatical works and a homiletical collection (*derashot*). Two of Immanuel's books focus on the Hebrew language and study its letters and grammar. In *Maḥberot Immanuel*, he references a work on the symbolism of Hebrew letters, long considered lost but recently identified in manuscript.[26] At least one of these works was popular in the early modern period, as the Renaissance philosopher Yoḥanan Alemanno (1435–1504) recommended Immanuel's grammatical text, *Even Boḥan* ("The Touchstone"), as a fundamental study tool for Hebrew grammar.[27] In addition to his books, there is a collection, attributed to Immanuel, of about a dozen fragmentary commentaries that emphasize three topics: the red heifer (*parah adumah*), wine preserved from creation (a cryptic topic), and the angel Metatron. Finally, Immanuel's supercommentary on Ibn Ezra's explanation of the Tetragrammaton (found in his commentary on Exodus 33:21) was extremely popular.[28] As Hebrew was solely a literary language in the Middle Ages, the Bible served medieval Hebrew poets and belletristic authors as a repository of vocabulary, imagery, and grammatical forms. These works demonstrate Immanuel's wide range and the centrality of the Hebrew Bible to his Hebrew writing, yet the two corpora—poetic and nonliterary—have never been brought to bear on each other. As becomes evident throughout this book, *Maḥberet Ha-Tofet V'Ha-Eden* demonstrates the ways Immanuel purposefully recycles texts—both others' and his own—to a didactic effect.

Authors and Authorities

Glancing sideways at Immanuel's Christian contemporaries, we note that the concept of authorship changed dramatically in the fourteenth century, which may have affected Immanuel's understanding of his role. Conveying hierarchical rigidity and a status of authority, the Latin term *auctoritates* (authoritative texts) refers to a closed canon of classical texts used and commented on by medieval writers. As bearers of that trusted and unquestioned clout, *auctores* (authors) are revered as mediators between an impersonal body of divinely given knowledge and a historically contingent audience.[29] Yet the financial expense of book production and the mediation of scribes and orators calls the very concept of an "authored text" into question.[30] Dante's *Divine Comedy*, claims one scholar, challenges regnant medieval ideas about authority and the texts that convey it, as Dante's nonclassical text commands the same gravitas and authority as the writings of Latin *auctores* but in vernacular Italian. The rapid dissemination of Dante's *Divine Comedy* in the first quarter of the fourteenth century through sermons, commentaries, visual arts, and textual legacies attests to its broad popularity.[31] As the only medieval vernacular text to generate a commentary tradition, Dante's *Divine Comedy* stands out for its disruption of a culture in which solely Latin texts gained authority, reflecting societal embrace of an educated lay culture.

One of Dante's earliest exegetes, his son Pietro (1300–1364), addressed the issue of scribal contamination and textual variation by "reading Dante with Dante," a technique that uses Dante's robust collection of writings to explain words and ideas in the *Divine Comedy*.[32] *Bridging Worlds* uses the same technique to "read Immanuel with Immanuel," an especially pertinent mode of reading given that Immanuel cites his own biblical commentaries explicitly in his tour of heaven.[33] To employ a sociological paradigm of bricoleurs who "combine their imagination with whatever knowledge tools they have at-hand in their repertoire (e.g., ritual, observation, social practices) and with whatever artifacts are available in their given context (i.e., discourses, institutions, and dominant knowledges) to meet diverse knowledge-production tasks," Immanuel's imaginary netherworldly realms cultivate authority and gravitas to ground his lessons about the importance of philosophy, ethics, and repentance for what he imagined to be a mostly unenlightened audience.[34]

The burden of conveying wisdom to others is addressed throughout Immanuel's commentaries and poetry alike, although we do not know whether Immanuel was ever employed as a teacher. Explaining the structure of Ecclesiastes, Immanuel identifies three audiences that could benefit simultaneously from the book: simpletons and youth can learn knowledge and skill from a literal reading; wise people can fathom the esoteric content; and discerning minds (*nevonim*) can impart the esoteric lessons through hints and parables.[35] For Immanuel, the ability to teach elevates the discerning one over even the sage. In the eighth *maḥberet*, for instance, Immanuel lambasts a fellow poet for leading students astray, while several characters in *Tofet* (Hell) suffer for withholding knowledge from others. Glossing Proverbs 10:6–9, Immanuel explains that "a righteous individual's name will gain acclaim each day, and his name will never be forgotten because he assists his contemporaries. He converts souls or he writes a book that will serve as an eternal memorial and aid to those that follow him. On account of his active production, his memory will be actively remembered forever, while the names of the wicked will be forgotten."[36] Writing a book, according to Immanuel, conveys immortality to its author, and Immanuel ends *Maḥberet Ha-Tofet V'Ha-Eden* with the guide's assurance that, as a *maskil* (intellectual), Immanuel is akin to "those who lead the many to righteousness, forever and ever, like the stars," a verse from Daniel 12:3 frequently used by medieval authors to refer to the afterlife and immortality.

Immanuel and Dante

It is no coincidence that Immanuel concludes his celestial tour with a biblical verse that mentions stars, as Dante (ca. 1265–1321) ends each canticle of the *Divine Comedy* with the words *le stelle* (the stars). Several features of *Maḥberet Ha-Tofet V'Ha-Eden* pay further homage to the *Divine Comedy*, Dante's celestial tour guided by the Roman poet Virgil, an epic poem that normalized vernacular Italian language when classical Latin was considered the standard for educated elites. Although the netherworld dream journey appeared in the Jewish context prior to Dante's *Divine Comedy*, Immanuel and Dante are linked by their geographical and chronological proximity. Both tours of realms of the dead, the *Divine Comedy* and *Maḥberet Ha-Tofet V'Ha-Eden*, offer the authors' omniscient views of characters in hell and heaven, highlighting the dissonance between private and public identities. Both works employ a literary medium to address the social and spiritual ailments of their respective religious communities, with a special focus on hypocrisy in religious praxis. Adopting similar tropes of extreme humility, each author affirms his special status as the chosen seer and scribe for posterity. Finally, there are correspondences in types of sinners, language, and imagery of specific sinners in hell

(*Tofet*) and *Inferno.* This resemblance has dominated academic studies of *Maḥberet Ha-Tofet V'Ha-Eden* since the nineteenth century, obscuring the study of this chapter within Immanuel's larger oeuvre. As this book shows, the didactic purpose and philosophical character of *Maḥberet Ha-Tofet V'Ha-Eden* merit particularly serious consideration within the history of ideas; the chapter's unique blend of literary conventions, social critique, and philosophical universalism serves as a testament to Immanuel's intellectual approach.

The association of Immanuel with Dante dominated early academic studies of Judaism because it fed an integrationist fantasy of German Jews seeking citizenship in nineteenth-century Europe who hailed Immanuel as a committed Jew, fully immersed in Italian culture, who kindled an interfaith friendship with Dante. After M. D. Cassuto (1883–1951) proved the idealized relationship fictional, studies of Dante and Immanuel's relationship pivoted to comparisons that recognized Immanuel's talent but subordinated it to Dante's.[37] Thus Immanuel was called "Dante's younger brother in talent, and close relative in the kinship of poetic spirit."[38] One modern scholar even laments the absence of personal storytelling in *Maḥberet Ha-Tofet V'Ha-Eden*, an evocative technique perfected by Dante in the woeful tale of the lovers Francesca and Paolo.[39] Yet this critique overlooks the tale of the miser in *Tofet* who personally bemoans his sin and tantalization in hell or the aggrieved father in *Eden* whose personal narrative evokes deep pity. Immanuel does powerfully grasp and deploy personal narrative in his tour, but he does so in vignettes that don't mirror characters from *Inferno.* Other scholars celebrate Immanuel's originality, especially as the netherworld journey genre has a long tradition within Judaism, predating the *Divine Comedy.*[40] Overall, studies of Immanuel reveal more about scholarly agendas and historical context than about the text or our author, a not unsurprising finding.

While it is unlikely that Immanuel and Dante knew each other, the promotion of their connection by both Jews and Christians reveals insights into the Jewish-Christian dynamic throughout the ages. Immanuel's Italian sonnets feature in a manuscript collection of "poets of Dante's circle," where Immanuel is conspicuously identified as "Immanuel, the Jew."[41] Although Immanuel divulges much information about himself, he remains strikingly silent on the topic of Dante and the *Divine Comedy.* However, a comparison of *Maḥberet Ha-Tofet V'Ha-Eden* with the *Divine Comedy* demonstrates how Immanuel integrally incorporates the *Divine Comedy*'s images into his own journey and idiosyncratically appropriates them for an educated Jewish audience. Immanuel's use of non-Jewish texts appears in two different ways: Either he neutralizes the foreign source through a direct translation of the material into Hebrew rhymed prose or poetry, or he imports images that appear in the *Divine Comedy* and refracts them through Hebrew analogs. As Immanuel was one of the first, if not the first, to translate the sonnet form into Hebrew, by necessity he integrates a plethora of Italian literary forms and themes into *Maḥberot Immanuel*, which showcases conventional lyrical forms like the *sirventese* and a verisimilitude reminiscent of Giovanni Boccaccio's *Decameron*.[42] He also engages in a *tenzone*, a poetic exchange, with the Italian poet Bosone da Gubbio (d. ca. 1349).[43] From Immanuel's commentary on Esther, it is apparent that he was familiar with other Latinate works of Dante's besides the *Divine Comedy*, although he likely did not know Latin.[44] These elements demonstrate Immanuel's awareness of Italian literary developments, a heritage that Immanuel vigorously defends against a Provençal poet who affirms the supremacy of his countrymen over Romans in all matters literary and intellectual.[45]

The Italian Historical Context

Immanuel's familiarity with Italian literary culture reflects his intimate awareness of his surrounding political and religious environments, highlighted by the mocking irreverence of his Italian sonnets. He mentions the rift between the Guelphs and Ghibellines, a power struggle at the highest levels of empire and Church, which spilled over into the towns and cities of the central and northern peninsula.[46] Rome was caught between the power politics of the papal forces and wealthy elite families until the 1305 death of Pope Benedict XI (1240–1305) and the election of the French pope Clement V (1264–1314), who never entered Rome and led the papacy from France.[47] The Avignon papacy, the seventy-odd year period during which the papacy was headquartered in France, reinforced the notion that Rome was dangerous because of rivalries between two families, the Orsini and Colonna, whom Immanuel mocks in another Italian sonnet. Absent imperial and papal rulers, and already fraught with civil strife, late medieval Italian towns and cities organized themselves into independent units, communes (*comuni*), governed by popular councils that rotated frequently to prevent corruption. As much as the late medieval Italian peninsula was wracked by violence, to which Immanuel alludes in his commentaries, it was also a place of growth and development opportunities, especially for Jewish businessmen who migrated out of Rome to Tuscany, Umbria, Veneto, and Le Marche.[48] Immanuel sets *Maḥberot Immanuel* in the city of Fermo, a trading hub on the Adriatic coast, where Jews had settled since the late thirteenth century. Due to the papal absence and crushing economic legislation, Roman Jews left Rome en masse in the thirteenth and fourteenth centuries.[49] It is likely that Immanuel was one such Jew who immigrated to the regions of Umbria and Le Marche. The Purim gathering at Fermo, which opens the narrative frame of *Maḥberot Immanuel*, hints at the existence of an established Jewish community, which is further supported by archival evidence.[50] Immanuel's concerns about his reputation, echoed in the chapter's opening lines, suggest that Immanuel's verses were widely known, attested by the long and checkered reception history of the book.

Reception History

Maḥberot Immanuel has had an uneven past, with approbations and condemnations issued since its release. Initially, the book was wildly popular, as attested by ten independent manuscripts and an incunable.[51] Additionally, numerous printed editions of portions of the *Maḥbarot* exist, suggesting that some chapters had more mass appeal than others. *Maḥberet Ha-Tofet V'Ha-Eden* is the most frequently excerpted chapter; other popular chapters include one on old age and the first chapter, which is set during a Purim feast.[52]

The popularity of *Maḥberot Immanuel* is also evidenced by the many condemnations of the book, including in Rabbi Joseph Karo's *Shulḥan Arukh* in the sixteenth century. Two centuries earlier, in his fourteenth-century Hebrew imitation of the *Divine Comedy*, *Mikdash Me'at* ("The Minor Temple"), the Italian author Moses Rieti (1388–1460) warns his readers about the vulgar content of Immanuel's poetry and denies Immanuel a place in heaven.[53] And later, in his seventeenth-century book on Hebrew verse, *Metek Sefatayim* ("The Sweetness of Lips"), the Italian Jewish poet Immanuel Francis (1618–1703) describes Immanuel as one "whose hand excelled at poetry, but he lost his way on earth through erotic poems that are forbidden to hear."[54] In the eighteenth-century work *Ben Zekunim* ("The Child of Old Age"), Hezekiah David Bolaffio advises readers to "put all his [Immanuel's] poems in the latrine."[55]

This longstanding modern disdain stemmed from a reading of *Maḥberot Immanuel* as a textual witness to the poet's own moral and religious laxity. Halakhists and poets alike, these readers were tricked by the verisimilitude of Immanuel's narrative and its tendency to venture into questionable situations, believing that it was autobiographical. His love poetry is lighthearted, even borderline vulgar, yet a greater concentration of frivolity and erotic imagery cannot be detected in Immanuel's poetry than in other literary works of the period. Dvora Bregman examines the rejection of Immanuel's poetry in the early modern period to understand why Italian Jews failed to produce love poetry and Hebrew sonnets for centuries after Immanuel's lifetime. While she attributes some hesitation to emerging traditionalist sensibilities, she ultimately claims that Immanuel's technical poetics proved too challenging to master.[56]

Against the early modern critical reading of *Maḥberot Immanuel*, later scholars viewed this work as a poet's rhetorical masterpiece, excusing vulgarity and ribaldry as elements of convention rather than as testimony to the author's actual behavior or moral values. Comparing Immanuel to Boccaccio (1313–1375)—whose tales were popular despite their licentiousness—in the nineteenth century, Joseph Chotzner railed, "Injustice would be done to Immanuel if his private life and character were judged in the light of his writings. In these he certainly appears as a thorough devotee of women and of Bacchus, and as a scoffer at religion and religious practices."[57] Chotzner understood that Immanuel, "adopting the style of the Italian novelists of his time whose works were great favorites with the general reading public, no doubt thought he would attract and amuse Jewish readers by reproducing in a Hebrew garb the popular ideas and modes of expression."[58] In another comparison of Immanuel to Boccaccio, Cecil Roth exclaims, "There is to be sure an air of unreality about all these erotic and skeptical verses of Immanuel. . . . One has the impression that he thought it fashionable to write love poems, and he wrote them; that he found that it was titillating both to himself and his hearers to describe amatory conquests, and he described them; but that in neither case did his compositions bear much relation to actuality."[59] This perspective dominates recent scholarship as scholars attempt to neutralize Immanuel's erotic verse through contextualization. Given the lack of new materials, it is no surprise that "the paradox of Immanuel's personality," which has remained an overriding but unnecessary approach to his work, has yet to be fully illumined.[60]

This book, by contrast, tackles Immanuel of Rome's intellectual and cultural profile by rejecting any notion of a paradox in his personality. Using new manuscript evidence and advancing a novel methodological intervention, *Bridging Worlds* reveals deep connections between Immanuel's "literature" and "exegesis," which have been bifurcated in all previous studies of this thinker. In its two parts, *Bridging Worlds* first investigates the social, political, and cultural contexts of *Maḥberot Immanuel* and then offers an analysis and novel reading of *Maḥberet Ha-Tofet V'Ha-Eden* itself. Chapter 1, "Of Fallacy and Fraud: Immanuel's 'Biography,'" addresses the thorny problem of Immanuel's life, the study of which has been muddied by misguided attempts to draw biographical information from the *Maḥbarot* and its two introductions. While giving these introductions due consideration, the chapter situates Immanuel in the late medieval Italian context using the prefaces to Immanuel's biblical commentaries and new manuscript evidence. This chapter also contains a revised biographical timeline of Immanuel's life, significantly later than previously believed, based on a new manuscript finding. The placement of Immanuel firmly in the fourteenth century, as opposed to the thirteenth century, helps to explain the realism of *Maḥberot Immanuel*, which is more characteristic of the methods of later fourteenth-century authors like Boccaccio.

Chapter 2, "Between the Eagle and the Lion," traces the relationship between Immanuel's exegesis and his poetry through the test case of Psalm 68. This psalm is the focus, in *Maḥberet Ha-Tofet V'Ha-Eden*, of a public display of Immanuel's erudition in heaven, where King David, the purported author of the psalm, publicly shames Rabbi David Kimḥi's (1160–1235) historical interpretation of the psalm and commands all the exegetes to adulate Immanuel for his brilliant allegorical reading. A close study of Immanuel's exegesis reveals his philosophical understanding of the natural world and the metaphysical workings of the universe as well as his insights into the soul and its ultimate purpose. This chapter considers Immanuel's philosophical orientation, shaped by both Maimonides (the eagle) and Judah Romano (the lion), acknowledging the ever-present tension between old and new philosophical ideologies in Immanuel's writings as an amateur philosopher.

Chapter 3, "*Shalom* and *Shelemut* (Peace and Perfection): Immanuel on the Ethical Life," explores the importance of ethics to Immanuel's understanding of human perfection. Unlike Maimonides and Samuel Ibn Tibbon, who viewed the role of the commandments as ancillary to the intellectual quest, Immanuel placed great emphasis on commandments and virtues as integral to human perfection. This chapter uses Immanuel's unpublished commentaries on the red heifer (Numbers 19) and the cryptic wine preserved since creation to demonstrate the importance of catharsis and reflection on the soul. This commentary, part of a didactic and previously unstudied philosophical primer, offers insights into Immanuel's conception of sin and punishment, furthering the argument that Immanuel's works must be studied synthetically rather than as unrelated texts.

Turning from Immanuel's context to a close reading of *Maḥberet Ha-Tofet V'Ha-Eden*, the fourth chapter, "Navigating the Afterlife," examines the impact of two disparate traditions on the narrative poem. The form and structure of *Maḥberet Ha-Tofet V'Ha-Eden* aligns it with Dante's *Divine Comedy*, one of the most popular literary texts in the Italian peninsula in the fourteenth century. Yet, as a disciple of the Maimonidean tradition—as transmitted through the Tibbonide scholars—Immanuel expresses his understanding of the postmortem experience as an immaterial one. This chapter demonstrates how Immanuel navigates between such divergent approaches to the postmortem experience while creatively marshaling both the *Divine Comedy* and the Maimonidean corpus. While this chapter claims that Immanuel translated complex philosophical and theological notions into an entertaining and edifying tale of eschatological realism, chapters 5 and 6 demonstrate that process by focusing on individual characters and vignettes within the tale itself. Although the *maḥberet* is spatially organized into the region of hell (*Tofet*) and that of heaven (*Eden*), *Bridging Worlds* takes a thematic approach to analyze salient leitmotifs in the tale. Utilizing a Maimonidean binary of body and soul, this book explores sinners and saints whose actions relate either to the social order or to the intellectual realm. It argues that Immanuel's characters were realistically crafted so that they might manifest complex ideas from his philosophical commentaries in an accessible narrative.

Chapter 5, "The World of the Body," focuses on two major themes that underlie both regions of Immanuel's hell and heaven. Maintenance of social order and communal wellbeing are Maimonidean requirements for a society that fosters intellectual advancement. This chapter explores how characters either hindered or promoted communal health through their actions. Throughout the chapter, the characterizations repeatedly draw on theories in Immanuel's philosophical commentaries to concretize those ideas using sympathetic anecdotes. The juxtaposition of the poem and the commentaries, therefore, reveals the richness of the *maḥberet* as a didactic text that inspires self-reflection through a dramatic literary experience.

Chapter 6, "The World of the Mind," continues the demonstration of Immanuel's intertextual methodology through a focus on sins or virtues of the mind. By exploring the human interior dimension, Immanuel offers novel insights into actions traditionally considered sinful, like gambling or taking one's own life. His use of verisimilitude conveys his sharp social critiques in sympathetic and compelling narratives. This chapter also examines Immanuel's spotlight on his own commentaries, praised by various biblical authors as useful tools to teach philosophical truths to the uninitiated. It is this ability, according to Immanuel, that earns his literary persona an eternal place in heaven.

The conclusion, "What Is an Author?" considers the pedagogical role of the tale through the prophetic persona that Immanuel crafted for his traveler, further examining the goal of such a narrative in a culture newly influenced by an emphasis on ethical refinement and penance. The chapter closes with a consideration of the act of writing as the primary vehicle of an author's immortality, demonstrating the ideologies advanced not only by *Maḥberet Ha-Tofet V'Ha-Eden*'s content but also by its placement as the concluding chapter of Immanuel's entire poetic anthology.

Immanuel and his otherworldly tale have fascinated lay and scholarly audiences alike since the Middle Ages, but both are due for a frank reassessment in light of new manuscript material and new methods. Utilizing Immanuel's entire oeuvre, *Bridging Worlds* demonstrates the intertextuality of Immanuel's writing, and argues that only an interdisciplinary approach can prompt a full understanding of this author's place within his intellectual and historical contexts.

I

The Historical and Intellectual Contexts

1

OF FALLACY AND FRAUD

Immanuel's "Biography"

> Immanuel was the Lipa Schmeltzer of medieval Italy.
>
> **—"Wine, Women and Song, Part 3," seforimblog.com**

> Immanuel may be called the Heine of the Jewish Middle Ages.
>
> **—Heinrich Graetz, *History of the Jews***

Immanuel of Rome's literary output was enormous. One might expect that it would be matched by an equally rich biographical record, yet beyond the fact that he was an author living in the Italian peninsula during the fourteenth century, almost nothing is known about Immanuel's personal life. A survey of the secondary literature, however, gives a very different impression. *Maḥberot Immanuel*, Immanuel's poetic anthology, is full of realistic scenarios and enticing details. Historians have seized on various remarks, quips, and comments therein to construct elaborate biographical sketches. But such sketches are, at their best, aspirational and—given their shaky foundations—have varied wildly. Among many examples, Immanuel has been likened, on the one hand, to a provocative contemporary Hasidic lyrical artist and, on the other, to a cynical nineteenth-century German poet. Overall, historians' biographies of Immanuel have used as their primary source the body of *fictional* writing produced by Immanuel himself.

Perhaps most troubling is that they induce a false sense of certainty in readers. The interventions presented in this chapter offer a more critical approach to Immanuel's biography, building on what solid documentary evidence there is, sparse though it is. That an author with such an impoverished biographical record was so compelling to scholars is a testament to Immanuel's literary achievement.

When Did Immanuel Live?

The dates of Immanuel's life and death are currently unknown. It can be generally established that he lived sometime in the fourteenth century simply from the fact that he was evidently aware of Dante's *Divine Comedy.* In addition, the earliest extant manuscript of Immanuel's biblical commentary was copied in 1342.[1]

Attempting to narrow down the dates of Immanuel's lifetime brings to light the problems involved with mining the *Maḥbarot* for biographical data into sharpest relief. The dating of the work, and particularly that of the order of composition of individual chapters, is difficult. Some scholars, for example, assumed that the order of the chapters in the *Maḥbarot* reflects the chronological order of their composition. (The order of the chapters, however, varies among the extant manuscripts.) Others used any apparent reference to a date within a chapter as proof of its composition in that year. A seeming reference to the 1291 fall of Crusader-ruled Acre to the Mamluks in the sixth *maḥberet* "indicates" that it was composed in that year, while an allusion to the year 1328 in a chapter that begins with the formulaic words "in the days of youth," "proves" that Immanuel was born in that year.[2] A passing note in praise of King Robert of Anjou (1276–1343) in the twenty-third *maḥberet* "attests" that Immanuel could not have written that chapter before 1312, during the period when King Robert was still only the count of Romagna and the papal vicar of the imperial state.[3]

Even more doubtful, however, are the theories about Immanuel's birthdate based on the fact that *Maḥberet Ha-Tofet V'Ha-Eden* begins with the phrase "After sixty years of my life had passed."[4] Although there is no consensus on the matter, most scholars take these words literally and date Immanuel's birth to sixty years before that chapter was composed. Assuming this chapter was written shortly after Dante's *Divine Comedy*, they conclude that Immanuel was born sometime between 1260 and 1270, sixty years prior to the publication of the *Divine Comedy* in 1320.[5]

Other attempts to date the *Maḥbarot* with these kinds of speculative calculations have marshaled inconsistent evidence. For example, Immanuel mentions a book, possibly called the *Sefer Tekhunah* ("The Book on Astrology"), which (if identified correctly) was translated into Hebrew in 1336; if the *Maḥbarot* is dated to that year, then Immanuel's birth can be reached—relying on the same phrase about sixty years having passed—by subtracting sixty years from that date instead.[6] If, as has been argued, *Maḥberet Ha-Tofet V'Ha-Eden* was written in response to an expulsion decree issued for the Jews of the papal states in 1321, then 1261 is claimed as Immanuel's birth year.[7] In this case, however, there is only flimsy historical evidence for such an expulsion; it was mentioned a single time in the liturgy for a public fast recorded in *Maḥzor Roma*, the holiday prayerbook for the Roman rite, and again by Samuel Usque (1490–ca. 1550s) in his sixteenth-century chronicle *Consolation for the Tribulations of Israel*, a work known for conflating several anti-Jewish events into one, undermining its historical reliability.[8]

While it is tempting to trust Immanuel's profession of "sixty years" in the *Maḥbarot*, few scholars have stopped to consider whether it might simply be a literary convention. Dante famously conveyed his own unstable emotional state in terms of chronological age and geographical location ("When I had journeyed half of our life's way, / I found myself within a shadowed forest, / for I had lost the path that does not stray"). It is very likely that Immanuel too used this chronological age symbolically to express his discomfort with aging and his intensifying fear of death. The author's age, in fact, sets the mood for the journey; there is no reason to think that it was meant to function as a realistic chronological marker. Even when scholars have intimated a comparison between Dante's midlife status to Immanuel's age of sixty, they have refused to see the number as anything but a historical datum.[9]

When one reads through Immanuel's writings, however, it becomes clear that the number sixty has a clear connotation of declining physical powers and increasing spiritual abilities; the body's physical deterioration around the age of sixty allows its mental powers to flourish. In his commentary on the Song of Songs, Immanuel remarks on the "rose among thorns" image in Song of Songs 2:2. Linking the word *rose* to the age of sixty, Immanuel explains that "the name rose [*shoshanah*] derives from the number six [*shishah*] alluding to sixty [*shishim*] years, that is the sixty years that an individual stands among the thorns, among the material faculties that hinder intellectual perfection which was hinted at when our Sages said, 'The son of David will not come until the souls [*neshamot*] in the body cease to exist.'"[10] Immanuel comments elsewhere on the Song of Songs that, "after sixty years, the intellect grows stronger in the diminution of the material faculties."[11] *Maḥberet Ha-Tofet V'Ha-Eden* is set in the twilight years of

Immanuel's life as he ponders the afterlife and his lack of spiritual preparation for that world. The narrator's age at the journey's outset thus signifies his readiness to leave his body behind and undertake the intellectual quest ahead. It is highly doubtful that this number has any relation to reality, and it certainly cannot be used for determining Immanuel's birth year.

Another potential source for determining Immanuel's lifetime has been an invective epistle allegedly sent by him to a Rabbi Hillel, whom Immanuel accuses of slandering a great scholar. Some historians have identified this Rabbi Hillel as Hillel of Verona (d. ca. 1290) and suggested that the letter is part of a protracted scholarly debate between Hillel of Verona and Zeraḥiah Ḥen of Barcelona (d. ca. 1290s). If this were true, it would situate Immanuel squarely in the thirteenth century.[12] As I have shown elsewhere, however, an earlier version of the epistle, lacking "Rabbi Hillel" as the addressee, indicates that it was not in fact written to Hillel of Verona; this eliminates the reason for dating Immanuel's lifetime before 1300 or entangling him in the Hillel-Zeraḥiah debate.[13]

Indeed, situating Immanuel in the fourteenth century is also more consistent with data drawn from Italian literature. A set of Italian sonnets exchanged between Immanuel and Bosone da Gubbio (d. after 1349), a lawyer and eventual magistrate of Rome, and another set, between the same Bosone da Gubbio and Cino da Pistoia (1270–1336), a jurist, point to Immanuel's acquaintance with Italian poets of the fourteenth century.[14] These sonnets are the only known non-Jewish contemporaneous sources that mention Immanuel, but they too are difficult to parse. In one sonnet, written in 1321, to "the Jew Manoello," Bosone mentions two "lights" that had recently been extinguished from the universe. One of these likely referred to Dante Alighieri, as the sonnet was composed in the year of Dante's death. The other, Bosone hints, seems to have been a personal loss for Immanuel, perhaps a woman who had been close to him. Bosone's words ("the beautiful face, of whom your tongue used to speak so well") have led to conjectures that Immanuel was lamenting the death of a mistress.[15] Immanuel's response expresses profound sorrow in terms that suggest the loss would have been felt by Jews and Christians alike.

The second set of sonnets was exchanged by Bosone and Cino da Pistoia, a professor at the University of Siena who was traveling through the peninsula in 1320 and 1321, from Macerata to Camerino, on his way to assume his university post. One of them refers to Immanuel's place in hell next to Dante, suggesting Immanuel had, by that point, died. It has been used to suggest *a terminus ad quem* of 1336 (Cino's death) for Immanuel's life.[16] But Cino was known to be a friend and admirer of Dante, and this sonnet, extant only in a late (fifteenth- or sixteenth-century) manuscript, places Dante and Immanuel together in hell, a denigration of Dante that casts serious doubt on Cino's authorship.[17] The author of the sonnet writes to Bosone of "his Immanuel," stating "he is not with the common crowd, but he is with Dante under the same hat."[18] Bosone's own response reveals his dismay that Dante could be consigned to hell: "And although it was in that place that you put him, he doesn't deserve it; your pen did not picture him in truth, him and Dante covered in that filth."[19] It is therefore unlikely this sonnet was written by Cino. It should be noted that, even if it were known to be his, sonnets are unreliable sources of historical data.

Despite these problematic sources of data, some solid evidence does shed light on Immanuel's dates. It shows that Immanuel lived in the fourteenth century but later than previously thought. First, in a fifteenth-century manuscript, the scribe Daniel Jael includes a family tree of Immanuel's descendants next to a recipe for ink.[20] Daniel identifies the ink-maker's great-grandfather as "Immanuel, wrote the twenty-eight *Maḥbarot* and commented on the twenty-four [books of Bible]."[21] Second, my recent discovery of a document mentioning an Immanuel ben Solomon in Fermo corroborates this family tree. In the spring of 1395, Immanuel ben Solomon sold a manuscript to Menaḥem ben Samuel Alatrino for thirty gold ducats in Fermo in a sale witnessed by four Jewish signatories.[22] The book, an edition of the Prophets and Writings with Masoretic notes, was resold by Alatrino's son Abraham in 1460.[23] The deed and the genealogy accord chronologically, accounting nicely for the generations between Immanuel and his great-grandson, whose reputation as a thriving producer of ink was already established in 1471.

If Immanuel was born in the early fourteenth century and died in the late fourteenth century, several things about Immanuel that have until now seemed anomalous become clear. These dates explain how Immanuel had enough time to become familiar with Dante's *Comedy*—and how the realism of *Maḥberot Immanuel* so strikingly resembles the writings of Boccaccio, who lived from around 1313 to 1375.[24] Situating Immanuel's life fully in the fourteenth century also better explains how Immanuel's sonnets largely conform to the classical Petrarchan model. This resemblance has seemed a conundrum, as Petrarch, the humanist poet who gave the sonnet its distinctive cast, lived from around 1304 to 1374. Bregman, who noted this phenomenon, has conjectured that both Immanuel and Petrarch drew their models of the sonnet from Dante, who composed sonnets in various forms, and decided independently to favor a particular iteration of the poetic form. It seems far more likely, though, that Immanuel's sonnets follow a Petrarchan structure because, by his time, it had already become conventional.[25]

As we have seen, focusing on reliable documentary evidence, no matter how sparse, is the only route to constructing Immanuel's biography. He wrote his *Maḥberot Immanuel* using a conventional trope of fourteenth-century Italian literature: verisimilitude. Recognizing this fact allows us to make real strides in understanding him.

Where Did Immanuel Live?

Immanuel Ha-Romi ("the Roman"), as he is known now, identified himself as a native Roman. His commentaries and treatise on Hebrew grammar are attributed, by himself, to "Immanuel, son of Solomon (Yedidyah) of the city of Rome." He also claimed to descend from the Kitim, a Noahide tribe mentioned in Genesis 10:4, who were described as "Roman residents of the Campagna plain on the Tiber River" by the southern Italian historian Jossipon.[26] In addition, *Maḥberot Immanuel* expresses a sense of pride in Roman heritage, especially when Immanuel's character engages in a battle of wits with a rival poet of Provençal background.[27]

It is unlikely that Immanuel lived in Rome his whole life, for he states in the introduction to *Maḥberot Immanuel* that he composed that work in Fermo, and elsewhere claims to have visited Gubbio, Orvieto, Camerino, Fermo, and Perugia. (The narrative frame of *Maḥberot Immanuel* opens at a Purim banquet in Fermo, demonstrating the importance of this town to Immanuel.) The earliest known manuscript edition of any of Immanuel's writings was copied in Ascoli-Piceno, a Marchegian town not far from the province of Fermo.[28] And if the Immanuel who sold a Bible at Fermo in 1395 was our poet, as seems very likely, the deed of sale would corroborate the literary evidence, which, as I have been arguing, cannot be taken on its own to be historically conclusive.

Aside from his own testimony, Immanuel has been linked to other parts of the Italian peninsula. Rieti, the fourteenth-century poet, calls him "the Zifronite," a surname that has been interpreted as meaning his ancestors came from Ceprano in the Frosinone province of the Lazio region, but there is no corroborating evidence for this origin.[29] And another group of sources places Immanuel on the opposite side of the Italian peninsula. A sixteenth-century superscript to Immanuel's Italian sonnets calls him "the Gubbian," referring to the town of Gubbio in Umbria. And Immanuel

Frances, a seventeenth-century Italian Jewish poet, refers to "Immanuel, son of Solomon, from La Marca," a reference to the Marche region on the Adriatic coast.[30] The thirteenth and fourteenth centuries were periods of immense change in the Italian peninsula, especially for the city of Rome. As Rome lost many of its Jews to newly emerging towns seeking commercial growth, it is possible that Immanuel spent extended time in Umbria and Le Marche, regions undergoing dynamic political and socioeconomic changes in the late medieval period.[31]

Less convincing is the mining of Immanuel's Italian poetry for biographical details, in particular the fact that Immanuel set his longest Italian poem, "Bisbidis," amid the visual and auditory fanfare of the Veronese court.[32] Based on this literary choice, scholars have commonly claimed that Immanuel spent some time living in Verona, at the court of Cangrande della Scala (1291–1329), Dante's patron. But this court famously served as Dante's home while he wrote the *Divine Comedy*, and it is thus far more likely that Immanuel, for literary effect, simply imagined his own presence there. That is not to say that Immanuel's Italian poems are not worthy of interpretation, but they are most valuable for the glimpses they offer of the peninsula's political freneticism, about which his Hebrew poetry is silent.

Political Turmoil in the Italian Peninsula

Historically, the Italian peninsula was divided into three zones ruled by three competing powers: the Kingdom of Sicily in the south, the papacy in the center, and the Holy Roman Empire in the north. By the early thirteenth century, the cities and towns of northern Italy, though nominally part of the German-based Holy Roman Empire, had gained independence from foreign rule and feudal overlords through the creation of popular governments called communes or republics.[33] The delicate balance of political ecosystems was suddenly and violently upset by the reign of Frederick II Hohenstaufen (1198–1250), a descendant of both the German emperor and the Sicilian king.[34] Fierce rivalry between Frederick II and Pope Innocent IV cascaded into a rivalry between Guelph and Ghibelline factions that turned cities and families against each other, resulting in bloody conflicts. Over the course of the thirteenth century, antagonism between the Hohenstaufen family and successive popes embroiled Italy in a series of conflicts involving external powers like France, Aragon, and Germany. Hebrew historical chronicles note the anarchy in the city of Rome during the 1260s, when the papal throne changed hands repeatedly and no secular leader was present in the city.[35] The papal absence likely unnerved some Jews, as the pope's presence in Rome usually afforded the Jews physical protection.

Immanuel was acutely aware of political turmoil: The lyrics of his sonnet "Io steso non mi conosco" ("I don't know who I am") sarcastically convey the author's shifting political alliances from Ghibelline to Guelph depending on his location.[36] The relationship between Roman Jews and the papacy was complicated, as the Jewish community, or *scuola*, in Rome served in an unofficial diplomatic capacity for Jewish communities abroad but also bore the brunt of humiliating public rituals and high taxes.[37] With the intensity of political chaos keeping the papal see absent from Rome between 1378 and 1417, many Jews immigrated to more hospitable locations.

Ample evidence of Jewish settlement in the Marche region in the last decades of the thirteenth century indicates that this region absorbed many of Rome's Jewish families. Both Le Marche and Umbria were nominally part of the papal state, a titular concession extended after Frederick II's downfall, but they lacked consistency in political organization or allegiance to the pope. As mini laboratories in municipal self-government, theoretically declaring equal rule for all free men but in practice restricting power to a privileged few, communal governments had individual needs and idiosyncratic structures.[38] Several loan documents demonstrate that the communal governments throughout the regions borrowed money from Jewish lenders, presumably to invest in municipal infrastructure or governance; Jewish creditors, noting the details of the loan in Hebrew on the reverse side of the documents, were nearly all Roman Jews extending loans to Marchegian communes. At the same time, Hebrew manuscripts were copied and written in many of these same towns, attesting to the presence of Jewish intellectual life alongside the earliest Jewish businessmen who settled in Le Marche.

Immanuel alludes to communal government in his philosophically oriented biblical commentaries but ultimately concludes that the dynamic of shared power is less than ideal. Expounding Proverbs 28:2 ("When there is rebellion in the land, many are its rulers, but with a man who has understanding and knowledge, stability will last"), Immanuel explains that God punishes sinful people by instituting many political leaders to rule together, and this results in injustice and bad governance. According to Immanuel, many leaders give rise to conflicting opinions about rule, ultimately causing the city's destruction, but if a discerning person rules the land, God will grant it political stability. Hinting at the strife characteristic of so many Italian towns and cities, Immanuel states, "For the businesses and the arts do not unite. Each one stands apart on a matter, and they cannot reach a favorable conclusion."[39] Presumably referring to the various guilds (*arti*) that vied for political power in medieval Italian locales, Immanuel states his preference for rule by a single man.

The tight focus on Rome and its neighboring regions of Umbria and Le Marche in *Maḥberot Immanuel* highlights these three zones as areas of importance to Immanuel. The documentary evidence from Marchegian archives, together with the production of Hebrew scholarly works in those towns, already in the early decades of the fourteenth century, indicate that there were financial and intellectual sectors in the burgeoning towns, but one wonders whether this audience could appreciate the wit of *Maḥberot Immanuel*.

Genre and Patronage

Immanuel was fully aware of fiction as a distinct genre, with the power to exaggerate and even falsify reality. Anecdotes and remarks about the role of the poet are peppered throughout *Maḥberot Immanuel*. According to Immanuel, a poet is meant "to exaggerate praise and denigration in poetry, but not to stray too far from the truth so as to pronounce the dead man alive and the living one dead."[40] Immanuel playfully repeats the statement, attributed to Aristotle, that the best poems are full of deceit and recites two poems that exemplify this Aristotelian notion.[41] Immanuel highlights the diplomatic utility of poetry, to flatter a patron or a desired love object, but he also notes the potency of verse in belittling enemies and avenging a poet or his patron. The delicate dance between an artist and his Maecenas is a recurrent motif in *Maḥberot Immanuel*, likely reflecting the social and historical contexts in the Italian peninsula.[42] Immanuel's awareness of rhetorical conventions emerging from humanist circles is especially noticeable in his inclusion of letters in the *Maḥbarot*.[43] In the thirteenth century, the identification of epistolary composition as a technical field restricted to *dictators*, professional letter-writers, shifted to a consideration of it as a humanistic art practiced by scholars educated in classical rhetoric. In letters included in the *Maḥbarot*, Immanuel deploys humanistic rhetorical conventions that suggest his overall familiarity with the nascent field of rhetoric.

The rhetorical field, reinvigorated by humanists of the Italian peninsula, was based on the ancient Greek and Roman conventions of oratory that were used in trials or public orations. By the late Middle Ages, such oral persuasion had transformed into textual conventions. The ancient orator

Cicero (first c. BCE) identified a nonlegal type of narrative "wholly unconnected with public issues, which is recited or written solely for amusement but at the same time provides valuable training."[44] These narratives, which explain and discuss different matters, can be classified into three types—fable, history, and argument. Fables are stories that include details that neither happened nor could happen, while historical accounts recount exploits that occurred. Argument (*argumentum*), according to Cicero, is "a fictitious narrative which nevertheless could have occurred," including not only events but also conversations between and attitudes of the characters.[45] Since rhetorical treatises circulated in the vernacular during Immanuel's lifetime, it is highly likely that he utilized this convention when composing *Maḥberot Immanuel*, with its realistic aura projecting a travel narrative of two interlocutors.

Maḥberot Immanuel opens with two different introductions followed by twenty-eight chapters of composite rhymed prose and poetry. Scholars are divided over whether these two introductions are original or whether two versions were composed, transmitted in various manuscripts, which eventually were fused.[46] In both introductions the narrative presents a savior character who encourages the poet to anthologize his poetry in a diwan modeled on the *Taḥkemoni* by the twelfth-century Iberian author Judah Al-Harizi. Immanuel rewards his patron, "the *Sar*," by making him an interlocutor—a fellow poet-intellectual—who accompanies Immanuel and improvises poetry throughout the twenty-seven *Maḥbarot* before being replaced, in the final chapter, with the celestial guide Daniel, who leads Immanuel through hell and heaven. In the context of medieval Italy's rapidly shifting economic and political landscape, a wealthy patron was an absolute necessity to a poet.[47] This is especially evident in Immanuel's choice of the title *Sar* for his patron, which is likely an analog of the Italian *Ser*, a title indicating nobility or wealth, and a word that was transliterated into Hebrew (שֵׁר, סִיר) on many of the extant loan documents of the period.[48]

Maḥberot Immanuel was traditionally regarded as a repository of available historical data. Scholars debated whether Immanuel meant to flatter an actual patron when he crafted the *Sar* character or whether the patron should be understood solely as a symbolic figure, with each position "supported" by the wide narrative scope of the *Maḥbarot*. In the most extreme positivist historical reading, the *Sar* was identified as a wealthy banker named Daniel of Gubbio, whose sudden death occasioned both the writing of *Maḥberet Ha-Tofet V'Ha-Eden* and Immanuel's abrupt substitution of a guide character named "Daniel" instead of the *Sar* as an ode to him.[49] Opposing this reading is a view grounded in the idea that Immanuel belonged to a group of mystically inclined philosophers, with the patron symbolizing the agent intellect, a faculty identified by medieval philosophers as the source of all knowledge in the sublunar world.[50] While it is possible that Immanuel sought to immortalize an actual patron, "why should his name have been left unmentioned in a work which contains so many other names?"[51] The biting irony of an unnamed patron suggests that Immanuel crafted the character as a foil to his own literary persona, the brilliant poet Immanuel.

The first attempt to use the *Maḥbarot*'s two introductions critically, by Matti Huss, argues that they demonstrate the deep influence of two vastly different literary cultures—Iberian Hebrew literature and Italian Romance literature—on Immanuel, who blended the two contradictory traditions in his *Maḥbarot*.[52] A major discrepancy between Hebrew literature of the Iberian peninsula and Romance literature of the Italian peninsula, claims Huss, lies in the authors' acknowledgment of fictiveness; where Iberian authors blatantly admitted that their characters were pure fictions, authors of Romance literature strove to maintain an aura of authenticity or historicity in their works. In the first introduction, the patron sheepishly admits: "For I have never composed a poem, nor has my intellect ever outlined rhymed prose with a stylus. Make me your companion in your book, and credit me with some of your tales and poems. And although my glory shall not stem from my own poetry and deeds, I chose to be your friend and confidant, so let my name be engraved on the folio of your book forevermore."[53]

The patron's expression of his intellectual and literary deficits, according to Huss, conveys an air of realism conventional to medieval Romance works, while the second introduction smacks of the imaginative fiction employed by Iberian Hebrew authors by crediting the patron as the talented composer of the *Maḥbarot*.[54] In it the patron "opened the conduits of his heavens and trickled his fragrant juices" while urging Immanuel to "feed your stomach and fill your gut, for I will reveals matters and riddles to you."[55] For Huss, the patron is but one example of Immanuel's rhetorical strategy to engender an aura of realism in his fictive work.[56] Huss's theory can be evaluated through an examination of the *Maḥbarot*'s two prefaces juxtaposed with Immanuel's introduction to his commentary on the biblical book of Job.

In his proemium to the commentary on Job, Immanuel describes the circumstances that led to his exegetical project—his arousal from a sorrowful and troubled state by a patron, Isaac ben Menaḥem of Rome, who had seen Immanuel's commentary on Proverbs and sought Immanuel's interpretation of Job. Immanuel writes:

> Pressured by the travails of the times, I stopped up my vintage and the manna ceased. The troubles built a sturdy house over me—not for one day or two. However, the hand of the distinguished intellectual [*maskil*], the holy crown and diadem who is more precious than wisdom and honor, the Rabbi, R. Isaac, son of the honored Menaḥem of Rome, may his memory extend to the world to come, was upon me. And it shook me onto my knees and soles of my feet. And he woke me as one who is roused from sleep, and made me flee the pit of shadowy thoughts. He strengthened and emboldened me to explain this book in a wondrously esoteric way when he saw the commentary I had written, the exegesis of the book of Proverbs. While studying some of its verses, he saw that I drew a line upon them, and didn't run away from their ambivalence, but that I waged a serious and deep war against every word to understand it and explain it with justice and charity. Shamelessly, he implored me to turn my face toward the fierce war in glossing this book whose meaning is far from the minds of the masses. And I, anyway, am reluctant to use full force, since I know my shortcomings. But he, through the benevolence of his mind, gave me a gift of his understanding, some balm and some honey. Upon my seeing his serious intentions, I knew that his merit would stand for me to tackle the exegesis of the book and perceive its stored treasures. So I set myself to this task, and my hands are spread out to the heavens to open the gates of this book and its hidden intentions for me.[57]

The only dedication of its kind in any of Immanuel's commentaries, this panegyric praises Isaac ben Menaḥem for inspiring and supporting Immanuel's commentary on Job. This dedication is significant for many reasons, as it attests that Immanuel's scholarship was funded by patrons, and it contributes significantly to establishing a chronology for Immanuel's commentaries, as the Proverbs gloss was presumably complete enough already for Isaac to know Immanuel's method and style.[58]

More important for our purposes, as a dedication to a named patron, it provides a template against which to compare the two introductions to *Maḥberot Immanuel*. The troubles to which Immanuel refers are vague, but his description of the cessation of manna alludes to an absence of patronage. In the preface to his *Maḥbarot*, Immanuel describes his noble patron with "the house of Israel called his name manna."[59] In fact, a comparison of *Maḥberot Immanuel*'s two introductions (which I will call A and B) with this panegyric dedication in the commentary on Job reveals many similarities in language and structure among the three. All begin with a narrative description of the author's woes. Introduction A presents an aged and wandering traveler named Immanuel who realizes that his poems and reputation are at risk while at a Purim banquet in Fermo. Introduction B features a bleak picture of a dull, unintellectual society that does not value literature. Finally, the introduction to Job dwells on Immanuel's personal challenges. In all three cases, the patron's support remedies the situation. The patron in Introduction A proposes a brilliant organizational scheme for the *Maḥbarot*, while the patron in Introduction B acts as Immanuel's muse. Isaac's emotional and financial support aid Immanuel in the introduction to Job. Most striking, all three prefaces end with the same linguistic construction: "And my hands are spread out to the heavens to . . ."; but Immanuel requests different aid in each one. In Introduction A he requests rational speech and that his tongue should not fail, while in Introduction B Immanuel asks that God be with "our mouth in whatever we compose and teach us that which we will say," using the plural form to indicate himself and the patron.[60] And Immanuel's request in the preface to Job is that God "open the gates of this book and its hidden intentions for me."[61]

Together with other fragmentary evidence, Immanuel's dedication to Isaac ben Menaḥem suggests that Immanuel relied on patronage to support his scholarship.[62] While *Maḥberot Immanuel* contains patron characters, both good and evil, one could never be certain that Immanuel knew one from personal experience. Classification within the rhetorical genre of *argumentum* is thus highly relevant to the discussion of patronage in the *Maḥbarot* and especially in the presentation of the *Sar*. As a wandering poet in real need of a patron, Immanuel knows how to properly address one. Although the interlocutor in *Maḥberot Immanuel* is certainly a fictional character, he is based on a real character in the medieval world—the wealthy patron.

Final Methodological Comments

In *Maḥberot Immanuel*, Immanuel casually mentions a brief hiatus in the adventures of the poet and his companion. This comment prompted myriad conjectures about the cause of ruptured relations between poet and patron in the real world, as though the literature reflected the circumstances of Immanuel's real life.[63] In this vein some have read the tale of Immanuel's seduction of a nun in the third *maḥberet* as a reference to a real patron's biological sister, with whom Immanuel "allegedly" engaged in an illicit affair, causing Immanuel's banishment by his *Sar*.[64] Most biographical studies explain Immanuel's exile, also mentioned solely in the *Maḥbarot*, as the result of economic misfortune that was used by his detractors to exile him from Rome as a heretic.[65] This historicist reading of Immanuel's literary *Maḥbarot* should be counterbalanced by Immanuel's biblical commentaries, which allegorize the act of lending money to a peer. Immanuel's reading of Proverbs 6:1–2 ("My son, if you have stood surety for your fellow, given your hand for another, you have been trapped by the words of your mouth, snared by the words of your mouth"), which warns against serving as another man's guarantor, identifies the borrower as the material faculty of the human soul, the lender as the divine emanation "which is the connection between a human being and his creator," and the guarantor as the soul's rational faculty in order to warn readers about their spiritual health.[66] The lesson of the verse, explains Immanuel, is to preserve one's rational faculty, which Immanuel presents as the only part of the human soul that can live eternally, against the harmful physical forces of the body that threaten the soul.

Scholars occasionally acknowledge that *Maḥberot Immanuel* is "the chief source from which information has been obtained about its author's biography. But, as such, the volume is not always quite trustworthy, as certain facts mentioned there have hitherto not been fully authenticated, and would indeed seem to be more fictitious than true."[67] Nonetheless, scholars continue to embrace the biographical fallacy. This trend continued well into the twentieth century with, for example, Moses Shulvass asserting that "the only fact *definitely known* is that Immanuel of Rome was blond," based on Immanuel's comment that his beard had turned from gold to silver.[68] Even recent studies on Immanuel have supplied biographical information that is only tentatively linked to the *Maḥbarot* or has been absolutely invented out of nothing. For example, Immanuel praises his wife in the first *maḥberet* but does not divulge her name. But since his description of her is laden with linguistic allusions to the book of Esther, one scholar identifies her as "Esther."[69]

With competing evidence from two literary sources—the fictive *Maḥberot Immanuel* and the allegorizing biblical commentaries—the methodological complexity of reconstructing Immanuel's biography comes into full view. Neither source can be deemed a priori more trustworthy than the other, and they offer conflicting evidence. Until more concrete historical data can be obtained, if ever, the best approach is to reject their content as nonbiographical and instead use the two corpora together as bases for reconstructing Immanuel's intellectual and cultural, rather than personal, biography.

Given the impoverished state of knowledge regarding Immanuel's biography, one might ask why his life has been imagined with such richness by various scholars since the dawn of professionalized academic Jewish studies. What draws scholars to highlight Immanuel, a seemingly obscure author, living in a time and place that were not particularly known for their contributions to the cultural fabric of medieval Judaism? Ultimately, the history of "Immanuel studies"—namely previous treatments of Immanuel and his writings—reveals more about the scholars and their contexts than about the subject itself.

Imagining Immanuel: Who and Why?

Immanuel's poetry and "biography" were among the earliest subjects fervently studied by nineteenth-century German scholars of the *Wissenschaft des Judentums* movement, the first exemplars of professionalized academic Jewish studies scholars; Immanuel was embraced by Jewish proponents of reform who sought European citizenship and cultural integration.[70] In the nineteenth century Immanuel was hailed as "the wonder of all times" and "an anomaly in the Jewish society of the Middle Ages" by scholars who idealized him as a successfully assimilated Jew.[71] To one Reform rabbi and scholar, "Immanuel illustrates that duality of character which Mr. Israel Zangwill and Dr. Martin Buber regard as typical of the Jew."[72] In their quest to find a model of a Jew who fully participated in both Jewish and secular worlds, German scholars demonstrated Immanuel's departure from the commonly held perception of a pious medieval Jew—that is, someone devoted wholly to Talmud and ritual law. He is described as one who "allowed himself to be influenced by the vivacity of the Italians and the Europeanized Jews, and put no curb on his tongue."[73] Described as a unique environment for Jews, especially after the demise of other western European environs, late medieval Italy was idealized as a tranquil place, especially for Jewish-Christian contacts.[74]

The nineteenth century saw the nationalistic struggles of peoples of Germany and the Italian peninsula, each of which unified as national entities in that same century. Within German university circles, an appreciation for Italian literature developed through particular interest in Dante's writings, especially the *Divine Comedy*. Viewed as a poet who united religion and poetry with society and the nation, Dante was hailed by German

Romantics as a prophetic and mystical figure from the past, "a high priest of Catholic literature."[75] Since German Jewish scholars of the *Wissenschaft* circles sought to promote the idealized Jew as deeply engaged with non-Jewish society and culture, and Germans already revered Dante as a poet, the "discovery" of a Jewish poet who could have known Dante proved especially tantalizing. In *Wissenschaft* biographies, the aspirational Immanuel, "although a Hebrew by descent and training, though he was eminently proficient in Jewish lore and tradition, was at the same time thoroughly imbued with the spirit of the Italian nation and literature."[76]

The invention of a personal relationship between Dante and Immanuel pervades the scholarly literature of the nineteenth century, insofar as one scholar notes an almost mystical connection between the two authors who by "a remarkable coincidence"—he asserts—were born in the same year.[77] Other biographical details perpetuate the biographical fallacy while revealing more about the scholars' context than Immanuel's or Dante's, such as the assertion that the two authors met at a secret literary and political society called "Young Italy."[78] While a medieval Young Italy society is unknown, one was formed in the 1830s by the Italian nationalist Giuseppe Mazzini (1805–1872) in his efforts to stoke nationalistic fervor during the Italian Risorgimento.[79] While the majority of *Wissenschaft*-era scholars embraced the lively, even raucous, tone present in *Maḥberot Immanuel*, some excoriated Immanuel "for that prostitution of the sacred tongue. The apparent wish to display so thorough a mastery of the Hebrew as to be able to mould it at will cannot excuse the obscene imageries with which the poetical work of the Italian Jew teems."[80] Sabato Morais (1823–1897), a Livornese rabbi, minister to Congregation Mikveh Israel in Philadelphia, and eventual founder of the Jewish Theological Seminary in New York, expressed his condemnation of Immanuel's poetry in a long piece that simultaneously displays his fascination with *Maḥberot Immanuel*, suggesting that Morais perceived the cultural openness of medieval Sephardic and Italian Jewry as offering an idealized model for American Jewish youth.[81] For nineteenth-century Jews outside Italy, Immanuel's poetry represents a model of successful engagement and integration with secular culture, while for contemporaneous Italian Jews it affirmed and expressed their continuous and ancient membership in the Italian collective.[82] In the putative friendship between Immanuel and Dante, Italian Jewish luminaries like Samuel David Luzzato (1800–1865), Moses Soave (1820–1882), and Alessandro D'Ancona (1835–1914) found their "proof" that, historically, Jews contributed integrally to Italian culture.[83]

As a prolific author and talented poet, Immanuel of Rome fascinated medieval Jews and Christians as well as contemporary ones. His ability to write poetry in both Hebrew and Italian excited Jews seeking European legitimacy and Italians who celebrated the universality of Dante Alighieri's writings. The popularity of Immanuel's poetry stimulated an entire body of literature about the author, but there is very little evidence on which to base such theories. Furthermore, Immanuel's thought extends far beyond his poetry, and scholars who seek to understand him must cross disciplines to consider his philosophically oriented exegesis and treatise on biblical grammar. In some cases—such as those demonstrating that he had formal patrons—the biblical commentaries "stabilize" the narrative transmitted in *Maḥberot Immanuel*. In other instances—such as the admonition against lending money to a friend or the choice of the traveler's sixty years of age—the commentaries "destabilize" the literary narrative by revealing a nonliteral interpretation of the biblical passage. For now, the only way to advance studies of Immanuel is a full consideration of Immanuel's oeuvre, with all its myriad textual genres, within its larger historical, cultural, and intellectual contexts of the fourteenth century. While Immanuel was a creative and prolific poet, his biblical commentaries far outweigh his poetry in length and breadth. To date, there has been no systematic exploration of the relationship between Immanuel's poetry and his philosophical biblical commentaries. To ground Immanuel's work in its intellectual context, we next turn to his voluminous philosophical commentaries.

2

BETWEEN THE EAGLE AND THE LION

He is my brother and my crown, bone of my bones and flesh of my flesh, Judah the lion's whelp . . .

Leave *The Guide* to the guide.

—Immanuel, *Maḥbarot*

Among the many theological debates waged in medieval Christian universities and Jewish study halls, the dispute about the fate of the human soul after the body's death was one of the most central. This problem was animated by various and sometimes conflicting interpretations of Aristotelian and pseudo-Aristotelian writings from the Islamic world. During the twelfth century, Greco-Arabic philosophical ideas entered western European Jewish intellectual culture. At the beginning of the thirteenth century, the growing influence of Maimonides' writings and their rationalist orientation stimulated higher levels of philosophical awareness and study among medieval Jews in Provence, Christian Spain, and Italy. Aristotelian psychology was first accessed through the Greco-Arabic tradition, but the thirteenth century saw an explosion of writing about the soul in both Latin and Hebrew. Some of these works followed a radical interpretive stance first posited by Averroes (1126–1198), a jurist from Muslim Iberia and one of the most important medieval commentators on Aristotle.

The deep impact of Aristotelian psychology, as distilled by Maimonides and others, is evident throughout Immanuel's philosophical biblical commentaries. It appears as well in some of the poetry in *Maḥberot Immanuel.* But Immanuel did not follow Maimonidean ideas about the soul unswervingly. As this chapter will explore, Immanuel's meditations on the soul and its afterlife emerge from the Maimonidean and Scholastic traditions but also make important deviations. The focus for the analysis is Immanuel's commentary on Psalm 68, his longest exposition on any single psalm. Immanuel's reading exposes multiple layers of meaning through a focus on grammar, idiomatic language, and imagery. In addition he discovers an allegorical stratum that reveals scientific truths about the universe and its metaphysical entities. In Immanuel's view, this psalm encapsulates universal truths about God, the cosmos, and the place of humans within the cosmos. His interpretation, which is singled out for special praise in *Maḥberet Ha-Tofet V'Ha-Eden*, provides an opportunity for Immanuel to lay out his metaphysics. A close analysis of Immanuel's exegesis thus demonstrates how the poetic narrative compellingly and accessibly draws on key Maimonidean and scholastic philosophical concepts.

Maimonideanism in Italy

Before we turn to Immanuel's particular philosophical orientation, which was, understandably, shaped by the broader influence of Maimonides, some general comments about the influence of Maimonides on Italian Jewish thought are in order. Maimonideanism, in fact, was a vital aspect of late-medieval Jewish intellectual life in the Italian peninsula.[1] Maimonides' harmonization of Jewish law and tradition with philosophy and Aristotelian science created a complex legacy. Various Jewish communities reacted differently to his ideas and writings. Some accepted the Maimonidean codification of *halakhah* in *Mishneh Torah* with ease but bristled at the rationalist interpretation of Jewish tradition in the first book of *Mishneh Torah* and *The Guide of the Perplexed.* In contrast to the Jews of other regions, Jews in Italy accepted Maimonides' philosophical writings more easily than his halakhic ones. Italian Jews tended to follow an interpretation of *halakhah* strongly influenced by the Franco-German (Ashkenazic) legal tradition, but they were relatively open to philosophical ideas.[2] The popularity of Maimonides' *The Guide of the Perplexed* in thirteenth-century Italy is attested by the fact that two of the earliest commentaries on it were composed there. In addition, the philosopher Zeraḥiah Ḥen of Barcelona (d. ca. 1290s) and the mystic Abraham Abulafia (1240–1291) both describe their experiences teaching *The Guide of the Perplexed* to students.[3] By the fourteenth century, Hebrew translations of Maimonides' philosophically oriented introduction to *Pirkei Avot* ("Ethics of the Fathers"), known as the "Eight Chapters," and his commentary on *Avot* were inserted into the Italian *maḥzor* to be studied on Sabbath afternoons during the period between Passover and Shavuot.[4]

The development of an intellectual orientation that might properly be called Maimonideanism began with the translation of Maimonides' works into Hebrew and blossomed into an ideological movement (or movements) that propounded a curriculum and a method of Torah study.[5] In the introduction to *The Guide of the Perplexed*, Maimonides differentiates multiple layers of meaning in scripture, which he claims is aimed at varied audiences with diverse intellectual capacities and educational levels. Yet he explains the esoteric significance of only selected scriptural passages and episodes.[6] A systematic allegorical exposition of scripture was undertaken by Samuel Ibn Tibbon and his school. Samuel developed the fragmentary allegories identified by Maimonides into full-blown systematic excurses and commentaries on biblical books. Samuel's translation of Maimonides' *The Guide of the Perplexed* from Arabic into Hebrew kindled interest in the study of natural and speculative sciences alongside traditional Torah study, particularly among southern French and Italian Jews.[7] It also spurred an ancillary translation movement from Arabic into Hebrew of the speculative texts that served as Maimonides' sources.[8] A devotee of Maimonides, Samuel pushed the boundaries on exposing Maimonides' esoteric teachings because, as he noted, the post-Maimonidean Jewish community was intellectually sophisticated and erudite.[9] In addition to expanding the theoretical realm, Samuel's translation of *The Guide of the Perplexed* and his glossary of its unusual words nourished a bourgeoning vocabulary of philosophical terms in Hebrew, which would be cultivated throughout the late Middle Ages.[10] As the first section of Maimonides' *The Guide of the Perplexed* is devoted to defining biblical terms through a scientific and philosophical lens, Samuel's disciples undertook a rereading of the biblical text, with sensitivity to the narratives, characters, and verses that might be interpreted allegorically, as referring to scientific concepts and principles.

The twelfth-century appearance of a new literary genre in Hebrew, the philosophical commentary, may signal the most tangible impact of Tibbonide Maimonideanism. Samuel's commentary on Ecclesiastes, which reads the biblical book as a narration of the intellect's struggle to attain immortality, alongside numerous scientific and philosophical digressions, was the earliest sustained commentary on a full biblical book.[11] Samuel's son Moses, following in his father's footsteps, wrote philosophical commentaries on the Pentateuch and Song of Songs, all exegetical works that would later inform Immanuel's commentaries.

Amid the literary output of the Tibbonide school, *Malmad ha-Talmidim* ("The Students' Goad"), a thirteenth-century collection of philosophical sermons related to the weekly Torah portion, aided in the dissemination of the allegorical reading mode favored by medieval rationalists.[12] Cited frequently by Immanuel, the *Malmad*'s author was Jacob Anatoli (1194–1256), a physician and resident translator in the Neapolitan imperial court of Frederick II, who translated the middle commentaries of Averroes on the logical works as well as Averroes' paraphrase of Ptolemy's *Almagest* into Hebrew, providing Immanuel and other non-Arabophone Jewish scholars direct access to many scientific and philosophical texts.[13] Anatoli's *Malmad*, likely written in the imperial court of Frederick II, was heavily influenced by Ibn Tibbon as well as by a fellow Christian translator in Naples, Michael Scot (ca. 1175–1232). Anatoli's congenial relationship with Scot likely informed his view that gentiles and Jews who studied science to ascertain universal truths were equal in status. Anatoli went to great lengths to praise his gentile friend and quoted several of Michael's exegeses to show the similarity between the two scholars' interpretations.[14] Anatoli's recollection of his cool reception at and dismissal from several Italian Jewish communities likely signals early hesitation about rationalist readings of scripture, but by Immanuel's time, the hermeneutical strategies and allegorical readings popularized by the Tibbonides and Anatoli were commonplace. Immanuel, in fact, incorporated large portions of the *Malmad* into his commentaries and treated non-Jewish rationalists in the *Eden* portion of *Maḥberet Ha-Tofet V'Ha-Eden* with an appreciation reminiscent of Anatoli's.[15]

In his biblical commentaries, Immanuel follows the Maimonidean-Tibbonide tradition in his approach to biblical narrative and in his integration of comments taken from both Samuel Ibn Tibbon and Moses Ibn Tibbon (1195–1274) as well as Anatoli. He blends this dense philosophical material with more traditional biblical insights, which are drawn from the commentaries of Abraham Ibn Ezra (ca. 1089–1167) and Rashi (ca. 1040–1105).[16] But as much as Immanuel's biblical commentaries reflect the influence of Tibbonide Maimonideanism, they were also written in a cultural environment that had already amalgamated Maimonides' legacy with elements from Christian Scholasticism.[17]

These Scholastics, who combined Aristotelian and Neoplatonic philosophy with Christian theology, were primarily members of theology faculties at universities or cathedral schools. While Aristotelian writings had influenced the medieval philosophical curriculum since the eighth century, the twelfth-century translations of most of the Aristotelian corpus from Arabic into Latin, especially the paraphrases and commentaries rendered by later Hellenistic and Islamic scholars, reenergized the study of ancient philosophy. By the thirteenth century, theologians like Albert the Great (ca. 1200–1280s) and Thomas Aquinas (1225–1274) engaged with Aristotelian works, especially mediated through the interpretations of Averroes. Averroes' most controversial reading of Aristotle posited that when humans acquire true knowledge, their rational souls conjoin with a single universal intellect, and that this conjunction constitutes the immortality of the soul. The "unicity theory" seeks to explain how humans, whose existence is compounded of both matter and form, can acquire and know the incorporeal universal truths. Averroes' theory rejects the notion of a unique afterlife for each individual, which led to his censure by several Christian Scholastics, and his writings were formally condemned as heresy at the University of Paris in 1277. Debate about the soul and its ultimate purpose moved from Christian circles into the Jewish world through Hebrew translations of Latin Scholastic writings. This Latin-Aristotelian corpus included texts not found in the Greco-Arabic tradition, like the *Liber de causis* ("Book of Causes"), an anonymous Neoplatonic text attributed to Aristotle that relays metaphysical and cosmological propositions through a focus on causes, substances that can shape reality and trickle their strength down to lower levels of reality.[18]

Maimonideanism in Immanuel

Not a philosopher himself, Immanuel was nonetheless an avid consumer of philosophical writings and scientific theories, which he reworked into his biblical commentaries and narrative poetry. It is likely that Immanuel learned psychology through Hillel of Verona's Hebrew *Tagmule Ha-Nefesh* (On the Recompense of the Soul), an accessible and organized handbook that summarized Aristotle's *De Anima* ("On the Soul"), while citing significant excerpts from both Thomas Aquinas and Averroes. It also included elements from the Latin translation of Avicenna's book on the soul, *Liber Sextus Naturalium*; Dominicus Gundissalinus's *Liber de Anima*; and *Three Treatises on the Intellect* by Averroes and his son. Immanuel's other main sources of Scholastic theory were Judah Romano's (ca. 1286–1330) translations of philosophical, medical, and scientific works, and the *Liber de causis*. Possibly Immanuel's relative, although the exact relationship is still unknown, Judah is the subject of a lengthy panegyric *maḥberet* and the recipient of a coveted spot in *Eden*.[19] Judah's writings and translations appear prominently in Immanuel's commentaries and poetry, mostly unattributed, leading to a heartfelt confession to plagiarism by Immanuel's literary persona.[20] Immanuel's reliance on Judah's writings was so great that, as he notes, "without the wisdom in his books—mine would never have existed."[21]

In Rome, Maimonides' *The Guide of the Perplexed* served as a foundational text for philosophers as well as mystics. Immanuel was additionally exposed to kabbalistic teachings disseminated in the biblical commentary of Menaḥem Recanati (ca. 1223–1290) but rejected them for their mystical justifications.[22] The application of *The Guide of the Perplexed* by disparate thinkers in medieval Rome led Giuseppe Sermoneta to identify the two Romans, Immanuel and Judah, as adherents of "philosophical faith," an intellectual trend in Rome that blended Maimonidean rationalism with mystical tendencies.[23] Both Immanuel's and Judah's writings do strongly favor the plausibility of achieving intellectual conjunction during one's lifetime, which differs from Maimonides.[24]

Immanuel can perhaps be characterized as a secondary intellectual, curating and condensing philosophical literature into comprehensible parts, rather than as a philosopher. In his own opinion, however, his poetry, which communicates philosophical concepts to a popular audience, was ancillary to his commentaries. Listing his intellectual achievements in the first *maḥberet*, Immanuel highlights his commentaries followed by his books on biblical grammar and the shapes of the letters, and only afterward does he mention his poetry.[25] The commentaries are also highlighted in the eighth *maḥberet*.[26] But by far the most dramatic spotlight on Immanuel's philosophical commentaries appears in his tour of heaven, where the biblical authors, one after the other, commend Immanuel's persona within the text for his deep understanding of their books. As the longest section of *Eden*, with the greatest potential to showcase Immanuel's philosophical understanding of scripture, this literary episode offers the reader a unique opportunity to compare Immanuel's exegesis and poetry.

The Aristotelian cosmos, as found in Maimonides' *The Guide of the Perplexed* and *Mishneh Torah* (and in Immanuel's writings), is structured as an indirect chain of being beginning with the First Cause (God) emanating existence through the separate intellects to the sublunar world.[27] In its desire to imitate the unmoved mover, a separate intellect contemplates God's essence, which generates a celestial sphere. The separate intellect also contemplates its own essence, which in turn generates the separate intellect below it.[28] Immanuel explains this process in his gloss of Psalms 18 and 19.[29] The tenth and lowest of the separate intellects, which Maimonides identifies as "angels" in religious parlance, is the agent intellect (also called the active intellect).[30] As the final emanated intellect, the agent intellect links the celestial and terrestrial worlds. Like Avicenna, Immanuel conceived of the agent intellect as the giver of forms, an incorporeal existent that confers form on sublunar matter and generates existent things, depending on the capacity of the recipient matter.[31] In his commentary on Song of Songs, Immanuel considers the idea of an agent intellect located within the human soul, a view upheld by both Albert the Great and Thomas Aquinas. He rejects it, representing the agent intellect as external to man.[32] The agent intellect appears both in the biblical commentaries and in *Maḥberot Immanuel*, sometimes recast in a traditionalist idiom as "the spiritual Eden" because it nourishes souls behind the curtain of the heavens while "tying crowns for its Maker, which are the crowns worn by the souls of the righteous."[33] The righteous wearing crowns of knowledge appear prominently in Immanuel's *Eden*, where crowns represent the accumulation of knowledge by a perfected intellect. The souls delight in the agent intellect's emanation, more so than in any other experience, and Immanuel reiterates the spiritual joy of "the souls that have been gathered into it."[34]

As for the human soul, Immanuel describes it as divided into three parts, the vegetative soul responsible for generation, nutrition, and growth; the sensitive soul responsible for perception and motility; and the rational soul responsible for cognition, which is unique to rational human beings.[35] He illustrates this division using an unusual metaphor of a walnut whose layers must be penetrated to reach the meat, which is the rational faculty.[36] Like most medieval thinkers, Immanuel was fascinated by the rational soul, "the most exalted part of them all," which animates the body but is also capable of engaging in incorporeal activities like reasoning and cognition.[37] In his comment on Genesis 1:26, Immanuel describes the first man, Adam, as created "in a rational form by which he can be likened [to the angels] in his immortality—for it [the rational faculty] alone, of all a human's parts, can render him immortal."[38]

The actualization of the human intellect and its ability to know universal truths, or intelligibles, differentiates the human being from the animals. Sensible perception is followed by the abstraction of knowledge and the eventual acquisition of truths. In these stages, the human intellect is merely potential until its actualization, when it intelligizes those truths.[39] Aristotle described the moment of actualization as one where "mind, when actualized, is the same as the things it is thinking of."[40] Maimonides posits that the intellect that has apprehended necessary truths, which are immaterial, thereby insures its immortality beyond the death of the body. In other words, intellectual perfection leads to immortality of the soul.

The cultivation of the rational faculty, therefore, which can be hindered by the material pursuits of the other faculties, yields, in Immanuel's words, "the virtue by which he shall cling to God and the intellects and he shall know truth without study, rather by casual thought."[41] What Immanuel describes here is conjunction with the agent intellect, which is the union of the agent intellect and the rational part of the human soul, an ideal state in which the human intellect cognizes all knowledge. As Immanuel describes it, immortality is the result of conjunction, since "the material intellect within the human soul desires to cleave to the agent intellect . . . and when the material soul apprehends it [the agent intellect], they will unite and conjoin in the manner common to each intellect and its actualized object of thought. The material intellect will become immortal and everlasting."[42] The acquisition of knowledge, therefore, is a lifelong endeavor leading to ultimate perfection, rewarded by immortality.[43] Immanuel returns to this idea again and again in his biblical commentaries, but perhaps his most explicit description of the process of acquiring knowledge is in his allegorical reading of Psalm 68.

Immanuel's Commentary on Psalm 68

In *Maḥberet Ha-Tofet V'Ha-Eden*, Immanuel's tour of hell is followed by a parallel visit to heaven. When Immanuel's persona first arrives in *Eden*'s heights, he is welcomed by a series of biblical figures who praise his exegesis, highlighting the readings of individual biblical verses. King David, the traditional "author" of the book of Psalms, commends Immanuel's interpretation not of a single verse but of an entire psalm, Psalm 68. In this striking scene, King David welcomes Immanuel, then charges all the earlier interpreters of Psalms, including David Kimḥi (1160–1235), the famous Provençal grammarian and exegete, to offer their own interpretations of Psalm 68, which he rejects. The king finally asks for Immanuel's interpretation, which Immanuel provides, to general acclaim. The psalm, traditionally read as a triumphal hymn celebrating the defeat of the Egyptians and the deliverance of the Israelites, uses mythological motifs to survey the journey of the Israelites from Egypt to Canaan, including their sojourn through the wilderness and their reception of the Torah at Mount Sinai.[44] It is "widely admitted as textually and exegetically the most difficult and obscure of all the psalms."[45] Immanuel's allegorical exposition of the chapter views it as revealing the structure of the universe and the soul's teleological goal.[46]

> David said to me, "Welcome in the name of my Lord! Are you the one who removes the decay from my pearls?" He hugged and kissed me, clung to me as a belt girds a man's waist. He said to me, "You have honored me with your interpretation of Psalms, and your comments revealed its exemplary greatness. You clarified its figures of speech that, until now, were unknown to man, like a virgin. By my life! After your soul is pleased with knowledge, I will truly honor you with my words and actions and I will do whatever you command." David dispatched one of the assembled men to gather all the exegetes who had interpreted Psalms with their commentaries. All came at King David's command, led by David Kimḥi. Upon arrival, they bowed before King David, prostrating themselves seven times, and extended their greetings to him. David said to the exegetes assembled before him, "Each of you shall recite the psalm, 'God will arise, his enemies shall be scattered, his foes shall flee before him' [Psalm 68:2], revealing its inner meaning and matters according to your reading." Then, each one arose and seized the opportunity to explain it this way or that way. David said, "While one exegete says: 'this is my interpretation,' another one says: 'this is my innovation,' but none of you bring comfort to my soul." David arose, kissed me on my forehead, and said, "This one is as delightful as a pouch of myrrh. He revealed the secret of this psalm so that no allusion or secret remains within its foundation or structure, from beginning to end." He commanded me to publicly recite my exegesis of the psalm, which I did. Neither did I hide any aspect of the psalm nor did I conceal anything. When the exegetes heard my interpretations, pondered their greatness, the exegetes were rendered mute. Then, David ordered the exegetes to honor me. They esteemed me and served me as though I was their king and their messiah.[47]

The culmination of this extended public performance, clearly intended to pique the reader's curiosity, is King David's exuberant praise of Immanuel's interpretation of Psalm 68. In this scene, the substance of the interpretation is not explained, but, as we will see, Immanuel understands the psalm to allude to the structure of the universe and the place of the soul therein. It should be noted first that in these scenes David Kimḥi is the only medieval exegete mentioned by name. And, as it happens, Kimḥi's interpretation of Psalm 68 is thoroughly historical; he sees it as an allusion to the Assyrian invasion of Jerusalem in the eighth century BCE. Immanuel's reading of this psalm, which begins with God and advances down the ladder of existence to the human experience in the sublunar realm, is, in fact, an outright refutation of Kimḥi's historical approach. But without knowledge of the episode in *Eden*, the full significance of Immanuel's interpretation is lost on the reader of the biblical commentary. Immanuel's larger purposes can, in fact, be appreciated only when juxtaposing the poetry and the philosophical commentary.

Immanuel's reading of the psalm finds multiple layers of meaning, but most important for understanding Immanuel's philosophies is the allegorical level that reveals scientific truths about the universe. Although Immanuel generally follows Maimonides' creation scheme, he does include newer material taken from Judah Romano. Immanuel explains that "the author of the psalm [King David] revealed that the psalm was composed in poetic style, like the Song of Songs, whose words cannot be understood according to their literal meaning. Thus, the author used hyperbole to allude to the intended matter through allusion [*remez*] which is distant from the literal meaning."[48] For Immanuel, that intended matter is the ordered structure of the universe. The opening verses thus refer to God's creation of all existents, both above and beneath the moon; the cosmos is divided between the sublunar existents, which "have no eternity and enduring rank" and the supernal existents, "which are above time, for they are eternal."[49]

Immanuel nuances the Maimonidean conception of God with integrated elements from Judah Romano's writings, but the basis of his philosophy remains steadfastly Maimonidean. Immanuel's use of Judah Romano is perhaps most evident when he incorporates Platonic and Neoplatonic concepts, as, for example, the concept that God contains all the ideas of existent things even before they were created. God is described in verse 6 as "a father of orphans, and a judge of widows." Immanuel sees the orphans here as "an allusion to the forms of species, in their being conceptualized first in the group of ideas." And, reflecting the standard philosophical principle that form is male and matter female, he sees the widows, who by definition lack husbands, as alluding to "matter abstracted from any form, in their being also [included] in the group of *hemshele ha-metsiut* [ideas]."[50] The forms of things and the *hemshele ha-metsiut*, for Immanuel, are thus conceptualized within the divine essence.[51] A similar view of preexistent exemplars, using the same terminology, appears in Judah Romano's *Commentary on Kaddish and Kedushah*. Judah describes the *hemshele ha-metsiut* as templates for existent things, which are *in potentia* within the divine essence, alluding to the Neoplatonic idea of all the intelligibles conceptualized in the divine being.[52] Immanuel's depiction of God in this verse, as conceptualizer of existence, differs from that of God as prime mover entailed by the previous verse.

In verse 7 ("God sets the solitary in families; He brings out those who are bound into prosperity; but the rebellious dwell in a dry land"), Immanuel explains: "God brought all the exemplars forth unto some of the qualities of existence and all of existence was good in general."[53] According to Immanuel, God created the world not out of necessity but out of kindness (*ḥesed*). The rain showers, in verse 9 ("The earth shook; the heavens also dropped rain at the presence of God; Sinai itself was moved at the presence of God, the God of Israel"), signify the hierarchical chain of emanation, from prime matter to lower forms of matter. Immanuel explains: "He called the descent of their emanation and goodness upon what is beneath them by the name of falling rain . . . he meant that they [the heavenly bodies] are not the First Cause of what is beneath them; rather they only emanate upon the sublunar beings from the emanation which they received from God, for He is the [most] distant First Cause."[54] In this comment, Immanuel acknowledges God as the creator, affirming that neither the celestial spheres nor the astral powers have generative power over sublunar beings.[55]

Immanuel interprets the first part of Psalm 68 as a reference to the divine creation of the universe and uses it to investigate the supernal processes that issue from God, emanating downward to create the universe, surveying its structure, and exploring the role of human beings within that universe. He explains, "After the poet [David] mentioned the three parts of the world and alluded to the sublunar world in his saying: 'she that tarrieth at home divideth the spoil,' he said 'when ye lie among the sheepfolds,' with regard to the human species, speaking of the individuals thereof."[56] Because humans have a rational faculty, which can exist eternally, Immanuel regards them as "at an intermediate rank between the noble existents and the rest of the animals—you have a noble and magnificent rank. . . . That is to say, [you have] a supernal, intellectual soul that in its matter resembles the spiritual substances and which has the potential to ascend in the ranks of intellect and resemble the angels on high and return, separate from all matter."[57] The next part of the verse ("Even for those of you who lie among the sheepfolds, there are wings of a dove sheathed in silver, its pinions in fine gold") reassures the downtrodden that they, too, can ascend like a dove of gold and silver. To Immanuel, this image assures a human being that despite the corporeality of the human condition, the rational soul can attain salvation. He notes: "He called the soul by the name of dove because the dove is not among the scavenging birds, nor is it among the birds that eat insects or any sort of filth. [He did so] to allude that through the soul, one aims at cleanliness and purity and the perfection of virtues, as well as distancing [oneself] from despicable actions."[58]

Equating the dove with the soul, Immanuel states, "It is in her [the soul's] power to ascend to the heights of the intellect, to be like the exalted angels, and to return divested of all matter."[59] Immanuel views the body and the soul as interdependent, working together to attain wellbeing during life and immortality in the afterlife. Immanuel explains, "For he shall know that he is composed of body and soul, and it is ideal for them [body and soul] to act in the manner of friends or lovers . . . to attain perfection, that is [eternal] life."[60]

Citing *The Guide of the Perplexed*, Immanuel reads the dove's two wings as representing the desired state of perfect body and soul. Echoing the Maimonidean distinction between physical and intellectual perfection, Immanuel states:

> The *wings covered with silver* are an allegory for the faculties that are in the soul of man, in order that he thereby attain the perfection of the body, through which the house and the city may be established. [As for] her *pinions* covered *with shimmering greenishness*, he alluded therein to the intellectual faculties through the intermediary of which the soul attains its final perfection, which consists in the intellectual apprehension of intelligibles and believing in true opinions and paying those duties incumbent upon one to God.[61]

The silver wings, of great value, symbolize the faculties of the soul that enable one to reach perfection of the body, which is needed for the proper management of one's domestic and political encounters. The golden wings, of even greater value, symbolize the rational faculty, which enables the soul to reach its ultimate perfection: the acquisition of intelligibles, having true beliefs, and repaying the Lord's debts.[62] Immanuel emphasizes that the preparation of the intellect and observance of the commandments were given to perfect these two realities. This Maimonidean binary of body and soul is evident throughout both realms of Immanuel's otherworldly journey in *Maḥberet Ha-Tofet V'Ha-Eden*.

The perfection of the soul, the Maimonidean "ultimate perfection," is attained through acquiring truths, eventually "knowing everything concerning all the beings that is within the capacity of man to know."[63] This cognitive process is intertwined, according to Maimonides, with the observance of Torah commandments because the dictates of the divine Torah regulate the social and political serenity necessary for intellectual development, and they also convey true beliefs. Devoid of any theurgic value, performance of the commandments, in Maimonides' view, has no effect on God. But as God never does anything in vain, they must have a rationale, and Maimonides points to their social and intellectual utility. Mosaic law, Maimonides notes, is exemplary for its attention to the needs of both body and soul.[64]

Immanuel imbibes Maimonides' rationalization of the commandments, evident in his enumeration of the commandments in his commentary on the Pentateuch, and views praxis as a fundamental part of human perfection. In his comment on verse 14, Immanuel states, "What is aimed at thereby is that its [the intellect's] faculties were prepared and the commandments were given to the holy people to perfect the two existences within us, that is, the perfection of the body and the perfection of the soul."[65] In his reading of Proverbs 31, Immanuel notes, "The reason by which this soul came to be bound in the bond of life is that beyond wisdom and attributes, it attained fear of God which includes the fulfillment of all the practical commandments for they are the roots that bear the intentions [*kavvanot*], propositions [*deot*], and beliefs [*emunot*]. This also includes avoidance of all that was prohibited to it. . . . Therefore, because it allotted time for these three matters, it clung to the Lord and it ought to be praised."[66] Thus, in addition to moral perfection and the study of the sciences emphasized in his commentary on Song of Songs, Immanuel considered the fulfillment of biblical commandments an essential precursor to the soul's ultimate beatitude. Although Immanuel embraced a Maimonidean immaterial vision of the postmortem experience, *Maḥberet Ha-Tofet V'Ha-Eden* demonstrates his idiosyncratic approach to perfection bolstered by the interpretation of Psalm 68.

Immanuel's reading of verse 15 delves into the details of emanation, for "through the Almighty's moving the emanation of the angels into the soul of man, it [the soul] shall be restored to illumination and whiteness, even though it is imprisoned in a place of darkness."[67] Immanuel outlines a course of preparatory studies. The Maimonidean course of study orders the seeker of perfection to "train himself at first in the art of logic, then in the mathematical sciences according to the proper order, then in the natural sciences, and after that in the divine science."[68] A potential problem is that "people whose mind stops short at one of these sciences . . . are cut off by death while engaged in some preliminary study."[69] Immanuel highlights the contingency of one discipline on another in his commentary on Song of Songs 3:6, where he explains that "one shall ascend in a straight path from the applied sciences to the natural sciences to the divine sciences which is the straight path. The one intending to ascend to Him, may He be blessed, should not learn them out of order."[70] A haphazard approach to study will render one's intellect unable to proceed to the goal of metaphysics.[71] This approach to intellectual training is praised and reinforced in the narrative of *Maḥberet Ha-Tofet V'Ha-Eden*.

Under "mathematics," one of the preparatory subjects, Immanuel includes the seven branches enumerated by Avicenna.[72] Though subordinate, they are "a ladder by which to ascend to the natural and divine sciences and therefore they are called 'points of silver,' small points to emphasize their value to the natural and divine sciences, and silver because they are pleasant to acquire and a ladder by which to ascend to the other sciences."[73] Immanuel cautions against excessive study of natural sciences, which have as their object things composed of form and matter and the four elements, since they are merely a prerequisite to attain understanding of metaphysics, the study of incorporeal entities like God, angels, and the separate intellects.[74] Surveying the levels of the divinely created universe, the spiritual, celestial, and sublunar worlds, Immanuel homes in on the human being and the rational intellect's ability to transcend the material nature of the soul. After this, about halfway into the chapter, Immanuel's commentary begins to distinguish between the celestial and spiritual realms, affirming the superiority of the spiritual angels over the heavenly bodies of the celestial realm that are in constant motion. This shift reminds readers that to Immanuel, as to Maimonides, the spiritual realm far supersedes the material one.

In verse 19, Immanuel praises the uniqueness of God and his loving emanation upon the supernal and terrestrial realms. He notes, "God is a God that graces those who love him with two salvations of the soul in the world of angels. The salvations are the deliverance of the body in this world and the deliverance of the soul in the world of the angels."[75] Immanuel reads subsequent verses as referring to postmortem reward:

> after the Poet mentioned that God *delivers* the soul of the righteous and *bundles* it *in the bundle of life* [1 Sam. 25:29] and that He punishes the soul of the wicked, he mentioned that God *awakens them that sleep in*

> *the dust of the earth* [Dan. 12:2], for His Wisdom decreed [for the] righteous and wicked, *some to everlasting life and some to reproaches and everlasting abhorrence* [ibid.]. Regarding the resurrection of the righteous, he said: *The Lord said: I will bring back from Bashan.* That is to say, God decreed and said: from *a mountain of God* [that] *is the mountain of Bashan*—for that is the world of angels where the righteous dwell—*I will bring* [the soul] *back* to the body a second time, to the place where its abode was initially, to see the downfall of the wicked. Similarly, *I will bring back* the soul of the wicked from the depths of hell unto the body, as it was in the days of reproach in order to punish it.[76]

Immanuel reads geographical locations in the psalm, like the mountains of Bashan, as referring to the world of the angels, but he offers no concrete description of that world other than to say that the righteous live there. He does, however, describe a process of punishment for the wicked that alludes to a second resurrection.

Immanuel's exposition of Psalm 68 thus introduces readers to the tripartite structure of the universe and the emanation that informs matter, generating the terrestrial world. As such, it reveals Immanuel's theory of the ultimate human goal. In identifying the rational faculty of the human soul as an entity that has the potential to imitate the immaterial cosmic spheres, this psalm explores the dynamic between the material and immaterial parts of the soul to claim that only the rational part of the human soul can perdure. These discussions also reassure readers with vague allusions to divine reward and punishment, important concepts that Immanuel nuances in his *Maḥberet Ha-Tofet V'Ha-Eden.* Though he mentions conjunction between the rational intellect and the agent intellect in his exegesis of this psalm, Immanuel depicts it more comprehensively elsewhere in his commentaries and poetry.

Immanuel's Theory of Conjunction

Maimonides concludes the *Guide* by outlining four levels of perfection that humans should strive to attain, where a person's greatest perfection refers to "the conception of intelligibles, which teach true opinions concerning the divine things."[77] He also describes "a human individual who, through his apprehension of the true realities and his joy in what he has apprehended, achieves a state in which he talks with people and is occupied with his bodily necessities while his intellect is wholly turned toward Him, may He be exalted, so that in his heart he is always in His presence, while outwardly he is with people."[78] For Maimonides, only the biblical Moses experienced this state, as he was a unique prophet-philosopher who reached the apex of human wisdom.[79] By contrast, Immanuel asserts that conjunction is indeed accessible during a person's life: "the conjunction of the human intellect with the agent intellect is possible, for man's soul does not desire and imagine an impossible thing."[80] Immanuel outlines the path to achieve conjunction. First one needs an inborn disposition, followed by a course of scientific studies, punctilious observance of the commandments, and finally intense ethical rehabilitation. Immanuel reads Song of Songs 1:1 to 5:2 as a textual unit, in which the lover, representing the human intellect, beseeches the beloved, or the agent intellect, to unite with her in the garden.[81] Immanuel also explicates the *Eshet Ḥayil* ("Woman of Valor") passages in Proverbs 31 as referring to a potential intellect that has reached its "ultimate perfection," as the spousal relationship in that chapter signifies the soul's willingness to acquire knowledge and fulfill the Torah commandments.[82] He states:

> When you shall reach this level He, may He be blessed, will emanate the light of the intellect upon you until you desire to climb the ladder of wisdom to approach God. You will find this path straight before you and this means that you will be aided by the heavens, for whomever shall intend to reach beatitude and orient his face toward it, he shall be supported by a generous spirit, that is intellect, granted by the Benefactor. The intellect grants this to anyone who prepared his thoughts for this.[83]

He notes that the soul, conjoined with the agent intellect, will be "above time and see the paths of time below it."[84] Immanuel describes conjunction as a quasi-mystical experience that is difficult to attain but theoretically accessible to any human being. As a close reading of *Maḥberet Ha-Tofet V'Ha-Eden* will show, Immanuel alludes to conjunction between his literary persona and the agent intellect at the chapter's end. This stance echoes intellectual developments current among other Roman Jewish philosophers, who blended Maimonidean theories with newer ones drawn from Christian Scholastic philosophy.

In *Tagmule Ha-Nefesh*, for example, Hillel of Verona (1220–1295) challenged Maimonidean theories on conjunction by attesting that conjunction with the agent intellect is possible during one's lifetime and by attributing supernatural powers to the conjoined individual. He describes the path to conjunction as necessitating a gradual subjugation of the soul's faculties and the perfection of moral and intellectual virtues. This allows one to apprehend divinely revealed secrets of human existence. Having reached an "angelic state," Hillel reports, the individual can perform miracles, such as killing someone or reviving them, creating people and animals, or controlling rainfall.[85] Furthermore, this individual could hear angels and heavenly hosts, even without invoking the holy name. No barrier, he posits, exists between the conjoined intellect and God other than a human soul's material state.[86] Immanuel, for his part, combines the standard Maimonidean naturalistic ideas of providence with Hillel's more radical approach to intellectual conjunction.

Based on Maimonides, Immanuel maintains that the conjoined intellect merits God's direct supervision and has foreknowledge of the future. Maimonides explains, "Providence watches over everyone endowed with intellect proportionately to the measure of his intellect. Thus providence always watches over an individual endowed with perfect apprehension, whose intellect never ceases from being occupied with God."[87] Immanuel imports this idea into his commentaries, establishing a hierarchy of providence where the more developed intellects enjoy greater degrees of divine providence, while nonintellectuals are governed by the vicissitudes of the natural world.[88] He says, "The blessed Lord protects the virtuous who conduct themselves on the path of virtue . . . for the virtuous are protected from temporal events by being above Time. God defends them against the suffering reserved for the blemished souls."[89] Thus, as the intellect amasses knowledge, it receives divine protection. Immanuel expresses this position in his commentary on Job, which is itself heavily indebted to the Maimonidean and Tibbonide readings.[90]

Immanuel's Job symbolizes a morally virtuous individual who lacks intellectual perfection and thus is subject to the rule of natural law. Over the course of the book, Job's friends, representing different philosophical schools, fail to explain reasons for Job's suffering, until Elihu reveals another dimension in which a soul can be rewarded or punished—the afterlife. Elihu's revelation of immortality and the soul's postmortem experience is the essential message of the book of Job. While Immanuel embraces the allegorical readings of both Maimonides and Samuel Ibn Tibbon in his Job commentary, he claims that physical suffering and illness serve as divine tools of reproach, causing human introspection and repentance.[91] Interpreting Job 33:30, Immanuel states:

> And the meaning is that God, may He be elevated, will spur man to return to him two or three times, either through a night-time dream vision or he

> will reprove him two or three times through bedridden illness "to bring his soul back from destruction that he may bask in the light of life" [Job 33:30]. That is to say, in order "to bring his soul back from destruction" is that he should not die a corporeal death, while in a sinful state, and descend to the grave. And in order that the light of his intellectual soul [behold] the light of life, he meant to say with the light of the celestial spiritual world which is the true light.[92]

There are two ways, states Immanuel, that God signals trouble to human beings—dream visions or painful illness. These signals alert an individual to repent so that "he should try to perfect his soul to take it from human potentiality to divine actuality until the rational faculty, from among the other faculties of his soul, shall merit to be called 'an angel.'"[93] In a position that completely negates the Maimonidean-Tibbonide view of the human-divine relationship, Immanuel stresses the importance of penitence to the intellect seeking conjunction. Whereas Maimonides and his Tibbonide followers conceived of conjunction solely as an intellectual experience, Immanuel nuances this by insisting on the importance of commandment observance and moral perfection as well. When Immanuel notes that immorality is addressed through a dream vision meant to spur introspection and penitence, it is striking that he crafted his *Maḥberet Ha-Tofet V'Ha-Eden*, a literary tale that spurs reflection about sin, as a dream vision. The commentary on Job clarifies the true introspective value assigned by Immanuel to dream visions, and thus should be read alongside Immanuel's final *maḥberet.*

Meditations on the soul are not limited to Immanuel's philosophical commentaries or celestial journey, but are peppered throughout his poetic anthology. A series of sonnets and connective prose in the fourth *maḥberet* addresses the fate of the soul after death in language and allusions heavily borrowed from moralistic works such as Baḥya Ibn Pakuda's *Ḥovot Ha-Levavot* ("Duties of the Heart").[94] A somber reflection on youth in the fourteenth *maḥberet* recounts, "I am composed of spirit and flesh and the soul is immaterial, whereas the body is mire and mud. While the soul follows the intellect, the body tends toward matter. One's fate is God, while another's is hell."[95] *Maḥberet* 26, a chapter on old age, finds the pair of interlocutor characters discussing the effects of death on body and soul.[96] Of a Neoplatonic inflection, suggesting that the body imprisons the soul, Immanuel's verses complicate his classification as an Aristotelian, but as medieval Italians attributed the Neoplatonic *Liber de causis* to Aristotle, some non-Aristotelian positions seeped into their writing.

* * *

Debates over the nature of the soul and the accessibility of the agent intellect were limited to the intellectual elites of both Jewish and Christian circles. The inability to harmonize Aristotelian theories of the soul with Christian theology led to vicious disputes that culminated with a condemnation of 219 propositions by Etienne Tempier (d. 1279), bishop of the University of Paris, in 1277.[97] Contemporaneous with Tempier's condemnation, several Hebrew translations of works related to the soul appeared in Provence and Italy, together with encyclopedias of science that included current soul theory.[98] Immanuel's biblical commentaries and poetry attest to his knowledge of these issues, and their distillation in *Maḥberet Ha-Tofet V'Ha-Eden* subtly urges his educated readers to probe deeper into the mysteries of existence.

Not so subtle, however, is the performance of Immanuel's literary persona in *Eden*, where King David's approbation is pivotal, and not only for Immanuel's self-image vis-à-vis other exegetes. The heavenly chorus of praise for Immanuel's reading of this specific psalm affirms the dominance of the allegorical reading mode over literal or historicist ones, and it confirms Immanuel's identity as a veritable rationalist because of his laudable commentary. Moreover, it goads curious readers to seek out Immanuel's commentary on the psalm, where they will find revealed secrets about the First Cause, the three realms—celestial, supernal, and earthly—and the relationship between humans and the divine. Furthermore, they will learn about the soul's form—the rational faculty—that alone can render itself immortal with proper training and education. It is no coincidence that Immanuel chose to highlight his commentary on this specific chapter; by spotlighting it in his celestial tour, Immanuel tempts his readers to expose themselves to philosophical wisdom. The intertwining of Immanuel's biblical commentaries and poetry allows Immanuel to address similar themes in different media.

Immanuel's views on the soul, the cosmos, and the human telos of true cognition and intellectual conjunction rest on a Maimonidean foundation. But his exposure to Scholastic philosophy through Judah Romano's translations and Hillel of Verona's handbook on the soul results in Immanuel's integration of ideas and philosophical positions that are not consistent with the Maimonidean-Tibbonide legacy. Intellectual conjunction, the apex of human attainment of knowledge, is not only acknowledged, as it was by Maimonides, but championed as a realistic possibility for one who trains himself in the proper moral, educational, and intellectual path. While for Maimonides and Samuel Ibn Tibbon the path is purely intellectual, prepared by ethical perfection and Torah observance, Immanuel maintains the importance of observance of commandments and ethics as equally important to the acquisition of true knowledge. In this he reflects both the aftermath of the Maimonidean controversy that concerned itself with the utility and purpose of the commandments, and also a Christian environment where ethics, free will, and penance were championed. In ethics, as in philosophy, Immanuel occupies a middle ground between the Maimonidean legacy and the newer Scholastic material emerging from Christian circles.

3

SHALOM AND *SHELEMUT* (PEACE AND PERFECTION)

Immanuel on the Ethical Life

> Literature, because it describes and dramatizes the behaviour of human beings in greater variety than moral treatises do, continually provides material for questioning the "right" values.
>
> —**Ruth Morse, *Truth and Convention in the Middle Ages***

The previous chapter explored *Maḥberet Ha-Tofet V'Ha-Eden*'s intellectual context, demonstrating that Immanuel's interest in the soul and its afterlife echoed Jewish and Christian debates about the topic, likely occasioned by recent translations of philosophical texts into Hebrew and Latin. This chapter examines the social context that grounded the ethical imperative of *Maḥberet Ha-Tofet V'Ha-Eden*, which was composed within a culture where ethical discourse about both the individual and communal spheres was prominent. To do this, we begin by examining the Maimonidean ethical substrate underlying Immanuel's approach to moral improvement and then move to locally written Jewish and Christian ethical works. Examining these will show that the focus on ethics and penitence likely emerged from the public preaching of the mendicants, which itself originated in Umbria. As is evident in his philosophical approach, Immanuel's fundamental reliance on the Maimonidean ethical tradition is nuanced by Hebrew translations of Christian scholastic texts.

Finally, having established the historical context, this chapter highlights an as-yet-unstudied work of Immanuel's, a homiletical anthology separate from his biblical commentaries, which includes an explication of the biblical ceremony of the red heifer (*parah adumah*). Immanuel's unique approach to this rite of purification amalgamates classical rabbinic interpretations, according to which the red heifer is a proxy for the sinner, with newer Christian ideas about public penance popularized by mendicant preachers. This homily about the red heifer reveals that Immanuel was convinced that introspection and penitence required an external stimulus. I argue, therefore, that Immanuel crafted *Maḥberet Ha-Tofet V'Ha-Eden* as just such a textual impetus, meant to stir readers to penance.

Maimonidean Ethics

As demonstrated throughout his commentaries and detailed in the previous chapter, Immanuel was a student of Maimonideanism as transmitted through the Tibbonide school, which viewed the union of the human intellect with the agent intellect as the final goal of human existence, constituting immortality of the soul. Like other Maimonideans, Immanuel believed that ethical behavior helps a person attain knowledge of God, insofar as such knowledge is possible for a human being, as it moderates human actions, conduct, and speech.[1] But Immanuel also diverged from this Maimonidean position in at least one crucial respect. For him the attainment of intellectual perfection is not just enabled by but fundamentally intertwined with the observance of the commandments and moral excellence.

In the "Eight Chapters," as his introduction to the Mishnaic tractate *Avot* is known, Maimonides focuses on the development of intellectual and moral virtues as the foundation for closeness to God, characterized as "the most perfect path of the ways of worship."[2] Applying Aristotle's concept of the golden mean to ethics, Maimonides defines virtue as a median expression of a particular trait and vice as the adoption of either extreme. For Maimonides moral perfection (i.e., a perfectly healthy soul) is possible but rare—among the Jewish prophets, only Moses was completely virtuous.[3] Moral and ethical behavior has two aspects in this view. First, one must subdue the faculties of the soul to the rule of the intellect. Second, all corporeal activities should be aimed at preserving the health of the body and the soul, and thus at enabling the intellect to function properly. A healthy body and a healthy soul are desired, but only for the sake of acquiring knowledge.

Notwithstanding Maimonides' focus on ethical behavior in the *Eight Chapters*, his later works suggest a more complex relationship between ethics and human perfection. In *The Guide of the Perplexed*, he describes true human perfection as a state where the individual cognizes intelligibles to obtain divine truths.[4] This state, which confers "perdurance" (i.e., immortality of the soul), requires two elements—total focus on God without material distractions and the apprehension of truths. Prayer and study are activities that train "you to occupy yourself with His commandments . . . rather than with matters pertaining to the world." And the commandments themselves are conceived as tools to support one's intellectual quest.[5] Intellectual apprehension, according to Maimonides, rests on a foundation of rigorous training, including the gradual moderation of character traits to subdue the material faculties.[6]

Ethics are discussed extensively in Maimonides' *The Guide of the Perplexed* and the section on the laws concerning character traits (*Hilkhot De'ot*) in his legal code, the *Mishneh Torah*. In both works he stresses moderation as the desired outcome, with a prescribed course of character development to create balance. Immanuel's commentary on Proverbs quotes extensively from *Hilkhot De'ot*, especially those passages that treat ethical problems as a medical condition to be cured, as is the case in the *Eight Chapters* as well. As a fever is counteracted by applying cooling medication, ethical behavior that inclines to one extreme or the other can be counteracted by practicing its opposite in the hopes of attaining the middle path. The irascible individual should train himself to absorb beatings and insults without becoming angry, whereas a haughty individual should accustom himself to personal degradation.[7] A proponent of moderation, Immanuel criticizes those who choose an ascetic life, cautioning that those enfeebled by excessive fasting nullify their ultimate purpose because they cannot fulfill the commandments.[8] Immanuel targets the ascetics (*perushim*) who unnecessarily subject their bodies to all sorts of tortures, sometimes even giving this claim a gendered tone, as when he concludes that "due to their stupidity, women subject themselves to fasting."[9] In his gloss of the nut garden in Song of Songs 6:11 ("I went down to the nut grove to see the budding of the vale"), Immanuel compares actualized souls to the fruit of the walnut, which is extracted after cracking the shell. Unactualized souls, by contrast, are compared to dry nuts that remain within their casings and cannot be extracted because their souls cling to physical matter until death. However, Immanuel notes, just as an unripe and bitter nut can be refined by boiling it in honey until it becomes a sweet delicacy, so too can human souls be refined during youth.[10]

Immanuel's allegorical reading of Proverbs 12:10 ("A righteous man knows the needs of his beast") interprets the term "beast" as the animal, or sensate, soul (*nefesh behemit*), one of the three parts of the soul identified by Aristotle.[11] Together with the nutritive soul, which facilitates growth, the animal soul is responsible for movement and sensation, while the rational soul engages in cognitive functions like imagination, volition, and rational thought. Typically, only rational thought is praised, but Immanuel encourages righteous individuals to provide the essential needs of one's animal soul.[12] While privileging intellectual conjunction as a goal, however, Immanuel's approach remains grounded in the knowledge that intellectual perfection is unlikely for most.

Ethics Among Italian Jews

Immanuel's focus on ethics can best be appreciated in the context of other Jewish ethical works from the Italian peninsula. At least three ethical works intended for Jewish popular audiences appeared in Rome in the thirteenth century. The first, composed around 1287, was Yeḥiel b. Yequtiel Anav's *Ma'alot Ha-Middot*, a practical moralistic handbook that examines twenty-four virtues and their corresponding vices through the lenses of biblical and rabbinic literature.[13] A handbook for young men seeking to improve the states of their souls and bodies through a study of virtues and modulation, *Ma'alot Ha-Middot* translates biblical, rabbinic, and philosophical wisdom on the virtues and vices into simple language for the masses and explores the consequences of virtuous or vicious acts.[14] Yeḥiel borrows heavily from Maimonides and Baḥya Ibn Pakuda's *Ḥovot Ha-Levavot* ("Duties of the Heart"), a popular, Sufi-inspired, moralistic treatise that distinguishes between the interior aspect of divine worship (the duties of the heart) and the exterior aspect (the duties of the body). Written in the late eleventh century in Arabic and translated into Hebrew by Judah Ibn Tibbon (1120–1190) in the late twelfth century, it—along with the works of Maimonides—informs many of Immanuel's moralistic meditations as well.

Two other ethical works, both by Benjamin b. Abraham Anav (ca. 1215–ca. 1295), also of Rome, sharply critique the ethical state of society and the individual, while attacking the wealthiest echelons of the Roman Jewish community. The first, *Masa Gei Hizayon* ("The Burden of the Valley of Vision"), a three-part satirical narrative in Hebrew rhymed prose, laments the opulence of the author's community. In a vision, Benjamin is charged by a celestial entity, an *ofan*, to gather his peers and teach them about ethics.[15] Benjamin constructs a genealogical tree of virtues and vices to map out various expressions of the character traits and to show the relationships among them. This tree was a convention of Christian moralistic literature on the virtues and vices, which filtered into the popular consciousness via vernacular sermons and visual media in the thirteenth century.[16] Benjamin's other work, *Sh'arei Etz Hayim* ("The Gates of the Tree of Life"), is a practical handbook that provides rabbinic maxims and biblical verses related to an alphabetically arranged list of the virtues and vices.[17] All three works evince anxiety about moral laxity, and all three exemplify a current trend among Roman Jews to write moralistic works alongside a swell of other practical methods for ethical rehabilitation. Like these practical ethical manuals, Immanuel's poetry relies on Maimonides and Baḥya, and, like them, is also aimed at making theoretical material more broadly accessible.

The image of a morally compromised community emerges, too, from *Maḥberot Immanuel*. The fourth *maḥberet* in *Maḥberot Immanuel* opens with a reconciliation scene between poet and patron after Immanuel's ten-year banishment from his patron's employ. Against this background, in a somber exchange full of meditations on old age, wisdom, death, and the afterlife, Immanuel's persona pits youthful folly against serene old age. Like most of the other *maḥbarot*, this chapter is written in rhymed prose punctuated by shorter metered poems. The poems in this *maḥberet*, ranging from couplets to sonnets to long poems, distill descriptions of the soul adapted from the related chapter in Baḥya's "Duties of the Heart."[18] To counteract the inclination to rebel against God, Baḥya's chapter suggests reflecting on the natural world and the human body, which dutifully follow natural law. Immanuel's sonnet, focused on the conflict between the speaker's rebellious soul and his dutiful limbs, echoes Baḥya's chapter but in the personalized voice of a speaker. Further, in the introduction of this sonnet, Immanuel's character depicts the creation of humanity as a drama wherein God imbued humans with natural dispositions to "worship Him and to investigate [God's] existence with all their potential" through observance of the commandments.[19] Immanuel adds observance of commandments to the list of things that help a human soul remain faithful to God. However, Immanuel laments, the human condition is rebellious, whether because of blindness to the truth or subordination to one's desires rather than mastery of them, as originally intended by God. So Immanuel recites a sonnet about this sorrowful state, in which he urges his readers to "let us impede our spirits and align our actions with all our might. If there is evil on our hands, let us disengage it, and if evil matters lie sweetly on our tongues, let us restrain them with our palates."[20] Although Immanuel incorporates Baḥya's moralistic rebuke into his *maḥberet*, the sonnet and its surrounding rhymed prose lines express that rebuke in a gentler tone, engaging the audience homiletically through a story of reconciliation after rupture between poet and patron.

In the fourth *maḥberet* the patron notes that Immanuel "composed poems about the matter of lust during one's youth, and pietistic poems, and lamentations during the ripening days of maturation."[21] Following this statement, he asks Immanuel's character, "Have you composed poems about matters of wisdom and the Torah's purest commandments?"[22] This exchange, I believe, is important for two reasons. First, it conveys the structure of chapters 3 and 4 of *Maḥberot Immanuel*, which, atypically, share a continuous plotline. Second, the exchange between patron and poet also reveals conventions of genre as understood by Immanuel.

The patron's question seems to refer to a tripartite division in life—youth, middle age, old age—which he associates with matters of lust, pietistic poems and lamentations, and matters of wisdom. The third chapter of *Maḥberot Immanuel*, tinged with the aura of a medieval romance, recounts the tale of Immanuel's epistolary pursuits of an unattainable, deeply pious woman who is cloistered. The story begins as a challenge, as the patron dares Immanuel to win the cloistered lady's affections—which he does—and the woman vows to abandon her sheltered life for Immanuel. When Immanuel regales the patron with his conquest, the shocked noble angrily reveals that the woman is his half-sister and implores Immanuel to reject her so she can continue her life of piety. At the tragic end, the lady dies by her own hand, and Immanuel is angrily banished by the patron for ten years. The frivolous machismo and passionate exchange expressed in the tale would certainly qualify as "matters of lust." After the passage of time and the reconciliation between poet and Maecenas in the fourth chapter, Immanuel's literary persona shares his sobering poems: those on the soul or what the patron calls "pietistic poems and lamentations during the ripening days of maturation." The final step in a poet's development, intimates Immanuel, is the composition of wisdom poetry, which he produces at the end of the fourth *maḥberet*. Thus the patron's question mirrors the framing of *maḥbarot* three and four while acknowledging the developmental stages outlined by Immanuel regarding an individual's intellectual quest—consumption by material concerns in one's youth, reflection on one's approaching demise with maturation, and devotion to intellectual matters in older age.

The genre of wisdom poetry, then, leads into Immanuel's seventy-two-line versification of Maimonides' thirteen principles of faith, *Eftaḥ be-khinor* ("I shall begin with a lyre").[23] This is the only poem found copied separately from the *Maḥbarot*; it appears in a thirteenth-century codex.[24] Often considered a forerunner to the better-known hymn *Yigdal Elohim ḥai* ("Exalted be the living God"), *Eftaḥ be-khinor* generated some debate about whether Immanuel authored the *Yigdal* prayer, but scholars today generally consider Daniel b. Judah Ha-Dayan to be its author.[25] In the preface to *Eftaḥ be-khinor*, Immanuel asks his reader to "understand my poem and its admonition," for the one "who finds it will find life, but the hater despises his soul."[26] The poem uses key terms from Maimonides' thirteen principles, expanding them with poetic imagery and language. The longest exposition, on resurrection, fortifies those who "observe His [God's] laws and ordinances" with the knowledge that those who don't worship God are like tinder destined for the flames.[27] The fourth *maḥberet*, whose devotional themes and introspective motifs are set in a realistic narrative, demonstrates the way complex theoretical material, like Baḥya's "Duties of the Heart" or Maimonides' principles of faith, were recast by *Maḥberot Immanuel* in a more accessible and entertaining format.

Allusions to Baḥya's chapter on examining the soul reappear in verse, in the eighth *maḥberet*, where Immanuel recalls his youthful carousing with a friend and recites a poem he later wrote to temper that friend's uncontrolled behaviors. In the poem Immanuel reminds the friend of tales about great men who died suddenly, asking him to repent of his ways and prioritize the pure soul, "which is prepared for important virtues, and its existence is in the bosom of Abraham and Sarah."[28] The bosom of Abraham is a rabbinic euphemism for heaven, which alludes to a concept of a material afterlife and, strictly speaking, conflicts with Immanuel's philosophical view of an immaterial state after death. Statements such as these show the fluidity of Immanuel's conceptual repository and the wide range of sources that informed his narrative poems.

Immanuel's wit and erudition are on display when he portrays, with impressive realism, emotional interventions between friends in which the dialogue is drawn directly from Baḥya's "Duties of the Heart." Speaking to his wayward friend, Immanuel pleads, "My chosen brother! Let us be jealous of holy people, bearers of pure hearts, those untroubled by their desires on whom Fate has no knotty hold. . . . Evil fate disguised itself to them but they recognized its empty actions."[29] Echoing the language of Baḥya's chapter on abstinence, which describes the world's attempts to entice pure souls, Immanuel's dialogue lacks the harsh admonitory tone of "Duties of the Heart."[30] Similarly, theoretical concepts from moralistic works are manifested in the characters of *Maḥberot Immanuel*, a technique we will explore closely in chapters 5 and 6. Citations of Baḥya's "Duties of the Heart" are not limited to Immanuel's poetry, as significant excerpts are interpolated into Immanuel's commentary on Proverbs and his commentary on the curses and blessings in Deuteronomy.[31]

The nineteenth *maḥberet* is a somber chapter that begins with the Immanuel character attempting to convey ethical wisdom (a sort of ethical will) to his son, continues with a meditation on retribution in the afterlife, and ends with a poem meant to rouse Immanuel's own soul from sin before his body's demise. Immanuel's son, he claims, was an admirably withdrawn boy who devoted himself to reading Hebrew literature—rhymed prose and poetry—instead of sporting with his peers. Immanuel's character was so moved by the boy's generous soul and efforts "to arouse love" (*le'orer ha-ahava*) that he sought to help his son "ascend the chariot" (Maimonidean shorthand for philosophical study). It may seem curious that Immanuel phrased his son's intensive reading of literature as "arousing love," a citation from the Song of Songs 2:7, but the reference becomes clearer with consideration of Immanuel's commentary on the Song of Songs, where he reads love as a symbol of conjunction with the agent intellect.[32] To aid the boy's intellectual development, Immanuel composed snippets of rhetorical prose "to open the eyes of the blind to acquire the discipline for success, righteousness, justice and equity."[33] The centerpiece of the *maḥberet*, however, is a series of poems on the vices and virtues, written to open the "locked gates of ethics" for his son. These poems list roughly the same vices and virtues as Yeḥiel and Benjamin Anav, and rework sections of Hebrew wisdom collections like Solomon Ibn Gabirol's (ca. 1022–1070) *Mivḥar Ha-Peninim* ("A Selection of Pearls"), or Hunayn Ibn Ishaq's (809–873) *Musrei Ha-Filosofim* ("Sayings of the Philosophers"). They also incorporate tales with moral content, like those in Ibn Hasdai's (1180–1240) *Ben Ha-Melekh V'Ha-Nazir* ("The Prince and the Monk").[34]

The abundance of contemporaneous moralistic handbooks, a medieval "self-help" literature of sorts, alongside Immanuel's literary didactic writings seems to reflect an interest in the subject among Italian Jews. One example of a sustained interest in ethics and repentance from extant material culture is a fourteenth-century Italian manuscript that contains Maimonides' "Eight Chapters"; an abridged version of Baḥya Ibn Pakuda's "Duties of the Heart"; Nahmanides' (1194–1270) *Sha'ar Ha-Gemul* ("The Gate of Recompense"); Solomon Ibn Gabirol's moralistic aphorisms, *Mivḥar Ha-Peninim*, and his treatise on ethical rehabilitation, *Tikkun Middot Ha-nefesh*; as well as biblical commentaries on Job and Ecclesiastes.[35] It is possible that this collection was intended for use during the high holiday season, when reflection and repentance are encouraged, because the manuscript also contains a sermon for the New Year (Rosh Hashanah) delivered by Nahmanides in the synagogue of Girona, Spain. However, the collation of all these works into a single manuscript demonstrates concerted interest in ethics that also emerges from Immanuel's poetry, philosophical commentaries, and homilies.

While the thirteenth century is known as a time of increased lay piety within Jewish and Christian communities, a new religious order aimed to inspire laypeople to penance and reform: the Franciscans. This movement, centered in Umbria, represented a dynamic and rapidly growing group that preached the need for penitence and morality in town squares throughout central and northern Italy. To properly understand Immanuel's approach to ethics, it is necessary to understand some of the changes that swept Italian society in its wake.

Penitence and Politics in the Italian Peninsula

The thirteenth century brought decisive political and spiritual changes to the Italian peninsula, with the growth of northern and central Italian towns and cities that embraced a republican or popular government in turn attracting emigres from the surrounding countryside.[36] In its effort to strengthen its hold on towns in the papal state, the papal curia deployed Roman Jewish businessmen to the regions of Le Marche and Umbria in the second half of the thirteenth century.[37] Although not much is known of the Marchegian Jewish communities during this period, the extant documentation suggests the existence of loan companies formed by groups of Jews and even cooperative business enterprises between Jews and non-Jews.[38] In *Maḥberot Immanuel*, Immanuel often mentions Marchegian and Umbrian locales, as when two Jews from the Umbrian town of Orvieto are praised in *Eden* for their support of the downtrodden, or where the origin story told of the *Maḥbarot* is conceived at a banquet in Marchegian Fermo. It is highly likely that Immanuel spent extended time in those regions, perhaps traveling between them to find work.

As Italian regions like Le Marche experienced demographic growth and economic transformation in the thirteenth century, communal governments struggled with factionalism, internal violence due to jurisdictional conflicts and foreign antagonism. Many of the nascent communal governments eventually found it unwieldy to operate without singular leadership, and they turned to electing a *podestà* as the highest-ranking communal official. A supporter of rule by a single person, Immanuel offers his own political commentary, explaining that God punishes people for their sins by allowing many political leaders to rule together, which results in injustice and bad government. Many leaders give rise to conflicting opinions about rule, ultimately causing the city's destruction. But if one person with knowledge rules the land, God will extend it political stability. Demonstrating an awareness of the strife characteristic of so many Italian towns and cities, Immanuel writes, "For the businesses and the arts do not unite. Each one stands apart on a matter, and they cannot reach a favorable conclusion."[39] Presumably referring to the various guilds (*arti*) that vied for political power in medieval Italian locales, Immanuel states his preference for rule by a single person.[40] In many instances, the *podestàs* could not overrule the guilds so that, by the early thirteenth century, several Italian towns were ruled by representative councils called "the people" (*il popolo*).[41]

Communal governments run by municipal councils sought creative ways to stem violence, for example, by requiring a city's highest-ranking bureaucrats to engage in formal peacemaking rituals (*pax et concordia*) before taking office.[42] Peace instruments, or the documents that individuals or communities created to resolve private disputes, began to appear in the late thirteenth century and circulated widely by the fourteenth century, revealing the ubiquity of public peacemaking rituals across social classes, genders, and faiths.[43] The great number of such instruments also exposed the rampant violence in late medieval towns and cities, which Immanuel seems to acknowledge in his commentaries, especially the comment on Proverbs 6:32–35.

Proverbs 6:32–35 states that an adulterer will meet with shame and disgrace (*negah v'kalon*) and that his shame will never be expunged. It declares that "the fury of the man will be passionate; he will show no pity on his day of vengeance." In his commentary, Immanuel explores the referent of "his shame," suggesting that it could refer to either the adulterer, whose shame results from the eternal memory of his evil deed, or to the cuckolded husband. Immanuel explains: "The reason that this adulterer will find affliction and disgrace is because it is human nature to be jealous of the man who strayed with one's beloved wife, and this jealousy comes with mighty fury. And if the opportunity for immediate revenge on the adulterer does not arise, and some time passes, do not think that he [the husband] forgot the disgrace caused to him, but rather that he waits for a time that he may avenge himself."[44]

Further exploring the shamed husband's emotions, Immanuel notes that no amount of money could ameliorate the husband's disgrace or compel him to forgive the adulterer. He suggests a second interpretation of "affliction and disgrace" to the adulterer—physical harm because "the wife's relatives will wound him and shame him."[45] Additionally, the husband will never rid himself of the image and thought of the shameful deed done by his wife and her lover. The husband will hold these thoughts tightly and recall them whenever the opportunity to avenge himself arises. Regardless of the mechanics, Immanuel assures readers that adultery leads to violence, even random violence, because one never knows when a husband will (rightfully) lash out. This comment seeks to explicate seemingly casual violence as a simmering tension borne of animosity. While Immanuel's reading of Proverbs is not testimony to social disorder, his nuanced exploration of violence suggests, at the very least, familiarity with it, a major concern of Italian municipal bodies.

Communal governments turned to the newly established mendicant orders, welcoming religious input into the lawmaking processes of maturing communes, like Fermo, in the first half of the thirteenth century.[46] Mendicant preaching was influential in the late-medieval Italian peninsula, and popular governments embraced the newer religious movements as they rejected institutions affiliated with the old imperial regime.[47] As engineers of a new Christian ethic—willing to engage businessmen and empower them to seek direct spiritual fulfillment without a clerical intermediary—the Franciscans and Dominicans offered a spiritual ethos consistent with new social paradigms.[48] Their religious input impacted republican policymaking, and their reframing of civic disorder as a consequence of sin and concupiscence spurred the reformulation of communal statutes targeting sinful behaviors.[49] As public religious figures, Franciscan friars emerged as important peacemakers in the communes, dealing with both intercommunal politics and private disputes.[50] Preaching pacifism through penance and moral rehabilitation, vernacular mendicant sermons helped forge a new cultural concept of peace, with formal ceremonies, verbal formulae, and prescribed rituals practiced by the developing communes.[51]

A significant innovation in the realm of medieval Christian spiritual life, the mendicant public oration popularized religious and moral ideas in a vernacular idiom. There were many approaches to homiletical sermons, but the major distinction was between those based on abstract lessons and universal statements and those that used detailed stories whose particularism rallied listeners to immediate action.[52] The more academic of the two, called "modern" (*sermo modernis*), was said to appeal to a more educated audience, as its orderly divisions mimicked the Scholastic method of study. The anecdotal style, called "humble" (*sermo humilis*), relied on exempla and was popular among less educated audiences.

As mendicant sermons became ubiquitous in thirteenth-century Italy, there arose a corollary literature of preaching manuals and handbooks. *De eruditione praedictorum*, a homiletical guide by Humbert of Romans, underscored the importance of offering a fitting rhetorical speech to a particular audience. Humbert identifies the preacher's main task as moving the will of the sinner to confession and penance, and his manual offers a plethora of rhetorical strategies to do so.[53] Drawing a direct link between the sermon and its effects, he writes: "The seed is sown in preaching, the fruit is harvested in penance."[54] Because friars took a vow of poverty, they were viewed as uninterested in financial gain and even to be above any political faction. Communal governments run by municipal councils therefore appointed friars to rewrite the municipal statutes and laws of the Italian towns, which had been plagued by violence and vendetta. With their focus on penitence, these mendicant lawmakers targeted civic chaos by focusing on private sin and communal disorder but, especially, on the nexus between individual and communal good.[55]

Individual and Communal Good

The friars' concern for social order appears most pointedly in the sermons of the Dominican preacher Remigio de' Girolami (early 1300s) that promote harmony (*concordia*) as the chief virtue of a healthy society. Applying the Aristotelian concept of humans as social animals, Remigio distinguishes between individual and communal good, maintaining that the wellbeing of the community is more important than that of the individual.[56] Synergy between individual and community was studied at the highest levels of the universities by masters like Albert the Great, Thomas Aquinas, and Giles of Rome (1243–1316). These Scholastics exposed a contradiction in Aristotle's *Ethics* about the definition of communal wellbeing. In the *Ethics*, common wellbeing refers to happiness and a life of virtue (*bonum commune*) and also to a state of peace, material security, and wellbeing (*communis utilitatis*). Depending on one's chosen definition, communal virtue is both superior to and inclusive of the individual good, while peace is the product of individual acts of virtue.[57] Both definitions outline the delicate dance between an individual and a society aspiring to virtue and peace.

Immanuel's otherworldly tour in *Maḥberet Ha-Tofet V'Ha-Eden* explores this dance at some length. The link between individual actions and the state of the community is a major theme of this *maḥberet*, which engages with the Maimonidean conception of Mosaic law as so comprehensive that it addresses both the physical and spiritual needs of individuals and communities. Yet the focus on penitence of the mendicant preaching movements penetrated the daily lives of medieval Christians and Jews. Sharing their religious interpretations and insights in the vernacular, the mendicants were ubiquitous in the Italian peninsula, and Immanuel was very likely exposed to orations on the importance of general morality and repentance, not only for the individual but also for the *bene comune* (common good). This awareness is evident in Immanuel's novel interpretation of the red heifer ceremony, a biblical sacrifice believed to expiate impurity from contact with a corpse. A more general examination of this biblical ritual and Immanuel's homiletical collection are necessary to appreciate the novelty of Immanuel's approach and its impact on *Maḥberet Ha-Tofet V'Ha-Eden*.

Immanuel's Homilies (*Derashot*)

The earliest extant dated copy of Immanuel's commentaries on Job and Proverbs also contains his exegeses of scattered verses, readings of aphorisms from *Pirkei Avot*, and meditations on thematic topics. This collection is important because it transmits Immanuel's interpretations of books that currently have no extant edition, confirming Immanuel's claim that he had glossed the entire biblical canon.[58] Immanuel's miscellany exists in at least ten manuscripts, differing slightly in order and contents; these are largely preserved within manuscripts of a kabbalistic nature.[59] In form and structure, this work resembles Judah Romano's *Be'urim*, short snippets of commentary on individual verses, with no apparent order. Immanuel admits to plagiarizing Judah's writing, as mentioned in Chapter 2; he also seems to have imitated Judah's exegetical style.[60]

Immanuel's miscellany, a philosophical anthology, exposes readers to speculative ideas about the three realms of the cosmos and the roles of the agent intellect, conjunction, prophecy, and providence—all through biblical prooftexts. One of its longer expositions, a treatise about wine saved from the days of creation, analogizes a human to a grape, as both possess great potential. As grapes contain humanity's greatest material pleasure—wine—so too do humans bear potential for knowledge, perceived as humanity's greatest spiritual pleasure.

The most extensive comment in the miscellany is that on the biblical ritual of the red heifer, described in Numbers 19:1–10. When mixed with living waters, the ashes of the sacrificed red heifer convey purity to those who have had contact with a corpse. The ritual itself is notoriously enigmatic and difficult to rationalize. The act of preparing the sacrifice paradoxically renders the ministering priest who prepares the sacrifice and all the other attendants impure, while the one who is sprinkled with the ashes is rendered pure. Immanuel reads this rite as an allegory of sin, identifying the red heifer as the human soul which, despite having been placed within a pure body, is still driven to wickedness.

The human body, states Immanuel, is ready to perform good deeds that accord with the intellect's will, but material appetites prevent the body from partnering with the soul for good. Although God gave humans all the faculties necessary to achieve perfection (*shelemut*), individual temperaments make actions easier for some than for others, a perspective that echoes Maimonides' *Eight Chapters*. The goal of perfection (*shelemut*) consistently arises throughout Immanuel's commentaries; it is the ultimate state following the transcendence of a materiality shared by humans and animals. In his commentary on Proverbs 29:27 ("the unjust man is an abomination to the righteous, and he whose way is straight is an abomination to the wicked"), Immanuel explains:

> For the wicked one is an animal in the form of a person and he is more loathsome than the animal because the animal was not expected to be anything besides an animal. However, the wicked man was expected to be a divine man and all the tools were prepared for him to receive the form of the intellect on top of perfection [*shelemut*]. And due to the way of the world that he embraced, he turned himself from divinity to bestiality, and he is an abomination before righteous ones.[61]

Intellectual potentiality, according to Immanuel, differentiates humans from animals. Likewise, Immanuel characterizes any human being endowed with a rational soul who denies the soul its ultimate perfection in favor of wickedness as "an animal in the form and shape of a man."[62] For Immanuel, the red heifer symbolizes the wayward human being, and he interprets each aspect of the sacrificial ritual allegorically.

The Red Heifer

In Numbers 19, the Israelites are commanded to offer a sacrificial cow that is completely red and unblemished and that never worked in its life. The priest slaughters the cow outside the Israelite camp and sprinkles its blood seven times toward the camp. Then the cow's carcass is incinerated together with cedar wood, hyssop, and scarlet thread, and the ashes are stored in a ritually pure location. Like Maimonides' paradigm of the parabolic narrative, in which every detail corresponds to the allegory, Immanuel invests each aspect of this ceremony with moral significance.[63] Immanuel's reading revolves around the need for individual self-reflection and repentance for nonobservance of the commandments.

The heifer, according to Immanuel, symbolizes the soul, whose choice and desire (*be-vekhirato u-virtzono*) led to actions that incur excision (*karet*). Immanuel reads the "red cow without blemish, in which there is no defect and on which no yoke has been laid" as a symbol of a sinner who cast off the yoke of heaven and the burden of Torah and its commandments, for both the sinner and the cow resist any encumbrances.[64] A classic rabbinic image, the one who bears the yoke of Torah and commandments is said to be free of the yoke of government and worldly concerns, but Immanuel connects the spiritual duty to an actual object, especially in the Song of Songs, where the beloved's body is praised.[65] There, he focuses on the neck as "the limb specialized to carry a yoke . . . which is an allegory for the soul . . . carrying the burden of Torah and commandments, and generally all the duties of the heart and the limbs which is true worship."[66] The heifer's physical state of perfection at the time of its ritual slaughter is a reminder that all God's creations eventually die, whether in old age or prematurely during youth. In the biblical narrative, the priest slaughters the heifer outside the Israelite camp and burns the cow's entire carcass, including its dung (Numbers 19:3–6). To Immanuel, this detail signals to the sinner that punishment does not end with physical death, but rather the soul shall be tortured by spiritual anguish before being destroyed and reduced to nonexistence. Immanuel notes that, like one whose suffering makes him yearn for death, the sinner, too, will desire a swift end to his torture, but his punishment shall endure. The setting of the ritual outside the Israelite camp, according to Immanuel, alludes to the existential banishment that the sinner's soul endures in the afterlife, as an impure soul (*nefesh teme'ah*) exiled from the bonds of life, sanctity, and God's Temple. Immanuel's views on hell and punishment after death, as expressed in his homilies and philosophical commentaries, differ substantially from the physical description of hell in his literary *Tofet*, which will be discussed in the next chapter. In Immanuel's view, the symbolic elements of the red heifer ceremony are part of an important ritual that targets sinners and moves them to repentance.

The ceremony, as Immanuel understands it, is meant to inspire reflection in the bystanders, for "at the time the sinners' souls will arouse while they still live their lives and they instill in their hearts what sorrows the sinning soul will endure. Then, their foolishness will depart from them and they will purify themselves after being impure."[67] As the ashes of the burnt heifer purify those in a state of impurity, so too the sight of the cow's slaughter and its incineration will inspire sinners to return to a pure life. Immanuel notes the paradox of the red heifer, in which the very preparation of the sacrifice whose ashes are used to purify the impure renders the ministering priests impure. ("The priest shall wash his garments and bathe his body in water; after that the priest may reenter the camp, but he shall be unclean until evening" [Numbers 19:7].) In his reading, this paradox alludes to the communal role of spiritual guides to help individuals in need of repentance.

Immanuel identifies guides who themselves have acquired truth, and he charges those guides to help the sinners repent. Explaining the expiating "water of lustration" (*mei niddah* and *mei ḥatat*) mixture, Immanuel notes that the living waters (*mayim ḥayim*), symbolic of Torah, were mixed together with the ashes by "those who have acquired truth and the arbiters of justice and righteousness." These people, serving as spiritual guides, will make sinners aware of the consequences of sin by teaching them that souls will experience spiritual immolation after the body's death and that they will turn into ashes after sustaining punishments tailored to their sins.

It is not enough for these righteous guides to preach about the tortures awaiting the wicked souls in the afterlife, states Immanuel, but they should also "emanate upon them the overflow of wisdom that is likened to living waters, and they should show them the path of uprightness according to their receptive abilities."[68] Immanuel is sensitive to different intellectual capacities and counsels the spiritual guides to adjust their messages according to the intended audience. Some sinners deserve eternal punishment, while others are so evil that their remains are ground up and sprinkled underfoot. In this homily, Immanuel marshals classical rabbinic images of postmortem punishment, like the physical destruction of souls, even though he espouses the Maimonidean idea of an immaterial afterlife. Immanuel was very aware of his audience and genre, and some of his rhetorical choices reflect the environment in which he wrote rather than his own philosophies. He demonstrates his engagement with his audience, for example, with the warning: "Do not regard these words as hyperbole and exaggeration to frighten the wicked and instill fear within them, and that they [the wicked] will not be judged forevermore, rather the matter is real and understandable to the intellect." Citing Daniel 12:3, the verse Immanuel often uses to refer to the afterlife, he explains that the good deeds of moral men add merit to the souls of the righteous while the sins of the wicked compound the sorrow of the souls of all those who led them astray.

Immanuel transforms the biblical ceremony of the red heifer and the purifying waters produced from its ashes into symbols of penitence and moral rehabilitation. With its cathartic nature, the rite stimulates viewers, in Immanuel's reading, to look inward and realize that the human condition can be transcended only through good deeds. But this is not enough, states Immanuel, who identifies wise and righteous guides as necessary elements to introspection and transformation. Although *Maḥberet Ha-Tofet V'Ha-Eden* is a fictional narrative, it establishes his literary persona as a visionary whose experiences stimulate self-reflection, if not fear, in his audience. Could Immanuel have considered *Maḥberet Ha-Tofet V'Ha-Eden* a textual substitution for the wise and righteous guides inspiring introspection and leading sinners onto the right path?

This question becomes especially relevant when considering the textual history and structure of the red heifer homily. Within the manuscripts, the homily has a complicated structure, starting with Immanuel's presentation of a long explication of the ritual, which he rejects for his own new interpretation. The rejected reading is likely the interpretation of Daniel b. Judah Ha-Dayan, whose versification of Maimonides' thirteen principles was canonized in the Hebrew prayer book as the *Yigdal* hymn after the fourteenth century, as discussed earlier in this chapter.[69] Daniel's interpretation views the sacrifice as inspiring repentance and observance of commandments, but Immanuel's novel approach, more introspective than Daniel's, also includes the spiritual guides as mediators between the performative ritual and its concealed messages. Neither Immanuel's nor Daniel's readings of the red heifer ceremony feature in Immanuel's comprehensive commentary on the book of Numbers where, instead, Immanuel integrates long citations from Rashi, Abraham Ibn Ezra, and Jacob Anatoli without alluding to his own innovative reading. The absence is quite striking, and one wonders if Immanuel regarded different exegetical readings as fitting for different genres.

The collection of verses that includes the red heifer homily may have also served Immanuel as a repository for homiletical purposes, like sermon composition, which might explain his compartmentalization of materials. In *Maḥberot Immanuel*, Immanuel boasts of his annual oration on Yom Kippur, and while this may have been an empty claim, it is also possible that he had experience as a preacher.[70] His distillation of ethical treatises, like Baḥya's "Duties of the Heart," into accessible verse demonstrates a sensitivity to audiences of myriad receptive capabilities. Vernacular manuals on preaching (*ars praedicandi*), circulating throughout central Italy, stressed the rhetorical conventions of different homiletical styles, which likely heightened Immanuel's awareness of preaching as a rhetorical art and led him to pen an ordered but powerful oration on the need for atonement.

The Rationalization of the Commandments

In his commentary on Psalm 1, Immanuel states that "every action in this world, whether important or trivial, must be motivated by the intent to reach true blessedness, as the Rabbis stated: 'All your deeds shall be for the sake of Heaven.'"[71] The observance of the Torah's commandments was always considered important in Jewish tradition, but the medieval desire to harmonize the Bible with contemporary philosophical and scientific theories stimulated a new style of thought called *ta'amei ha-mitzvot*, characterized by a firm belief that all the commandments have reasons that are intelligible to the human mind.[72] This approach is explicitly clear in Maimonides' enumeration of the commandments, the *Sefer Ha-mitzvot* ("The Book of Commandments"), as well as in the classification of commandments into broad categories in *Guide* II:25–49.[73]

Immanuel's idiosyncratic approach to observance of the commandments demonstrates his fidelity to two different thinkers, Maimonides and Judah Romano. Immanuel maintains a unique approach to biblical exegesis that simultaneously validates the literal sense and the esoteric interpretation of a biblical verse. His reading of the red heifer ceremony offers a useful case study to examine the purpose of the Torah commandments in Immanuel's worldview, especially because he offers divergent views on this commandment in several of his works.

Explaining the purpose of Torah commandments, Immanuel invokes the Aristotelian doctrine of the golden mean from Maimonides' *Eight Chapters* and *Mishneh Torah, Hilkhot De'ot* when he states, "They moderate the virtues [*middot*] and distance [one] from the extremes."[74] Interpreting the erect columns of smoke in Song of Songs as symbols of the straight ethical path taken by the blessed soul, Immanuel affirms that "the median and straight virtues are sweet for they are the path by which to reach you [God]."[75] While most medieval exegetes identify the beloved's breasts in

Song of Songs as Moses and Aaron or as the Written Torah and Oral Torah, Immanuel labels them the moral and intellectual virtues "through which a person's intellect is actualized, for this is the end expected from a person."[76]

Advancing multiple views of the commandments and their purpose, Immanuel's commentary on Song of Songs preserves conflicting ideas about the role of commandment observance that demonstrate the impact of various ideologies on the relationship between actions and intellectual perfection. When Immanuel reads the beloved's unrequited passion for the lover in Song of Songs as her desire to observe commandments and pursue moral rehabilitation as preparatory steps to intellectual conjunction, he accords with the Maimonidean view that correct actions moderate one's character traits away from extremes as a precursor to intellectual perfection.[77] In passages reproduced verbatim from Moses Ibn Tibbon's commentary, Immanuel suggests that a person's lack of virtue prevents the material human intellect from conjoining with the agent intellect.[78] Elsewhere in the same commentary, Immanuel identifies observance of the commandments and moral perfection as ends unto themselves for the human intellect that will never conjoin with the agent intellect.[79] Other parts of the commentary, however, suggest an entirely different position, one that locates esoteric philosophical secrets at the core of the *mitzvot*, which only a philosopher can unlock through observance of those actions in purely practical ways. This stratum is entirely foreign to a Maimonidean reading and must be explained through the influence of Judah Romano on Immanuel's thought.

Immanuel compares Torah commandments to a pomegranate, whose seeds are fragrant but concealed within a thick rind. So too, states Immanuel, are the internal meanings of Torah commandments significant to the soul, although they are obscured by praxis of a commandment.[80] This position assigns *mitzvot* a new role that deviates from a Maimonidean stance. No longer merely conveyors toward a philosophical end goal, commandments have theurgical significance that disseminates philosophical truths.[81] To illustrate this point, Immanuel identifies the wreaths of gold in Song of Songs 1:11 as "the inner meanings of the practical commandments and the knowledge of tenets of faith through logical demonstration."[82] Because the wreaths in Song of Songs are golden, Immanuel associates that verse with Proverbs 25:11 ("Like golden apples in silver showpieces is a phrase well turned"). The apple of gold inlaid in silver filigree, an image interpreted by Maimonides as an allusion to allegorical reading, represents a verse whose literal sense compares to silver while its esoteric intention is likened to gold. But where Maimonides uses the esoteric-exoteric paradigm to convey inner philosophical meanings hidden within biblical verses, Immanuel applies this image to the commandments to assert that the performance of the commandment conceals its secret significance.[83]

Such a non-Maimonidean stance is further evident in Immanuel's reading of Psalm 19, recited as part of the morning liturgy on Sabbaths and festivals. The psalm contrasts God's magnitude, evident in the celestial luminaries and the perfect law, with the humble requests of a human supplicant. Critiquing other exegetical readings that interpret praise of the heavens as material speech, Immanuel affirms the Maimonidean view of Psalm 19 as expressing the immaterial praise of God by the souls of the celestial spheres. Immanuel's commentary sketches out the general order of the cosmos, charting the process of supernal emanations that exude divine efflux through a chain of separate intellects to generate the natural world. Although the separate intellects and the related spheres affect the sublunar, elementary world of human beings, Immanuel insists that human free will is not under their control.[84] After the emphasis on cosmological processes, the psalm shifts to praise the perfection of God's laws and ordinances, which Immanuel claims "give superior qualities to the bodies as well as to the souls."[85] The interpretations mentioned thus far accord with Maimonidean concepts, but Immanuel's statements on the commandments radically abandon Maimonidean perspectives for those of Judah Romano, who invests Jewish liturgy and Torah commandments with the ability to bring one closer to intellectual conjunction.[86] Immanuel's willingness to entertain the possibility of conjunction during one's lifetime demonstrates that late medieval thinkers, especially in Italy, ascribed a more active part to humans than Maimonides had done.

Immanuel emphasizes the apotropaic nature of observance of the commandments because, according to him, observance entails the reunification of body and soul at the resurrection.[87] Moreover, the judgments of the Torah are eternal, in contrast to astrological judgments, which Immanuel considers avoidable due to the protective nature of conjunction.[88] As the Torah conveys universal truths—about the creation of the world, providence, conjunction, transcending materiality, as well as reward and punishment—Immanuel affirms that observance of its commandments yields eternal reward.[89] Thus Immanuel views the Torah's commandments as sites of true wisdom and models of ethical perfection, two elements essential to a person's quest for perfection. At the end of Psalm 19, he writes, "The man who follows the paths of Torah is certain to be among the group which is described as 'Many of those that sleep in the dust of the earth will awake, some to eternal life' for the observance of Torah's ways are the reason that their souls return to their bodies at the time of resurrection."[90] In other commentaries, Immanuel maintains that the protective power of Torah observance has benefits in this world as well as the afterlife. He states, "For the one who observes the Torah of God and its leaders will be celebrated in this world, for he will not receive worldly punishment and he won't know any malice."[91] Called a "philosophical performance of commandments," Immanuel's approach to observance requires the actor to possess knowledge of the commandment's philosophical reason and intentions.[92]

This very sentiment, that observance entails knowledge of philosophical rationales, is expressed in Immanuel's homiletical anthology, through the cryptic image of wine preserved since the days of creation. He explains:

> And it is known that wine is a thing found in grapes in potentia, and it is actualized through manufacture and stomping, and he who eats grapes as they are has not reached the strength of wine. And when he crushes the grapes and elicits wine from them, then he shall reach the pleasure of drinking wine and its benefits. This is similar to the practical *mitzvot* of the Torah, which resemble grapes as bearers of hidden intentions, true knowledge and the divine wisdoms like the grapes are bearers of wine. And he who observes the practical *mitzvot* without acquiring the knowledge of their intentions and their purposes is similar to one who eats grapes, which is a great joy, but through these actions he has not reached the joy of one who toils and strains the wine from them. For the drinking of wine after it is vinted is the greatest physical pleasure because it renews his state to happiness.[93]

Using a very practical example, Immanuel describes the mechanism through which observance of the Torah's commandments, with true philosophical understanding, refines one's soul to experience a profound state of happiness and perfection. The process of transforming a neutral grape into delightful wine represents, for Immanuel, the actualization of the human potential energy. The wine from creation also serves Immanuel as a parable of the true knowledge and divine secrets that have been hidden from people since the creation of the world, intimating that the Torah's commandments and stories contain esoteric matters and hidden secrets that have not all been revealed. In this stance, Immanuel sharply differs from his Tibbonide predecessors who sought to unpack the Maimonidean allusions to esoterica and further explain that which Maimonides did not.[94] Immanuel's acceptance of unrevealed meanings within the commandments smacks of a traditionalist conservatism that is threaded throughout his commentaries.

Immanuel's comment on wine also reveals an awareness of his audience, which supports the idea that these fragmentary comments were homiletical in nature. Immanuel notes:

> It is well known that our Sages, of blessed memory, spoke in their explanations [*midrashim*] in the manner of a parable and riddle, in the same way as the Prophets, peace be upon them, so that the masses would not orient their minds solely to the intelligibles. And their intentions and purpose is to take pleasure in bodily delights, so they satisfy themselves with the exoteric meaning. And those who seek to know [*maskilim*] shall radiate as the light of the firmament and they will understand the lesson of their words, which is truly intended. And wine that pleases God and people is a parable of the divine wisdoms which are the goal of a person's strife, and his knowledge of them is expected of him.[95]

Explaining his choice of metaphor, Immanuel reveals his sensitivity toward the masses who are limited in their understanding of the message. The knowers (*maskilim*), however, are skilled at distilling the intended message from the parable to spur actualization of human potential. The schema presented here, of a scripture containing multiple levels, has roots in the rabbinic, Talmudic, and Maimonidean traditions. This comment, however, reveals Immanuel's regard for an intellectual archetype Immanuel highly regards, the *maskil. Maskilim*, mentioned in this book's introduction, represent the intellectual apex for Immanuel. He may draw this concept from Hillel of Verona's *Tagmule Ha-Nefesh*, which describes *maskilim* in potentia and actual *maskilim*.[96] Immanuel's allegorical reading of Song of Songs 6:10 ("Who is she that shines through like the dawn, beautiful as the moon, radiant as the sun, awesome as a bannered host"), wherein the lover's beauty is analogized to the luminaries, spurs a comparison between a thinker (*maskil*) and a traditional Jew (*ha-yodeah m'tzad ha-kabbalah*). The *maskil* forges his own intellectual path, like the sun, which generates its own light. The traditional Jew, whose knowledge is transmitted from others (*kabbalah*), resembles the moon, which reflects the sun's light and does not generate its own.[97] But, as Immanuel's homilies show, the *maskil* is a philosopher endowed with two capacities: to read scripture allegorically and to observe *mitzvot* philosophically. A close reading of *Maḥberet Ha-Tofet V'Ha-Eden*, in the next several chapters, demonstrates how the concept of the *maskil* is significant to Immanuel's conception of the afterlife and to his literary journey.

As will be discussed in the next chapter, Immanuel maintains a unique approach to biblical exegesis which simultaneously validates both the literal sense and the esoteric interpretation of a biblical verse. Taken together, Immanuel's divergence from Maimonides on the topic of commandments and his affirmation of the literal reading suggest a reaction to the radical rationalism of certain Maimonidean thinkers. In the wake of a fourteenth-century controversy over philosophy and scripture, critics of the Maimonidean side attacked those who excused themselves from observance because of their rationalizations. According to these critics, when such Jews determined that the reasoning behind a commandment did not pertain to them, their observance lapsed. It is possible, then, that Immanuel's diffusion of such a hybrid position on the commandments reflects his negotiation of the disparate ideological camps.

* * *

In light of Immanuel's two independent exegetical treatises, explicating the red heifer and wine from creation, it is clear that Immanuel was deliberately considerate of his audience and genre, especially when delivering messages of repentance and moral rehabilitation. Immanuel wrote during a time of Jewish cultural wars over Torah observance, when rationalists viewed commandments as tools for moral habituation to condition a person toward the end but as ancillary to that goal. Those in his environment were fixated on the discourse of virtues and vices as developed externally by the mendicant friars and communal governments and internally by the Jewish moralists. Although Immanuel offers harsh critiques of sinful behavior and material pleasures in his poetry, and certainly in his biblical commentaries, *Maḥberet Ha-Tofet V'Ha-Eden* conveys the same message through an entirely different medium—the narrative tale. Familiar with the ethical works of Benjamin and Yeḥiel Anav, and likely aware of the penitential sermons occurring in random settings throughout town, Immanuel sought to convey the gravity of vicious sin and the serenity of reward to a mixed audience through a realistic tale set in a hell and heaven. Throughout the journey tale, he establishes his literary persona as authoritative and relatable. Immanuel must have already been familiar with Dante's *Divine Comedy*, which quickly spread within the decade or so after its writing in 1310. The real challenge, for Immanuel, remained how to amalgamate a thoroughly Christian work about the afterlife with a rich Jewish tradition in a way that empowered Jewish readers to pause and reflect. Having established Immanuel's intellectual and historical contexts, we now turn to a close reading of the otherworldly poem to explore the mechanisms of adaptation.

II

Maḥberet Ha-Tofet V'Ha-Eden

4

NAVIGATING THE AFTERLIFE

Having examined Immanuel's biblical commentaries in their social and intellectual contexts, we now turn to *Maḥberet Ha-Tofet V'Ha-Eden* to illustrate the interplay between the *maḥberet* and Immanuel's exegetical works. The final chapter in Immanuel's poetic anthology, *Maḥberet Ha-Tofet V'Ha-Eden* stands apart from the other *maḥbarot* in both form and content. It is the only chapter with a single, sustained plot, and the only one without metrical poems interspersed in the rhymed-prose narrative. This chapter prefaces a close reading of *Maḥberet Ha-Tofet V'Ha-Eden* with a survey of the structure and general content of Immanuel's netherworldly realms. It also explores the relationship between this Hebrew tale and its twin sources of inspiration: Dante's *Divine Comedy* and the Maimonidean philosophical tradition. The confrontation between Dante's hypermaterialist vision of the beyond and Maimonides' outright denial of a materialist understanding of the afterlife, which led him to invest rabbinic concepts with immaterial significance, undergirds *Maḥberet Ha-Tofet V'Ha-Eden*. Amalgamating such starkly opposed ideologies about the beyond, *Maḥberet Ha-Tofet V'Ha-Eden* presents a unique otherworldly vision important for the history of Jewish thought and literature.

Literary Models

Contrary to popular opinion, which maintains that Jews don't believe in hell or heaven, rabbinic and medieval Jews believed that an individual was punished for sins or rewarded for virtues after death; some seem to have imagined the experience of the human soul after death in ways that imply a material place.[1] Likely a result of Greek or Persian influence, biblical acknowledgment of reward and punishment in an afterlife is evident in the book of Daniel, where Daniel indicates that the souls of the wicked will go to eternal damnation while the beatific souls shall shine like the stars (Daniel 12:2–3).[2] Fleeting statements and fragments found in the Talmudic corpora, Midrashic collections, and the early exegetical Targums (Aramaic translations of the Bible) provide additional details. With the influence of the Greco-Arabic philosophical tradition on Jewish thought, Jewish philosophical writings examined the afterlife through studies of the soul's relationship to the divine and earthly realms, often pitting the rabbinic tradition of physical reward and punishment against philosophical views of immaterial postmortem experiences. Maimonides, for example, rejected the traditional views of reward and punishment as recompense for good or evil deeds in favor of a purely spiritual realm in which no physicality exists.[3] Following his theory that human "happiness" consists of the actualization of the human intellect, Maimonides saw biblical or rabbinic references to reward and punishment as alluding to the fulfillment (or failure) of the intellectual goal. Consequently, the very conceptualization of reward or punishment shifted from physical to incorporeal, a position that Immanuel expresses throughout his biblical commentaries.

As a tour of hell and heaven, *Maḥberet Ha-Tofet V'Ha-Eden* draws on Jewish predecessors from the late-antique and rabbinic periods as well as from allusive Talmudic references to salvation in the next world (*Olam Ha-Ba*).[4] Abraham Ibn Ezra's *Hayy ben Meqiz*, a medieval Hebrew adaptation of an Arabic visionary tour by Avicenna, is perhaps the closest Jewish analog to Immanuel's work. In many of these earlier works, however, the next world is envisioned as a pastoral utopia, or a heavenly academy where enthroned souls engage in eternal study.[5] Common to all these texts, despite their attempts at description, is an insistence that the next world is indescribable, obscure, and nothing like this world.[6] Immanuel echoes this sentiment in his Proverbs commentary, stating that at least as far as the experience of the soul is concerned, "the soul's pleasure is concealed and unknown to the eyes of our intellects, and we have no way to understand its true nature."[7] Yet, strikingly, in *Maḥberet Ha-Tofet V'Ha-Eden*, Immanuel depicts the afterlife in physical terms, as a world shaped like a cone, in which the souls of the dead experience bodily tortures or enjoy a glowing light as a consequence of wicked or good behavior during their lifetimes.

None of Immanuel's Jewish predecessors was as seminal an influence on this work as the Christian vision of the beyond found in Dante's *Divine Comedy*, one of the longest medieval poems written in vernacular dialect. This influence is evident, first and foremost, in the structure of Immanuel's narrative, which is split into the realms of hell and heaven. Given that, in his philosophical biblical commentaries, Immanuel rejects the idea that hell and heaven are real, physical places and instead adopts a radically different vision of the soul's experience from Dante's tale, it is reasonable to ask why the *Divine Comedy* might have provided so much of this final *maḥberet*'s imagery and form. As Dante's shadow looms large in *Maḥberet Ha-Tofet V'Ha-Eden*, as well as in scholarly treatments of the poem, a closer examination of the relationship between the two literary works illuminates the dynamics of adaptation employed by Immanuel.

Literary Structure

The conceit of Immanuel's *Maḥberet Ha-Tofet V'Ha-Eden* is that it is a dream vision experienced by a character named Immanuel, who is grieving the death of a younger friend. In the vision Immanuel's literary persona tours hell and heaven, led by a guide named Daniel. Immanuel's hell and heaven are complementary spaces, both in structure and in content, although hell (*Tofet*) is far more elaborate. Hell is broken into twenty-three distinct regions, followed by a region for collective punishment, housing twenty-five sinners, while heaven (*Eden*) has only seven regions altogether. Both spaces begin and end with areas for collective punishment or reward; they both start with individuals drawn from traditional scriptural and rabbinic traditions and end with contemporary sinners or saints. And whereas *Tofet*'s collective burns in a bonfire, *Eden*'s group of righteous glows with the splendor of celestial light.

The narrative progresses as a traditional tour, with stops for the guide to explain the traveler's sights. While the absence of an apparent organizational scheme in *Maḥberet Ha-Tofet V'Ha-Eden* has been contrasted negatively with the highly structured *Divine Comedy*, the *maḥberet* in fact displays Immanuel's deep engagement with both the *Comedy* and the rabbinic tradition.[8]

Throughout the tour, the traveler, Immanuel, registers extreme emotions, often expressing surprise in his encounters or anxiety about the torments and rewards he witnesses. Anxiety bookends the literary journey, as Immanuel opens the chapter grief-stricken over the fate of his soul. In a tearful opening scene, preceding the dream vision, he is plagued with self-doubt and fear of eventual divine retribution. He laments his lack of spiritual provision (*tzeidah*), fearing to experience death suddenly (*el-al yikra-uni*), and calls himself an "ignorant fool" (*sakhal*), weeping until he falls asleep. The language and allusions draw from the author's reading of Proverbs 30:25 ("Ants are a folk without power, yet they prepare food for themselves in summer"), in which an unprepared fool is contrasted with an efficient and diligent ant. In his commentary, Immanuel invokes the fool (*sakhal ha-mekatzer*) who has not behaved properly. He explains:

> He will not know when they shall call him to the beyond [*el-al yikra-uhu*]. Behold, when a man is called before one judge in this world, he is fearful and afraid. How shall a man not fear when called by God and brought to trial for every hidden action, whether good or bad? How can he not be roused by the tale of the ant to prepare provision [*tzeidah*] for his orphaned soul? How can he not find a place of rest for her to stand among those who stand there?[9]

The overlapping terms and images highlight an interplay between Immanuel's narrative poem and biblical commentaries: the characters and interactions of *Maḥberet Ha-Tofet V'Ha-Eden* find parallel in and, indeed, manifest the speculative material presented in the commentaries.

Pregnant with Immanuel's personal misgivings, the poem's opening scene also subtly channels Dante's *Divine Comedy*, which similarly opens with a lost poet's personal reckoning. Dante's poem is a tripartite work chronicling a lost traveler's quest, beginning when he finds himself in a dark and frightening forest. The traveler, named Dante and guided by the Roman poet Virgil, voyages through the realms of Hell (*Inferno*) and Purgatory (*Purgatorio*), until they reach the outermost limit that a pagan like Virgil may reach. Dante continues his journey led by his beloved lady, Beatrice, ascending through the celestial spheres (*Paradiso*) until he reaches the final realm where he expects to have a vision of God. While Dante's material human condition prevents him from actually beholding God, the journey is not fruitless, for it has enriched his knowledge, understanding, and purpose. The tour defies genres, conveying scientific, philosophical, and moral theories alongside historical narratives and social commentary, all set against a solemn, otherworldly backdrop. Dante's material depiction of the netherworld, with topographical features and a distinct geometric shape, synthesizes ancient afterlife imagery with more contemporary Christian accounts to foster a realistic literary experience.

Throughout his hell and heaven, Immanuel manipulates classical eschatological language and imagery from both the scriptural and rabbinic traditions and from Dante's poem in service of his allegory. Immanuel's engagement with traditional rabbinic ideas appears most clearly in the heavenly realm of *Eden*, whereas the influence of Dante's *Comedy* is most evident in *Tofet*. Before highlighting specific instances of the *maḥberet*'s engagement with Dante's work or the Maimonidean tradition, we will take a brief look at Immanuel's exegetical approach to clarify his perception of the authorial role, which is echoed in Immanuel's choice of place names for his netherworldly realms.

Terminology and Methodology

As a narrative embodiment of Immanuel's philosophical ideas, *Maḥberet Ha-Tofet V'Ha-Eden* is intimately connected with his philosophical biblical commentaries. This sentiment is evident in Immanuel's choice of the terms "*Tofet*" and "*Eden*," which, I would argue, reveals one item on his agenda for writing the narrative, which dovetails with the *Divine Comedy*. Both the Italian and Hebrew celestial tours feature a tourist who experiences a personal quest, and for both the frightful content of the tales insinuates that the audience, too, is at risk and should be engaging in repentance. Describing his discomfort at witnessing the sights of hell, Immanuel asks Daniel, his celestial guide, for further elucidation of the sinners' crimes. Daniel responds, "Now pay attention to my words and admonish the hearts of the wayward with your writings."[10] Affirming the tale's utility as a potential corrective for a wider public, Daniel's words express the moralism of this narrative. We cannot know for certain, but Immanuel's choice of the term *Tofet* may signal something about his intention. This rare word appears in the book of Job, where Job states that he (Job) should be displayed as a parable (*mashal*) and *Tofet* for the nations.[11] Puzzled by the use of *Tofet* as a state of being, Immanuel explains: "If Tofet comes from '*Tofteh Arukh*' [Isaiah 30:33], then this verse means that my sorrow made me speak words of allegory and hellfire [*Tofet*] among the nations, so that I am as a drum [*tof*] and a flute before people."[12] Immanuel thus reads Job as an ethical model, whose story—the book of Job itself—serves as a warning drum calling neighbors to repent. His choice of *Tofet* for his narrative, over any of the plethora of biblical terms for hell, like *Sheol* or *Gehinnom*, indicates that he saw his story—the *maḥberet*—as similarly meant to awaken people to their iniquity. Both Dante's and

Immanuel's fantastical narratives, then, foreground an ethical imperative using an otherworldly setting.[13]

As the name *Tofet* gestures at the *Divine Comedy*, Immanuel's use of the term *Eden* for heaven points to his Maimonidean intellectual orientation. In his commentary on the creation narrative in Genesis, Immanuel describes the *mashal*, the parable: the Garden of Eden as a lush habitat for human beings where "the Lord, may He be blessed, planted good trees gathered together in one place called a garden."[14] Later, however, Immanuel uses *Eden* not as a place name but as a reference to abstract intellectual concepts. On Genesis 2:10, Immanuel reveals the *nimshal*, the interpretation of the parable, or its allegorical meaning: "a wondrous matter," namely that "the spiritual Eden is the Agent Intellect, that is sanctified souls' Eden, for it stands behind the veil fashioning crowns for its Maker. These crowns are the ones that adorn the heads of the righteous souls as our blessed Sages said: 'the righteous souls sit with crowns upon their heads.'"[15] Rejecting the rabbinic vision of eternal material reward, Immanuel's philosophical position equates Eden with the union between the human rational intellect and the agent intellect, the lowest of the separate intellects. Reading Psalms 36:9 allegorically, Immanuel compares the souls of the righteous to "a bountiful garden" that draws the intellect's emanation from an overflowing spring. Again he explains the intended meaning: "He [the Psalmist] called the intellect whence emanation will flow onto the righteous souls, Eden."[16] As evident from Immanuel's commentaries, the term *Eden* poses hermeneutical complexities to an exegete and poet who writes in several modes.

Immanuel confronts his apparently contradictory explanations of *Eden* by focusing on the four rivers that emerge from it (Genesis 2:10) as paradigms of multiple modes of reading and exegesis. He states:

> He disclosed the locations of the aforementioned rivers for a reason, since the entire Genesis narrative reflects matters as they [actually] are, according to the simple reading, as well as their wondrous secrets, which cannot be imagined. So that a person should not say that the matter of creation did not happen [in reality], as is plainly stated, but rather is [merely] an allegory of esoteric matters, Scripture mentioned the names of the rivers and their locations. For they are famous and well-known rivers to all. Even though the narrative of the Garden of Eden and the rivers that flow from it allude to esoteric matters, nevertheless the details are as they appear in the simple reading. There is a Garden of

> Eden on Earth and those rivers flow from there, and yet they are also an allegory for divine matters as we will mention.[17]

This interpretation of the four rivers encapsulates Immanuel's exegetical method, allowing multiple truths to coexist depending on the mode of interpretation deployed. Although Immanuel does not doubt that the four rivers exist in the world, a symbolic reading of the rivers reveals esoteric truths, while at the same time maintaining the integrity of the literal verse. Immanuel cites the number 4 as an allusion to the material elements (earth, air, water, fire) whose admixture forms all matter.[18] As an embodiment of an actual place in nature and a symbol of the four elements, the Edenic rivers serve as a potent allegorical figure for Immanuel, especially in light of the general Jewish debates over the value and utility of allegorical readings of the Bible that raged during the early decades of the fourteenth century in southern France.[19] One of the anxieties expressed by more conservative medieval Jewish exegetes was that allegorical readings of the Bible might lead Jews to doubt the truth of the entire biblical narrative, a position rejected by Immanuel. His "four rivers" approach affirms the legitimacy of an allegorical reading while asserting the unquestioned reality of the verses' literal meaning.[20] This methodological statement was of such importance to Immanuel that he repeated it verbatim in most of his commentaries.[21]

The recourse to allegorical reading was also a strategy employed by Maimonides, who redefined the after-death experience as immaterial but nevertheless sought to maintain the authority of traditional sages and the integrity of their statements on the afterlife. Throughout *Maḥberet ha-Tofet V'Ha-Eden*, Immanuel uses multivalent terms like "crowns," "radiance," and "ladder" to refer simultaneously to real objects and to deeper philosophical truths, an approach that displays an exegetical hermeneutic consistent with the paradigm of the four Edenic rivers in Genesis. A closer look at Immanuel's manipulation of these terms in *Eden* demonstrates how his tour exemplifies ideas about the soul's experience, reinvested with philosophical significance.

Crowns

The concept of the blessed wearing crowns in heaven is reinvested with intellectual significance by medieval Jewish rationalists. Maimonides interprets a well-known talmudic portrait of the afterlife—a vision of blessed souls wearing crowns—allegorically in his legal code, *Mishneh Torah*.[22] Maimonides explains:

> The phrase "crowns on their heads" refers to the knowledge they have acquired, for which they have attained life in the world to come. This is their crown, in the same sense as where Solomon says: with the crown wherewith his mother hath crowned him [Song of Songs 3:11]. And just as in the text: everlasting joy shall be upon their heads [Isaiah 51:11], joy is not to be understood as a material substance that actually rests on the head, so "the crown" of which the Sages here speak, is not to be taken literally but refers to knowledge.[23]

Immanuel quotes this passage in his gloss on Proverbs and paraphrases it in the commentary on Song of Songs, where he also cites Moses Ibn Tibbon's commentary to explain that "their crown is a known idea through which one merits eternal life."[24] Elsewhere in his Proverbs commentary, Immanuel adds that the crowns worn by the righteous in *Eden* represent the public acclaim earned by their knowledge. On Proverbs 4:9, Immanuel states, "Whoever attained knowledge of the divine . . . treads the path of true beatitude, and his soul will be glorified in the spiritual world together with the righteous who sit with crowns upon their heads."[25]

Throughout *Maḥberot Immanuel*, crowns (*atarot*) symbolize wisdom. Another word for crown, *keter*, also appears in both literal and figurative senses. Referring to decorative headpieces, a "crown of royalty" (*keter malkhut*) adorns some of the blessed souls in *Eden*.[26] And crowns can refer, metaphorically, to the possession of an attribute, as in "the crown of humility" or "the crown of glory" or "the crown of pride."[27] Similarly, the biblical authors whom Immanuel meets in heaven praise his literary persona for returning the "crown of Torah" to its former glory.[28] In his commentaries, too, crowns have multivalent meaning; Immanuel's interpretation of Psalms 122:5 as a reference to the soul's experience after death compares the "heavenly thrones" of judgment to the rabbinic notion of crowns for the souls, reading both as metaphors for rational wisdom. The crown serves Immanuel as both a useful object with which to declare a soul's righteousness in *Eden* and an indicator of deeper truths acquired by the seeker of knowledge.

Light and Radiance

The association of righteousness with light, particularly with respect to the afterlife, permeates biblical and midrashic literature. One concept is that of the primordial light (*or ha-gamur*), a soul-sustaining light fashioned on the first day of creation. Philosophically oriented Jewish thinkers, and perhaps especially Saadia Gaon (ca. 882–942), reworked scriptural and rabbinic references to describe the soul's experience after death.[29] Immanuel, too, deploys biblical and rabbinic language to describe the afterlife as a place of light. On arrival in heaven, Immanuel "saw new heavens and a new terrain. This place had no stench or rotten smell, just holy and purified earth. . . . There, one sees the ultimate light, called by the sages 'the sevenfold light,' like the light of the seven days of creation. . . . There, the pure souls bound in bonds of life reside, those who shine like the light of the firmament, those who have become luminaries."[30] The souls of the righteous are thus transformed, as it were, into astral bodies and glow like the splendor of the firmament. An instructive parallel is found in Immanuel's commentary on the Song of Songs, where he compares the luminescence of the righteous in this world to the light of Venus, which intensifies when souls move beyond this life.[31] In his comment on Psalms 118:27, Immanuel writes that the newly ascended soul is brought to "the great light and that pleasure because the souls of the righteous shine like the splendor of the firmament, and those who lead the many to righteousness are as stars forever and ever."[32] Here too the philosophical idea of the immortal soul and its experience after death is embodied in his literary depiction of a material heaven suffused with physical light.

The Ladder

Immanuel ascends to heaven via the ladder from Jacob's dream, which straddles earth and heaven. Since late antiquity, Jacob's dream of the ladder in Genesis 28:10–19 had been interpreted allegorically by both Jews and Christians. By Immanuel's time, Maimonides' rationalistic interpretation in *The Guide of the Perplexed* and Samuel Ibn Tibbon's exposition in *Ma'amar Yikavu Ha-Mayim* ("A Treatise on Let the Waters Be Gathered") had established that the ladder was an allegory of the workings of prophecy.[33] Immanuel, however, when he uses the ladder metaphor in his commentaries and the *Maḥbarot*, employs it either in its literal sense as a means of ascending to *Eden* or, allegorically, as an individual's pathway to God.

In its plainest sense, the ladder represents the process of acquiring knowledge, with each ascending step symbolic of the advancement of knowledge. Immanuel explains that "study of the applied sciences sharpens the mind; it is a ladder by which to acquire the remaining sciences."[34] Narrating a tale about a verbal joust with a presumptuous man in the *Maḥbarot*, Immanuel exclaims, "I showed everyone that his thoughts were not my thoughts, his ways were not my ways. His recollection of memories left him ashamed and disgraced, and my recollection ascended to the highest step of the ladder where I received an everlasting name."[35] Immanuel invokes the image of the ladder to signal the completion of steps in the intellective process.

Immanuel's "ladder of wisdom" refers to the intellectual path one must follow to reach God, who is stationed at the top. Immanuel identifies the rungs of this ladder as crafted from the wooden beams of the Tree of Life, equating the acquisition of wisdom with immortality.[36] He states, "Wisdom is a ladder that the thinker [*maskil*] climbs to reach God, and the more steps he climbs, the closer he approaches God. Whoever merits reaching the top of the ladder shall find the Lord's angels ascending and descending, and the Blessed God stationed above it."[37] Immanuel also mentions the ladder of wisdom in his commentary on the Song of Songs, when he expounds the verse "Who is she that ascends from the desert?" (Song of Songs 3:6) as "ascends the rungs of the ladder of wisdom, which is stationed on the ground and its top reaches the heavens and divine angels ascend and descend it, and God is stationed above it. He mentioned 'ascending' in the way that he mentioned the spirit of humanity that ascends upward, and this ascension is the ascension of a step and attainment of a glorified and high level."[38] The "ladder of wisdom" is identical to Jacob's ladder, and Immanuel states that "the path of life ensures that its travelers will live eternally and this road, beyond the thinker, is the ladder which our patriarch Jacob saw. . . . This path is good for the thinker [*maskil*], who bypasses his descent to *Sheol* by ascending the ladder of wisdom."[39] By introducing the ladder as the bridge between hell and heaven in *Maḥberet Ha-Tofet V'Ha-Eden*, Immanuel finds a concrete object to link the two realms, while alluding to wisdom as the only way to reach the Lord, as is evident in Immanuel's revelation that "when we were on its highest rungs, God was revealed to us."[40]

These central examples demonstrate how philosophical concepts about the postmortem experience are embodied in the narrative of Immanuel's poem. Having introduced the value of multivalence, established in his reading of the four Edenic rivers, Immanuel deploys terms that have been read both materially and allegorically, claiming simultaneous truth for both reading modes. The importance of the Maimonidean tradition to Immanuel, for ideas as well as imagery and terminology, is almost matched by the influence of Dante's *Divine Comedy* as a source of language and imagery. As opposed to *Eden*, mostly animated by the Maimonidean tradition, *Tofet* contains several Dantesque elements that Immanuel adapts by use of Jewish analogs. This likely reflects Immanuel's perception of his *Eden* as a celebration of intellectual worship; a stance that mirrors the Maimonidean ultimate goal.

The Gate

The closest parallels to Dante's *Divine Comedy* appear in the opening and closing lines of the *Maḥberet* and the vignettes of the first two regions of hell. It is possible that Immanuel began his narrative intending to mimic the structure of *Inferno* but could not meaningfully sustain the effort for the entirety of his work. Still, the examples of *Tofet*'s gate, the bonfire of rebellious souls and the lustful women, as well as the story's conclusion demonstrate that Immanuel usually sought out biblical or rabbinic analogs for concepts in the *Divine Comedy.*

Dante's gate to hell is inscribed with the phrase "Abandon hope all you who enter." Immanuel's literary persona, for his part, passes through *Sha'ar Shaleḥet* ("gate of dispersal") at *Tofet*'s entrance, the name of a biblical gate to the Temple (1 Chronicles 26:16). The root of *Shaleḥet* (ש.ל.כ), signifying casting something off, refers to the dispersal of leaves from a tree, which aptly fits the displacement of sinful souls from their bodies as they pass through. Like Dante, Immanuel's literary persona hears the shrill sound of the souls howling, "Our hope is lost, we have been judged," a phrase from Ezekiel that recalls the inscription on Dante's gate.[41] The phrase packs a double punch, evoking the *Divine Comedy* while also drawing on the original scriptural locus of Ezekiel's vision, which was itself frequently cited in rabbinic discussions of resurrection of the dead.[42]

In his commentaries as well, Immanuel associates this verse from Ezekiel with the notion of a punitive afterlife. Immanuel's comment on Proverbs 15:11 ("*Sheol* and *Abaddon* lie exposed to the Lord, how much more the minds of men!") reads this verse as a confirmation of God's omniscience, explaining that:

> [Solomon] says that even though *Sheol* and *Abaddon* [Pit and Despair] are esoteric and hidden matters, they are exposed before God. This means that individuals who descended to *Sheol* and those *who lost all hope* are apparent before him. Moreover, living individuals who have not descended to *Sheol* are apparent and known before him, the Blessed One. . . . One who died should not think that he has escaped, for those who are in *Sheol* after their deaths—whose hope has been lost, and they have been banished from the land of the living—have not escaped his hand. They are before God, to reap the fruit of their deeds.[43]

In comforting the spirits of the dead by referring to the doctrine of resurrection, the verse also affirms God's omnipotence for the living, imparting the belief that God does not abandon the dead. The use of Ezekiel in this part of *Tofet* is particularly potent because it resembles the inscription on Dante's gate while invoking classical Jewish beliefs about God's omnipotence and the justness of the afterlife. Immanuel's choice of a scriptural verse with theological significance that is reminiscent of a scene in the *Divine Comedy* attests to his deep biblical knowledge. Having passed *Tofet*'s gate, Immanuel and his guide, Daniel, proceed to the first zone of punishment, a massive bonfire filled with the souls of the rebellious.

Bonfire of the Rebellious

Dante's first circle of *Inferno*, called Limbo, holds a crowd of sinners, including unbaptized infants and non-Christians. Similarly, the first sinners encountered in *Tofet*—those who possess a rebellious soul—also appear as a group. Immanuel never directly defines a "rebellious soul," but his cast of characters aligns for the most part with typical biblical and rabbinic characterizations of wicked personae. With their names etched on their foreheads, reminiscent of the seven P's that are engraved on the forehead of Dante's eponymous character in *Purgatorio* (which were themselves possibly drawn from the events in Ezekiel 9:2–6), these rebellious sinners are drawn from a range of classical Jewish texts, such as the Bible and the Apocrypha. The sinners are not categorized by type of sin or level of guilt; rather, they appear according to Immanuel's need to maintain his rhymes. When we come across these sinners, they are being burned in a pyre. Unlike the case in Limbo, the pyre inflicts suffering, but, as in Limbo, it includes "virtuous adults of different faiths."[44] Both Limbo and the bonfire lump together a motley group of sinners, and both also permit their authors to quietly acknowledge the intellectual legacy of the ancients.

Alongside the biblical and apocryphal figures in the bonfire, Immanuel depicts a more contemporary cast of characters, including ancient and medieval non-Jewish philosophers who are denigrated for their misguided beliefs, excessive pride, and lack of reverence for the biblical Moses. The ancient physicians include Galen (ca. 200s), who maligned Moses, and Hippocrates, who hid his medical books.[45] Among the ancient philosophers, Aristotle is condemned for his belief in the eternity of the universe, which contradicted rabbinic belief in creation *ex nihilo*. Plato burns in hell for his belief in the existence of the world of the forms, an immaterial realm containing the perfect form of everything in the sublunar universe. The medieval Muslim philosopher Al-Farabi (ca. 870–951) is criticized for his mockery of conjunction and his belief in the reincarnation of souls, and Avicenna's flawed understanding of geology led him to argue that mountains can be naturally formed.[46] On the other hand, as seen throughout *Maḥberot Immanuel* and his commentaries, Immanuel considered Aristotle a sage, and even sermonized on the importance of accepting true wisdom from a non-Jewish source.[47] With its buoyant rhyme scheme and terse descriptions, the depiction of this region of collective punishment did not offer much opportunity for cross-genre fertilization, but as an analog to Dante's Limbo it testifies to the impact and early reception of Dante's *Divine Comedy* in Jewish circles. Descriptions of the next region, however, contain striking allusions to both the commentaries and the *Divine Comedy*, making it an excellent example of Immanuel's compositional method.

The Adulterous Women

In the second circle of Dante's *Inferno*, both men and women suffer for their sins of lust. In the parallel scene in Immanuel's tour, only female sinners are tortured. A host of angels hurls a group of adulterous women into a cauldron full of bubbling, liquified metals. Commanded by a disembodied voice, the angels set the pot on the fire and prepare to release predatory beasts. The voice scolds the sinners, "Eat, stuff yourselves with the bounty of the abyss that lurks below!"[48] Female sexuality has an ancient history of legislation, regulation, and punishment, as classical midrashic depictions of hell included in the Talmud feature women hanging by the particular limbs involved in their sins, for immodestly displaying themselves to attract young men. But Immanuel is the first to identify, as a group, female adulterers.[49] Most interesting is the way Immanuel marshals seemingly unrelated allegorical scriptural readings into a Jewish adaptation of the circle of the lustful in Dante's *Divine Comedy.*

Without knowing Immanuel's Proverbs commentary, readers might be confused by the choice of the pot and meat image as depicting torture. But Immanuel's gloss of Proverbs and its warnings about the "foreign woman" (*ishah zarah*) and her wily ways is key to grasping the significance of the punishment. Reading Proverbs 30:20 allegorically ("such is the way of an adulteress: She eats, wipes her mouth, and says 'I have done no wrong'"), Immanuel compares the adulteress to matter, which, like the woman who moves from man to man, moves from form to form, an explanation straight from Maimonides' *The Guide of the Perplexed* (III:8). Immanuel prefers a different interpretation, however, which rests on the principle that "eating is a euphemism for adultery," a theme integrated into the punishment of the adulterous women. Like the so-called *contrapasso* method in Dante's *Comedy*, in which sinners are punished in a manner related to their sin, these women are punished in a cooking vessel due to their sin of "eating."[50] This imagery is reinforced by the demonic command, "Eat, stuff yourselves,"[51] an explicit association of their sin and a corresponding punishment.

Adding further nuance to the narrative of adulterous women, Immanuel layers allusions from different literary corpora to highlight the sinners' betrayal of God. A double allusion that engages with both the Jewish scriptural tradition and Dante's *Comedy* is Immanuel's characterization of the adulterous women as doves. The women "all moaned like doves of the valleys, with tears flowing down their cheeks."[52] Later, they "moaned like the sound of doves while beating their breasts."[53] The dove appears in many biblical passages symbolizing the beloved, peace, and innocence, but, less positively, the biblical prophets in particular emphasize the dove's noisiness in connection with its foolishness. Drawing on Hosea 7:11, Immanuel equates the weakness of Israel with the meekness of the housewife, and in turn, with the pettiness of the foolish dove. The association of meek women and doves is also expressed elsewhere, in Immanuel's commentary on Psalms 68:13, where "housewives sharing spoils" after the defeat of an unnamed army in the Land of Israel signifies the Israelites' resounding victory. The next verse prominently mentions the wings of the dove. The linkage of weak women and doves also appears in Dante's *Inferno* V, where the sinful lovers Paolo and Francesca are likened to "doves whom desire has summoned, with raised wings steady against the current."[54] Recalling Dante's lovers, while also noting the bird's stupidity and weakness, Immanuel's characterization of adulterous women as doves acknowledges both his Jewish literary heritage and the *Divine Comedy*. The ambiguity of the dove symbol would also seem to suit Immanuel's desire to represent wayward women as once-innocent doves who have transformed into wailing and petty creatures.

As discussed in Chapter 2, Psalm 68 bears significant allegorical meaning for Immanuel. The psalmist compares God's scattering of the kings to a snowstorm in Zalmon, which led medieval commentators, including Immanuel, to interpret this psalm as an affirmation of Israel's final eschatological victory. Immanuel reads this psalm as a narrative of Israel's unlikely victory after the final battle between Gog and Magog (Armageddon). The housewives collecting the spoils of the war symbolize the "tribe of Israel," whose dejection and weakness are like the woman who remains, tending to the home, and the miracle of Israel's final victory is conveyed in its gathering of the spoils of war despite its subjugated condition. Immanuel comments, "If you are in a place of inferiority and subordination, like the place [where one] sets the pots in between the stove and the grill, then you too shall reach the wings of a dove sheathed in silver."[55] Reverting to a domestic metaphor, Immanuel equates the housewife's meekness with the intermediate space between stove and grill, explaining that "if you are weak and debilitated and you lie in between the stove and the grill, like the woman who dwells in the house over a pot of meat, its contents will be filled with gold and silver from the volume of spoils that you shall inherit from the army [*ḥayil*] of Gog and Magog."[56] Extending the domestic imagery, in his commentary on Psalms, Immanuel interprets the scattering of the kings on the basis of the verse "and they scattered as in a pot and as meat within a cauldron." In *Tofet* Immanuel recasts the battle between Israel and its foes into a battle between the adulterous women and the ministering angels. Instead of the army (*ḥayil*) of Gog and Magog, there is the army (*ḥayil*) of the adulterous women that sweeps in like the storms of the Negev desert. Rather than God scattering the anonymous enemy kings, the angels of death consign the women's bodies to scatter like meat in a cauldron.

Read in this manner, Immanuel's biblical commentaries clearly serve his poetry as a rich source of language, imagery, and ideas. His adaptive techniques enrich the literary characters in *Tofet* by blending gendered imagery of the weak, petty-minded housewife of Psalm 68, the seductive temptress of Proverbs 30, the rebellious talmudic characters, and the lustful sinners of Dante's *Inferno.* Immanuel, a textual omnivore, deftly utilizes multiple streams of text to craft a creative and entertaining narrative that also highlights his understanding of morality and biblical texts.

Immortality and the Stars

Maḥberet Ha-Tofet V'Ha-Eden concludes with a dramatic spectacle, the clearest example of his addressing both Jewish traditional imagery and the *Divine Comedy.* On waking at the end of his journey, Immanuel's literary persona beseeches God: "At my end, may divine kindness be right beside me, sustaining me. May it give honor to the place where I shall be stationed, alongside those who lead the many to righteousness [*maskilim*], forever and ever, like the stars."[57] Drawing on Daniel 12:3 ("And they that be wise shall shine as the brightness of the firmament; and they that turn many to righteousness as the stars for ever and ever"), Immanuel ends his celestial journey with a prayer for immortality, a verse that would have resonated with both Jews and Christians in medieval Italy. For medieval Christians, this biblical phrase subtly acknowledges the *Divine Comedy*, whose three canticles (*Inferno, Purgatorio, Paradiso*) each finish with the words *le stelle* ("the stars"). For medieval Jews, especially philosophically inclined ones, Daniel 12:3 was read as a shorthand reference to the soul's eternal delights after death.[58] Throughout his commentaries, Immanuel refers to the verse as code for intellectual immortality. For example, in his explication of Proverbs 24:20 ("For there is no future for the evil man; the lamp of the wicked goes out"), Immanuel contrasts the eternal fates of the wicked and the righteous, stating, "The righteous soul will shine and radiate like the splendor of the firmament and the stars forever and ever. It will savor all that it has accomplished. The wicked soul will remain in darkness and gloom, judged in accordance with its iniquity."[59]

Yet Daniel 12:3 also had practical resonance for medieval Jews, who used this verse as a scribal formula commonly found in the colophons of medieval Hebrew texts to bless the scribe and his family.[60] It is, therefore, doubly appropriate that Immanuel used this verse to end not only *Maḥberet Ha-Tofet V'Ha-Eden* but the entire poetic anthology. By using Daniel 12:3 to conclude the work, Immanuel finds an expressly Jewish way to acknowledge the concluding verses of the *Divine Comedy* while at the same time alluding to rabbinic and philosophical ideas about eternal reward and intellectual perfection. The potency of this verse, for Immanuel, lies not only in its content but also in its practical scribal application.[61] A scriptural allusion filled with resonances, Daniel 12:3 exemplifies the cultural currents washing over Immanuel in late-medieval Italy.

Having idealized the *maskil*, who attains immortality by virtue of leading others to wisdom in Daniel 12:3, as a perfected intellectual in *Maḥberet Ha-Tofet V'Ha-Eden*, Immanuel sets his encounters with biblical authors in heaven to cement the notion that a *maskil* leads others to wisdom through biblical commentary. After witnessing the torments of *Tofet*, Immanuel's literary persona is stricken with significant fear and self-doubt. In a tearful confession, he laments the sullied state of his own soul, expressing fear at its eventual fate. Daniel, the guide, reveals that Immanuel's commentaries have redeemed him, for "you earned a reputation among the greatest men of the land and saved your soul. How the world would suffer were you to be shamed! The sweetness and richness of the Torah ceased until you arose and returned the crown of scripture to its former state."[62] While Immanuel's biblical commentaries subtly undergird his narrative fantasy of hell throughout the text, they play a leading role at its conclusion. Praising Immanuel's exegetical efforts, Daniel states:

> You denied sleep to your eyes and slumber to your eyelids until you had gathered all the pearls of wisdom and arranged them in a commentary on God's pure Torah. Although a kingdom of commentators rose against you, you did not forsake grammar, literal definitions, innovations, hidden secrets, and wonderful riddles throughout your books, so much so that your words were words of prophecy. You have banished and neglected the names of other exegetes who are embarrassed and ashamed upon encountering your exegesis. Even the priest who declares war fears your words![63]

While disparaging other biblical exegetes, Daniel highlights Immanuel's nuanced exegesis, with its multiple reading modes, to pose a causal relationship between biblical interpretation and eternal salvation. What Immanuel seems to be saying in *Tofet*'s conclusion is that his commentaries can be considered counterweights to his own moral indiscretions, and their worth may ensure his own immortality. Immanuel believes scriptural exegesis to be a vehicle for acquiring universal truths and achieving eternal beatitude. Such a position explains why much of *Eden* is devoted to encounters between Immanuel's literary persona and the biblical authors who praise his scriptural readings above those of all other exegetes.

* * *

In a striking artistic move, Immanuel, otherwise a predominantly Maimonidean thinker, appears to have disavowed the Maimonidean immaterial conception of afterlife in favor of a realistic and material space heavily influenced by the *Divine Comedy*. Perhaps Immanuel made this bold move because he viewed the poetic genre as one of embellishment and exaggeration, as an allegory (*mashal*) of his own, with its own interpretation (*nimshal*), or a popularizing vehicle for big, intangible ideas. It seems clear enough that, at the very least, a Jewish poet was mesmerized by a magisterial Italian poem and sought to imitate it. Whatever Immanuel's reasoning, *Maḥberet Ha-Tofet V'Ha-Eden* serves as a textual site of cultural deposits, cross-cultural amalgamation, and creative adaptation.

Accessible in its vernacular, Dante's *Divine Comedy* rapidly gained in popularity, as evidenced by numerous vernacular and Latin commentaries, a robust visual arts tradition, and allusions to the poem in vernacular sermons already in the mid-fourteenth century.[64] Jewish attitudes toward Dante's work did vary, but one cannot doubt the importance of the text for medieval Italian Jews.[65] For Immanuel, the *Divine Comedy* served less as a source of theological content and more as a framing device for imparting his own moral lessons in an imaginative and comprehensible fashion. As both Dante and Immanuel creatively adapted classical authoritative texts to address the ills of society, each author presented himself as a quasi-prophet tasked to save the living from eternal punishment and damnation.

The fertile exchanges between ancient Jewish texts and medieval Italian ones, embodied in the verses, images, and characters of Immanuel's poem, attest to the hybridity of our author, who meaningfully engaged with the philosophical writings and literature of his time. An understanding that he did so not only enriches the significance of the text, but requires knowledge of the philosophical ideas couched in Immanuel's commentaries. The next two chapters demonstrate how Immanuel's philosophical commentaries enhance the characterization of figures in *Maḥberet Ha-Tofet V'Ha-Eden* to highlight Immanuel's iconoclastic hybridity.

5

THE WORLD OF THE BODY

It would be easy to argue that the rendering of hell and heaven as actual physical spaces in *Maḥberet Ha-Tofet V'Ha-Eden* constitutes a rejection of the Maimonidean conceptualization of the soul's immaterial postmortem experience. Although Immanuel's Maimonidean affiliation is expressed clearly in his biblical commentaries, the previous chapter demonstrated how the colorful rhymed prose narrative of *Maḥberet Ha-Tofet V'Ha-Eden*, whose characters likely engendered voyeuristic schadenfreude in its consumers, is a closer analog to Dante's *Divine Comedy*. Nevertheless, in this chapter and the next, we turn to the philosophical underpinnings of *Maḥberet Ha-Tofet V'Ha-Eden* to argue that it also concretizes theoretical philosophical concepts by embodying them in its carefully crafted characters and vignettes. The richness of the narrative—and Immanuel's literary skill—therefore, can be truly appreciated only by juxtaposing it with Immanuel's philosophical biblical commentaries. By virtue of this novel methodological approach, the *maḥberet* is transformed from a merely aesthetic work into a delightful didactic morality tale, an accessible narrative that disseminates philosophical ideas about ethics, sin, and immortality in an entertaining otherworldly tour.

The Maimonidean Tibbonides conceived radical ideas about the final purpose of the human intellect and society's role in promoting intellectual perfection. Maimonides himself identified divinely revealed Mosaic law as nourishing both body and soul, terms that he generalizes to refer to an ordered body politic and correct ideas, or truths.[1] Maimonides notes that "even though the practical well-being of society is less exalted than its intellectual perfection, practical communal order must be achieved before intellectual knowledge can be obtained."[2] Although not adopted by Immanuel himself, the Maimonidean division between body and soul is the organizational scheme of chapters 5 and 6 of this book, to highlight the *maḥberet*'s deep reliance on Maimonidean thought. Chapter 5 examines characters whose actions either promoted or hindered the health of the body politic, while Chapter 6 focuses on the consequences of characters' thoughts. Together, both chapters offer a detailed case study of an entertaining tale that communicates complex philosophical ideas alongside biting social critique.

Maimonides' *The Guide of the Perplexed* classifies prohibitions related to "perfection of the body" as those that curb individual desires, those that compel behavior useful to the collective, and those that teach moral qualities so that the affairs of the city are ordered.[3] These categories, I argue, are reflected in *Maḥberet Ha-Tofet V'Ha-Eden* through Immanuel's pervasive concern for social order and his condemnation of hypocrisy. Immanuel values a harmonious social ecosystem; many of the sinners in his text threatened communal health and communal adherence to *halakhah*, and many individuals are considered righteous because they ensured communal wellbeing. Many of the characters in *Maḥberet Ha-Tofet V'Ha-Eden* seem, in fact, to have been crafted to embody theoretical ideas raised in the philosophical commentaries. Other characters, however, appear to reflect contemporary people or groups within Immanuel's orbit, and the relationship between their vignettes and the philosophical commentaries is less evident. Immanuel, a master of scriptural allusion, carefully deploys biblical words and phrases for various literary purposes. Juxtaposing the two genres—entertaining literature and commentary—highlights Immanuel's creative application of biblical language. The following examples, focusing on collective wellbeing, illustrate the fundamental links between Immanuel's narrative and his commentaries.

Maimonides and the Social Contract

In addition to maintenance of general communal order and propriety, Maimonides defines control of the body as including, along with the positive acquisition of moral qualities by individuals, the negative correlate: "every individual among the people not being permitted to act according to his will and up to the limits of his power, but being forced to do that which is useful to the whole."[4] In other words, it aims at "the governance of the city and the wellbeing of the states of all its people according to their capacity."[5] This idea, that the individual has power to affect the collective, is captured in *Maḥberet Ha-Tofet V'Ha-Eden* by Immanuel's wide-ranging vision of communal chaos as including individuals whose sins affect only themselves or their immediate families as well as those whose sins have wider societal implications.

Tofet: *The Abusive Son*

Perhaps the best example of a character in the narrative of *Maḥberet Ha-Tofet V'Ha-Eden* who seems created merely to embody theoretical ideas is the son who verbally and physically abused his parents. Proper treatment of one's parents is frequently discussed and legislated in rabbinic tradition; the Talmud condemns children who physically or verbally abuse their parents to strangulation or stoning. But discursive admonitions and even threats of punishment do not compare to an anecdote that causes an audience to recoil, such as in the vignette where the "right hand and tongue [of the abusive son] were shredded."[6] This whole story turns out to be a pastiche of Immanuel's exegetical comments on Exodus and Proverbs. When he interprets Proverbs 20:20 ("One who reviles his father or mother, light will fail him when darkness comes"), Immanuel highlights the biological and emotional roles played by parents, explaining that a child is "obligated to honor them [i.e., his parents] because of their collaboration with the Lord in creating him," paraphrasing the Talmudic idea that children are created through a partnership between a couple and God.[7] In *Tofet*, acknowledging the biological aspects of parenthood as well as its tremendous emotional investment, Immanuel casts the son's cruelty and ingratitude as especially grave sins. He reminds the reader that parents "fed them their milk and suckled them with their blood," while his comment on Exodus 20:12 ("Honor your father and mother") notes that parents "made their blood and tissue his food and drink."[8] Dwelling on the spiritual ramifications of abusing one's parents, Immanuel explains, "It is fitting that the light of divine providence should depart from him while he stands in the valley of sorrow and despair. He shall find no comfort when he is in distress. His [i.e., the son's] soul will be severed from the bundle of life[9] and it shall not be among those who 'shine like the splendor of the firmament.' Rather, his darkened soul shall be destined for the spiritual punishments that lie in the gloom of death."[10] Marshaling traditional allusions to immortality, Immanuel concludes that children who abuse their parents will be subject to a terrible demise.

Unlike the commentaries' focus on the spiritual ramifications of parental abuse, *Tofet* highlights physical torture, likely reflecting *Tofet*'s task to entertain and enthrall its audience. In delivering justice, *Tofet* adapts Christian and Jewish paradigms in an original way. The physical punishment of the specific parts of the body that sinned, especially the mouth, evokes Christian moralistic literature that classifies spoken vices as "vices of the tongue" (*vitiae linguae*).[11] Immanuel's sinner is initially described as having "a tongue that spoke in arrogance, but in his heart he devised wrongdoing," and using his mouth, "he cursed at his father, spit in his face."[12] In chastising the son, Immanuel wonders how he can abuse those who facilitated his "entering into the atmosphere of this earth," a quotation from a Talmudic discussion of how the navel closes and the mouth opens when a fetus exits the uterus.[13] Punishment was exacted on the son's mouth by shredding his tongue and muting his voice on the mountains of Israel for blaspheming his father.

Incidentally, Immanuel's comment on Proverbs 10:18 ("He who conceals hatred has lying lips") offers an insight into his general approach to speech acts. For Immanuel, echoing Maimonides, speech distinguishes people from animals. He explains that "through speech, a human being is likened to angels, and therefore it is fitting that the human part developed by God above all other creatures should be used for pleasant and purposeful matters, while leaving indecent matters, and certainly detrimental and negative matters, to others."[14] Immanuel's sinner, then, is chastised for improperly using this potent faculty to harm his parents.

Since medieval Hebrew was a literary language, it is possible to read the biblical turns of phrase in *Maḥberet Ha-Tofet V'Ha-Eden* as either supplementary vocabulary or rhetorical flourishes. A closer evaluation of the intertextual language and biblical allusions reveals that Immanuel's biblical interpretation served as a conceptual bedrock for the *maḥberet*. While the sinner's behavior is disgusting, the full gravity of his actions is only hinted at by the biblical turns of phrase in the narrative. One must turn to the commentaries, which convey how abuse of parents is tantamount to disgrace of the Lord and that the faculty of speech separates humans from animals, to truly appreciate the depth of this character's sinfulness. Although initially it seems that the effects of this sin are "limited" to the family unit, when read in conjunction with the moral principles expressed in Immanuel's commentaries, it becomes clear that the author conceived of such sins as extending beyond the family to the wider social order. Marshaling the commentaries in service of the narrative's significance elevates it beyond that of a pure social critique and shows how the *maḥberet* is infused with philosophical and moral significance.

Tofet: *The Miser from Ancona*

Turning to a vignette with a weaker link to the commentaries but a stronger sense of similitude, we find the tale of the miserly sinner from the Adriatic coastal city Ancona, suggesting that the sinner's characterization might have been drawn from an actual figure known to Immanuel. The story revolves around an old man who, "In past times, he loved me [Immanuel], and I loved him," and who, when he was alive, focused on amassing material wealth to the neglect of spirituality or social conscience. The theme of this sinner's vignette is his squandered potential, as he was a wealthy man with so much ability to share his wealth and devote himself to spiritual and intellectual pursuits. Yet he did none of these things, for which he incurred great suffering. Although the Anconitan sinner was married, he had "neither son nor daughter, inheritor nor heir, and no relative for whom I could hope to be happy in his wellbeing." [15] The sinner, whom Immanuel calls "a diamond crown on the heads of men of your [his] generation" mentions his childless state three times in his monologue, the longest sinner's monologue in *Tofet.* He highlights the fruitlessness of his life as he asks, "How did I not serve portions from my table and gifts to orphans and widows, to the miserable souls, those oppressed, tortured, enveloped by hunger, conspicuous in every district?" [16]

Instead of the grand home that he built and furnished, the man wistfully wishes that he had devoted time to spiritual pursuits, which he describes as "construction of a house in the heavens." The Anconitan abode is meticulously described, with special attention to the windows, using terminology from the biblical account of the Tabernacle and Temple. The sinner laments, "I thought to build a Temple as high as the heavens, with recessed and latticed windows." [17] Bewailing his punishment, the sinner states:

> Instead of my bath and my oven, I see a river of fire. Instead of my lily-lipped crystal, I see fiery torches and a smoking kiln, fistfuls of futility and furnace soot. Instead of the birds prepared for me, I see a great, dark dread descending upon me. Instead of drinking sweet things and eating choice foods, with bearers of tribute before me, I stumble about at noon as if in darkness, like the dead in the daytime.[18]

Here it is evident that Immanuel marshals Temple-related language—architectural flourishes, sacrificial vessels and rites—to designate this residence as distinct and palatial. The cadence of the section, established by Immanuel's repeated use of the formula "Instead of . . . I see . . . ," indicates rhetorically savvy verse. Interestingly, however, Immanuel mentions a ritual bath within this domestic space, which was a rare amenity in a private home. This demonstrates the technique of similitude, as Immanuel likely chose architectural elements that could have been part of an actual house in Ancona.

Both the home and the sinner's wife are objectified as trophies; both, fittingly, serve important roles in the sinner's punishment. In describing his house, the sinner recalls how he sought "to fill it with treasures kept in chests, to showcase its beauty to the generals and nations," a citation from the book of Esther 1:11 that recalls King Aḥashverosh's desire to display Queen Vashti's beauty to his peers, the exploitative act that sets this book in motion.[19] Despite the sinner's attempts to master both house and woman, he is tortured by watching another man enjoy the delights he had amassed. The sinner recalls that, two years after his death, his soul was resurrected and forced to watch his wife and new husband enjoying the grand house and the ritual bath. The sinner was taken to their bedroom, where he witnessed the new couple sleeping in an affectionate embrace, his former wife "voluptuous and luxuriant," likely hinting that she was pregnant.[20] By contrasting the Anconitan physical home with the ultimate Jewish "spiritual home," the Temple, Immanuel frames the sinner's materialism as a rejection of God that consequently affects his relationships with other human beings, like the poor or his wife.

In this case, although link between Immanuel's biblical commentaries and this sinner's vignette is weaker, a leitmotif of both the commentaries and the poetry is the relationship between a sinner's deeds and his punishment in the afterlife. On Psalm 107, Immanuel states, "A person should know that all that happens to him like an evil blow and a sorrowful thing should be linked to his prior iniquities."[21] The sin of the wealthy miser from Ancona is personal, insofar as he misused his copious funds to build an opulent home and to secure a beautiful wife rather than to support Torah scholars or to care for the poor in his community. And, according to the Maimonidean definition of perfection of the body, the sinner's lack of restraint harmed communal health in his abandonment of the needy. In the view of Immanuel's commentary, neither the impoverished nor the nonexistent heirs will advocate on behalf of the sinner's memory. On Proverbs 21:13 ("Who stops his ears at the cry of the wretched, he too will call and not be answered"), Immanuel remarks:

> The man who closes his ears to avoid hearing the cries of a poor person begging for sustenance will, himself, cry like the poor person cried. He

> will plead and beg another but will not be answered because God grants money to those who care for the indigent, as it says: for one who is generous to the poor [Proverbs 28:8]. If a person will not be compassionate toward the poor, God will take his wealth and give it to another man who will sustain the poor. He, relinquished in poverty, shall call out to people for mercy, but they will not answer him. This is a divine punishment issued by the blessed God that he shall call out but not be answered, in addition to the people who know him as a cruel man will act cruelly to him and not pity him.[22]

In the miser's case, there is no obvious allusion to Immanuel's exposition of Proverbs 21:13, as there is no blatant connection between the sinner's personal sin and its wider reverberations. Yet Immanuel's comment bridges that conceptual gap, positing a direct link between an individual's cruelty and societal repercussions. It also advances stinginess as a sin against God, a nuance that can be gleaned only by juxtaposing the miser's vignette with the biblical commentaries.

Tofet: *Stalkers of the Ritual Bath*

In the next example, certain "lawless men," voyeurs who once stalked the ritual baths, leering at the Jewish women who came to immerse, are eternally consumed by flames and trampled by fiery horses. Like the miser just discussed, these characters committed a personal sin, but one with widespread reverberations, even affecting communal observance of *halakhah*. Pious women were embarrassed by the male spectators, and some of them refrained altogether from engaging in ritual purification.[23] Select women, states Immanuel, lived their entire lives without immersing in a *mikveh* because of their self-imposed modest standards. As ritual bathing is necessary to resume spousal relations after menstruation, it is an essential feature of Jewish communal religious life.[24] As in the previous case, there are no clear allusions to the philosophical commentaries, perhaps suggesting that Immanuel included this vignette as a social critique to address real issues.[25] The language of the tale, however, demonstrates Immanuel's creative application of biblical verses. Since the sinners prevented the women from immersing in water, their punishment is fiery thirst. Immanuel phrases their lechery as "catcalling at another's wife," a reference to Jeremiah 5:8, in which the prophet compares the men to lusty stallions. Thus, being trampled beneath fiery horses was a fitting punishment for this group.

Tofet: *Cascading Sin: The Adulterer and the Murderer*

Some of the tales in *Tofet* feature characters who seem to combine social critique with philosophical paradigm. In general, Immanuel reifies the family constellation as an important source of support; for him, the absence of a supportive network contributes to the breakdown of social order. Immanuel highlights this through two particular male sinners. A naked man shackled in chains is immersed in a cooking vessel brimming with lead and tin, then dunked into an icy pit. Though called an adulterer, he has committed a sin that extends far beyond forbidden sexual relations. Daniel explains:

> He sinned in that he taught his friend's wife to commit adultery with others, to desire strangers. She birthed bastard children from them, so her husband, who did not regard these boys as his sons, refused to acknowledge them. He hid himself so as not to take responsibility for them, nor did he teach them wisdom and morals. The boys, upon knowing they had no protection, trod a path of evil consumed by their wickedness. Occasionally they meant to sin while sometimes they inadvertently strayed, but at the end, they took others' lives and lost their own lives. It was as if that adulterer had killed them all with his sword, so the collective sin rests upon him.[26]

The illegitimate children, claimed by no man, lacked the education and discipline needed to keep them from a life of crime. Daniel says, "It was as if that adulterer had killed them all with his sword, so the collective sin rests upon him."[27] The theme of cascading actions is explored in Immanuel's commentary on Proverbs 14:25 ("A truthful witness saves lives; he who testifies lies [spreads] deceit"), where he explains that, in addition to the impact of a life-saving witness on a defendant, the witness indirectly saves the members of that defendant's household and the progeny that will issue from him.[28] The language used to describe this sinner acknowledges the devastating effects of adultery on a family and on society.

Immanuel's characterization of the adulterer as a sacrificial animal implicitly acknowledges traditional venues of expiation while also highlighting his gendered approach to the sin of adultery. Like the female adulteresses who were boiled in cooking vessels, this adulterer is scalded in a pan, but, as opposed to the former, the language and images in this vignette are drawn from biblical descriptions of Temple sacrifice. The tools used to punish the adulterer are the same ones used in the priestly preparations of sacrifices. The griddle (*maḥavat*) in which the sinner is scalded was used for flour offerings while his shackles (*ḥaḥim*) refer to those shackles chained to animals' cheeks or noses that were used to pull them toward the sacrificial altars. The angels take the sinner from the "strange fire" to immerse him in the ice, a reference to the sinful sacrifice offered by Aaron's priestly sons Nadab and Avihu (Leviticus 10:1). Daniel describes how the sinner "strayed unfaithfully from God,"[29] referencing a type of sinner in Leviticus who must bring a specific type of sacrifice, a guilt offering.[30] He compares the adulterer to one who "scorned the Lord's word and violated his commandment,"[31] whose sins led to the issue of children who "meant to sin" (*zadu*) or "inadvertently strayed" (*shagagu*) because they lacked education and proper behavioral modeling.[32] Daniel's discussion of the "weight" of sins, invoking traditional legalistic jargon, together with a description of the sinner as an expiatory sacrifice, express the rabbinic maxim "one sin begets another."[33] There is a measure of irony in the sinner's characterization as a sacrificial animal, insofar as this sinner shunned the rabbinic premise and has now become an embodied sacrifice, the very vehicle of communal expiation.[34] The principle "one sin begets another" lies at the heart of another set of characterizations that are drawn from the Davidic tales.

Allusions to adulterous exemplars from the Bible underlie Immanuel's description of this sinner, as he is called a "wretched man," the epithet for Abigail's husband Nabal in I Samuel. The medieval commentary tradition censures King David for his affair with Bathsheba and previous encounter with Abigail. Both women are sources of scandal for King David, and the talmudic sages suggest that his propositioning Abigail led to her vision that David would become embroiled in the affair with Bathsheba because "one sin begets another."[35] The language and imagery in the adulterer's vignette reifies the concept of sin begetting sin by exploring the social ramifications of his adulterous union on civic society, since the adulterous union created fatherless children who, lacking guidance, caused mayhem and discord. Unlike the circle of adulteresses, this sinner is not held accountable for sexual indiscretion. By gendering the sin of adultery, Immanuel reveals a nuanced understanding of guilt that distinguishes the male adulterer from the female one, revealing conventions about the roles of men and women in both the family unit and society. Such conventions are more fully explicated in Immanuel's biblical commentaries.

The nexus between adultery and civic disorder is explored extensively in Immanuel's commentaries on Genesis and Exodus. Explaining the order of the Ten Commandments in Exodus, Immanuel notes:

> The prohibition of adultery follows the prohibition of murder because, like murder, adultery is similar to the destruction of the lower world, for an abundance of illegitimate children will increase the number of bad people in the world. And they will harm and steal and kill. Many of those will die in deficit for they had no known fathers to support them and to rebuke them, thus they steal and rob and kill. Adultery also incites homicides because men fight jealously over a woman.[36]

Without fathers to discipline and morally train them, says Immanuel, illegitimate children grow up with no understanding of how to function as upstanding members of society. Immanuel's gloss of this biblical prohibition examines both sides of the parent-child relationship, as adultery impairs both the child's ability to honor a parent and the parent's responsibility to educate a child. This insight is mapped onto the adulterous sinner's vignette in *Tofet.* The theoretical link posed by Immanuel to explain the juxtaposition of the prohibitions against murder and adultery in Exodus is manifested in this adulterer character in *Tofet* who suffers the sins of his uneducated and unsupervised illegitimate children.

In Immanuel's commentary on the Judah and Tamar affair in Genesis, he explores the sociological history of marriage through a long digression about prostitution. Immanuel borrows citations from two sources—Maimonides and Thomas Aquinas—to construct a sociological argument for the necessity of marriage. Excerpting Maimonides' *Guide* III:49, Immanuel offers a sketch of prostitution in antiquity, claiming that, as common property, prostitutes ignited violent outbreaks, which were curbed only by the institution of marriage.

Maimonides' historical justification for marriage is supplemented by a defense of marriage lifted directly from Aquinas's *Summa Contra Gentiles.*[37] In it, Aquinas argues for the legitimacy of marriage by drawing parallels to the animal kingdom, where, in some species, females are responsible for raising offspring, and the male and female don't stay together, "but in the case of animals of which the female is not able to provide for the upbringing of offspring, the male and female do stay together after the act of generation as long as is necessary for the upbringing and instruction of the offspring."[38] According to Immanuel, since humans require both physical and spiritual nourishment to thrive, "it is an appropriate thing according to human nature for a man to remain with a woman after pregnancy and delivery, and not to hide from her as adulterers do."[39] In Immanuel's view, human mothers provide infants with nourishment and bodily comfort, but human fathers serve a greater purpose—the soul's activity—which includes education and moral guidance over a long period of time, necessitating a family unit. Therefore, Immanuel, following Aquinas, states, "Sons should be taught by their fathers and guided toward goodness and truth. The female cannot provide this guidance. The actions of a man are more appropriate for this since he is a master of science and intellect more than the woman."[40] According to Immanuel, the job of raising a responsible child requires two capable partners with different roles, and a married union between a man and woman encapsulates this natural relationship. Sex outside of this union, whether with a prostitute or another woman, is considered unnatural and harmful to an individual and to society. The medieval reflections on the origin and utility of marriage, which today would be called sociological theory, are nestled into Immanuel's reading of the biblical tale of Judah and Tamar and used to shape the character of the male adulterer in *Tofet.*

Adultery and violence were documented social ills in medieval Italy, but the correlation between this sinner and the theoretical ideas in Immanuel's commentaries suggests a creative characterization that may have been loosely based on social reality. Realized through the heart-wrenching details of the character's tale, Immanuel's discursive admonitions are anecdotally compelling in a manner that the commentaries are not. The philosophical and moral meditations scattered throughout Immanuel's biblical commentaries have been transformed into characters in his tale.

The sinner Immanuel's literary persona sees immediately after the adulterer, a murderer whose act caused a cascade of crime, offers a similar message. His scorched body was stripped by ministering angels who hanged him on a tree, where poisonous snakes would consume him. Daniel explains that this sinner did not realize how the death of one would cause the deaths of many. Although this sinner killed only one man, his murder led the victim's wife and children to a life of crime to survive. When caught, some of the family members were banished and others were executed. Thus the father's death triggered the eventual deaths of many family members. Like the adulterer, the murderer did not realize that "sin begets sin" and that his one deed would multiply into the deaths of so many. While adultery and murder are classic sins against other humans, their familial and societal repercussions are rarely explored in medieval writings. Using theoretical ideas from his commentaries as well as examples from his society, Immanuel has crafted characters whose individual sins erode the communal fabric and hinder the Maimonidean "perfection of the body."

Eden: *The Grieving Father*

Turning to *Eden*, where many of Immanuel's characters are rewarded for sustaining and advancing communal welfare, the same mix of philosophical concepts and social contextualization obtains. While touring heaven, Immanuel's character and Daniel encounter a man dressed in sackcloth, with dirt on his head, who appears to be in a state of mourning. The man is known to Immanuel's literary persona, who registers disbelief that such a great person could appear so dispirited and promptly inquires into the character's circumstances. The man depicts his former life as one of spiritual and intellectual devotion that slowly eroded because he chose to "abandon the enterprise of study, in which I was engaged, because it is utter futility! Buy yourself wealth and property that exceeds the value the treasuries of Egypt and Nubia!"[41] The man's sudden death ended his pursuit of materialism. Mourning his poor choices, the man abashedly relates the consequences of his sudden death on his family. Like the adulterer and murderer, whose actions cascaded to yield disorderly children wreaking havoc on society, this man's prioritization of wealth over Torah study also resulted in a broken family, especially after his distraught wife died by suicide. As the man notes, "My widow, who panicked when utter destruction occurred and her protection disappeared, ended her life with her own hands, casting her soul aside and abandoning her children as though they were not hers."[42] However, the generosity of Immanuel and others prevents the most devastating effects.

In an emotional exchange between the two characters, the mournful character pleads, "I pray that my son, such-and-such, should merit to learn and teach, to observe and to fulfill. Never should he wander from his worship, and may he keep his covenant and religion. Knowing that I loved him fiercely, and disciplined and educated him according to his capacities, I beg of you to encourage him in ethics and wisdom."[43] He begs Immanuel "to encourage him in ethics and wisdom. For I know that you can do anything, and that nothing you propose is impossible for you."[44] Tearfully, Immanuel's character assures this man that his son is a devoted Jew who has been educated by pious teachers, and he beseeches the man to exchange his sackcloth for royal garments, threatening to withhold the son's education if the man remains in mourning. This exchange highlights the importance of communal responsibility by providing an example of a successful communal intervention into the life of an orphaned youth. It also reinforces the idea that both moral and intellectual training are requisites for sanctity and beatitude as well as ancillary components of social order. Immanuel, self-positioned as the font of wisdom, emerges as the only one who can provide that training to the man's son.

Immanuel's devotion to education is as evident in his harsh critiques of corrupt teachers in *Tofet* as it is in his philosophical commentaries, where the educational process is accorded philosophical import. His allegorical reading of Proverbs 11:24 ("One man gives generously and ends with more; another stints on doing the right thing and incurs a loss") celebrates the "generous, giving, granting soul that wants the best for itself and its peers."[45] The commentary on this verse promises that "the one who guides his peers to divine worship by bestowing his knowledge upon those prepared to receive it will be blessed with increasing wisdom."[46] Immanuel's reading of this verse transforms it from a general maxim about generosity to an explication of the intellectual process in which the agent intellect grants knowledge to the human being's rational intellect. Framing his reading according to rationalistic ideas about the acquisition of knowledge, Immanuel finds philosophical significance even where it is absent from the literal reading of the verse. The master, in Immanuel's reading, resembles the Tree of Life, which medieval Jewish rationalists identified as a symbol of immortality. In the same comment, Immanuel casts the master-student relationship as an earthly exemplar of the transcendent relationship between agent intellect and human-rational intellect. This comparison is evident in the language and imagery of this vignette in *Eden*, where Immanuel uses philosophical terminology traditionally applied to discussions of conjunction with the agent intellect.

Attempting to compel the father to don festive clothing, Immanuel threatens, "By my life, I swear that if you do not place the pure crown on your head nor bedeck your robes with jewels of gold, I will never connect with your son so-and-so. My mouth will never converse with his."[47] Immanuel's term "connect" (ח.ב.ר) is the same one used in Hebrew philosophical treatises to denote conjunction (*ḥibbur*), reinforcing the image of teacher as agent intellect. Ultimately, the character dons festive garb and accompanies the traveling pair of characters to other areas in heaven, but he disappears from the narrative. Besides this character's reinforcement of the idea that education, and even religious observance, is vital to social order, it is unclear why this character is among the righteous. In addition to these two aspects, Immanuel reveals his desire for a well-ordered society through portraits of idealized and still-living characters at the end of the tour.

Eden: *The Canopy Crowd*

Toward the end of *Eden*, Immanuel's literary persona comes upon ten canopies (*ḥuppot*), richly covered in gold and sumptuous textiles, containing ten empty golden thrones. Daniel explains that the thrones are reserved for the ten martyrs of the Hadrianic persecution, who accompanied the archangel Michael and a Rabbi Samuel to plead Israel's case before God. The archangel Michael, depicted here as an advocate for the Jews in *Maḥberet Ha-Tofet V'Ha-Eden*, is elsewhere portrayed by Immanuel as a heavenly priest who sacrifices the souls of the righteous in heaven. Since celestial *ḥuppot* appear both in midrashic accounts of heaven and in Immanuel's comment on Psalms 68:21, a verse that asserts God's deliverance of his nation even from death, their appearance in Immanuel's *Eden* is not surprising.[48] But, adding philosophical nuance to the classical image of celestial canopies, Immanuel notes that God assigns different types of salvation to his creations based on the differences in their intellective capacities. He explains, "Each and every righteous person has a canopy to suit his glory, that is to say, a unique spiritual salvation."[49]

The canopies at the end of *Maḥberet Ha-Tofet V'Ha-Eden* feature five characters whom Immanuel considers virtuous even if they bear little intellectual significance. This book argues for the general disentanglement of *Maḥberet Ha-Tofet V'Ha-Eden* from historicist readings; this cluster of righteous figures in *Eden* offers an instructive counterexample. The individuals who earn his highest accolades for valuing the acquisition of wisdom are all generous patrons who are portrayed as sustaining medieval Jewish communities in the Italian peninsula. As much as Immanuel expresses Maimonidean ideals of communal health and wellbeing through his characters, he also captures the pragmatic challenges of a delicate patronage system that needs finances and agents to run smoothly.

The first canopy, reserved for "the Perugian," rewards a charitable and upstanding individual involved in communal affairs. Immanuel praises the Perugian's magnanimity, his open home, and his religious devotion in the face of personal challenge. Immanuel says, "Although he experienced some unfortunate events, too lengthy to recount here, he always says 'blessed be the name of the Lord.' He never raged about the circumstances of fate, and he suffered for the love of the trustworthy God."[50] Against the background of *Tofet*'s sinners, eternally damned for misinterpreting divine punishment as determinism, the praise of this individual reveals Immanuel's sense of symmetry between *Tofet* and *Eden*. The Perugian is "generous to the poor and nourishes them from his bounty. When faced with throngs of impoverished and destitute people, overwhelming as a squall, he reduced their neediness to a sprinkle. He relieves them with the rich fare of his house, and quenches their thirst with his refreshing streams."[51] His vigorous involvement in communal affairs, together with his willingness to lend his home to elders and Torah scholars, stand in stark contrast to the Anconitan miser in *Tofet* whose palatial home remained silent and empty. Displaying virtue in his individual life and involvement in communal burdens, the Perugian serves as an idealized portrait of a benefactor for most of Immanuel's audience.

The second canopy is reserved for "the army commander," who defended the Lord's nation and is "second only to the Hasmonean" in bravery.[52] Like that of his predecessor, the officer's personal valor is balanced by his genuine concern for the public. Together with his wife, who "is both mother and nurse to every passerby,"[53] this man provided shelter and sustenance to the needy. Immanuel describes his home as "generously open, there is no breach in his house, no sortie, and no wailing. Liberation is there for those spent ones, and tired ones repose and find a resting place."[54] Knowing that Immanuel was a poet, and recalling his praise of his patron in his commentary on Job, one can see the possibility that Immanuel sought to memorialize generous individuals who had supported him. Immanuel's frequent discussion of patronage and the burden of securing support resonates in his praise of open homes and limitless beneficence. Positing another communal model, Immanuel praises the involvement and virtue of this hospitable couple.

Immanuel emphasizes the third character's advocacy on behalf of Israel in addition to his piety, as "he [the Rabbi] removed idolatry from the earth, as well as anything contaminated by an unclean animal,"[55] suggesting that Jewish ritual observance is a necessary component of a healthy social ecosystem. The fourth and fifth canopies are reserved for individuals identified by the term "intellectual" (*maskil*), Immanuel's friends, who combined a life of letters with communal devotion. For Immanuel, the combination of public service and personal study ranks highest on his list of virtuous characters. In his emphasis on specific characters' attributes, Immanuel reveals that the individual who has perfected his religious and social life is certainly praiseworthy, but the human telos remains an intellectual acquisition of knowledge and truth.

Immanuel's description of the fourth character is laden with idiomatic phrases charged with philosophical significance from the Maimonidean register, overlapping with those Immanuel deploys earlier in the *Eden* section to describe Judah Romano. The canopy is reserved for the intellectual, "who climbs the ladder's rungs, stretching out his hand to take fruit from the Tree of Life, and eating it to live forever."[56] In Immanuel's commentaries, the temporal life is represented by the Tree of Knowledge of good and evil, while immortality is represented by the Tree of Life. Immanuel explains, "The one whose intellect triumphed to cast his hand, pluck fruit, and eat from the tree of life, shall live the eternal life forever."[57] For Immanuel, the Tree of Life symbolizes conjunction with the agent intellect and immortality, and an individual's challenge is to identify, pick, and eat from the correct tree. According to Immanuel, "the righteous man [*tzadik*] makes fruit for himself through the work of the blessed Lord and through acquiring wisdom [*ḥokhmah*], the Tree of Life, that is to say conjunction with the blessed Lord [*devekut*], who is the bundle of life. He likened this matter to the Tree of Life so that those who eat from it will live forever."[58] Immanuel's use of two symbols typically associated with the acquisition of knowledge signals his respect for this individual's intellectual quest.

Beyond his personal investment in knowledge and truth, this man's involvement in communal affairs is noted as a factor in his ultimate reward. The character transformed his home into a "Tent of Meeting for Torah instruction and moral instruction."[59] His greatness merited eternal life among the righteous of the world, shining like the stars of the heavens, referring to the verse about the afterlife in Daniel 12:3. Daniel, the guide, also reveals this character's regard for Immanuel's biblical commentaries: "He copied a bit from your commentaries, because of his love for them, and he sealed them on his heart. He will not be calm nor rest until he copies the remainder of them to ponder them and to understand their legacy. They are exemplars for him to see and imitate."[60]

Immanuel designates the fifth canopy for a master of poetry and politics also called "the intellectual" (*ha-maskil*), "whose own poetic display wiped out the memory of contemporary poets."[61] The poet was as adept in Hebrew verse as he was in Arabic and the "Christian tongue," probably Italian or Provençal. This character is praised for his deft use of weapons, as Immanuel notes that "with his sword, he accomplishes terrorizing feats and wonders of wonder with his spear."[62] Unlike his peers in these canopies, whose learning and generosity earned them their noble spots, this person represented Jews in Provence before the chief of Magdiel. The writing and poetry of this character, who served as a diplomat, impressed non-Jews, and he engaged in battles with "prophets of Ba'al and priests," a presumable reference to polemical exchanges with Christian clergy.[63] Perhaps, as relayed by historical treatments of this poem, this figure was a "Jewish troubadour or jongleur" who represented the Jews of Rome before the pope in hopes of reversing the decreed expulsion of Roman Jews in the 1320s.[64] Regardless, the characterization valorizes a diplomat-poet whose writings are appreciated by non-Jewish audiences, perhaps a furtive fantasy for our author.

From these canopies, Immanuel proceeds to another set intended for two individuals from Orvieto, "the pious ones, the pride of this world," who sheltered, clothed, and fed the poor and the exiled.[65] The exceeding kindness of these two Orvietans, who dowered orphans, cared for widows, and ransomed captive prisoners, earned them entrance into the "sanctuary of my Lord."[66] It is notable that in Immanuel's *Eden*, these characters alone are rewarded for acts of service rather than intellectual accomplishment. While some of the "canopy crowd" exemplify devotion to study, their charitable and diplomatic acts in service of communal well-being are what determines their celestial placement.

Hypocrisy: Public vs. Private Personae

Another major theme emerging from those vignettes in *Maḥberet Ha-Tofet V'Ha-Eden* that relates to communal health, or what Maimonides calls perfection of the body, is the chasm between public and private spaces. The *maḥberet*'s otherworldly setting enables Immanuel's literary persona to access the raw truths in the hearts and minds of his characters, which he contrasts with their public façades. Whereas, in medieval Christian circles, the disparity between public and private personae was acknowledged in the rite of private confession, mandated annually for all Christians by the thirteenth century, Judaism lacks a formal outlet for the reconciliation of thoughts and deeds. Instead, *Maḥberet Ha-Tofet V'Ha-Eden* serves as a type of textual confession box where Immanuel's encounters, as mediated by the celestial guide, offer us a "bird's eye view" of his social circle; he is frequently surprised at seeing characters who were seemingly blameless during their lifetimes.

Immanuel addresses hypocrisy in his commentary on Proverbs 19:22 ("Greed is a reproach to a man; Better be poor than a liar"), in which he states that people seek public recognition for their deeds, often by self-promotion. He qualifies, "They boast about the kindness they have done and that which they have not done, for people desire that other people speak about their kindness."[67] In the commentary on Proverbs, Immanuel designates such hypocrisy by the term “a spring whose waters fail,” a sarcastic emendation of Isaiah 58:11, which compares humans guided by God to a spring whose waters do not fail. Several vignettes in both *Tofet* and *Eden* explore the dissonance between the public and private realms, and they all share two consistent elements: First, the mechanism of sin or virtue is internal, and, second, nearly every tale repeats Immanuel's expressions of surprise.

Tofet: *The Mental Sinners*

Our first examples are people about whom Immanuel observes: “While they were alive, I considered them righteous people.” But Daniel notes that these people had iniquitous thoughts.[68] He explains, “They appeared asleep, but their hearts were awake, storming and burning in the fires of jealousy and lust. When the chance arose to act malevolently in secret, they did it.”[69] This revelation shatters the naiveté of Immanuel's literary character, who asserts that as far as he knew “these people never sinned, nor did they divide others' money.” Daniel, however, stands in for the divine gaze, offering a contextual portrait of human actions and thoughts. He reveals that their apparent “innocence” was occasioned by a lack of opportunity, but that sin was ever present in their minds.[70] These sinners directly challenged God's omniscience, believing that they could conceal sinful thoughts and behaviors from him. As Immanuel repeatedly affirms, hiding from God is impossible.

Tofet: *The Doubting Martyrs*

Another group that provokes surprise in Immanuel's character consists of “holy ones” (martyrs) who “gave up their lives and sanctified the Lord.”[71] Immanuel is puzzled by their appearance in *Tofet*, but, Daniel reveals, these martyrs did not accept their martyrdom wholeheartedly, expressing doubt at the final second of death. He compares them with paradigmatic Hadrianic martyrs,[72] stating: “They were supposed to receive their cruel death with love, viewing it with sweetness and delight. They should have said, ‘How fortunate we are! How great is our portion! How pleasant is our fate to have been tested!’”[73] Instead of a joyful acceptance of death, they “became upset because of their miserable souls.”[74] The martyrs' “upset” about their miserable souls suggests that their death was characterized by rage against God, a vice that Immanuel identifies as heresy.[75] Overtaken by rage, the martyrs' thoughts transformed into heresy. This vignette is startling, as martyrdom is rarely, if ever, criticized in Jewish or Christian writings. While it is possible that this tale criticizes the violent behaviors of Ashkenazic Jews during the First Crusade, it primarily exemplifies that a clash between appearances and reality can exist in anyone, reinforcing the idea expressed in Immanuel's *maḥberet*.[76]

Tofet: *Hypocritical Cantors*

In our next example, Immanuel continues to explore the dissonance between the public and private personae in the vignette of the hypocritical cantors, who, hanging by their tongues, are pierced by archers' arrows. Guilty of excessive pride and irreverence, "these people were not like their fathers, who were hallmarks on the tablet of time's heart."[77] Characterized by fraudulence, the hypocrites disregard God during the week and vainly participate in public synagogue rituals to entice women and attract flattery on sabbaths and festivals. The tone of this vignette is playful, as Immanuel describes the sinners' squabbles over prominent synagogue positions, especially during the holidays. Immanuel's use of an omniscient narrative mode, alternating between the sinners' discussions of the Jewish liturgical calendar and Immanuel's revelations of their true intentions, allows him to reveal the sinners' most private thoughts and actions, creating the illusion that the reader occupies the sinners' minds: "They said, 'Who is like us? Who can summon us? Who is the shepherd that stands before us?' . . . On the day of atonement [Yom Kippur], they rose in the early morning, but fasted in strife and contention. They said no man knows the prayer *'Shoshan Emek Ayumah'* ("Rose of the valley, standing in awe") like them."[78] Immanuel underscores that appearances can be deceiving, and that social status and prestigious parents do not guarantee piety. This theme is also explored in Immanuel's explication of Proverbs 28:9 ("He who turns a deaf ear to instruction, his prayer is an abomination"), where he explains that one who rebukes his teachers and parents cannot pray meaningfully because he does not know God. Immanuel calls his prayers "an abomination" since "his heart does not intend what emerges from his mouth, and when he prays, he mostly thinks about his desires and unsavory actions."[79] These insolent sinners are manifestations of moral insights from Immanuel's commentaries. The contrast between the cantors and their fathers in the *maḥberet* is bolstered by Immanuel's explication of Proverbs 28:9, which links rejection of one's parents to rebellious actions.

Exposing the hypocritical cantors' true motivations, namely female admiration and communal stature, Immanuel declares, "Because pride adorned their necks, this evil infected them,"[80] a phrase from Psalms 73:6 ("So pride adorns their necks; lawlessness enwraps them as a mantle") in which the psalmist laments his jealousy of the wanton ones who live with ease. Immanuel's interpretation of this psalm layers philosophical significance onto the literal reading of the wicked men who arouse the psalmist's jealousy. Where the psalm targets proud men who luxuriate in extravagances, Immanuel's reading portrays the men's pride as stemming from their doubts about God and the celestial existents. Fostering an association between the necklace of pride with "their tongues that wander about the Earth, speaking with pride about the existent things in the heaven," Immanuel's reuse in the Psalms commentary of the same necklace of pride image in *Tofet* is layered with philosophical implications.[81] In this case, recourse to the commentaries reveals that these sinners' actions were far graver than "simple" pride.

Tofet: *Hypocritical Communal Leaders*

For Immanuel, hypocrisy is particularly offensive in communal leaders who command prestige in public. The punishment for a group of elders who prayed devotedly in public but never uttered a word of prayer in private is being eaten by lions and bears. Immanuel's comment on Proverbs 28:15 ("A roaring lion and a prowling bear is a wicked man ruling a helpless people") compares the ideal religious leader to a kind shepherd who tends to the sick and bandages the wounded among the flock.[82] But, Immanuel reveals:

> These accursed ones, when they prayed in public, their prayers were as solemn as the Yom Kippur service, with 120 bows and genuflections. They make a display of fervent concentration over every word, subservience and trembling from the beginning to the end, and utmost genuflection, so that each disc in the spinal cord could be seen. But when alone, in their own palaces and courtyards, nary a word of prayer exited their mouths. Mentally meandering the streets of their sinful thoughts, they gave their hearts over to sin.[83]

The corruption and hypocrisy of leaders, suggests Immanuel, threatens the spiritual health of a community. Elsewhere in *Tofet*, too, Immanuel explores the nexus of hypocrisy, political corruption, and synagogue leadership.

Tofet: *Corrupt Communal Elders*

Yet another group of public figures are "leaders of their ancestral houses" who were "chief speakers in all places, discerning and prominent; these were famous men!"[84] These men of stature, Immanuel reveals, deceived the community by choosing unfit men as prayer leaders. The intellectual and moral fitness of a person chosen to lead public prayer services is discussed in the Mishnah as well as by medieval halakhists like Maimonides.[85] Ideal prayer leaders, or public representatives, are imagined as pious and modest, known for their good deeds and erudition in Jewish texts.[86] Immanuel describes the ideal representative as one "with abundant stores of knowledge, supplying produce of all kinds, whose lips and heart should be one, collecting his ideas for God, not the lustful type who was raised on love tales."[87] His comments about the blundering prayer leaders chosen by vindictive elders are expressed in a comic key, calling their candidates "Jeroboam's calf who stands before the Ark as if disturbed."[88] Sinful prayer leaders who pray loudly to impress women bear the brunt of Immanuel's wrath elsewhere, in the final pits of *Tofet*, where they undergo the four rabbinic punishments, but Immanuel's critical gaze here rests on communal leaders who appear to be respectable but are actually not.[89]

Immanuel's critiques of spiritual and political leaders in *Tofet* also embody more general positions on leadership expressed in his biblical commentaries. Immanuel's recognition of the importance of good governance is articulated in his comment on Proverbs 16:8 ("better a little with righteousness than a large income with injustice"), which notes that "a smaller monetary portion in a well-governed and just city or state is preferable to a bountiful lot in a lawless state where justice is not exacted on criminals."[90] Immanuel's appreciation for stable and just governance reflects the Maimonidean insight that, even though the wellbeing of society is less exalted than its intellectual perfection, practical communal order must be achieved before intellectual knowledge can be obtained.[91] In his Proverbs commentary, Immanuel emphasizes that leaders should guide the masses toward ethical perfection and eventual divine reward, and he attributes a bad political situation to a society's sinful state.[92] In these examples Immanuel casts his sharpest critiques of spiritual and political leadership, intimating that the powerful bear an especially heavy burden as individuals responsible for communal health that prompts spiritual or intellectual perfection.

Tofet: *Ḥiel the Bethelite*

About halfway through *Tofet*, Immanuel's literary persona and Daniel reach an area containing a unique sinner. The only named sinner in *Tofet*, Ḥiel the Bethelite suffers a multilayered punishment in a distinct region called *Taḥtiot ha-Tofet* ("hell's underside"). Following his torture by burning coals, arrows, and preying animals, Ḥiel is ground seven times daily in a mortar with a pestle. Structurally, this sinner's discernable alterity suggests that he is especially evil, but this is also confirmed by Immanuel, who exclaims, "Truly, he was deserving of that place, and that place was deserving of him and those evil ones of his age. It is no wonder if his soul mourns itself and his flesh is pained over itself."[93] Ḥiel is *Tofet*'s only sinner whose punishment is approved by Immanuel's literary persona.

Ḥiel was guilty of fraud and deception, sins that affected every aspect of his intellectual, personal, and business pursuits. A cunning liar, Ḥiel slandered several righteous individuals and squandered others' funds. Others were aware of his depravity, guarding their funds and distrusting Ḥiel. Immanuel claims that Ḥiel annulled contracts and engaged in illegal business practices, so his family "never placed him in charge of their accounts, lest he steal their meager rations."[94] Yet, to cover these crimes, Ḥiel assumed a pious posture, studying Torah. In omniscient narrator mode, Immanuel reveals Ḥiel's deepest thoughts: "I made myself crowns of falsity and deception because the goal is to nullify contracts forever."[95] A look at Immanuel's commentaries shows how Immanuel concretized theoretical ideas within Ḥiel's character.

Ḥiel suffers various forms of torture but is ground in a mortar as a second layer of punishment. In Immanuel's commentary on Proverbs, he identifies the simpleton (*'evil*) as one whose actions cannot be refined, regardless of attempts to educate, threaten, or even pound him with a pestle. Other sinners in *Tofet* had moral potential that could have been channeled to righteous ends; but Immanuel implies that Ḥiel's temperament made that impossible. On Proverbs 27:22 ("Even if you pound the fool in a mortar with a pestle along with grain, his folly will not leave him"), Immanuel states:

> If you pound a man who is a simpleton [*'evil*] in the mortar amongst the wheat that is pounded by the pestle means that you intensify his suffering to admonish him, but his foolishness will not depart from him. This verse does not come to say that one should despair of rebuke, for reproach and rebuke will not succeed. Rather, he said this because sometimes one finds a man exhausted by his stupidity and if you continue to torture him and admonish him, his foolishness will not depart from him.[96]

In *Tofet*, the sinner is called "a foolish shepherd" (*ro'eh 'evili*), utterly wicked.[97] As we saw in the exposition of Proverbs, stupidity is impossible to expel, even with extreme torture, and Immanuel uses both the image and the terminology in his characterization of the sinner.

Why, for example, would Immanuel use a named biblical character, and who is Ḥiel? The biblical Ḥiel the Bethelite violated Joshua's prohibition against the rebuilding of the fallen Jericho, and he lost his children because of Joshua's curse.[98] It is possible that Immanuel refers to an actual person, even a contemporaneous nemesis, but attaches the moniker of a biblical character to conceal his attack. The patronym "Beit-El" translates into the Italian "Casadio," a name found among several late-medieval scribes in Italy.[99] There are at least four different Jewish scribes named "Yeḥiel" in the various branches of the medieval Beit-El family.[100] Whether Ḥiel's vignette is a scathing critique of a real person is currently unknowable, but Immanuel likened him to numerous archetypical sinners in the biblical and rabbinic traditions. Immanuel notes that Ḥiel is "an arrogant man like Balaam, a stain on humanity and the scorn of the nation. He sinned and caused sin like Jeroboam. He is as fitting a replacement for David as Doeg the Edomite."[101] This passage alludes to Mishnah Sanhedrin 10:2, which excludes three biblical kings (Jeroboam, Ahab, Manasseh) and four commoners (Balaam, Doeg, Ahitophel, Gehazi) from a share (*ḥeleq*) in the world to come. Like these seven figures, Immanuel claims that Ḥiel "has no part in loyalty," a clear reference to the words of the Mishnah.[102] Immanuel's recourse to his own biblical commentaries and to rabbinic eschatological statements, for vocabulary as well as imagery, demonstrates a fluid intertextual dynamic between these corpora. Both corrupt communal leaders and fraudulent individuals who appear righteous, in Immanuel's view, can jeopardize a community's health. This is reinforced in *Tofet*'s final realm, where pits contain several types of sinners, including hypocrites.

While many of the final pits in *Tofet* reiterate scenarios mentioned earlier in the text, they offer more generalized portraits of sins or more specific examples of sinful behavior. The pits of the hypocrites criticize public displays of piety motivated by internal desires for material things. They contain sinners who appeared upright and humble only to win others' trust and money, as well as preachers and cantors motivated solely by the ladies. There are sinners who donned religious artifacts, like phylacteries and ritual fringes, only to ensnare people, while others gave charity only in public. One atypical example is the pit of sinners who appeared "well intentioned, with their eyes cast heavenward," but these men built ritual baths in their homes in order to bed wayward women.[103] Other pits include false witnesses, liars, and false prophets who claimed to have heard the voice of God. Corrupt judges and law officials who did not judge a matter truthfully are punished in these pits alongside fraudulent physicians who cited Hippocrates and Galen though they had no medical wisdom. Two other pits, containing sinners who refused to aid distressed members of their community because they believed God should help them, and individuals who watched others sinning but didn't correct them, are present in this region too. Akin to Dante's Neutrals, who refused to take either side of a debate, these sinners relinquished their communal responsibility to help their brethren.[104] Possessing less connection with the biblical commentaries, these brief sketches offer more examples of sinful behaviors. Resounding throughout the vignettes that address hypocrisy is the assertion that human knowledge of another's interior realm is limited if not impossible.

Eden: *Repentant Sinners*

The luminescent souls that occupy heaven's highest heights (*Ma'alot Ha-Eden Ha-Gevohim*) provoke further confusion in Immanuel's literary persona, as he knew them as evil men who died untimely deaths, presumably as punishment for their wickedness. Daniel confirms that, indeed, these sinners' premature and disgraceful deaths were punishment for despicable acts committed during their lives. But, Daniel reveals, it was their state of mind at the time of death that led them to their coveted eternal abode. Daniel explains, "When they reached the bitter end, contemplating their evil deeds, they accepted their bitter demise with love, knowing that it came upon them as judgment and obligation. To them, death became more pleasant than life, as they envisioned a worse evil for themselves."[105] Seemingly, just preceding or upon death, these sinners repented in fear of hell's torments, embracing their deaths as one would accept a tiara. Like the surprising characters in *Tofet*, this vignette also teaches Immanuel's character that both positive and negative appearances can deceive, reinforcing the traditional idea that only God knows the truth about humans. Related biblical passages in Immanuel's commentaries further enrich our knowledge about this group.

Daniel's elucidation of the group's actions is phrased using words from Ecclesiastes 7:17 ("Don't overdo wickedness and don't be a fool, or you may die before your time"), a verse that correlates excessive wickedness and foolishness with premature death. Immanuel's commentary explains this verse as part of a textual unit (Ecclesiastes 7:15–7:18), which tackles the complicated problem of the pious dying early while the impious live long lives by questioning traditional conceptions of piety and impiety. He offers examples of behaviors typically considered righteous, like temperance, which, when exaggerated into full-blown asceticism, is criticized. Altogether in this comment, Immanuel reassesses the terms "pious" and "wicked" equivocally, reading this textual unit as a clarion call for moderation.[106]

Returning to Daniel's praise of the saints, Immanuel notes that, when they were sinners, they did not "rage at their souls," a verse from Isaiah 8:21 ("he shall rage and revolt against his king and his divine beings") that appears in Immanuel's exposition of Psalm 112:10 ("The wicked man shall see it and be vexed; he shall gnash his teeth; his courage shall fail"). The psalmist describes the wicked man's anger in seeing the honor given to the generous man. Immanuel reads the psalm allegorically as a reference to the afterlife, so he interprets this verse as the attitude of the wicked souls when they witness the rewards of the righteous. He explains: "The verse alludes to the evil soul who beholds the bliss experienced by the souls of the righteous after death. They [the evil ones] rage at their souls when they see those eating while they starve, those drinking while they thirst, those jubilant while they are humiliated, those melodiously rejoicing while they painfully cry out in anguish."[107] Yet, as noted in this vignette, the souls of the wicked that ascended to heaven did not rage; they accepted punishment for their misdeeds gracefully and penitently, meriting an eternity in heaven with the blessed souls. The tale of the repentant sinners is instructive, as it optimistically conveys the power of penitence even for the wicked. Both the language and the characterization of these figures echo the concepts expressed in Immanuel's commentaries. Here the commentary enables a deeper appreciation of the sinner's repentance when juxtaposed with the other sinners who could not acknowledge the depths of their depravity.

* * *

As the vignettes analyzed in this chapter demonstrate, Immanuel's philosophically oriented biblical commentaries served as an important source of ideas, imagery, and language for his poetry. While the physical realms of *Tofet* and *Eden* stand in contrast to Immanuel's conception of an immaterial life after death, he likely marshaled such verisimilar narrative elements not to elucidate his theory of immortality of the soul, but rather to criticize behaviors that could jeopardize the health and wellbeing of the community. Disturbing the social order and hypocrisy emerge as two important themes in both *Tofet* and *Eden*, indicating that Immanuel considered these significant issues. The characters encountered by Immanuel's literary persona reveal a concept of community as a fragile environment, impacted as much by private individual acts as by public, collective ones. He bridges the gap between the realm of private intentionality and public performativity. Only in *Tofet* does Immanuel forge a connection between the sinful action and the characters' punishments, while the rewards of *Eden* remain general and disconnected from righteous action.

Reverberating throughout the tales of all these sinners and saints, however, is the sentiment that human knowledge of others is limited and insufficient. This is expressed in Immanuel's cast of characters, which includes communal and religious leaders, as well as in his character's repeated exclamations of surprise as he wends his way through the two realms of the netherworld. It is this sentiment, perhaps, that subtly but clearly reinforces the plea of Immanuel's biblical commentaries for an individual to be "one who is God-fearing, observant of the commandments of his [God's] Torah . . . [and who] will progress toward the right path and truth with all his virtues and deeds."[108] The vast corpus of Immanuel's biblical commentaries expresses divergent views about whether human perfection is solely conditional on intellectual accomplishment or whether the Torah commandments, which shape one's deeds, are a necessary component of perfection as well. A focus on the toxicity of sin to the communal body in the *maḥberet* emphasizes the importance of the observance of the commandments to maintain the social order and to inculcate values in individuals—in Maimonides' words, again, to ensure "the governance of the city and the well-being of the states of all its people according to their capacity."[109] The sinners and their punishments examined in this chapter manifest Immanuel's philosophical views as presented in his biblical commentaries. Deploying tremendous creativity with his commentaries, Immanuel incorporates sharp social critique in his narrative poem, obscuring some of its harshness with the fantastical setting. Yet Immanuel's commentaries also affirm the importance of the intellectual world, to which we turn next.

6

THE WORLD OF THE MIND

This chapter, like the previous one, examines how Immanuel's philosophical commentaries informed his *Maḥberet Ha-Tofet V'Ha-Eden*, but here the focus is on the processes of intellectual conformity. The Maimonidean "welfare of the soul" consists of "the multitude's acquiring correct opinions corresponding to their respective capacity," so that one can know "everything concerning all the beings that it is within the capacity of man to know in accordance with his ultimate perfection."[1] Throughout Immanuel's works, the rational intellect is championed as the most sublime aspect of the human soul and the only part capable of immortality. In fact, Maimonides identifies sinful thoughts as more grave than sinful actions because thought, with its transcendent potential, is considered a nobler process than action.[2] The purpose of human existence, according to Maimonides and his Tibbonide disciples, is intellectual actualization, which is attained by an individual choosing virtuous behavior and also having a supportive social context in which to pursue the arduous intellectual path. *Maḥberet Ha-Tofet V'Ha-Eden* is populated by some characters who appear to be merely manifestations of theoretical ideas, while the depiction of others conveys a sense of realism. Throughout, however, Immanuel marshals the philosophical material in service of a definition of sin that includes transgressions of the mind.

Tofet: *Efratim and Misguided Thoughts*

In hell, the characters of Immanuel and his guide, Daniel, encounter a group called the "Efratim," people who suffered terribly in their lives and who, one would think, should have a blessed afterlife to make up for their worldly troubles. It turns out, however, that they were not entirely innocent. Daniel reveals that the Efratim ignored the divine messages encoded in tragic events that befell them and denied their own guilt, which is why they suffered in the first place. In telling their story, Immanuel layers complex ideas about divine retribution and penitence, which also appear in his commentaries, onto these characters. Daniel explains: "These are the people who, when found by evil, proclaimed: 'We are innocent! Neither for our sins nor for our crimes have we have endured punishment.' For as they suffered the loss of money and children, they attributed it to the natural way. When evil accosted them with physical pain and illnesses, they did not say: 'It is because of Miriam!'" Just as the biblical character Miriam, whom the Talmud calls Efrat, was stricken with leprosy after disparaging her brother, so too, do these sinners fail to examine their own sins when assailed by physical punishment.[3]

In his commentary on Proverbs 12:25 ("If there is anxiety in a man's mind let him quash it, and turn it into joy with a good word"), Immanuel explores the loss of possessions or children as events that force one to "remember and recognize one's creator and to humble one's soul before him."[4] He identifies anxiety about one's future as expressions of inadequate trust in God, and suggests that material punishment is meted out in accordance with sin. Whether Immanuel crafted these characters in response to a particular situation is unknowable, but the motifs in the Proverbs comment expand and clarify the narrative in *Tofet.*

In *Tofet*, Immanuel conveys trust in God using transactional language and imagery, as Daniel advises that one should treat both the death of children and the loss of money as repayment of an outstanding debt (*ḥov*), fulfilling it willingly and lovingly. To demonstrate his point, Immanuel marshals the talmudic tale of Rabbi Meir and Bruriah, who lost their two sons on the Sabbath, but Bruriah concealed their deaths from her husband until after the Sabbath. Bruriah is praised for her insight, restraint, and shrewd method of revelation, as she asked Rabbi Meir about the legal requirement to return a deposit (*pikadon*) to its rightful owner and only afterward revealed the children's fate to him. Rabbi Meir's laments are eased by Bruriah's reminder that children are only a pawn from God, to be kept safely until the owner claims repayment.[5] Using the Hebrew word *pikadon* to refer to an individual's material lot in *Tofet*, Immanuel draws on a formal legalistic relationship between the owner of the *pikadon* and the individual assigned to use it temporarily, to convey that all people and things should be considered temporary loans from God.[6] Here the relationship between the punishment and the crime is clarified in Immanuel's commentary, but the anecdote in the poem reinforces the importance of trusting God through a heart-wrenching narrative.

Tofet: *Gamblers and Suicides*

Rabbinic texts have long identified both suicide and gambling as problematic behaviors, so the presence of such sinners in Immanuel's *Tofet* is no surprise.[7] However, the language and biblical allusions in *Tofet* rather surprisingly link these sins to misguided beliefs. "Burned in a kiln and hacked with saws," the faces of the suicides resemble "the edges of a cauldron."[8] While the image of a sinner's face covered in ash has early origins, *Tofet* connects it specifically with suicide. Wrongly believing that taking their own lives would release them from pain and sorrow, the suicides have, instead, provoked God's anger. In imagery related to the blackened cauldron metaphor, divine wrath billows over the suicides. The region of the gamblers, too, has analogs in early Jewish writings, as the Mishnah invalidates witnesses if they are "players of dice," and numerous rabbinic authorities issued communal bans and refused to annul vows in order to curb this vice, although exceptions were made on Jewish festivals and other times.[9] However, as Immanuel's literary persona reaches lower hell (*sheol taḥtiah*), where a deep pit is filled with lions, tigers, and scorpions, the narrative focuses on the internal implications of gaming. The gamblers "faced upward while they played, and cursed God with their lips and their hearts when their vessels returned empty," suggesting that their sin was in blaspheming God's name, a biblical prohibition (Exodus 22:27), rather than gambling per se.[10]

That gambling was a local problem in Italy is well attested by both Immanuel and Franciscan sermons. In the eleventh *maḥberet*, when the patron asks Immanuel's literary persona to compose a letter about his family, the patron identifies his brother, Abraham, as a "wicked, hypocritical man" who squandered his inheritance through gambling. Betting and dicing were also condemned as social maladies by Franciscan friars, who viewed such forms of entertainment as a direct threat to communal and individual health. The fifteenth-century preacher Bernardino da Siena accuses gamblers of blasphemy and idolatry because they frequently invoked divine aid or cursed it depending on the outcome of the game.[11] Although Immanuel preceded Bernardino chronologically, his critique of gamblers echoes Christian views more than traditional rabbinic discussions of the vice.

Immanuel's phrase "their vessels returned empty," from Jeremiah 14:3 ("they came to the cisterns, they found no water. They returned, their vessels empty"), refers to a time of drought in Jerusalem when the Israelites found empty wells. Although Immanuel's comment on this verse is not extant, it is referred to in his explication of Proverbs 30:4 ("Who has ascended heaven and come down? Who has gathered up the wind in the hollow of his hand? Who has wrapped the waters in his garment?"), a verse that highlights the power of God through a series of rhetorical questions. The verse stimulates Immanuel's discussion of individuals "who caused their intentions to sin" (שהחטיאו כוונתם) by attempting to acquire wisdom by sidestepping the traditional route. Although such individuals had good intentions, they were distracted by the pursuit of material delights, and their empty vessels represent the futility of seeking out wisdom while still mired in materialism.[12] Together with its implied philosophical significance, Immanuel's striking characterization of the gamblers in *Tofet* elevates his critique of gamblers from a local problem into a more serious spiritual flaw.

Tofet: *The Blind Elders*

Immanuel's literary persona and his guide, Daniel, witness a group of communal elders blindly ambling about *Tofet* because they refused to follow the light of true wisdom. The elders, of whom Immanuel knew about 120, "had eyes with which to see, but they did not see. They knew the levels of wisdom, its value, but they could not see light in its luminescence."[13] Daniel explains that they rejected the intelligibles (*muskalot*), "unchanging essences of existents," for conventional ideas (*mefursamot*).[14] Intelligibles are universal truths, while conventional wisdom is characterized by widespread acceptance regardless of any independent value.[15] Desirous of prominence but too lazy to apply themselves, the blind elders recycled common theories rather than pursuing challenging cognitive truths.

Both the description of the group and of the sin appear paradigmatic, as the number of men that Immanuel recognizes is 120, a stock number that alludes to the number of sages in the great assembly, a legislative body traditionally believed to have existed in the Hellenistic period or earlier. Echoing previous Greek and Jewish models where blindness is a punishment for lack of self-awareness, Immanuel introduces intellectual lethargy as a sin.[16] The contrast between intelligibles and conventional ideas was standard in philosophical writing, and Immanuel explores it in his commentary on Psalm 49:20 ("he will join the company of his ancestors, who will never see daylight again"). There, he considers Adam's attraction to conventional ideas despite his favorable placement in Eden and identifies that attraction as the direct cause of Adam's expulsion from the garden. For Immanuel, Adam's rejection of his divinely granted discernment and rationality signals the victory of his bestial aspect (his animal soul), but he notes that Adam exercises free will and thus could always rehabilitate his bestial state. Immanuel's exegetical understanding of Adam, who abused his potential to learn divine truths, is repurposed as a description of the elders in *Tofet* who preferred the comfort and ease of their knowledge rather than toiling to actualize their potential knowledge. Immanuel reads Psalms 49:17–20 as assuring the reader that even rich men cannot take their wealth to the next world and are, therefore, destined to join their ancestors "who will never see the daylight again." Both the language and theme of Immanuel's comment underlie his characterization of this group, demonstrating how the ideas in the commentaries are manifested in the *maḥberet*'s characters and tales.

Tofet: *The* Shovavim

Another group enveloped in total darkness, the "wicked ones" (*shovavim*), were learned scholars who used their erudition to gain money and pride. Daniel explains, these ones "made the Torah and knowledge into crowns and axes: crowns by which to glorify themselves and axes by which to feed themselves. They did not love Torah and knowledge for their intrinsic value, nor for the splendid glory of their majesty."[17] This tale affirms the primacy of Torah study as a path to God and eternal life rather than as a tool to gain material benefits. Daniel notes:

> Therefore, whosoever intends to reach any material end by means of Torah and knowledge, to know the ways of the living God, or to glorify himself amongst the living, has dreamed a dream and not trodden a safe path. His actions will not be desirable, for Torah and wisdom are the essential life. As Solomon said, "For he who finds me, finds life." He did not say, "For he who finds me finds something that causes him to merit life," just he who finds me finds the thing of life. For the words of Torah are life to those who find them.[18]

Immanuel's purposeful misreading of Proverbs 8:35 ("for he who finds me finds life and obtains favor from the Lord") demonstrates his disgust for the misuse of Torah study in service of worldly status. Immanuel's comment on this verse, to which the *Tofet* tale alludes, identifies the term "life" as a referent to eternal life, so the sarcasm expressed in the vignette is even more biting when the poem and commentary are juxtaposed.[19]

The value of Torah study for spiritual, moral, and intellectual edification is a topic frequently explored by Immanuel's commentaries. Reading Proverbs 10:4 ("negligent hands cause poverty but diligent hands enrich") allegorically, Immanuel notes that one who studies wisdom not for its own merit "will be punished by divine judgment because he cheated wisdom, placing it as a crown by which to glorify himself, and an ax by which to feed himself. This demonstrates that he does not recognize wisdom's intrinsic value. His desire to use wisdom for the attainment of a greater goal also exposes his complete foolishness in using wisdom as a means to attain a worldly object."[20]

Using the same language in his commentary and poem, Immanuel reveals that studying the Torah study for material purposes is a punishable offense, as this should be done only by those who value Torah and wisdom for their own sake. The dark setting of this vignette, embodying the sinners' spiritual condition, reflects their inability to appreciate the light of the Torah in and of itself. By condemning these men, communal leaders who guide others, for their misappropriation of trust and knowledge, Immanuel casts his social critique as an intellectual sin.

Tofet: *The Jesus Figure*

Immanuel and Daniel encounter a sinner wearing a crown of thorns, who hangs as a target for bowmen. The guide reveals that this sinner, whom I identify as a Jesus figure, was a heretic with an insatiable sexual appetite. As I have argued elsewhere, this sinner's vignette reveals the dangers of intellectual deviance to a community through a character crafted—from Immanuel's commentaries as well as other Jewish texts—to embody theoretical ideas.[21] Immanuel fashioned the character of the old man crowned with thorns, a former rabbi who shunned Torah for a life of physical pleasure, by conflating sexual deviance with heresy. While it is possible that Immanuel's description of a sexually deviant heretic alludes to an actual figure whom he sought to denigrate by characterizing him as another Jesus, the parodic and paradigmatic aspects of the vignette obscure any identification of an actual target. In Immanuel's comment on Proverbs 2:22 ("while the wicked will vanish from the land and the treacherous will be rooted out of it"), a verse that describes the potential harm of treading the wrong path, he explores the interplay of physical and spiritual sins. He explains:

> It is possible that the sage interpreted "forbidden and foreign woman" to mean the path of apostasy [*minut*], false doctrines, and invalid assertions. He explains that wisdom saves a person from believing in false doctrines and invalid assertions. Any faith beside the Torah of Moses is false doctrine and apostasy, which leads a person to abandon the living God and the Torah, the covenant between God and us. They say: "Her house sinks down to death, and her course leads her to the shades" [Proverbs 2:18] means that heresy and deficient faiths imprison a person's soul, impede it from attaining eternal life, and consign it to utter destruction. The path of heresy is such that none of its travelers return, and none attain the path of life. Since he is not given the opportunity to repent, they will not attain the path of life until the afterlife [lit. "the world that has been arranged"]. "So follow the way of the good" [Proverbs 2:20] means that wisdom will save you so you are not tempted to follow those who believe in false doctrines, for you shall follow the paths of Torah and "keep to the paths of the just."[22]

Immanuel's allegorical reading of the foreign woman's temptation of the youth in Proverbs as spiritual ensnarement links the threat of sexual temptation with that of apostasy, an idea manifested in the Jesus character in *Tofet*. The thematic and linguistic affinities between Immanuel's *maḥberet* and his commentary on Proverbs demonstrate that Immanuel used sexual deviance rhetorically, symbolizing apostasy, to explore the damage of charismatic teachers who cause real spiritual and intellectual damage to followers.

At *Tofet*'s conclusion, more than half of the twenty-five pits of punishment focus on the educational sector, perhaps reflecting Immanuel's role as a teacher. Some sinners extracted foreign ideas from the Torah "to deceive people and trip them in a fowler's trap."[23] Others refused to share their wisdom with students or withheld it from them because they feared a diminishment of their own stature and reputation. Immanuel remarks that, just as clouds and candles bestow freely their bounty and their light, teachers can certainly share their knowledge with no diminishing effect. Some teachers relished their rabbinic title but did not care about delivering any meaningful educational content, while other "mindless" teachers were satisfied with food, drink, and merriment while mocking those who truly imparted wisdom. Other pits in this region contain idle chatterers who devoted their time to talk of politics and gossip instead of prophetic wisdom and were punished for withholding true knowledge from their intellects. With their brevity and lack of intertextual allusions, the descriptions of these pits offer social critiques that seem local and targeted as compared to the longer vignettes in *Tofet* in which the characters manifest theoretical ideas from the commentaries. This bolsters the verisimilitude that Immanuel deploys throughout the *maḥberet.*

Tofet: *The Miserly Brothers from Maresha*

The element of corrupt scholarship, expressed in comic textual misreadings, characterizes a tale of the two brothers Immanuel recognizes in *Tofet.* They are from Maresha, which could allude to the Italian region of Le Marche, and are initially described as "pioneers in the kingdom of wisdom and understanding."[24] Through Daniel, however, Immanuel's literary persona learns that these men squandered their intellectual potential through parsimony, as their tightfisted hands are compared to virgins "unknown by a man."[25] The brothers mangle biblical verses in support of their abusive mistreatment of the poor, scattering beggars who come before them with "flee, impure one," a phrase from Lamentations 4:11.[26] Immanuel's exegetical creativity is evident in its fullest force here, as the brothers contort biblical phrases traditionally associated with charitable giving into justifications for their stinginess.

> "Furnish him" [Deuteronomy 15:14] was erased from their books. They said that they tried to "send your bread forth upon the waters" [Ecclesiastes 11:1] once or twice, and on most days, they did not find it. Thus, they erased it from their books. Their hands faithfully followed the verse, "Distribute portions to seven or eight" [Ecclesiastes 11:2], and said that the best of interpretations was to divide a piece of poultry between seven or eight people rather than dividing a whole chicken between two people, as fools do. They expounded "You must open your hand to him" [Deuteronomy 15:8] as meaning: One must open the five fingers of the hand and slap the face of the poor man with them, to frighten him, since frightening him was God's intention. One of them swore to God, his Creator, on the life of his eldest son, that in his copy he found the word "lo" ["to him"] spelled with an aleph [meaning "not"]; while the other explained the verse: "You must open your hand to him" [Deuteronomy 15:8] to show the poor man that there is nothing in your hand that belongs to him. They said that the meaning of "You must lend him" [Deuteronomy 15:8] is to confiscate a pauper's pledge when you lend him enough for whatever he needs.[27]

This exegetical parody, filled with fantastic puns and hilarious misinterpretations, attests to Immanuel's linguistic capabilities while displaying his awareness of traditional rabbinic interpretations of the biblical verses.

"Furnish him," the decree to sustain a manumitted Jewish slave when his or her period of slavery ended, was codified by Maimonides in the *Mishneh Torah* and glossed as "not to send him empty-handed."[28] Medieval exegetes like Rashi and Abraham Ibn Ezra use the verse "Send your bread forth upon the waters once or twice" to encourage almsgiving to all—even to strangers who won't ever return the charity—while a midrashic tale of a man miraculously saved from drowning because of his benevolence invokes this verse to explain his redemption from a watery death.[29] Immanuel notes that these two verses were erased from the brothers' bibles, not to charge textual corruption but to playfully mock his subjects while displaying his own exegetical prowess. Immanuel's reading of Ecclesiastes 11:1–2 in his commentary encourages charitable giving by assuring its eventual repayment to the lender. When the verse directs a person to give "to seven or eight," Immanuel's exegesis interprets this as a call for benevolence during the seven days of the week and beyond, into the following week, but the brothers' misreading in *Tofet* suggests splitting one piece of poultry seven or eight ways.[30] Maimonides explains the directive "You must open your hand to him," which the brothers used to justify violence against the poor, as the supreme form of aid to one who has not yet asked.[31] Contorting classical references to charity and generosity to justify the castigation and shaming of the indigent, Immanuel's satirical vignette exposes the ugly underbelly of irresponsible scriptural interpretation. Here, the juxtaposition of the misreadings with the commentaries heightens the *maḥberet*'s comic effect.

For Immanuel, the brothers' exegetical contortions are only one symptom of a general disregard for wisdom. He explains, "They said that they found a maxim in Greek wisdom [literature], 'Mine is mine and yours is yours—this is the golden mean,' but they forgot that this is a principle of Sodom and Gomorrah."[32] In a parodic amalgamation of Mishnah Avot 5:10 with the Aristotelian concept of the golden mean, Immanuel affirms the brothers' wickedness and distortion of knowledge. He says, "They regarded wisdom as baseness and infamy, the pursuit of wisdom as madness and folly."[33] The brothers' lack of appreciation for wisdom serves as a perfect platform for Immanuel to discuss the true value of wisdom since, according to Immanuel, "wisdom is a ladder, set upon the ground, whose top reaches to the lord of the universe. As a person ascends its high rungs, he approaches God by his ascent. As he retreats, he shall be distant from him, the Exalted One, and his soul and body will be consumed."[34] The symbol of Jacob's ladder, to which Immanuel alludes, was glossed by Maimonides in his *The Guide of the Perplexed* as a "prophetic parable" (*mi-mishle ha-nevuah*) where "every word occurring in this parable refers to an additional subject in the complex of subjects represented by the parable as a whole."[35]

As we saw in Chapter 4, Jacob's ladder is understood by Immanuel, in the Tibbonide manner, as an educational curriculum through which one attains increasingly abstract knowledge.[36] "The one who walks blamelessly" in Psalms 15:2, for Immanuel, is "the individual who ascends the ladder of wisdom according to his capabilities, and did not spare the obligations of the Torah or the rational mind."[37] In *Tofet*, the brothers' derision of wisdom provokes Immanuel's meditation on the unique intellective capacities, divinely imprinted on the human soul, which can be actualized. Following this comment, Immanuel laments that these miserly sinners wasted their intellectual potential on material wealth, for "had these arrogant people, resting untroubled in their spots, full of sap and freshness, only sought out wisdom as silver and hunted it like treasure, then they would have collected tons and tons of it."[38] Possessing the requisite intellectual dispositions, as Immanuel concedes, in their manipulative readings, these brothers could have reached the pinnacle of intellectual perfection, but they failed and are eternally punished. The punishment of exile from the divine palace for "those who could have climbed up the ladder of wisdom and did not ascend" is seemingly benign, yet the commentaries reveal its harshness, especially in a philosophic idiom.

The image of the king's palace, a recurrent symbol among medieval rationalists and mystics, was employed by thinkers like Solomon Ibn Gabirol and Moses Maimonides to symbolize the human quest for God.[39] For Maimonides, who devoted an entire chapter of *The Guide of the Perplexed* to expounding this image, the palace signifies varying levels of intellectual proximity to God, represented by a person's distance from the king in his inner chambers. Since, according to Maimonides, each individual was imprinted with only a certain intellective capacity, each person stands at a different degree vis-à-vis knowledge of God.[40] After acknowledging that these wicked brothers did not fully engage their divinely imprinted abilities for the correct intellectual pursuit, Immanuel banishes them from the king's palace, effectively severing any chance of a relationship with God.

In the vignette of the brothers from Maresha, Immanuel tackles the complex issue of intellectual capacity and its unique individual expression due to natural disposition. The brothers display a rare ability to intelligize truths, but they dwell in *Tofet* because "they forgot that when true knowledge is absent, espousing foreign ideas from Edomites, Sidonites, and Hittites is graver than monetary theft. Stealing the rational part from the intelligized parts of the soul and from the exalted sciences is worse than any theft or robbery."[41] While their actions toward the impoverished were especially cruel, it is the crime of intellectual theft from their own rational intellects that ultimately banishes them from the king's palace. The tale of these two misers is inversely mirrored in Immanuel's *Eden*, where Immanuel offers a corrective example to counteract their behaviors. In *Eden*'s "heights" (*Ma'alot Ha-Eden*), Immanuel's literary persona sees celestial thrones surrounding a magnificent throne and footstool, but all are empty. Immanuel's narrative deviation from a tour of characters in hell and heaven is striking, but the purpose of this strange digression becomes clear when one considers it an opportunity to extol two of his mentors who, though still alive, have already secured themselves prominent places in heaven through their intellectual activity.

Eden: *The Thrones of Daniel and Judah*

Daniel, the guide, indicates that one throne is intended for "Judah, the lion's whelp," an epithet used in the twelfth *maḥberet* for Judah Romano, the philosopher, translator, and exegete. Immanuel confesses to having stolen his words and used them to ornament his own exegetical comments, because "without the wisdom in his books—mine would never have existed."[42] In his commentary on Proverbs, Immanuel calls him "the godly, wise philosopher Rabbi Judah, my brother."[43] The familial relationship between the two Italian thinkers is unclear, but the textual relationship is evident from the hefty portions of Judah Romano's commentaries that Immanuel incorporated into his own.[44] Judah's view of the possibility of intellectual conjunction during one's lifetime, together with his novel scriptural and liturgical interpretations, strongly influenced Immanuel; there are quotations from Judah's writings, acknowledged and not, laced throughout Immanuel's exegetical and poetic works. While Daniel reserves the throne for Judah, he points to the footstool as intended for "the scribe" (*ha-meḥokek*), a reference to Immanuel himself. This title links Immanuel to the biblical Moses; Maimonides calls Moses "a scribe to whom it [the Torah] was dictated, while he transcribes all the events that transpired—the narratives and the commandments. Therefore, he is referred to as a *meḥokek*."[45] Like Moses, Immanuel has transcribed his own ineffable experience in hell and heaven for the edification of his readers. The subordinate position of the footstool in relation to the throne indicates that Immanuel's station is inferior to that of Judah Romano.

Judah's throne stirs emotions within Immanuel's literary persona, who suddenly remembers his companion Daniel—calling him "my brother" (*aḥi*)—and asks where he will reside in heaven. The reference to Daniel, both here and at the beginning of *Maḥberet Ha-Tofet V'Ha-Eden*, is ambiguous. Does it refer to the celestial guide or to the close friend whose death inspired the *maḥberet*, or to both at once? It is striking, though, that Immanuel's request of his literary persona, to see Daniel's final celestial place, echoes his initial grief-stricken lament at the outset of the journey. Immanuel learns that his eternal station in *Eden*'s heights was assigned because of Daniel's vicarious merit, as the guide reveals:

> Supreme Wisdom knew that without you he would neither settle nor be calm, so she positioned his tabernacle by your tabernacle. Even though your worth is beneath his, She knew that your company would delight him. He will be a Moses to your Joshua. Thus, all who will see your souls together, united, enmeshed, and inseparable, will say, "Can two walk together without previously having met?"[46]

After expressing self-doubt and fear, Immanuel expresses joy "knowing that my lot had been favorably cast, aware that my salvation is because of him."[47] Again, acknowledging and welcoming his subordinate position vis-à-vis Daniel, Immanuel accepts his station gracefully. The reference to the relationship of the biblical Moses and Joshua offers a corrective to the miserly brothers in *Tofet*, about whom Immanuel states, "If one cannot be like Moses, his heart shall not compel him to act as Manasseh. He should try to be like Joshua."[48] Here, in *Eden*, Immanuel's literary persona models the very mentality Immanuel the author promotes by embracing his vicarious salvation rather than questioning his place or worth. This point is reinforced by the next stop on Immanuel's character's journey, at the tent of Oholiab, son of Aḥisamakh, an assistant builder of the Tabernacle, who is joined by Betzalel, son of Uri, the Tabernacle's master builder. En route to see Daniel's final resting place, Immanuel beholds this pair of builders who—like Moses and Joshua, and, presumably, like Daniel and Immanuel—share a master-apprentice relationship. Whether Daniel represents a real figure, such as a patron, is unknowable, but the regard shown for his character is undeniable. Lacking any characters, this region is structurally distinctive, a feature that might functionally reflect its purpose as a panegyric to a real personage; but it inverts the depiction of the brothers from Maresha and offers a corrective: acceptance of one's natural disposition and station.

Eden: *Righteous Gentiles*

Another example of souls in *Eden* who used knowledge to the best ends is found in "the righteous gentiles of the world who so triumphed in their knowledge and intellect."[49] The presence of non-Jewish individuals in heaven may surprise avid readers of Dante's *Divine Comedy*, which bars non-Christians from blessedness, consigning even important figures like Virgil and other poets to the first region of hell known as Limbo.[50] In contrast, Immanuel quotes the famous line of Maimonides: "We need to accept the truth from anyone who states it."[51] While the category of "righteous gentiles" is not by any means original to Immanuel, it is striking that he collapses the Maimonidean distinction between righteous gentiles and gentile sages into a single category by considering how these gentiles reached their beliefs.[52] Gentiles are called "pious ones," who ruminated over the nature of the creator and their earthly existence and whose backstory Daniel reveals. They were people searching for answers about their existence on earth and their creator, spurning the unsatisfactory "deceptions" provided by their own elders and sages.[53] Their earnest search for knowledge brought these gentiles to survey world religions and assemble their own creed. Fearing that naming God would somehow limit the deity, they describe God as "the First Cause, authentic and giving life, who was, is, and will be. He created the world at the moment that his wisdom ordained it. The intensity of His light renders him invisible to us. He neither tires nor does he become weary, and his wisdom cannot be fathomed. The one who is merciful toward his creations sustains them with the care of a shepherd tending to his flocks. He recalls us to him at our end, and his glory shall gather us."[54]

Guided to universal truths by logic and reason rather than reliance on familiar tradition, the righteous gentiles earn tremendous praise for scrutinizing their faiths and challenging their ancestral leaders. In stark contrast to the ancient philosophers burning in the bonfire at the beginning of Immanuel's *Tofet* for their misguided beliefs about the eternity of the universe, these gentiles "were intellectually curious about their Maker and Creator, who mercifully created them, the one who transformed them from nothingness to existence, and brought them to this world."[55] In praising non-Jewish thinkers who approach religion rationally, Immanuel deviates from Dante, and even from Maimonides, but reinforces a philosophical approach to religion.

The vignette of the righteous gentiles reflects tensions in Christian intellectual circles that had been percolating over the course of the thirteenth century at the University of Paris and which culminated in the harsh condemnation of Aristotelian texts and tenets in 1270 and 1277.[56] Chief among the topics of debate between members of the faculties of the arts and theology was that of creation *ex nihilo* versus the Aristotelian belief in the eternity of the world. As noted in Chapter 4, the major philosophers whose works influenced Immanuel were nevertheless placed in hell specifically because of their belief in the eternity of the world. And Immanuel returned to this point several times in his biblical commentaries. In his comment on Psalm 111, for example, Immanuel identifies the eternality of the universe as a false supposition. To combat that "foreign belief," Immanuel explains, Jews were commanded to observe the Sabbath, commemorating God's creation of the world.[57] The righteous gentiles in *Eden*, therefore, who came to correct conclusions rather than erroneous ones, held those philosophical ideas espoused by Immanuel in his commentaries. Their characterization gives our author the opportunity to craft an ideal non-Jew who, nevertheless, embraces rationalism.

When we juxtapose Immanuel's exegetical corpus with his *maḥberet*, it becomes possible to appreciate the delicate details of adaptation and transfer between textual genres and corpora. A focus on the Maimonidean category of the soul, however, demonstrates that Immanuel isolates the mental space as independent of the body and only knowable by God. This concept enables him to redefine actions traditionally frowned upon, like gambling or suicide, through a new prism—the mind. While his commentaries provide the conceptual framework for Immanuel's *maḥberet*, the spirit of verisimilitude ensures that enough narrative details maintain a sense of realism. As in the previous chapter, where individual and collective actions equally impact the social order, so too here can individuals and groups promote or hinder the intellectual journey. But, claims Maimonides, social wellbeing is only a prerequisite to the real challenge of acquiring truths and intelligibilia. For Immanuel, this intellectual task is embodied in the meetings between his literary persona and the biblical authors.

Eden: *The Biblical Authors*

A considerable part of Immanuel's *Eden* chronicles the encounters between Immanuel's literary persona and various biblical authors, cementing the importance of biblical exegesis to our author. The authors initially declare, "Here comes Immanuel—it is time to laugh,"[58] highlighting the perception of Immanuel as an entertaining bard, but the individual meetings between Immanuel's persona and the prophets and sages confirm Immanuel as a venerable exegete. The introductory character, King David, accompanied by musicians like Asaf, Heiman, Jedutun, and Korah's sons, welcomes Immanuel, "holding a harp and the lute."[59] After David, Immanuel's character meets Ezekiel, Jeremiah, and Isaiah, prophetic authors of biblical books which, in addition to Psalms, were also read as containing mystical secrets about the universe and its creation. Then, in an interlude of sorts, Immanuel's persona meets Solomon and a band of prophetic authors who escort him to *Eden*'s "highest heights" (*Ma'alot Ha-Eden Ha-Gevohim*), where he encounters Moses, Solomon, and Joseph. Joseph's inclusion in this group is strange, as he did not author a biblical book, but his exchange with Immanuel's character nevertheless highlights Immanuel's moralistic readings of the Joseph narrative.

As author of the Psalter, David embodies the intellectual philosopher and religious devotee praised by Immanuel in *Eden*'s canopies (Chapter 5) and in his biblical commentaries. David's accompaniment by the Levite musicians might seem to be an aesthetic choice, but Immanuel's commentaries reveal a deeper significance to their presence.[60] Asaf, Heiman, and Jedutun, Levites known in biblical and postbiblical literature for their musical talent, are identified in Immanuel's commentary as early *maestri* of the "science and art of music," which he identifies as having Jewish origin. Immanuel notes, "Today, there is not one among us who knows anything about it and it remains entirely in the hands of the Christians," suggesting that, over time, Jewish knowledge of art and music had been lost to the Christians during numerous exiles.[61] Other literary features of this encounter further reveal connections to Immanuel's philosophical commentaries. David greets Immanuel with a verse from Psalms 118:26 ("Blessed is He who comes in the name of the lord"), saying, "Welcome in the name of my Lord!"[62] Although this biblical phrase supplies a useful greeting, its significance lies in Immanuel's identification of this phrase as an angelic exclamation declared by angels accompanying a soul newly released from the "lower world." Immanuel reads the psalm, allegorically, as a dialogue between the eternal souls ("stored in the bundle of life") and the newly ascended soul, where the greeting phrase also praises the soul for abandoning its physical body and worldly pleasures.[63] This specific greeting scene between David and Immanuel thus serves as a manifestation of a celestial process imagined by Immanuel in his philosophical commentary on Psalm 118. In fact, most of the exchange with King David in *Eden* serves this role.

David asks Immanuel's literary persona, "Are you the one who removes the decay from my pearls?"[64] As with his greeting, David's complimentary question acquires newfound texture when considering Immanuel's comment on Psalm 119:59 ("I have considered my ways, and have turned back to your decrees"), where David's strength comes to "remove the rust of doubt from their hearts."[65] Immanuel reads the psalm as a tale of King David's jealousy of wicked men and his desire to follow their ways. Defending King David, Immanuel claims that his professed jealousy and temptation is only a rhetorical strategy to fortify the hearts of the weak, as his task is to remove and refresh rusted material. In *Eden*, Immanuel emphasizes the virtuosity of his literary persona by analogizing him to King David, using David's character to assert the traveler's exegetical abilities. These abilities come into full view when King David summons all the exegetes who have glossed the book of Psalms, especially David Kimḥi. After proper veneration, David asks each to recite his interpretation of Psalm 68. Not satisfied with any explanation, David requests Immanuel's public presentation of his reading, instructing the other exegetes to worship Immanuel's persona as their "king and their messiah." It is ironic and revelatory of Immanuel's self-pride that King David insists that the exegetes worship Immanuel of Rome as king and messiah when he himself is the king and ancestor of the messiah in classical Jewish lore.

As mentioned in Chapter 2, Psalm 68 is known as a particularly difficult psalm to interpret because of its complex syntax and language; Abraham Ibn Ezra calls it "a most exalted psalm." It is usually glossed as an Israelite victory song culminating in the granting of the Torah at Mount Sinai. Immanuel explains that David wrote it, in the manner of Song of Songs, as an allegorical work referring to exalted matters. In Immanuel's interpretation (explored at length in Chapter 2), the psalm surveys the sublunar and celestial worlds, the divine, and the place of the human intellect. David Kimḥi's gloss is extremely literal, identifying Hezekiah and Sanḥerib's army as the historical referents of this psalm, and it is no surprise that Immanuel singles him out as the exegete who missed its significance. King David bestows much praise on Immanuel for his interpretation of Psalm 68, calling him "a pouch of myrrh," the same term used for the lover in the Song of Songs 1:13. This commendation is especially significant for Immanuel, who read that phrase in Song of Songs as an allegory for the agent intellect "that is the bundle of life which holds the souls of the righteous."[66] By highlighting his allegorical reading of Psalm 68 and making it the object of King David's praise, Immanuel broadcasts the importance of this particular psalm for its scientific-theological content.

The conversation between King David and Immanuel is interrupted by the prophet Ezekiel, who lauds Immanuel's commentary on his own book, calling it "a veritable cure for the disease of the commentators." He highlights Immanuel's reading of the chariot passages, traditionally glossed by both rationalists and mystics.[67] Immanuel's commentary on Ezekiel is partially extant in marginal notations surrounding Kimḥi's commentary, offering allegorical insights in a brief, terse style. In *Eden*, the character of Ezekiel states, "Your interpretation of the chariot episode, extended like the staff of Moses, paved a way through a sea of doubt. All the springs burst out of their depths, and the children of Israel, that holy flock, crossed the waters of wisdom on dry land."[68] Ezekiel calls Immanuel's commentary "the staff," the hermeneutical enabler that split the "sea of doubt" and revealed the dry, paved road that lies within. This image is particularly relevant to Immanuel for two reasons. Water, in rationalist idiom, signifies wisdom, so Immanuel's commentary enabled people to securely acquire wisdom.[69] Even more significant, Ezekiel's words liken Immanuel's literary character to Moses, an idealized figure in both Maimonidean writings and Immanuel's thought.[70]

Jeremiah praises Immanuel's literary persona for properly interpreting specific verses in his biblical book, highlighting Jeremiah 1:5. Flanked by the prophets Elijah, Elisha, and Barukh ben Neriah, Jeremiah complains that "contemporary exegetes failed to grasp its meaning," but Immanuel "uncovered its branches and roots, feeding the sweet nectar of its truths to the hungry."[71] While the correlation between a tree and honey seems nonexistent, Immanuel's comment on Proverbs 25:16 meaningfully connects the two motifs. The verse in Proverbs ("If you find honey, eat only what you need, lest, surfeiting yourself, you throw it up") advises a cautious ingestion of excessively sweet foods, which Immanuel relates to the realm of knowledge, advising that one must study only that which one can fully understand. The attempt to grasp knowledge beyond one's intellectual capacity, states Immanuel, will trigger a knee-jerk reaction. Immanuel reinforces his point with the talmudic exemplum of Elisha ben Abuya, or *Aḥer*, who entered an orchard (*pardes*) with three other sages. Of the four sages, only Rabbi Aqiba emerged unscathed, but Elisha ben Abuya was described as "cutting down saplings," which was interpreted in several different ways.[72] To Immanuel, Elisha's cutting down the saplings signifies an inability to respect intellectual boundaries in the celestial realms.[73] In his Proverbs comment, eating excessive amounts of honey is compared to the act of cutting down young trees, a pastiche of images that reappears in Immanuel's celestial tour to the opposite effect of its initial significance. Jeremiah's praise of Immanuel celebrates his exposing the roots and leaves of a tree and feeding honey and nectar to the hungry, connoting an appropriate and measured type of teaching.

The highlighted verse from Jeremiah 1:5 ("Before I formed you in the belly, I knew you, and before you came forth from the womb, I sanctified you") does not have a related comment in Immanuel's extant marginal notations. Yet Immanuel alludes to his interpretation of the verse in his brief comment on Mishnah Avot preserved in his collection of homilies, the source for Immanuel's exposition of the red heifer, analyzed in chapter 3.[74] There Immanuel advances a novel reading that counsels authenticity and virtue in both private and public domains, since God is ever present and omniscient. Immanuel warns that "although a person can hide his thoughts and ways from his peers, he cannot conceal them from his Creator who knew him before he was formed in the womb."[75] The encounter with Jeremiah thus condemns the very hypocrisy targeted by Immanuel in *Tofet.*

The appearance of Jeremiah's attendants in this vignette alludes to the Maimonidean reading of this verse, which relates it to three ideologies regarding prophecy. Prophets, according to Maimonides' *The Guide of the Perplexed* II:32, are born with a natural disposition that becomes actualized with proper training and preparation, but not every child born and prepared becomes a prophet. To demonstrate this, Maimonides cites Jeremiah 1:5 as well as the example of Barukh ben Neriah, who was born with a suitable disposition and trained by Jeremiah but prohibited from prophecy because it was too burdensome.[76] Later in that chapter of *The Guide of the Perplexed*, Maimonides establishes divine will as a factor in bestowing prophecy, and he cites the example of Elisha the prophet from II Kings 6:18 to prove that God can intervene in natural processes. The appearance of these particular attendants flanking Jeremiah serves as a visual manifestation of the Maimonidean idea of prophecy as a natural process mediated by God. Perhaps, then, it is no coincidence that the next biblical figure, Isaiah, greets Immanuel with the epithet, "O exegete, who prophesied amongst the prophets."[77]

Isaiah praises Immanuel's reading of Isaiah 1:5 ("why do you seek further beatings, that you continue to offend? Every head is ailing, and every heart is sick"), affirming Immanuel's prophetic status while repudiating other exegetical interpretations. Though Immanuel's exegesis of Isaiah is extant as marginal notes in a manuscript of David Kimḥi's commentary, no comment on Isaiah 1:5 exists.[78] Isaiah confirms that Immanuel has merited *Eden* because of his exegetical compositions, stating, "Your commentaries have earned you life in the world to come!"[79]

The shift to *Eden*'s highest heights brings Immanuel's literary persona face to face with Moses, whose face radiates such an intense light that he must veil his face to protect Immanuel's vision. Praising Immanuel's interpretation of Moses's own work, the book of Job, Moses says, "You will come to the grave at a ripe old age, having redeemed your soul from destruction and your lifeforce from the sword."[80] Highlighting Immanuel's reading of the esoteric Behemoth and Leviathan, Moses announces that Immanuel's exegesis is salvific, having redeemed him from unworthiness. As mentioned in Chapter 2, Immanuel's commentary on the book of Job follows the Maimonidean characterization of a universal tale about providence, with the Tibbonide inflection that interprets the tale as a reference to immortality.[81] However, Immanuel reads the textual unit about the beasts (*Behemoth*; Job 40:15) and the sea creature (*Leviathan*; Job 40:25) as an allusion to celestial existents, because "it is known to every person of intellect that the way of the prophets is to speak about lowly things and to allude to exalted things."[82] For Immanuel, the secret of Behemoth and Leviathan is a hermeneutical key to understanding the otherworldly visions of Ezekiel (Ezekiel 1) and Isaiah (Isaiah 6) and to explain the splitting of the four rivers from Eden in Genesis 2. Immanuel's digression is lengthy—approximately five full pages—and he often asserts the esoteric nature of the truths he reveals.[83] Like the meeting with King David, the encounter with Moses emphasizes an exegetical passage of which Immanuel is proud, but the attribution of this allusion to the greatest of prophets maintains the humble façade of Immanuel's character.[84]

In the spirit of self-promotion that began with the King David encounter, King Solomon also plays a prominent role in *Eden*, both as an admirer of Immanuel's erudition and as a motivating force that conveys Immanuel's literary persona from one realm of heaven to another. The exchange with Solomon leads to more inter-Immanuel allusions, as Solomon's character is "amazed at how you were able to tie together the verses of Proverbs and to write wondrous things on the 'Woman of Valor' narrative [Proverbs 31]."[85] Solomon's phrase "to tie together the verses of Proverbs" echoes the rabbinic comparison of Solomon's composition of Proverbs to one who ties ropes together in order to draw water from a deep, inaccessible well, which Immanuel cites in his introduction to the commentaries on Proverbs and Ecclesiastes. Here, in *Eden*, Immanuel appropriates rabbinic acclaim of Solomon, converting it into Solomonic praise of Immanuel. Of all his commentaries, Immanuel's reading of Proverbs 31 contains the most explicit references to afterlife and intellectual union with the agent intellect. Besides his grammatical and literal readings, every verse of the chapter is explicated "according to an esoteric reading."

Addressing Immanuel's Song of Songs commentary in *Eden*, Solomon says:

> Your innovative reading of Song of Songs is a wonder of wonders that does not fail to satisfy anyone who sees it. On the verse "O maidens of Zion, go forth and gaze upon King Solomon wearing the crown that his mother gave him on his wedding day, on his day of bliss" [Song of Songs 3:11], all the wise men of the age failed to glean my intention nor could they solve my riddle until you arose, increasing wisdom and honor, you exposed the glory of its secrets about the truth.[86]

Solomon's words reveal an exegetical point that Immanuel seeks to highlight, an identification of Solomon's mother with Torah and wisdom, the means by which a felicitous soul reaches its perfection and conjunction with the agent intellect. Expanding on Moses Ibn Tibbon's interpretation of Solomon's crown, Immanuel views it as a reference to one's knowledge that merits one an eternal life.[87] Solomon also praises Immanuel's commentary on Ecclesiastes, disparaging other exegetes who didn't see "any utility in it."[88] Each biblical author homes in on a specific instance in Immanuel's commentaries that proposes an original reading, even if that reading is a composite of unattributed sources. As I have demonstrated elsewhere, Immanuel engages in this self-referential intertextuality frequently in *Maḥberot Immanuel*, but this is the only instance where a speaker other than Immanuel refers to his commentaries.[89]

Immanuel employs a similar tactic with the biblical character Joseph, though he was not a biblical author. Appearing in *Eden* wearing a golden diadem and called "the righteous Joseph" (*Yosef Ha-Zadik*), Joseph greets Immanuel's literary persona as the one who "memorialized me favorably in his commentaries. It was as though he crowned my head with royalty when he judged me meritoriously with his words and wrote lengthy praise about me and my actions."[90] Truly, against all other medieval biblical exegetes, Immanuel interprets Joseph's informing his father of his brothers' behaviors as a sign of Joseph's integrity, for "we should believe that Joseph did this because of a good quality within him. For the ugly behaviors were evil in his eyes and rejected by him."[91] Here too Immanuel's novel interpretation of a biblical passage is stressed, luring audiences into reading this comment in its original context. Joseph explains that Immanuel is renowned in heaven for his humorous verse, but his praise of Immanuel is as an exegete.

Initially, the encounters with the biblical figures seem haphazard. But as each biblical figure isolates particular biblical verses, episodes, or chapters, there emerges a portrait of important concepts that Immanuel chose to spotlight. David's praise establishes Immanuel as a philosophical exegete while elevating allegory as the premier mode of reading. Next, Ezekiel's comment compares Immanuel to Moses, wielding his commentary like a hermeneutical staff. Jeremiah affirms that Immanuel is a generous and authentic teacher and person while acknowledging the uniqueness of prophecy in general. Isaiah identifies Immanuel as a prophet. Following these encounters, Immanuel's literary persona meets Moses, whose verses allude to the immortality of the rational intellect and its familiarity with the celestial existents. Solomon's praise, the apex of this vignette, revolves around the chapter that most clearly refers to the union of human rational intellect and agent intellect. In short, teasing out the exegetical significance of the verses highlighted in Immanuel's *Eden* reveals a hierarchical order of ascending importance that mimics the general trajectory of actualization as it had been envisioned by medieval Jewish Maimonidean philosophers and adapted by Italian Jewish thinkers. The outlier example, that of Joseph, conveys the importance of moral virtue, as Immanuel's portrayal of Joseph emphasizes his upstanding character that exposed his evil brothers despite the threat of interpersonal discomfort.

The region of the biblical authors confirms Immanuel's literary persona as an intellectual who successfully understood the inner meanings of divine scripture. The episode demonstrates that Immanuel envisioned biblical exegesis as a competitive enterprise, confirmed by his derisive language about other exegetes—David Kimḥi in particular. As the prized exegete in the narrative, Immanuel insinuates that his glosses best embody the true message of the prophets and wise men. To understand why this is so, we must turn to Immanuel's intellectual context, specifically Judah Romano's view of prophecy, and to Immanuel's commentaries where the exegetical process is championed.

Prophecy and Commentary

As demonstrated throughout this book, the thought of Judah Romano, the philosopher and translator, affected not only Immanuel's own philosophy but also Immanuel's approach to Maimonideanism. Judah's exegetical methodology, evident in his *Be'urim*, offers multiple and equally authoritative interpretations of the same biblical verse, phrase, or word. Although deeper analysis of this method or text is not within the scope of this book, the exegetical approach draws on Judah's perception of the prophet as a philosopher endowed with supernatural ability to cloak universal truths in the figurative language of the biblical narratives. According to Judah, then, the biblical books must be decoded by a philosopher-exegete trained to extract the truths encoded by the prophets from their textual containers.[92] Thus both prophet and philosopher-exegete treat the biblical text as a vehicle conveying universal wisdom, but they approach the biblical text from different directions.

For Immanuel, then, a narrative about a philosopher-exegete who is not only vetted by the prophets but acclaimed as the supreme exegete symbolizes the intellectual apex. This symbolism is clarified in more detail in Immanuel's commentaries. There, he introduces the concept of a divine aide (*ezer elohi*) extended to an individual for various purposes. The term *ezer elohi* appears in Samuel Ibn Tibbon's comment on Ecclesiastes 2:12 ("For what will the man be like who will succeed"), where Samuel explains that no human alone can fully apprehend God. Rather, states Samuel, the individual can apprehend God only with the assistance of a divine aide.[93] Immanuel, however, extends this concept to the philosopher-exegete, championing the composition of a philosophical commentary as a direct road to immortality. The commentary on Proverbs 31, the Woman of Valor narrative, states: "The soul that volunteers to dwell and influence its environment will guide other souls and facilitate their beatitude by means of education. God will lend it a divine aide [*ezer elohi*] to rouse it [the soul] to compose a book on the topic of wisdom and the Torah or its interpretation. This book will stand for generations and people will enjoy it."[94] The reward for educating or edifying others, claims Immanuel, is divine inspiration to write a biblical commentary or book of wisdom for posterity. As a symbol of an author's generous bestowal of knowledge, the commentary represents an author's intellectual apex as well as his ticket to immortality. The power of the commentary resounds in Immanuel's comment on Proverbs 10:6–9, where Immanuel explains that "a righteous individual's name will gain acclaim each day, and his name will never be forgotten because he assists his contemporaries. He converts souls or he writes a book that will serve as an eternal memorial and aide to those that follow him. On account of his active production, his memory will be actively remembered forever, while the names of the wicked will be forgotten."[95]

Immanuel perceives of the authorial act as a sacred enshrining of wisdom for future generations, but it must be aided by a divine spirit. On Psalm 119, Immanuel explains that "man needs a divine aide [*ezer elohi*] to reach the joy of the world to come. Without God's kindness, which rules over his creations, man would never be entitled to reach him."[96] Elsewhere in his Psalms commentary, Immanuel explains that humans are indebted to God, and any goodness that they experience must come via a divine aide. He notes, "When an individual places all his trust in the blessed God and attempts to perfect himself to his greatest capacity, God will lend him a divine aide [*ezer elohi*] and the King of all Kings will extend his scepter. For this, the person will reach this highest level."[97] The divine aide, as conceived by Immanuel, extends inspiration to the commentator and immortality to the perfect individual. As this close reading of *Maḥberet Ha-Tofet V'Ha-Eden* has shown, Immanuel's literary persona is the recipient of both.

Immanuel ends his tour of *Eden* circumventing any description of God or his presence. Instead of a focus on God, as in the culmination of Dante's *Divine Comedy*, Immanuel dwells on the didactic value of the journey for his audience, highlighting the moralizing agenda that underlies the literary tour. The journey through *Tofet* and *Eden* embodies the process of moral improvement and intellectual training, as articulated by Maimonides, that must be undertaken by an individual desiring intellectual perfection. Once Immanuel's literary persona has traversed the tortures of *Tofet* and understood that individual good and communal wellbeing are inextricably linked, he is granted an opportunity to ascend to the next level required in an individual's quest for truth, knowledge, and conjunction with the agent intellect. The Maimonidean focus on perfection of the body and the soul are foundational concepts behind Immanuel's literary tour, which culminates in the area of the biblical authors. Those authors, mostly prophets, have generously provided the keys to universal wisdom and knowledge encoded in their biblical narratives, and only a trained philosopher-exegete can access them to distill those truths for the uneducated. Surrounded by thoughtful and generous moral people, Immanuel's perfected literary persona is impressed with a didactic mission to arrange his vision into a usable and accessible book. From *Maḥberet Ha-Tofet V'Ha-Eden* it is clear that he views himself as a *maskil*, one who conveys wisdom to others, through either his didactic morality tale or his biblical commentaries.

At the tour's end Daniel marvels at the good fortune of Immanuel's character, who has seen "wondrous things from the past and present" as well as the stations of the righteous and the evil spirits. He says: "All this was revealed to you, by the Heavens, so that people on Earth should be aware of what is to come. And, thus, preserve all the things that you have witnessed in your mind, and inscribe them in a book for posterity. You shall keep it close to the ark so that future generations may know the words of this book. Now, while you still walk among the living, cry out and tell the people of your age all the things that your eyes beheld and that your ears heard."[98] Akin to Maimonides' philosopher, who has achieved perfect knowledge to return with it to the people, Immanuel's character is mandated by Daniel to translate his journey into an inspirational text. Recalling his self-identification in *Eden* as a scribe (*meḥokek*) in the area reserved for Judah Romano, here too in *Eden*'s final wisps, Immanuel's persona is assigned a Mosaic role to mediate between the audience of the earthly life and the immaterial ideas of the beyond. Deploying biblical allusions to Moses as divine scribe, splitter of the Red Sea, and God's personal confidant, Immanuel proves in his self-descriptions that he has been appropriately chosen and granted this special status of seer of the netherworld. For this, Immanuel pleads that he should merit reward together with "those who lead the many to righteousness [*maskilim*], forever and ever, like the stars."[99]

Immanuel's belief in the power of authorship to bestow immortality is echoed several times in *Eden*, as Moses remarks: "It has never been heard or seen before that a man like you, a sullied and polluted soul, can interpret the prophetic scriptures as clear as day. You have not earned eternal life through your own righteousness and decency, but only by virtue of your commentaries that explain concealed secrets."[100] In the final moments of *Tofet*, Daniel admits: "you doubtlessly sinned, committed crimes, and transgressed, cursed God and people, and were satisfied with shame rather than glory. Yet, in your tireless effort to interpret the prophetic books, to exhibit their power among the nations, you have publicized their wonders. You earned a reputation among the greatest men of the land and saved your soul."[101] These comments affirm Immanuel's worth as a fount of knowledge. When taken together with the anecdotal "evidence" of Immanuel's erudition, expressed by the incomparable praise of the biblical authors in *Eden*'s heights, the narrative insinuates Immanuel's attainment of that indefinable goal—conjunction with the agent intellect.

* * *

Whereas Chapter 5 explored the sinful or righteous actions that affected social order and communal health, this chapter has highlighted Immanuel's exploration of the mind as a venue for sin or righteousness. Such a focus, which develops the Maimonidean notion that sinful thoughts are far worse than sinful actions, results in Immanuel's redefinition of the concept of "sin" from a wrongful deed to a misguided or erroneous interior process, which leads to harmful consequences for individuals and society. This redefinition results in surprising characterizations in *Maḥberet Ha-Tofet V'Ha-Eden*, such as those of the gamblers and suicides whose sins stem not from their wrongful actions but rather from their lack of trust in God. As in the previous chapter, the biblical commentaries serve as a rich source to clarify or enrich the poetic narrative, heighten the poem's effect, or elevate a local tale into one with universal significance.

Although not directly employed by Immanuel in his *Maḥberet Ha-Tofet V'Ha-Eden*, the Maimonidean dichotomy of corporeal and intellectual perfections serve as a useful analytical frame when analyzing Immanuel's poem. As in the previous chapter, many of the characters and vignettes are concrete manifestations of philosophical ideas from the biblical commentaries, while other characters or situations display verisimilar details projecting an aura of realism onto their tales. A prime example of an idea embodied within Immanuel's characters is that several of *Tofet*'s sinners are stricken with blindness as a physical manifestation of their misguided intellectual states.

Some characters engender surprise in Immanuel's literary persona, reinforcing the notion that only God knows the truth about individuals, especially their intentions. In *Tofet* there is a plethora of communal leaders, officials, and teachers whose insincerity or purposeful misleading causes much damage. In *Eden*, Immanuel's character is surprised to encounter righteous gentiles whose intellectual honesty and integrity led them to espouse rationalism. In the vignettes discussed earlier, the language of the poem alludes to Immanuel's commentaries that discuss related issues, enriching the poetic narrative with more details.

Immanuel's focus on the intellectual perfection of others in *Maḥberet Ha-Tofet V'Ha-Eden*, however, is superseded by the meetings between his character and individual biblical authors. These encounters affirm the importance of the exegetical enterprise to Immanuel, as he explicitly forges intertextual connections between the poem and his commentaries. While the meetings are crafted to appear casual, each biblical figure introduces an important philosophical concept. Thus the meetings with the biblical figures reinforce a core set of beliefs about prophecy and knowledge held by Immanuel and other rationalists. Through Immanuel's blatant self-promotion, his persona is styled not just as comparable to that of the prophets but as an alternate Moses, the ultimate prophet and scribe who translates the ineffable experience for his readers. Conflating the ultimate rationalist telos, intellectual immortality, with the immortality of an author, Immanuel transforms his persona from timid tourist to the ultimate source of knowledge, a substitute agent intellect, mediating between humanity and God.

CONCLUSION

What Is an Author?

Reflecting on the act of composition, Immanuel, in his commentary on Psalms, remarks: "It is customary for people to tell entertaining jokes and amusing riddles to amplify the heart. So too, I recount the sentences that you [God] verbally assign them, that is the punishments you inflict on sinners, so that the nation will hear them, cower, and sin no more."[1] With its sympathetic characters and memorable narrative details, *Maḥberet Ha-Tofet V'Ha-Eden* concretely manifests the authorial role envisioned by Immanuel in his commentary on Psalms. For the armchair traveler, the *maḥberet*'s dramatic vignettes impart moral guidance more effectively than the admonitions of moralistic literature—an insight that may have informed Immanuel's infusion of ideas from his philosophical commentaries into *Maḥberet Ha-Tofet V'Ha-Eden*'s characters. At a time when the term "author" was fraught with multiple meanings, Immanuel projects a clear vision of an author as one imbued with authority (*auctoritas*) to educate his audience. Shaped by Maimonideanism on one hand and by Romance literary conventions on the other, Immanuel negotiates multiple streams of influence and inspiration to craft his poem. To best appreciate *Maḥberet Ha-Tofet V'Ha-Eden*, however, we must step back and contextualize it within the larger structure of *Maḥberot Immanuel*.

Authority and Leadership

Maḥberot Immanuel unfolds with its myriad adventures, riveting tales, and somber meditations on the soul and old age amid a pastiche of verisimilar characters from Italian cityscapes. Immanuel develops his literary persona from a young, inexperienced, and insecure poet to an authoritative model of wisdom and knowledge. *Maḥberot Immanuel* rests on a literary conceit of Immanuel's reputational concerns. His character was shaken by other poets publicly reciting his poems as their own and attributing inferior poetry to him. In response to the character's laments, a noble patron emerges, encouraging Immanuel to collect his poems and invent connective framing prose around preexisting poetry, following Judah Al-Harizi's model in *Sefer Taḥkemoni.* Although the nobleman claims, "I never composed a poem, nor did I ever outline rhymed prose with the tool of my mind," he asks Immanuel to make him a character in the *Maḥbarot* so that "my name shall be engraved upon the tablet of your book eternally."[2] The resounding irony of the nobleman's request is, of course, that while Immanuel honors it, enshrining him eternally in a book, the character remains anonymous, never called anything but "the nobleman" (*Ha-Sar*). The request itself, however, reveals that Immanuel values the act of composition and its ability to immortalize personae.

Immanuel's character responds to the nobleman's suggestion meekly, offering myriad excuses not to follow it. This plotline, together with allusive language and imagery (*shibuzim*), recalls Moses's initiation scene at the burning bush, where a timid shepherd is unwillingly charged with the mission to lead the Israelites and confront Pharaoh. Immanuel's initial plaint is answered by the nobleman, who approaches Immanuel after "the God of the Hebrews chanced upon me," to rouse Immanuel to "go and gather the camp of your poems and rhymed prose," both allusions to Moses's initiation scenes in Exodus.[3] Immanuel's fear, "may I not fail with my tongue," also aligns him with Moses, whose deficient speech makes him hesitant to lead the Israelites. As though responding to Moses himself, the nobleman charges Immanuel to "rise, you of golden tongue and mantle!"[4] By the end of the anthology, Immanuel's persona resembles an aged and experienced Moses.

Throughout the final *maḥberet,* Immanuel compares himself to Moses by identifying himself as a "divine scribe" (*meḥokek*), a splitter of the sea of knowledge, and an intermediary between God and the people. It is not surprising, then, that Immanuel's character, a self-styled revealer of truth, is charged by Daniel, the celestial guide, to preserve his experiences for future generations because "all this was revealed to you, by the Heavens, so that people on Earth should be aware of what is to come."[5] As celestial agent and guide, Daniel imbues Immanuel's persona with *auctoritas,* the medieval measure of authority, gravity, and trustworthiness that truly transforms only the worthiest of individuals into authors.

The development of Immanuel's character, over the course of the anthology, from a timid, youthful bard into a fount of wisdom and knowledge suggests that Immanuel crafted *Maḥberot Immanuel* with an envelope structure, wherein the book's introduction and conclusion overlap in theme and content. Although the order of individual *maḥbarot* differs in the manuscript tradition, *Maḥberet Ha-Tofet V'Ha-Eden* remains the final chapter in every version, because it addresses the very fears and values expressed at the outset of the frame tale. By the end of *Maḥberet Ha-Tofet V'Ha-Eden*, the poet fearing a bad reputation has transformed into a veritable source of truth, recognized and lauded even by biblical figures.

For Immanuel, as expressed in his commentaries, writing a book is a sacred act with sublime consequences. On Proverbs 10:5 ("He who lays in stores during the summer is a capable son, but he who sleeps during the harvest is an incompetent"), Immanuel compares the writing of a book to winning converts to Judaism. He notes that "the memory of a righteous man increases daily and is never forgotten because he aids his fellow man, either by establishing souls during his lifetime [converting people] or by writing a book that that serves as an eternal testament and utility to those who follow him."[6] Elsewhere in his Proverbs commentary, Immanuel describes the act of writing a biblical commentary, especially one revealing philosophical truths concealed within the Torah, as proof of the author's acquisition of universal knowledge. Immanuel's commentary on Proverbs 31, perhaps, is his most explicit exploration of the link among writing a commentary or wisdom book, intellectual actualization, and immortality. There, the exegetical act itself is a reward for granting knowledge and imparting moral instruction to the unlearned.[7] The act of writing constitutes both the reward for his dissemination of knowledge and the vehicle by which Immanuel gains immortality.

In light of the high status assigned by Immanuel to the act of composition, it is no surprise that his character's ultimate act in heaven is the composition of the *maḥberet*, recounting the experiences of Immanuel's persona to edify and inform the living while they still have time to repent. By conflating the philosophers' goal of intellectual conjunction with the immortality of an author, Immanuel's otherworldly tale affirms his ideological position that morality and true cognition lead to intellectual immortality. Despite his quip that the best poetry is deceitful, Immanuel's angelic exhortations to warn the living, amplified by the frequent, almost megalomaniacal, declarations of his self-worth, indicate that *Maḥberet Ha-Tofet V'Ha-Eden* is not mere poetry to him but rather a tale to be understood allegorically. In fact, Immanuel's classification of his poem *Eftaḥ be-khinor* ("I shall begin with a lyre")—a versification of the Maimonidean creed explored in Chapter 3—as wisdom poetry suggests that Immanuel conceived of poetry that conveyed philosophical ideas as a distinct genre. As mentioned in Chapter 6, Immanuel specifies that immortality and a divine aide are extended to the author of a book of Torah interpretation or a matter of wisdom. This book contends, then, that *Maḥberet Ha-Tofet V'Ha-Eden* should be viewed as a matter of wisdom, and, like all texts in Immanuel's eyes, it is multilayered for different types of audiences. Immanuel's view, enshrined in his commentaries, that multivalent texts appeal to audiences with different capacities and interests, is expressed in a comment on Proverbs 15:14 in which Immanuel advises:

> When studying the prophetic books which are allegorical and allusive, one should not be satisfied only with the exoteric meaning, derived from a literal interpretation. Rather, one should rationally seek the concealed secret by peering through the apertures of encased apples of allegory to behold the gold within. For the value of the exoteric interpretation of the text is like silver compared to gold. Foolish people only seek the rind, the literal interpretation of Scripture, and they do not consider its implicit significance.[8]

Recognizing the potency of allegory, Immanuel encourages his audiences to dig deeper to truly appreciate the sense of the biblical passage. While *Maḥberet Ha-Tofet V'Ha-Eden* is not a biblical book, its structure and themes reinforce the Maimonidean idea that communal health and virtue are key social and political precursors to an individual's quest for intellectual perfection.

Demonstrating Immanuel's creativity in marshaling multiple streams of ideas and texts, this *maḥberet* attests to the popularization of Maimonidean philosophy in a more accessible narrative. But Immanuel's commentaries play a key role in understanding *Maḥberet Ha-Tofet V'Ha-Eden*, as the poem draws language and allusions from the philosophical discussions throughout the commentaries. In addition to linguistic links, the characters and plot details embody theoretical ideas expressed in the commentaries by concretizing abstract concepts in sympathetic characters and memorable vignettes. The lessons imparted by Immanuel's character in *Maḥberet Ha-Tofet V'Ha-Eden*, together with the verisimilar tone of the narrative, convey a vivid social critique.

Social Critique and Verisimilitude

Immanuel's tale addresses the merits and deficiencies of communities in Immanuel's own time, although the substitution of the term "so-and-so" in place of actual names makes such corroboration challenging. Vignettes in both *Tofet* and *Eden* feature specific details that were likely meaningful to Immanuel's audiences, and his attacks on enemies and praise of friends resonate strongly even among contemporary readers. As a social critique, *Maḥberet Ha-Tofet V'Ha-Eden* highlights problems in society, entertainingly mocking stock characters while simultaneously elevating the discourse to address universal human anxieties about sin, death, and the soul. Immanuel's interest in ethics is expressed in his homilies on the red heifer and wine preserved from the days of creation, two expositions within a larger independent collection of homilies. In his homily on the red heifer, Immanuel identifies spiritual guides who lead individuals to repentance and change. As this book demonstrates, *Maḥberet Ha-Tofet V'Ha-Eden* serves as a textual substitute for the red heifer ritual. Instead of the biblical ritual stimulating self-reflection and repentance, the *maḥberet*, with its frightening vignettes, serves as a sobering reminder of the ramifications of sin. The ethical imperative expressed by Immanuel's *maḥberet* may reflect a greater emphasis on individual and communal morality kindled by the founding and rapid growth of the mendicant Franciscan order.

The importance of morality is underscored in the transition from *Tofet* to *Eden*, where Immanuel's character is assured of his ultimate blessedness despite his occasional transgressions. Daniel, the celestial guide, reveals:

> The sweetness and richness of the Torah ceased until you arose and returned the crown of scripture to its former state. Added to this, you have crowned your soul with precious attributes. You were never a vengeful or resentful man. If someone wronged you, you immediately forgot it. If someone was kind to you, you remembered it forever. You were not serene nor did not rest until you paid that person back. You were a basket of manna that did not rage about the events of fate. You blessed the merciful Lord for the good and the bad. On account of these things, you have built yourself an enduring house in the angelic world. You never withheld anything good from one who deserves it, and you bestowed your radiance upon anyone who approached you. You were never stingy with your knowledge. You said, "Let me care for all your needs, Whoever is for the Lord, come to me" to anyone who asked. You were a faithful lover,

> a gracious and merciful brother. You never heard of a man mentioning God's name and didn't answer "Blessed is he and blessed is his name."[9]

Daniel asserts the supremacy of intellectual perfection, culminating in Immanuel's composition of Torah commentaries, whose "grammar, literal definitions, innovations, hidden secrets, and wonderful riddles . . . were words of prophecy."[10] But, he adds, the precious attributes of Immanuel's soul compounded his intellectual perfection. Following an extensive narrative that maintains the importance of one's public and private personae consistently striving to live a spiritual, ethical, and intellectual life, Daniel's assurance that moral excellence is a component of blessedness likely addresses the many who will not attain intellectual perfection.

Medieval notions of verisimilitude, derived from classical legal contexts, prepared audiences to receive stories that, today, we would call fictional. The cultivation of a realistic narrative was not for an audience to believe the tale to be truthful so much as it was "knowing the author claims to be realistic, [to] allow themselves to be influenced (attracted or repelled) by the claim."[11] Set in a dream vision, the realistic descriptions of *Tofet* and *Eden*, then, ask the audience to accompany Immanuel's literary persona on a fantastical journey where the audience fuses with the omniscient narrator to learn important, if sometimes harsh, truths about the human experience.

The verisimilar structure and details, inspired by Dante's *Divine Comedy*, offered Immanuel an accessible and compelling literary frame, despite his ideological rejection of a material postmortem experience for the soul. Yet, as Dante's own eponymous traveler achieves authority and worth over the course of his literary journey, Immanuel crafted his *Maḥberet Ha-Tofet V'Ha-Eden* to achieve a similar effect. One of the many differences between these two works is the motivating impetus for the traveler character in each tale. Dante's traveler endures the difficult journey motivated by his love of a beloved lady, Beatrice, who resides in heaven. Despite Joseph Karo's critique of *Maḥberot Immanuel* as an erotic work, this element is completely absent from Immanuel's *maḥberet*. However, the journey of Immanuel's character is, in fact, motivated by love: a love of wisdom and truth revealed through scripture.

* * *

When one considers the legacies of the Iberian Hebrew literary canon, traditional rabbinic literature and exegesis, contemporary philosophical debates, Romance literature, and the *Divine Comedy*, Immanuel's amalgamation of these diverse textual corpora to produce an entertaining and meaningful tale is an astounding compositional feat. Readers of *Maḥberet Ha-Tofet V'Ha-Eden*, however, have yet to appreciate the magnitude of Immanuel's poem, because its richness is appreciable only when juxtaposed with his biblical commentaries. A repository of his philosophical ideas, *Maḥberet Ha-Tofet V'Ha-Eden* conveys complex theoretical notions in embodied characters. Yet Immanuel also inhabited the late medieval Italian peninsula, where maturing communal governments deployed moral rectitude as a corrective to a longstanding culture of violence and vendetta. The centrality of penance and virtue in Immanuel's tale must be read in that context as well. While inspiration is a key factor in *Maḥberet Ha-Tofet V'Ha-Eden*, it is not the defining feature of this poetic narrative.

Working from one chapter of *Maḥberot Immanuel*, this book recasts Immanuel of Rome as an intellectual in his own right, demonstrating that a classification of this individual solely as a poet or imitator misconstrues his intellectual biography. Instead, approaching Immanuel's work as a coherent body reveals that he was actively involved in bridging the cultural, religious, and intellectual worlds of his time, responding to them through a harmonization of philosophy, spirituality, and belletristic literature that is *Maḥberet Ha-Tofet V'Ha-Eden*.

APPENDIX

English Translation of *Maḥberet Ha-Tofet V'Ha-Eden*

Thus spoke the author Immanuel, son of the honorable Rabbi Solomon, may the memory of the righteous be blessed.

After sixty years of my life had passed, the sharp pangs of death hurriedly approached me. Suddenly, a living man passed through death's door: a man of many deeds, a descendant of devout ancestors, but he was younger than me. Seeing this, fears engulfed me, and I said: "Woe is me, ignorant fool! How am I not shamed and disgraced? For I have transgressed, sinned, ruined, rebelled, and drowned in the depths of the sea of the time. I have cursed God and people. My guilt and transgressions have far surpassed those of my ancestors. When, suddenly, I will be beckoned to the beyond, hoisted onto shoulders and carried to the grave, those who know my name will seek me and not find me. What provisions have I prepared for my day of departure, for my discarded soul? What shall I say; how shall I justify myself, and for what shall I hope, if the mercies of the Forgiver and Absolver do not aid me?"

With my mind occupied with such matters, my heart blazed within me, the floodgates of my tears opened, and my howling cries rushed forth like water. I mourned, deeply and bitterly, as I realized that my dejected soul was fated for destruction, because I served my impulse like a toiling slave. I said, "Where, then, is Daniel, the precious man? Where is your wisdom? Would that I knew how to find you, I would come to your dwelling place to question you, and you would answer me. From the streams of your Edenic delight, you would satisfy me, revealing the length of my life and my demise. You would show me my place of final rest and repose."

While drowning in the depths of the sea of sorrow, with my tears flowing like a stream, I slept, saturated with sorrow and despair. A great, dark dread descended upon me, and a vision appeared to me. I was on the River Ulai. My heart went to and fro, flickering like a flash of light. Lifting my eyes, I saw a strong and wild windstorm, hovering and gaining strength, shattering mountains and smashing boulders. After the wind, there was thunder. My ears tingled at its sound, and my eyes shed streams of tears. And after the thunder, there was fire, a sound of stillness, and light shining seven times brighter than the light of the sun. Behold! An ancient man, wearing a cloak, passed before me, looking like an angel of God. Upon seeing him, I was overwhelmed. I fell prostrate on the ground, silenced. When the man saw that I had no strength, he said to me:

"What of you, O Sleeping one? Wouldn't I seek refuge on your behalf! Rise! For this is not time to rest. Today I will help attain respite for you so that agony and despair shall flee." As he spoke to me, I felt stronger. Holding the corner of his cloak, I licked the dust of his feet while kissing them. I said to him, "By my life, Lord, if I have found favor in your eyes, I and your nation, reveal your name!" He said to me, "I am Daniel, the precious man whom you called while tears fell from your eyes. At the start of your supplications, a word went forth to show you terrible things. Today I shall show you mysteries, in figures and secrets, so open your eyes and look around. Mark the word and understand the vision, because I was sent on your behalf. Now, I have arrived, gone forth to teach you wisdom. Shall we descend to the depths of *Sheol* or ascend to the heights? I cannot tarry." I said to him, "My lord, I desire you to show me the world that is everlasting, and the Tofet that has long been established for the wicked. Tell me the place of my post after my death! What type of house will you build for me? Where is my place of repose? Draw me after you and I shall chase you." He said, "I will do as you say!" The man asked me, "To where shall we go first?" I answered, "Tofet will be first, and Eden will be at the end."

Tofet

The man, Daniel, said to me, "Take hold of the edge of my cloak and grip it well, so that no wind shall come between you and me. For the land to which we turn is a scorched land of gloom and disorder. It is called the 'Vale of Corpses.'" As I clasped the corner of his cloak, my mind was terrified. We proceeded, descending down an unpaved path, clouded with distress and gloom where the routes were roundabout. We saw nothing there but lightning and thunder; we heard nothing there but the sounds of women writhing in pain and anguish, like a woman birthing her first child. I called that day "a day of wrath." When we finally reached a rickety bridge, with a stream flowing under it, it was as though the stream snatched up and pinched the onlookers' hearts. Then, my spirit began to wither. At the top of the bridge stood a gate where the revolving sword blazed. The man said to me, "This is called the gate of Shalekhet [Forgetfulness] through which all who depart from the world to find their station in Tofet come this way. Were we not to move from here for an hour or two, we would see those who have departed the world in multitudes; they would cover the surface of the earth twice over. We shall see how the angels of death lead them to a land of waste and desolation, and after that, we shall query them about their pitfalls, and you shall see their fates. There is nothing surprising about their misery, their tremendous ruin, or their pain, for they are a perverse generation, among whom I would not trust my sons. Thus, the angels' swords shall strike them in their hearts."

While sitting there, listening to reverberations of terror, we were stunned by a sound resembling an anguished woman. In unison, the souls said: "Our hope is lost, we have been judged!" When they approached us, we saw a band of evil angels passing by, carrying hundreds and thousands of corpses. When they passed through the gate, the angels said to each one of the souls, "You human! Sated by the bounty of the world, you have cursed humans and God and flouted the rule of ethics. Here you shall vomit that which you swallowed, and reap the fruit of the deeds which you planted. Here you will receive your comeuppance. One who enters may enter, but one who departs is stuck!" Those souls, dragged and carried about, shouted in a bitter voice, shrieking like dying soldiers upon knowing that they would suck the poison of asps.

So, the man, Daniel, said to me, "Have you seen the lost sheep destined to be a target for Tofet's arrows? You will return and soon see that those lost ones number greater than the multitudes of stars." When we had crossed the bridge, and arrived at the underside of the earth (*Taḥtiot aretz*), all those who saw me asked me, "What breach have you committed?" And there, in the land of gloom, we saw a prominent pyre whose darts are darts of fire, like a divine blaze. Its flame is so full of fire and wood that it does not extinguish, neither by day nor night. So said the man, Daniel, to me, "This bonfire, which burns like a river of sulfur, is for those souls who calculated their acts of rebellion. Should you desire to know the names of the sinners within it and their tales, study the names engraved on their foreheads."

When I gazed into the fire, I saw and observed there the people of Sodom and Gomorrah, and Esau, who belittled the birthright. Shimi, son of Gera, is there, as well as Athaliah, who terminated the seed of royalty.

Avshalom, son of Maaḥa, is there, along with the Levite who stood in the house of Micah. Aḥazya, who fell through a trellis, is there beside Sisera, crouched under covers. Haman, son of Hamdatha, enemy of the Jews, is there, together with Amalek, who battled Israel at Refidim. Also, there are Yaazaniah, son of Shafan, Joab, and Yoyakim. The men of Kozeva, Yoash, and Saraf are there for ruling over Moab. I see Yoḥanan, son of Kareaḥ, and Hoshaya's son, Yaazaniah, as well as Ishmael, son of Netanyah. Pharaoh Neḥo and Pharaoh Ḥofra are there. There, I see Gehazi, afflicted with leprosy. Balaam, is there, a son of Be'or, for the Kosbi affair and the thing with Peor. Abimelech, son of Jerubbaal, is there with all the prophets who prophesied in the name of Ba'al. Aḥitofel, the Gilonite, is there, as is Sheva, son of Bichri, a Yeminite. There is Zimri, son of Salu, chieftain of the ancestral house of Simeonites, and there is Sanvalat, the Horonite, and a slave, Toviah, who is Ammonite. There is Geshem, the Arab, and Naval, the Carmelite. Pinḥas and Hofni, the sons of Eli, are cast into pits of dung because they slept with women in their impurity. I see Ahab, son of Kolaia, and Zedekiah, son of Maaseiah, a blight upon the nation, whose actions came to inspire a malediction. Doeg, the Edomite, is there. May all memory of him vanish from the land, for killing eighty priests, bearers of the linen tunic with his hand. Cain is there for killing Abel; Ahab is there, as is his wife, Jezebel. I see Zedekiah, son of Kenaanah, as well as Rehav and Baanah, murderers of Ish-Boshet.

Tziva, Saul's servant, is there for spying on Mefiboshet. Ham is there, too, who saw his father's nakedness exposed. This, to his two brothers outside, he urgently disclosed. The daughters of Lot, impregnated by their father, are there, as well as Pashkhur, the priest, son of Immer.

I see Sihon, king of the Emorites, and the sons of Seir, the Horite. Og, king of the Bashan, is therein. May his ashes rise like the smoke of a kiln. Nevuzaradan, chief of guards, is there with Sanherib and Nevuḥadnezar, who destroyed the Lord's sanctuary. Berah, king of Sodom, and Birshah are there, as well as Kushan Rishataim and Meishah. And evil Titus is there. Ahiman, Sheshai, and Talmai, sons of the titan, are there alongside Antiochus, may he imbibe the poison of pythons. I see Reḥum, the commissioner, and Shimshai, the scribe, as well as the cursed Shlomit, daughter of Divri. There is Uzziah, king of Judah, with leprosy on his brow, and there is Ḥiel the Bethelite, who built Jericho. Jeroboam, son of Nevat, is there for his golden calves and for the month that he devised. The priests of the Bamoth are rife; innumerable licentious women are there, led by Potiphar's wife. I see Amon, who denied God, spurned the Lord's word, and disobeyed his commands. There is Yehoyakim, with his guilty gains, and there are Amnon and his friend, Yonadav, son of Shimah. Peninah is there for angering Hannah, and Shekhem, son of Ḥamor, is there because he tortured Dinah. Yehoash is there for the blood of Zekhariah, as well as Ahaz, son of Jotam, the son of Uzziah. Ba'ashah, son of Ahiayah, is there, together with Azariah, son of Amaziah. Yehoyakim, who caused strife and oppression, is there, along with Zimri, who had Tirtzah in his possession. Evel Merodakh, the dunce, is there, too. Belshazar is there, heaping coals upon his head. He displayed the Temple vessels in a drunken stupidity, to drink with the king, his consorts, concubines, and the nobility. I see Canaan, the cursed, whose sin is concealed and whose guilt is covert. He is grounded with millstones, pounded with a mortar, and boiled in a cauldron. The enemies of Judah and Benjamin, the backbiters, are there on account of their provocations against the builders. I see Aristotle, mortified and mute, for his belief that the universe is eternal. Galen, chief among physicians, is there for casting his tongue to speak ill of Moses, chief among the prophets. Abunazar [Al-Farabi], his day far spent, is there for saying that the conjunction of the human intellect with the agent intellect is an old wives' tale, and for believing in the reincarnation of dejected souls, severed from their nations. He said that they would be supplanted by other people in their stead. I see Plato, a leading adherent of philosophy, for pronouncing genera and species to have an external reality and for thinking of his teachings as words of prophecy. Hippocrates is there for being crafty with his wisdom and concealing his books of medicine. Ibn Sina is there, an object of ridicule and mockery, for saying that the birth of a human not from a human can potentially happen in the future. And he said that the formation of the mountains happened naturally. If only he who is drawn after the belief in the eternality of the world were muted. I see countless people, new and old, who died, long ago or recently, whose number prevents them from being counted faithfully.

From there, we traveled on, and we saw a boiling pot overflowing from the outer edge, which contained copper, iron, tin and lead. A voice commanded: "Set the pot, set it, and place it on the burning coals. Prepare the beasts of prey, for here comes the legion of licentious women whose guilt lures them into hell.[1] They did not desire the eternal life, so they shall be reproached!" The voice was still speaking, and they came through,

1. Immanuel interprets the word מדחפות as a synonym for hell in *Commentary on Psalms* 140:12 in Parma, Biblioteca Palatina, MS. Cod. Parm. 2844, fol. 98v.

enveloping, extinguishing, and embarrassed, as storms that pass through the Negev. They all moaned like doves of the valleys, with tears flowing down their cheeks. They moaned like the sound of doves while beating their breasts. Thrust, quite suddenly, into the boiling vat by a band of evil angels, they broke up in that spot just like meat in a pot. A tremendous voice howled at them: "You did not want any part of the bounty of heaven above, so here is the pit of perdition below: trap, terror, and trench for you! Eat, stuff yourselves with the bounty of the abyss that lurks below!"

From there, we traveled on to find a deep pit: desolate, devastated, and destroyed. No sound resonated from within it but the sound of weeping and the sound of shrieking. Within it were lions, tigers, and spotted scorpions. So said Daniel, the man, to me, "This is called the land of Oblivion, or by another name, Nethermost *Sheol.* It is the place for people who play dice because they said, 'God will not see,' and their blood requires sprinkling. Therefore, the hand of the Lord strikes them, in spirit and body. Because they faced upward while they played, and cursed God with their lips and their hearts when their vessels returned empty, therefore their actions will be handed back to them, and they will not be pitied on the day of revenge."

From there, we traveled on and reached another part of Tofet. I saw a man, a noble of the land, overtaken by hardships, his skin shriveled on his bones, and his face was dull. Burning in a consuming fire, a blaze that does not consume him, he recognized me, and I recognized him. In past times, he loved me, and I loved him. When he saw me walking around and observing, he heaved a sigh from his body. He said to me, "What have you here, who have you here? Have you fallen like the fall of treacherous men; have you too been stricken like us? Have you become like us?" Daniel, my righthand man said, "I swear by my pride that this man, whom I guard like the pupil of my eye, shall not be compared to you. When he runs, he shall not stumble." Then I asked the man who was burning in the fire of Tofet, and I said to him, "Please tell, O pained and raging one, what is the matter that brought you here? For you were a diamond crown on the heads of men of your generation, and now you are nowhere near peace and salvation?!" From within the tempest and the burning flame, the man responded with a bitter sound. He raised his voice and said, "Woe to me, the embittered, disturbed, and pained one, whose soul mourns my existence and whose flesh is pained. What an utter fool I was, for building a house with a synagogue in a place where I will not be able to dwell. If only I had built it in the sky, laying its foundation in the heights of the eternal mountains. Woe to me, woe to me, the foolish shepherd, who abandoned my castle irresponsibly.

I multiplied my things, but did not say: 'Where is my lord, my God, my maker?' I built gardens and orchards, amassed silver and gold, wealth and property, fattened geese and the finery of ornaments, but I forgot the shield of those who seek refuge. I refused to give bread to the poor man, but was generous to several worthless and reckless fellows who ate at my table. Instead of my learning the decrees and the directives, I ate delicacies and drank sweet things. In exchange for good deeds, I had sweet fruits, Helbon wine, and white wool.

"Regarding Torah and its message, I proclaimed them murky matters. I said in my heart, 'To the skies I shall ascend,' but I spiraled downward in the end. Time ensnared me, and I was trapped.

"Like a weaver, I snipped my life short; in darkness I have made my bed. I lamented my decline on account of not serving [God] properly. What is done, is done.

"I left my castle to others, and nothing will remain from all my efforts. How do I profit if all my work is for the wind? As I have been bereaved, so am I bereaved. Who allowed me to buy estates, homes, and fields, for I felt pressured to amass wealth? I had neither son nor daughter, inheritor nor heir, and no relative for whom I could hope to rejoice in his wellbeing. I abandoned everything to a man whom my wife will bed, and on my territory he shall trample and tread. How could I have failed to marry off a grieving widow with my fortune or to satisfy the desires of orphan boys and girls? How did I think to fortify myself in the world of death, when I have built neither house nor courtyard in the heavens? For I know that the effort is enormous while the time is short. Thus, I presently reap what I sowed, and I am in the hand of my Maker like material in the hand of an artisan, in a constricted place with no way to stray right or left. As I had no mercy on the impoverished yesterday, so today there is no man who has mercy on me. There was neither a grandson among my people nor a great-grandchild. Why did I not delight the heart of a widow? For what I spent on the windows, I could have wedded some widows. Woe to me! For a foolish heart led me astray when it wrapped me in a cloak of pride.

"I thought to build a Temple as high as the heavens, with recessed and latticed windows, and to fill it with treasures kept in chests to showcase its beauty to the generals and nations. I made my actions known among my people for I said: 'I have no son [so this] shall be in order to remember my name.' The ritual bath in which I thought my wife would immerse for me was used before me, for someone else, to my shame and disgrace. I planted a vineyard that I did not redeem, and I saw that which I never expected to see. I built an abode that I did not dedicate. My borderlands were filled with olives, but I did not anoint myself with their oil. Upon seeing me build the sanctuary, onlookers said, 'You are praised!' They did not know that I would leave it to the man who would follow me. I did not even sleep in it temporarily. I began to build it, and another completed it, for I did not know that my name would be expunged from among my brethren and from the public square. What is the value of building a vast palace with spacious upper chambers, of coating the locks in silver and gold, of filling my homes and storehouses with florins,[2] with the bounty of the sun's crops and the bounty of the moon's yield, when I lack a father or brothers, sons or daughters? How did I not serve portions from my table and gifts to orphans and widows, to the miserable souls, those oppressed, tortured, enveloped by hunger, conspicuous in every district? Of the evil things that happened to me and weakened me after death, one is this: Approximately two years after [my death], two men frightened me and raised me from my grave. They carried me on the wings of eagles to the city of Ancona and into my abode. When I saw this, I said, 'Perhaps the end of days is here, and the blessed Lord bore the guilt of the many and made intercession for sinners. Perhaps, from this day forth, I shall be at peace.' While thinking about this and that, they said to me, 'Listen, oh wicked One! It is not as you think, for you sit upon scorpions, and you shall go from evil to evil, and you shall find bitterness beyond death.' When I heard this, the light within me extinguished. I extended my hand to them, and I was drawn by them until I was brought to the house of immersion. There, they showed me my wife and her new husband. I saw her disrobing from her embroidered clothes while her new husband stood beside her. She immersed in the ritual bath that I had prepared for the attendant women while I watched with my own eyes.

"Then my eyes began to tear, and I suffered pain and sorrow in ways that neither the mouth can convey nor the ear can hear. Then they said to me: 'What is it to you, O lawless man? If you race with foot-runners who exhaust you, how can you compete with horses? If you stood in shock at the sight of your wife immersing, you will yet be enraged by the vision that your eyes are about to see!' They brought me to the bedroom, and when my eyes glanced about, I saw a blissful couch where my wife slept with her new husband; she was voluptuous and luxuriant.

2. While the Hebrew term פרחים completes the rhyme scheme, it is also used to refer to florins, the Florentine currency.

"His left hand was under her head, while his right arm embraced her. A voice called out, 'You will pay the bride price for a wife, and another man shall lie with her.'[3] Then, from on high, He sent a fire down into my bones. Afterward, they brought me here stricken and stupefied as my lord sees.

"Now my soul wants to pour out of me, for I cannot turn from side to side because my sins and transgressions set a net to entrap me, and rot has set into my bones.[4] At noon my skies darkened, and all that my fathers and forefathers had collected, in the midst of my days, I neglected. Naked I emerged from my mother's belly, and naked I returned to go as I came. I bore nothing from all my toil beside worn rags that were my destiny. My estate has been turned over to strangers and my homes to gentiles. Why build a home for the summer and one for winter when everyone turned their backs on me? Instead of my bath and my oven, I see a river of fire. Instead of my lily-lipped crystal, I see fiery torches and a smoking kiln, fistfuls of futility and furnace soot. Instead of the birds prepared for me, I see a great, dark dread descending upon me. Instead of drinking sweet things and eating choice foods, with bearers of tribute before me, I stumble about at noon as if in darkness, like the dead in the daytime. Instead of being fed fattened swans, I am fed on as sheep feed on meadows. I am engulfed by troubles as the sea is engulfed by water. Instead of the fresh bed, I shall lament as sadly as the jackals, as mournfully as the ostriches. In the evening, I shall sleep in tears and keen in the morning. Instead of the ivory tusks, ebony, gold, many pearls, drinking from golden vessels, vessels of many kinds, rings, hoops, multicolored carpets, fields, and vineyards, I shall see the spreading of nets, lightning and thunder, and a glowering face. Instead of my home's flat roof, I shall lie in sackcloth and ashes. Instead of its sides and its support beams, my name has been banished from among its nation. Instead of the hall, I shall sit humiliated and humbled as an everlasting disgrace. Instead of the barrels and the tower built to hold weapons, birds, and animals, I have the nethermost pit, desolation, and ruins. Instead of the flour, the wheat, dolphin skins, and acacia wood, here I am imprisoned in troughs where my soul lies down among predatory lions. I see nothing but the sacrificed and the slaughtered, those being led to death and left to slaughter. Instead of the presence of a carousing and corrupt crew

---

3. A clever way to use the direct citation of Deuteronomy 28:30 from the litany of curses.

4. Immanuel defines "my soul pouring out" (תשתפך נפשי עלי) as "my soul wants to pour out of me" in *Commentary on Job* 30:16, Paris, Bibliotheque National MS. 235, fol. 53v.

in my home, speaking profanities, here is the fire and the wood, and I am the sacrificial lamb. I dawned from the womb with the dew of my youth, but now my skin has blackened beyond black. Fire consumed me from both sides, and my middle is charred, and it shall be like this tomorrow. If only the days of remembrance happened in my life, I would not have come to this decree. Go and tell whomever still lives their lives about the tales of the sons of the dead, and their stories, so that they can understand their own prospects."

From there, we traveled on and saw a group of blind men, of whom I knew approximately one hundred and twenty. These people were wise, sensible, and known among their tribes as leaders of thousands of Israelites. Daniel, my righthand man, said: "By your life, delight of my eye! These people wore themselves out, for they had eyes with which to see, but they did not see. They knew the levels of wisdom and its value, but they could not see light in its luminescence. When they were once well known on earth, they wasted their wisdom on conventional knowledge, and they mocked the knowledge of the pleasant intelligibles.[5] Therefore, at noon, they must feel around as though in darkness. They must stumble about as though they lack eyes. The conventional knowledge, to which they adhered and which they loved, was abandoned outside of the camp, its charm like a failing spring. Those who recline on ivory beds with their women, abandoned by conventional knowledge, were positioned as a target for the arrows of their maledictions. Here today, they are empty of any delight, for looters have laid them waste, and they are festering in their offenses."

From there, we traveled on and saw an old, large man affixed as a target. His head bore a crown of nettles and thorns, and his nose was stuffed with human excrement, like incense. He was tortured with whips and scorpions, while bowmen gathered around him, spilling his bile to the ground. A cruel viper pulled at his genitals. He was taken to the top of a tall tower and cast from there onto the rocks below. From time to time, he was burned in a strange fire, and from time to time gnashed by wolves of the steppe. At times, a shot from a bronzed bow penetrated him, and at times rivers of tar and sulfur swept him away. Sometimes, the torrents of Belial flooded him, and sometimes the horns of wild oxen gored him. They broke his neck like a firstborn ass. He was thrust about from light into darkness, and hurled as though from the hollow of a sling. They said to him, "Praised is

5. Intelligibles are universal divine truths, while conventional knowledge is wisdom generally accepted by society.

the one who will seize you and smash you against a boulder, O one who loved all pernicious words." He was beaten with the force of battering rams, and given no rest. This happened through the day and night, ceaselessly and with consistency. They added to his suffering constantly, daily. Upon seeing these terrible blows, I cowered away so as not to hear; I was scared off from seeing. I said, "Who is that man whose great suffering I witness?" Daniel, my righthand man, said, "Do you not know who this one is?!" And I said, "No, my lord!" He said to me, "This man is wayward, defiant, and an imposter; in the past, he was called by the title: Master. A sinner like him has not appeared since the days of the [Temple] destruction. He studied Torah not for its own sake. He, like Ammon, incurred much guilt. No amount of licentious behavior was enough to please him. Infected by evil, he targeted every animal to mate with it. Inebriated with intoxicating wine, this man sullied the Torah of Moses with his abominations. He devoted himself to doing evil in the eyes of the Lord. He profaned what is holy to the Lord—that which he loves—and espoused the daughter of a foreign god. He became infatuated with the foreign women, groped the gentile ones. He never let any woman escape, neither a handmaiden, a gentile, an Ammonite, a Moabite, a Jew, a Christian, or even an Egyptian maidservant. He violated the covenant, deflected blame, thus his fate is excision of his name. His soul is sullied and polluted, lacking knowledge. He put it in every woman regardless of her status: menstruating, impure, diseased, or leprous. He banged both the saddled she-ass and the pig, sticking it in its mouth and rear end. He sought out slave girls, neither fully owned nor free, pierced professional handmaidens, foolish and insane women, the wicked Queen Athaliah, the prostitute demanding it orally, the impoverished, the limping woman, even the pregnant woman crouching down to give birth. There is no woman who had ever been with a man, from here to Jahaz, Kedemoth, and Mephaat, that had not been mounted by him. This was made known through all the land, thus it is no surprise that he drinks the dregs from a cup of poison. He knew his Maker—and intentionally rebelled against him. He sinned and led the multitudes to sin, so the guilt of the many hangs on him. His face is fat and fleshy. He is another Antiochus in his deeds and another Haman in his heart. His is a Jeroboam with his golden calves and a Manasseh with his sword. He profaned the Name [God] for days and years. His abominations and his blasphemies, both old and new, are written in the book. Go and tell the easily tempted fool that Tofet has long been appointed, and he will drink from the wrath of Shaddai. He will neither be favored nor be pitied, like the cities razed by the Lord with no mercy.

For he denied God above and begot the base plotter, the one who thinks badly about the Lord. Therefore, he should know that hail and flashing fire, terror, pit, and entrapment is laid out for him. When one advocates on his behalf and says, 'Redeem him from descending to the Pit,' his fruits will be severed from above and his roots from below on account of his rebellious soul that refuses to return."

From there, we traveled on and saw two men trapped in Tofet's snares. When I perceived their silhouettes, I recognized them, and I was stupefied! How, I wondered, did they reach such an evil state? For these were pioneers in the kingdom of wisdom and understanding, followed by the people. I asked Daniel, my righthand man, "Why have such things befallen these two, my lord?"

The man said, "These are two brothers from Maresha whose stinginess was their legacy. They deemed tightfistedness sanctity and generosity, foulness and stench. Their hand was modest, untouched and unknown by a man.[6] They renamed charity: Beriah, Misfortune and anything like it, Maḥlah and Noa, Ailment and Wandering.[7] Their hands are like leeches, always demanding: 'Give, Give!' They fashioned gods of silver and gods of gold for themselves, which they loved with all their hearts, all their souls, and all their might. They said, 'This is the way of man.' They did not link their wealth, honor, and precious objects to the kindness of their creator and restorer, He whose kindness extends to every living being. Nor did they reckon that life was a loan in their hands. They did not serve anyone other than themselves, and they did not want anyone aware of their secrets to serve them. Already from the day that God created man, they have had no matters with men. They said that they found a maxim in Greek wisdom [literature], 'Mine is mine and yours is yours—this is the golden mean,' but they forgot that this is a principle of Sodom and Gomorrah. As though they cut a sprig from those places, their intention was set to gather and hoard money until their demise. They said, 'By our own might, we prepared all this loot through our own wisdom, for we are clever.' When they saw paupers, too mortified to beg, they averted their eyes, calling 'Flee, Impure One' after them. They despised the destitute poor as Muslims despise pigs, as pretty girls monks, and as cats mice. They felt no qualms about the ruination of the poor, the naked, and destitute homeless. When a poor person

6. The Hebrew reads "virginal, unknown by a man."

7. These are names of female characters in the bible but can also connote an evil daughter (Beriah = Bat Ra'ah), illness, and wandering.

would plead before them, they fled from him beyond eyeshot. And to every needy and destitute person they would say, 'How foolish you were in wasting all that you inherited from your ancestors!' Never did they ever give a coin to a pauper that did not lead to regret, an angry face, and alarm. It was sheer horror to grasp the message. When they would hear that someone was down on his luck, they would say, 'His actions caused this, for he did not pinch pennies like us. Nor did he order his affairs as we ordered ours.' They guarded their eyes from the impoverished, and shielded their faces from seeing the exiles. Every relative and acquaintance distanced himself from their house. If they saw a traveler, they berated him until he fled far away. 'Furnish him' [Deuteronomy 15:14] was erased from their books. They said that they tried to 'send your bread forth upon the waters' [Ecclesiastes 11:1] once or twice, and on most days, they did not find it. Thus, they erased it from their books. Their hands faithfully followed the verse, 'distribute portions to seven or eight' [Ecclesiastes 11:2], and said that the best of interpretations was to divide a piece of poultry between seven or eight people rather than dividing a whole chicken between two people, as fools do. They expounded 'You must open your hand to him' [Deuteronomy 15:8] as meaning: One must open the five fingers of the hand and slap the face of the poor man with them, to frighten him, since frightening him was God's intention. One of them swore to God, his Creator, on the life of his eldest son, that in his copy he found the word 'lo' [to him] spelled with an aleph [meaning not]; while the other explained the verse 'You must open your hand to him' [Deuteronomy 15:8] to show the poor man that there is nothing in your hand that belongs to him. They said that the meaning of 'You must lend him' [Deuteronomy 15:8] is to confiscate a pauper's pledge when you lend him enough for whatever he needs.

"When he read scripture, he only wanted to know the Midrash, the Hebrew text and the translation, but any rational matter was driven out like the stormy sea. They had reason, foresight, and shrewdness, but they did not use it for any wisdom. If they heard a matter of wisdom, they mocked it, and if they saw one, they buried it. They regarded wisdom as baseness and infamy, the pursuit of wisdom as madness and folly. They said that the study of logic is null and void, worthy of scorn. Regarding the students of philosophy, which is sweeter than honey and flowing nectar and is forged in the forge of reason, those brothers said that they are merely plucking scrubby shrubs. They thought that, by distancing themselves from looking at a matter of wisdom, they would be placated, as though just by gathering at wisdom's gates, they would break through. They did not know that wisdom is a ladder, set upon the ground, whose top reaches to the Lord of the universe. As a person ascends its high rungs, he approaches God by his ascent. As he retreats, he shall be distant from him, the Exalted One, and his soul and body will be consumed. Every man is mandated to act in accordance with his capacity, and so, a person who wallows in the ocean of ignorance harms his soul. There is no justification for the negligent and indifferent one, who shall pay for that which he stole from the sanctuary. Had these arrogant people, resting untroubled in their spots, full of sap and freshness, only sought out wisdom as silver and hunted it like treasure, then they would have collected tons and tons of it, just like when silver was as plentiful as rocks in their homes [1 Kings 10:27]. How did they not wake from their slumber, as they are in their seventies, and yet unable to stop gathering wealth and hoarding? The sorrow in their hearts increased, because it was said, 'But I will leave a poor, humble folk among you' [Zephaniah 3:12] to frighten them, lest their honor diminish. They thought that a man can sin only in sleeping with a married woman, or worshipping the [idol of] Ba'al, stealing others' money, immersing oneself among the children [ways] of the gentiles, or worshiping foreign gods. They forgot that when true knowledge is absent, espousing foreign ideas from Edomites, Sidonites, and Hittites is graver than monetary theft. Stealing the rational part from the intelligized parts of the soul and from the exalted sciences is worse than any theft or robbery. They recognized that their intellects were naked, but did not cover them, and they detached them from any logical matter. They said that they do this because of what is written in Ecclesiastes, 'For what will the man be like who will succeed the king over what was built up long ago?' [Ecclesiastes 2:12]. For since a human lacks the capacity to reach the level of an ideal man, it is preferable to remain on the lowest stair, for he shall toil to no purpose, he shall not bear children for terror. They did not know that he who cannot become the king—it is more desirable to be his adviser than on par with the man who takes out the garbage. He who cannot be an adviser—it is more desirable to be an officer or cavalry than a carpenter or smith. He who cannot be an officer—it is more desirable to be a merchant rather than an ironsmith or a carpenter. It is better to be a vizier and administrator than a trader or peddler; and better to be a trader or physician than a cook or baker. It is better to be head chef than to be one who goes door to door. It is preferable to be a judge or scribe than a weaver, tailor, or gravedigger. It is better to be a silversmith than one who sacrifices sheep and breaks the necks of dogs. If one cannot be like Moses, his heart shall not compel him to act as

Manasseh. He should try to be like Joshua, with God's consent, and if not, he shall be like Samuel. If one does not merit to be an Elijah, he should be like Elisha rather than like Birsha and Mesha[8] and like one who steals for a piece of bread. If one cannot be like Jeremiah, he shall be like Barukh ben Neriah rather than an Ahaz, son of Jotam, son of Uzziah. Therefore, those who could have climbed up the ladder of wisdom and did not ascend are expelled from the palace of the king, my Lord of Hosts, and their feet are trapped in this pit where they fell."

From there, we traveled on and saw a man whose right hand and tongue were shredded. Placed as a target for the drawn arrows of bronzed bows, his bile spilled to the ground. He was roasted in an iron pan, drowned in bitter waters, hanged on a tree, and stoned with rocks. I asked the man who spoke to me about his circumstances and the reason for his exaggerated suffering. He said to me, "This man had a tongue that spoke in arrogance, but in his heart he devised wrongdoing. He cursed at his father, spit in his face, and ran to him defiantly with his thickly embossed shield. He struck his father once and twice until his father's cry ascended to heaven. Thus, he endures fire and water, for the Lord has done with him as he planned. His name, and those of his friends, will never be mentioned again, for the Lord, our God, has silenced them. How could this accursed one, a wicked man deserving of death, not realize that those who curse their fathers and mothers, who fed them their milk and suckled them with their blood, shall be stricken by the hand of the Lord to uproot them from the camp until their demise? This fool forgot that, through that same father and mother, whom he hit, he entered the earth's atmosphere. Therefore, one should not be amazed at his eternal embarrassment. On account of cursing his father, his tongue was shredded, and on account of hitting him, his right hand was mutilated, so that his voice should no longer be heard on the mountains of Israel. May his wealth cease, except for his anxieties and troubles that he suffers because of his attributes."

From there, we traveled on and reached another place of Tofet, where we saw Hebrews hanging by their tongues. Surrounded by people wielding bows in order to torture them, they were shot and struck suddenly by arrows. When I was confounded, confused, and perplexed by the depth of their malevolence, the man speaking to me said: "Do not be confounded by their abandonment and by the wicked spirit of God that abuses them.

---

8. Birsha was the king of Gomorrah mentioned in Genesis 14:2, and Mesha, king of Moab, in 2 Kings 3:4.

For these people were not like their fathers, who were hallmarks on the tablet of time's heart. Rather, they lay on ivory beds, sprawled out on their couches. Every weekday they slept, curled in comforters, until the fourth hour. They said, 'All of Israel are the sons of kings only on Sabbaths, New Moons, and on the sanctified festivals of the lord.' They said, 'Shall we arm ourselves hastily? Who is like us? Who can summon us? Who is the shepherd that stands before us?' Only three times a year did they rise for the first sin offering. On the day of atonement [Yom Kippur], they rose in the early morning, but fasted in strife and contention. They said no man knows the prayer *'Shoshan Emek Ayumah'* ["Rose of the valley, standing in awe"] like them, for it is their legacy from their fathers. They fought over prayer places; their throats called out that only they are worthy to sit beside the ark. This one said, 'I will pray on Yom Kippur,' while that one said, 'I will read the scroll [of Esther] on Purim.' These mournful ones said, 'Is it possible that those poor Jews recite "There is none like You" [Ein Kamokha] on the three pilgrimage festivals? Who shall complete the five [books of Moses] on the festival of Simhat Torah if not men of power and authority? Who shall pray on the day of the Sabbath and New Moon if not people of sanctity? Who shall recite the vision of Isaiah, son of Amots? Only those who aid the wronged! Who shall pray on the day of Hoshana Rabbah? Only us, sons of the next world! Who shall pray on the feast of unleavened bread? Only those who repair breaches, who are a gazelle among all the lands! Who shall pray on holidays and festivals? Only the clan chiefs in charge of numbers! If we don't amplify the splendor of our voices in the choirs, in the delightful yotzrot [liturgical poems] and prayers, when will the she-goats hear our voices?! With what shall we crown our heads if not with the splendid reading of the Haftorah portions on the festivals and holidays?' These men said such and such about themselves. They thought that this was the way of man. Because pride adorned their necks, this evil infected them."

From there, we traveled on and saw tyrants hanging from trees with severed thumbs and big toes. The birds picked at their flesh, while ravens and eagles gouged out their eyes. Hail and flashing fire rained down on them, destroying their fruits from above and their roots from below. Upon seeing this, my heart melted like wax, and I queried the man speaking to me about them. He said to me, "These people! The smoke of folly rose in their nostrils, they hardened their hearts and stiffened their necks. They roared like young lions and seized their prey; therefore, the stars of their twilight have darkened. They were the Lord's nation who left his land, but when they went out to gather [grain] and found none, they coveted and seized fields and houses. They cast off the yoke of heaven, for they are enemies with destructive plans. They stole, deceived, and put things in their bags, not gathering from what you gave them, but twisting their paths. Because they stripped the mantle with the cloak, they were stricken with madness and blindness. Even though the tablets and the tablet shards rest in the ark, these men will have no part or memory in the Lord's sanctuary, for their fate is a banquet of drunkenness and destruction twice over."

From there we traveled on and saw wrath, indignation, and trouble when we saw men burned in a kiln and hacked with saws. With faces as black as the edges of a cauldron, they cried in anguish, howled with broken spirits, magnified their bitter mourning. When I saw the depth of their evil, I was resistant, too anguished to hear, too frightened by the sight; I almost fell to the ground. Daniel, the man speaking to me, said, "These people went astray from birth, they were defiant from the womb. Their hope was lost, and they were banished from the land of the living when they acted cruelly against their souls, having gathered the fortitude to kill themselves. Their bones, therefore, were scattered at the edge of She'ol and they were expelled from the nest, spurned from ever seeing goodness, inheriting fire consuming fire. Mindlessly, they thought that their deaths saved them from trouble and wrath, but these dismal ones did not know that they went from evil to evil, for my Lord's anger billowed at them and they reaped the fruits of their labors."

From there, we departed and arrived at Tofet's depths. We saw a pit that was so much worse than the others, that to describe it is beyond the power of the tongue. In that place, there were white-hot coals and sharpened arrows,[9] venom of asps and poison of vipers, a serpent, a snake, and spider's poison. In that place was every illness and every plague, even those not inscribed.[10] In that place was the pestle with the grain. There fiery creatures prey, and there fiery flames burn, almost snatching the hearts of all who see them. I inquired about the pestle and the grain, so as to know their purpose and function. The man said to me, "This pit, called the 'pit of destruction,' was prepared in advance for all the children of the foolish shepherd, especially Ḥiel the Bethelite. He is ground seven times a day in the mortar with the grain by the pestle. This is besides what the preying animals did to destroy

9. See Immanuel's *Commentary on Psalms* 120:4, in Parma, Biblioteca Palatina, MS. Cod. Parm. 2844, fol. 61v.

10. In Deuteronomy 25:61, God threatens the Israelites with a litany of curses, including ailments they know and unnamed ones yet to come.

him, and besides that which the consuming fire did to him." I asked about Ḥiel's tale to see whether I would recognize him from his details. The man speaking to me said, "His beginning was shameful, and his ending was shameful. Throughout his life, he never fulfilled any part of a vow he made. Faith, in his eyes, was heresy, while lying and deception were regarded as wisdom and understanding. He fashioned axes from Torah's words, which he learned for the sake of cheating and craftiness. In his heart, the fool said, 'I made myself crowns of falsity and deception because the goal is to nullify contracts forever.' He spewed out any secret entrusted to him, and he fabricated and spread lies about men more righteous than he. If others' monies reached him, he squandered them. A ferocious beast, he was evil to the heavens and evil to humanity. An arrogant man like Balaam, a stain on humanity and the scorn of the nation. He sinned and caused sin like Jeroboam. He is as fitting a replacement for David as Doeg the Edomite, and he is a troublesome one who alienates his friend. A man of crooked heart, he is an avenger and enemy. Any fellow city-dweller of his pays dearly with his soul. When the man admits his myriad faults, surging like the ocean's roar, it is only a drop in the ocean of his errors, for he has collected embarrassment, shame, and crimes. Not stingily either. For he has no part in loyalty. Go out and see how the nation talks if you want to know how his cruelty resembles ostriches in the desert, what his abominations and blasphemies are, how he destroyed and smashed the intellect's gates, how he became furious with my Lord and his anointed one, and how he is a man who is not a man. Knowing that he is a lawless man, his ancestors and father's household considered him as one of the men who plundered the threshing floor. They never showed him the registers, never sent him to the storage trunks, and they concealed the secret of the hidden things from him. Out of fear lest he lose these things to looting and to plunderers, his family gave their treasures to their heirs. They never placed him in charge of their accounts, lest he steal their meager rations. Therefore, it is no wonder that his head was harpooned and the fruits of his land and his property were inherited by locusts. He never denied himself whatever his eyes desired, nor did he bestow any of his wealth on the disaffected. Since he couldn't bother to do good deeds, by my life, if such and such should happen to him, or his day shall come and my Lord shall strike him and this pit shall be his final resting place, then he will receive double for each of his sins." When I heard the man's words, I recognized Ḥiel the Bethelite from his details, and knew that it was not for nothing that he was caught in his own traps. Truly, he was deserving of that place, and that place was deserving of him and those evil ones of his age. It is no wonder if his soul mourns itself and his flesh is pained over itself, for he is a son who spurns his father. Destined from birth to be an instrument of havoc, he, therefore shall receive evil from God.

From there we traveled on and saw about one hundred and fifty men trapped in Tofet's snares. When I examined their silhouettes, I knew them as leaders of their ancestral houses. I was truly astonished at the depth of their evil, especially when recalling their exalted and splendorous status, their good deeds, and their righteousness. These were chief speakers in all places, discerning and prominent; these were famous men! When I asked the man speaking to me about their tale, especially the matter that turned them evil, he said to me, "These were great men of the generation. But where they should have, wholeheartedly, given support to repair the House of the Lord and mend its breaches, instead they sent drunkards and gluttons, who profaned the sacred in the eyes of the Lord, to lead prayers before God. Men like the one who hollers before nations, who, while he recites prayers, winks his eyes and shuffles his feet like an ass carrying books. A wicked man, who gloats about his soul's desires, but when he raises his voice, he causes hinds to calve. One does not know whether he blesses or curses. Anyone who hears his prayers says critically, 'What is this sheep bleating in my ears?' They should have chosen a prayer leader with abundant stores of knowledge, supplying produce of all kinds, whose lips and heart should be one, collecting his ideas for God, neither the lustful type nor one who was raised on love tales and not one who sought arrogance. Rather, he should be God-fearing and straying from evil, but instead they chose a polluted and wicked man, a veritable Gehazi the Leper. How is this man, this boor, fit to be a representative for prayers? Addicted to images, he is submerged in graves of lust. He understands nary a word of what he recites, for his ancestors did not stand at Mount Sinai. Shall a thief curse and scorn the Lord? Should a man who does not speak with knowledge and whose words lack understanding be dispatched to a prince or admiral? How were they not ashamed to send an impure soul and a trickster, who hauls sin with cords of falsehood, before the king of kings? Just offer it to their governor! Will he accept them, or will he turn to their offering? If they have a matter before a patron, prince, or a scribe, they should choose a moral man, a counselor, or skilled artisan to advocate on their behalf and to save them from a fowler's trap. How can they choose an everyman? Jeroboam's calf who stands before the Ark as if disturbed? It is no wonder if evil approaches and overtakes them." It was sheer horror to grasp the message.

From there, we traveled on and saw people whose sun and moon became dark, and the light was dimmed because of them. Possessing neither form nor beauty, they stood in a place of darkness and gloom like a degraded kingdom. As though defying God above, breakers of death encompassed them, while torrents of Belial terrified them. Upon seeing them drowning in the mire of the depths of sorrow, like people who steal from God and humanity, I inquired about their actions and about the matter that brought them to see such things. He said to me, "These are the wicked ones who learned Torah, Prophets, Writings, Mishnah, Talmud, Sifrei, Sifra, the Tosafot, commentaries, compilations, and novelties. But they made Torah and its wisdom into crowns and axes, crowns by which to glorify themselves and axes by which to feed themselves. They did not love the Torah and wisdom because of their greatness and for the splendid glory of their majesty. They just made them tools by which to reach other things. With their deficient and damaged minds, they thought that things reached by virtue of Torah and wisdom have a higher value than Torah and wisdom. They did not know that Torah and wisdom are like ships fully stocked with merchandise, themselves meant to be reached and sought after, their grandeur craved and chosen, not to be used as a means to reach other things. For they are the things that place us closer to God, 'to dwell among the cherubs.' Therefore, whosoever intends to reach any material end by means of Torah and knowledge, to know the ways of the living God, or to glorify himself amongst the living, has dreamed a dream and not trodden a safe path. His actions will not be desirable, for Torah and wisdom are the essential life. As Solomon said, 'For he who finds me, finds life.' He did not say, 'For he who finds me finds something that causes him to merit life,' just he who finds me finds the thing of life. For the words of Torah are life to those who find them."

From there, we traveled on and saw lawless men trampled by the hooves of fiery horses, inundated by anguish as water inundates the sea. I said, "Who are these men seized by a curse and annihilated by judgment?" The man said, "These treacherous men stalked the doors of the ritual bath to see the comings and goings of women purifying themselves from impurity. They chased vanity but they were naughty. Each man catcalling at another's wife, their filthy mouths demanding to know about the women. Therefore, they bob about beneath a bonfire. As the swagger of lust has embraced them, so has evil infected them. So many modest women were prevented from immersing because of them. With their eyes spent with tears, the women looked to heaven to inflict vengeance upon the men. Those fools did not know that they take someone's life as a pledge. For of the modest women, there are some who refused to immerse then because of them, and never merited to immerse at all. Thus, God said to overwhelm them."

From there, we traveled on and saw people bound in shackles and deposited into the mouths of lions and prowling bears, destroying them. When I studied their feeble figures, I saw that they were communal leaders, known among all the people on earth for their fame and renown.

I said, "How can the law destroy the righteous ones of their age? For these men were a treasure to the people of their generation. How can they toil vainly and bear useless children?" The man speaking to me said, "These accursed ones, when they prayed in public, their prayers were as solemn as the Yom Kippur service, with 120 bows and genuflections. They made a display of fervent concentration over every word, subservience and trembling from the beginning to the end, and utmost genuflection, so that each disc in the spinal cord could be seen. But when alone, in their own palaces and courtyards, nary a word of prayer exited their mouths. Mentally meandering the streets of their sinful thoughts, they gave their hearts over to sin. They were as grievously corrupt as in the time of Gibeah, proclaiming murder and raising battle cries, acting impiously and preaching disloyalty against the Lord. They were sanctimonious among their contemporaries; they stood up staunchly for sin, like Dathan and Abiram. They forgot their maker, clung to their inclination, exchanged their worth for disgrace. Therefore, God's anger was incensed at them, and he left them neither root or nor branch."

From there, we traveled on and beheld pits filled with snakes, flying serpents, hundreds and thousands of preying lions and tigers. Surrounding them, angels of death drew their swords, releasing a surge of rushing waters while snatching the hearts of all those who saw them.

I said, "For whom are these [pits] that desire to destroy?" He said to me, "These are for the diviners, the sorcerers, those who consult ghosts, family spirits, diviners, soothsayers, evil, idolatry, and the use of idols that chirp and moan. These are thrust by the fury of the Lord, pushed away at the decree of the king, my Lord of Hosts. On account of their deeds, the land is defiled, and, therefore, God's anger became incensed at them."

From there, we traveled on. Glancing here and there at all the places in Tofet, we saw people ensnared in locks of hair, taken to death, and condemned to slaughter. Angels of death placed them on trial, flogging them with whips and scorpions. When I studied their silhouettes, I recognized them, and I was stupefied at seeing them destroyed. For these were Efratim, settlers of the land regarded as men of ethics and humility. I thought they would have a hopeful future because of what these doleful ones suffered in their lives, from the loss of money to the death of their sons. I asked the man speaking to me about them, to know who tripped them in their traps.

He said to me, "These are the people who, when found by evil, proclaimed: 'We are innocent! Neither for our sins nor for our crimes have we have endured punishment.' When they suffered the loss of money and children, they attributed it to the natural way. When evil accosted them with physical pain and illnesses, they did not say: 'It is because of Miriam!' Therefore, even though the loss of children is an atoning sacrifice, to rage and roil against heaven is absolute rebellion. Although one who fears the word of my Lord, and gushes at his goodness, shall not rage when his suffering grows great. Rather, he should consider it repayment of his debt, which he should accept willingly with love. Then, it will be regarded as a voluntary burnt offering. Should he lose his wealth, he should think that the blessed God will accept his collateral object, and not be enraged at giving up the object that was placed in his possession. He should know that while money in his hand is a pledge, he is required to use it in service of the Lord, who gave it to him. When he will fulfill his duty with it and return it to its owner, he should show the joy in his heart and his words and intend to rectify his actions. He should not think an object was taken unlawfully from his possession, but that he is returning a pledge."

From there, we traveled on and saw people rotting in their sin, for marauders had laid them waste. While they were alive, I considered them righteous people. Here, they were impaled on a tree, then torn apart like a goat-kid being torn. At times, they were slung in the hollow of a sling. I said to my righthand man, "Tell me, my lord! These people never sinned, nor did they divide others' money. Why have they now been brought to see this?" He said to me, "Son of Man! These people, whom you defend by saying that they never sinned, nor did they have dealings with others, did so because the opportunity never reached their hands. But their thoughts, to act impiously and preach disloyalty against the Lord, were of an evil nature. They appeared asleep, but their hearts were awake, storming and burning in the fires of jealousy and lust. When the chance arose to act malevolently in secret, they did it. When other people's money came to their hands, they divided it. They devised lies, things they neither heard nor saw, about righteous men and spread them. These fools did not know that the Lord's eyes scan all throughout the land. When they commit evil, they hide themselves, for they fear people. They appear righteous, but they are wretches. They were not cautious and not prudent before the one who examines hearts and minds, the Lord of the world whom nothing escapes, the one who will take them out of this world and will bring them to judgment after their deaths. They did not fear his wrath, and they disobeyed him. Therefore, their faces are reddened by tears."

From there, we traveled on quickly and saw people in Tofet whom I considered holy, because they gave up their lives and sanctified the Lord, their holiness. Having turned their bodies into burnt offerings and sacrifices, no perverse words escaped their lips. I was amazed to see them in such a bad way, so I asked the man speaking to me about this event. He said to me, "These people bear a debt, for they were supposed to receive their cruel death with love, viewing it with sweetness and delight. They should have said, 'How fortunate we are! How great is our portion! How pleasant is our fate to have been tested! Today, we will merit to take refuge in the celestial mysteries, and today we exit the vale of tears, standing to receive blessing with the ten royal martyrs. Today, we will see our sanctity and the beauty of our inheritance. Today, we will inherit eternal lives and be saved from Tofet, which is reserved for the wicked.' But, at the last moment, they became upset because of their miserable souls. They regretted their original stance, and they forfeited both their original merit and the merit of their martyrdom. They said: 'We participated in the Lord's guard and walked at the end, and what is the outcome of keeping his guard, for we walked with sadness?' Therefore, ruination adhered to them, and it shall be sheer horror to grasp the message."

From there we traveled on and saw the outer edge of a bronze pot brimming with tin and lead. Inside it, a naked man was imprisoned in fetters. A constant fire burned under it; surrounded by fire and wood, the flame never extinguished. Near the pot, there was a deep and narrow pit filled with terrifying ice, and the angels of fury and wrath removed him from the strange fire and buried him in the ice. Then, they cast him from the ice back into the pot. They did this daily to frighten him and gave him no rest. I asked the man speaking on my behalf about him and the reason for his anxiety. He said to me, "This wretched has man strayed unfaithfully from God and committed adultery with another man's wife. Overtaken by the curse, he is shamed and humiliated, since he scorned the Lord's word and violated his commandment. He sinned in that he taught his friend's wife to commit adultery with others, to desire strangers. She birthed bastard children from them, so her husband, who did not regard these boys as his sons, refused to acknowledge them. He hid himself so as not to take responsibility for them, nor did he teach them wisdom and morals. The boys, upon knowing they had no protection, trod a path of evil consumed by their wickedness. Occasionally they meant to sin while sometimes they inadvertently strayed, but at the end, they took others' lives and lost their own lives. It was as if that adulterer had killed them all with his sword, so the collective sin rests upon him. These wild animals did not know that grave sins occur because of a single sin. No one knows this except He who penetrates hearts and minds; He whose counsel is profound; He whose wisdom is marvelous. From a single insignificant misdeed come multiple repercussions. As wise men say, one should not regard the meekness of sins, because when we view the majesty of the commanding Lord, the troublemaker's smallest unintentional act will be as grave to him as if he had done it on purpose."

From there, we traveled on and saw a man whose face was blacker than soot and whose skin had shriveled up on itself. His skin was stripped off him, and he was hung on a tree where vipers and snakes devoured him. When I saw this, I was terrified and seized by fear of death; I was almost destroyed. I asked the man speaking to me [Daniel] about the reason for which this man experiences such malevolence. He said to me, "This man spilled innocent blood, and, therefore, it is no wonder that he vomits what he swallowed. Thinking that he killed only one soul, really, he killed many. For the pained wife and sons of the murdered victim, having lost their protection, stole, broke the faith, and took other people's things in their bags. When their deeds became known and evident to others, some of them were exiled afar, while others were hanged on a tree. Those who lost their money lamented with great and heavy sorrow, like the laments of the victim of Haddadrimon, son of Tabrimon. They were slayed by the flickering flame of poverty and lack. Since one transgression begets several transgressions, one should not be amazed at how sinners are dragged to a day of wrath and engulfed with suffering, as waters cover the seas. The sinner's wickedness is so great that it occasions mighty and weighty sins."

From there, we traveled on and saw deep pits filled with suffering, distress, and flaming fire. All who saw these despaired of ever seeing goodness again. In that place, there were trials of different design, angels of death as cruel as ostriches, and judges sitting on saddle rugs judging sinners to the four judicial sentences. In that place, neither mercy nor compassion ruled, just weak hearts, and the sounds of crying and lamentation like the distress of a woman birthing her firstborn child. In that place is the sound of shrieking, like the groaning sounds of corpses, and those whose hearts are expiring. In that place, the spirits of the dying cry out, howling from heartbreak, wailing in brokenness, and intensifying their bitter grief. Ears just quiver at that sound, while eyes spill tears. When I saw them, I was seized with tremors. My heart wandered; I shuddered in panic. I was too anguished to hear, too frightened to see what happens to sinners' souls. I said to the angel speaking to me, "My lord! This vision has turned my insides out, and my heart is not strong enough to see each and every soul and the judgment meted out on it. However, after having seen some specific examples of their suffering, please tell me the general nature of these souls' sins. Why are they here, and what are their tales? Let this be an admonition to the generations that follow them." The man said, "Your verdict is true, and I will listen to you. Now pay attention to my words and admonish the hearts of the wayward with your writings.

"Know, my son, that some of these people you see in such distress extracted foreign, non-Jewish ideas, insights, and premises from the sciences and traditions. They used them to deceive people and trip them in a fowler's trap, as though the traditions and the sciences were nets and utensils for deception. Therefore, the sinners bear the same confusion. Some people had deaf ears, and concealed sins in their hearts, but were evil and sinful in their minds. Projecting respectability, justice, and humility in all their dealings, they sought to gain people's trust and stewardship of their wealth. In the end, they were treacherous; a trap was set, people were caught in a net. Some of them never used their knowledge to enrich others, because they thought that sharing the sweet secrets of knowledge with others would diminish their own store. They forgot that when clouds are engorged with rain, they shower upon the earth. Those who bestow of their glory onto others and support them are like people who light one candle from another. Some did not want anyone else in the world to be wiser. They feared that another person's reputation would overtake theirs. So, their marrow turned to dung, and the souls that did this were cut off from their people. Some intended to frequent choirs, to offer delightful prayers, so as to penetrate the hearts of the does and to earn the trust of the gazelles. No one knew their remotest intentions, except He who examines hearts and minds.

"Some of them kept company with criminals. Even if they did not join in, they observed and appreciated the crimes. It was in their hands to quash, but they did not squash them. Thus, they were banned from the land of the living, and they received double punishment for all their sins. The hearts of others, like ovens, were warmed by intrigues. The matters that caused them to lie in torment were their suspicions about other people that were not true. Therefore, their hearts are dashed by the sword. Some ensnared people by donning phylacteries on their heads and fringes on their clothes. They crafted nets and traps out of the lofty commandments, laws, and decrees. Thus their faces remain turned toward evil. Others didn't give even a penny to poor and miserable people except when they were in choirs and other public places. In places where other people would not see, however, the poor were chased away or verbally harassed. Thus their possessions are carried away by the river of willows. Some of them did not desire to teach others so that a stranger would not come close to them. As long as they were regarded by others as wise men, being called 'Rabbi' or 'Master' sufficed, whether their words were truthful and straight or mute like idols. How great is the foolishness of man whose heart rejoices to be praised for qualities he completely lacks? If only the falsely praised man were wise and sensible, that adulation would cause him misery and sadness. If only he regarded the praise as an affront, so as to go around and ask for reckoning from each person. Then people's true impressions of him would come out, and he would not rest until he actualized himself and perfected himself.

"For some, their punishment was justified since they spoke slander. The defamation they contrived was counted against them as though they had committed it. Others denied the Lord's existence and said: 'He does not exist!' Therefore, they are in that place where the evil ones are. They neither feared divine punishment, nor did they tremble. They followed neither the Lord nor his pious followers, because their hearts were blocked from apprehending and their eyes grew weary. It was as if they made a pact with She'ol, sealed a deal with death. Thus their names were expunged from the universe, and they were excised from the land of the living. Some were false and fraudulent witnesses. With their lies and extravagances, they lost the dwellings of Ahzib to deception. They thought that the blessed Lord left the land. They did not know that one who participates in violating the Sabbath is considered as guilty as the one who violated it. The one who holds the hide taut, in violation of the Sabbath, is considered akin to the skinner himself. Thus the faithful Torah pronounces, 'The hand of the witnesses should be on him first' so that all should know that he who testifies falsely against a man—it is as though he personally killed him with his sword. Some were mindless, only thinking about food, drink, and merriment. They did not dwell too much on any matter of wisdom, and mocked the important men, those with well-known reputations. Thus their frightful surroundings are no surprise. Some of them prophesied falsely, inventing teachings and laws from their minds. My Lord never spoke to them, yet they called out in his name. They related matters they had not seen, nor things they had heard. Having trained their tongues to speak falsehood, they exhausted themselves with telling lies. They are deceptive dolts, thus they have been detached from the earth. Their bones are rubbed away until they are no longer seen.

"For some, oaths were always on the tips of their tongues, oaths upon oaths. When they were summoned as witnesses to a vow, they swore that they had never sworn nor known about the matter, since they voided most vows in their hearts. Others would utter God's name in vain, dropping it alongside profanity as though it had no holiness or value. Thus every sanction rained down upon them. Some had sat on street corners, recounting tales of kings, dominions, dreams, trifles, and numerous other such things beyond measure. They responded, 'How annoying!' to wonderful wisdom or to word of prophecy. Because they withheld understanding from their souls and a bunch of beliefs from their thoughts, their unintentional sins were counted as intentional ones, as though they were plundering the threshing floors. Some of them were judges and officials, but they did not adjudicate the law truthfully. Truly, they were vengeful and bore grudges, chasing and closing in on just men like one chasing a partridge in the hills. Some of them were quacks, wearing their folly like a crown. They never studied medical books, and their follies depressed many patients. The 'physicians' said, 'No one is like us; No one can appoint us! Which physician will stand in our way? No one can withdraw our right hand, and no one can move us! Such-and-such said Hippocrates, and so-and-so answered Galen. If you do not believe us, then surely you cannot be trusted.' Those fools established themselves on the basis of those things. The dunces did not know that, with their delusions and dreams through which they deceive, they destroy lives, and their actions are considered as guilty as murder. Some stayed away from the plight of the public, avoiding it in words and deeds. They said, 'What are troubles to us?' The Lord should guide them and come to their aid, for what happened there will not happen eventually here. Thus they will be mowed down by death, remembered, and expelled. Relief and deliverance shall come to the Jews from another place. For the fate of the foul ones is to be effaced, while sulfur shall be strewn upon their homes.

"Some falsely swore, cursing God and men. Therefore, they drown in the mire of Tofet, sated by bitterness. For the blessed Lord finds falsehood loathsome and foul, thus a sudden arrow will pierce their innards. Some blocked their eyes from seeing, appearing well intentioned, with their eyes cast heavenward. In their courtyards and castles they built ritual baths, to sleep with the attendant women. So, therefore, they were cast into latrines by the fury of the Lord of Hosts. Some of them, rascals and rogues, never extended themselves to enliven the hearts of the depressed. On account of their wickedness, they sunk appallingly. He struck them in the public eye, and their souls lie among preying lions. Others became infatuated with strange women and attached themselves to gentiles. Although they had a charming wife, thriving like a flowering vine, they erred with their eyes. They stumbled in judgment, and thus my Lord's hand has struck them. Some pursued powerful positions, fashioning crowns for themselves out of pride. They regarded humble people as a spectacle; meek and modest people were objects of scorn and derision in their eyes. Thus, they are a parable, a mockery, and a horror."

My eyes shed tears upon hearing the words of Daniel, the precious man, together with the groaning sound of the burning souls and the wailing sound of lamenting souls beating their breasts. My thoughts were absent upon seeing the corpses of the people who sinned, whose seeds have shriveled. I was afraid that in my death, judgment would be executed upon me, and my soul would lie among fierce lions. I saw that the size of my sins surpassed me in height, and my soul had no refuge. Daniel, the precious man, saw that I was horrified, submerged in caverns of consternation, having driven my horn into the dust, and dragged my dignity to the ground. I had never expected to see goodness again, and I cursed the day on which I was born. He said to me, "Why are you afraid from what you see? For you bear the Lord's wrath, and yet you still stand there agape? Have you grown weary from seeing the Lord's revenge on his enemies?" I answered and said, "By your life, O crown of the age, my holy one! I recall my iniquities, and overwhelmed by them, I pour my heart out onto itself. For I, your servant, know the evil which I have done and how I traded dignity for dishonor when I turned my heart away. I had a pure soul; I sullied it with my deeds. I did not say: 'Where is my God, my Maker? If he judges me according to my actions, woe to me!' I was a foolish shepherd who relied on gold. I became as bloodthirsty as a leech who says 'More, more!' My soul sought more, and I became transfixed on white gold, property, and wealth.[11] I increased my sins and my crimes well beyond those who preceded me. After I sinned, committed crimes, and transgressed, the Lord is righteous

11. לבן חצרות ודי זהב are biblical place names; Immanuel uses them as puns here, because they also mean different types of wealth.

because of all that He bestowed upon me, for He is truth and I have transgressed."

Daniel, the precious man, said to me, "Banish anger from your heart, and strip yourself of fear. Honorable things are spoken of you, and, despite what you thought, no evil will touch you. You heeded the Lord's command, even though you doubtlessly sinned, committed crimes, and transgressed, cursed God and people, and were satisfied with shame rather than glory. Yet, in your tireless effort to interpret the prophetic books, to exhibit their power among the nations, you have publicized their wonders. You earned a reputation among the greatest men of the land and saved your soul. How the world would suffer were you to be shamed! The sweetness and richness of the Torah ceased until you arose and returned the crown of scripture to its former state. Added to this, you have crowned your soul with precious attributes. You were never a vengeful or resentful man. If someone wronged you, you immediately forgot it. If someone was kind to you, you remembered it forever. You were not serene nor did not rest until you paid that person back. You were a basket of manna that did not rage about the events of fate. You blessed the merciful Lord for the good and the bad. On account of these things, you have built yourself an enduring house in the angelic world. You never withheld anything good from one who deserves it, and you bestowed your radiance upon anyone who approached you. You were never stingy with your knowledge. You said, 'Let me care for all your needs, Whoever is for the Lord, come to me' to anyone who asked. You were a faithful lover, a gracious and merciful brother. You never heard of a man mentioning God's name and didn't answer 'Blessed is He and blessed is His name.' While your friends and peers mocked you while eating, drinking, rejoicing, slaughtering sheep, killing cattle, and delighting in worldly, material delights, your thoughts were like a thirsting hind on the riverbanks of Torah. You denied sleep to your eyes and slumber to your eyelids until you had gathered all the pearls of wisdom and arranged them in a commentary on God's pure Torah. Although a kingdom of commentators rose against you, you did not forsake grammar, literal definitions, innovations, hidden secrets, and wonderful riddles throughout your books, so much so that your words were words of prophecy. You have banished and neglected the names of other exegetes who are embarrassed and ashamed upon encountering your exegesis. Even the priest who declares war fears your words! How the prophet, Isaiah, rejoiced when you interpreted his book. By my life! When he saw the exegesis of 'why do you seek further beatings' [Isaiah 1:5], he swore by his creator that your interpretation was exactly the one intended by his words. He swore to be a mouthpiece and advocate on your behalf, to slake your thirst in parched places and to give your bones strength. If only you knew how Solomon, king of Israel, rejoiced when [the angel] Michael said, 'Immanuel has interpreted your books.' How he prayed to the Lord for your wellbeing. Now, you know that you have a good and redeeming advocate. By your life, when he heard that you interpreted 'The morsel you eat you will vomit' [Proverbs 23:8] using the verse "If a man seduces" [Exodus 22:15], he said, 'It is time to be merry!' He opened his mouth in a measureless gape, and the sound that emerged was heard from afar. He swore that such was his intention, and that was no other exegete understood his rhetoric. Fate anointed you, alone, with its sacred anointing oil. When the two of us shall ascend from Tofet and turn our faces toward Eden, his heart will be warmed. Behold, he, too, comes to greet you. When he shall see you, his heart will rejoice. There, you will receive endless honor and glory. By your life, you will not believe what is told, for you will achieve happiness and joy there. Arise and let's go, for this is not a place of repose!" I answered and said, "Please, my lord! Do as you say, drag me and I shall follow you, for I am inexperienced in such places. Take me out of the valley of corpses, for I have become ill." The man said to me, "Quickly! Hold the corner of my cloak. Don't look backward, and don't stand still anywhere." We set out on our way, placing our spirits and souls in the hand of God.

Eden

From Tofet, we traveled on. My mind was blank; my mind was wandering, disconnected, and detached. After departing from Tofet, we looked forward to Eden. We reached the top of a ladder set on the ground whose top reached the sky. When we were on its highest rungs, God was revealed to us, and there were new heavens and a new terrain. This place had no stench or rotten smell, just holy and purified earth. Stations were prepared for sacred souls, staggered like first, second, and third stories. There, one sees the ultimate light, called by the sages "the sevenfold light," like the light of the seven days of creation. How beautiful and how good it is! Because of it, no one tires or stumbles. There, the pure souls bound in bonds of life reside, those who shine like the light of the firmament, those who have become luminaries. The souls of the innocent poor are there, as is the eternal life, constant joy, and endless happiness.

Sarah is there, hugging her son, Isaac. Rebecca, kissing Jacob. Rachel, clinging to Joseph. Leah, knocking on her sons' doors. Abraham, our father, is there. He is the reason for our joy, the majesty of our elders and the crown of our glory. Moses and Aaron are there, as well as the Levites who carried the ark of the covenant. David is there, reciting his psalms out loud, while the kings of Judah pass before him rank and file. Adam, the first man, is there with the delicate and lovely Eve. Mordekhai is there, as well as Hadassah. Atniel is there, and so is Aḥsah, Avner, Amasah, and Asaf, minister of song. Jehoshaphat and Asa are there, together with Michiyahu, son of Yimlah. Elisha, son of Shefat, from Avel Mekholah, is there, as well as the Shunamite, a noblewoman. There, one sees the men of the Great Assembly. Micah the Morashite and Sibhai, who killed the Philistine, are there. Zephaniah, son of the Cushite, is there, along with Nahum the Elkoshite.

Zekhariah, son of Berekhiya, the son of Ido, is there with the prophet Isaiah, and Hezekiah, king of Judah. I see Josiah, who died at Meggido, Gad, the seer, and Ido. Joshua is there; Jeremiah, too.

Barukh, son of Neriah, Nehemiah, son of Khakhlaya, and Ruth, the Moabitess, are there, along with Enoch, Noah, and Samson, son of Manoah. Here is Amos, a sheep breeder from Tekoa, and there is Jonathan, who was at Mount Gilboa. Rahab, the prostitute, is permitted to move among these attendants for hiding the messengers. Miriam, the prophetess, is there with Tolah, daughter of Puah. Elijah, son of Barakh-el, the Buzite, is there, with Rabbi Judah Ha-Levi and Rabbi Judah Harizi. I see the rabbi, our teacher, Moses son of Maimon, servant of the Lord. Matthias, the high priest and Hasmonean, is there. Merciful women are there, like Shifrah and Puah, the Hebrew midwives, and Yael, wife of the Kenite, Hever. Ehud, son of Gera, the son of the Yeminite, is there, and so is Solomon Jedidiah, Jehoshaphat, and Obadiah. Jehoyada, the high priest, is there with his son, Zekhariah. There are Reu'el, Hovav, and Jethro. There is Gideon and Purah, his servant, as well as hasty Harvonah, always ready to serve, who exclaimed, "Here is the tree prepared by Haman." Both Shem and Japhet are here, for placing the garment on their backs as they covered their father's nakedness. Here, the lame jump around like rams, and the mute tongues exult.

Malkizedek, king of Shalem, is here, together with Phineas, son of Eleazar, a zealot for his Lord who fortified himself to attack Zimri, son of Salu, and Kozbi, daughter of Zur. I see all the tribes of Israel here, along with Hannah and Samuel. Shekhaniah, son of Yeḥiel, of the sons of Eilam, is here. He was the leader of the group that confessed their sin of bringing foreign women into their homes to Ezra. They said, "Is there any hope for Israel after this?" Bezalel, son of Uri, is here, as well as Beniayahu, who stole the sword from the Egyptian's hand. Caleb, son of Jefuneh, is here, with Eldad and Meidad, who are prophesying throughout the camp. I see Abraham's servant, who stood at the water well, and Elijah, who ascended to the heavens in a storm. Tamar, who sat at the crossroads, is here, with Judah, son of Maccabee, the hero. I see the servant of the Cushite king who raised Jeremiah from the pit. Yedutun, Heiman, and Eitan the Ezrahite are here, with Elifaz, the Yemenite, Zofar, the Naamite, and Bildad, the Shuhite. Elisheva, daughter of Aminadav, is here with other pious women. I see Deborah, the prophetess, Lapidot's wife. Here, I see Hananiah, Mishael, and Azariah, Hosea, Joel, Amos, Obadiah, Jonah, Micah, Nahum, Habakuk, Zephaniah, Malachi, Haggai, and Zehariah. I see Cyrus, the Persian king, who turned Babylonia into a desert and destroyed its cities. Shmaya and Avtalyon are here alongside Joseph, son of Gorion, and Rabbi Haninah, son of Teradyon. Rabbi Judah the Prince, compiler of the Mishnah, is here, along with Rav Ashi and Ravina, compilers of the Talmud. Abaye and Rava are here with Rabbi Joshua and Rabbi Aqiba. Here, I see Rav and Samuel, Hillel and Shammai, Rabbi Ishmael, and Rabbi Simon, son of Gamaliel. Here, are the deceased Rabbi Solomon Jedidiah and his son, Solomon. The aged Rabbi Judah, the judge, sits on his right side. I see the pious Rabbi Shabtai, son of Rabbi Matityah, and his father-in-law, Rabbi Joab. Here, sit the deceased, Rabbi Samuel, my father-in-law, Boaz and Naomi, Justa, my righteous mother, and Brunetta, my pious mother-in-law, whose glory illuminated the world. I see the master, Rabbi Benjamin, my teacher and my master, who taught me Torah in my younger days. Rabbi Zedekiah Anav and three of his sons are here. The pious Rabbi Menahem, the humble physician, is here, with the pious physician, Rabbi Isaac, and his son, Rabbi Benjamin. I see Rabbi Menahem Bozzecho and his son, Rabbi Shabtai, to his right, who are destined to receive their reward in the coming days. I see the pious master, Rabbi Shabtai, Leo, and his brother Rabbi Menahem next to Rabbi Judah the Leader and the phoenix, Milḥam. Here are Master Rabbi Abraham and his brother Rabbi Meshullam, surrounded by a pious army on their left and their right. Pharoah's daughter is here, with an illuminated face, because she drew Moses from the Nile river. Eshkol and Aner are here, as well as Avner, son of Ner. Here, there are tannaitic sages, Amoraic sages, and all the sons of the prophets. I see Nehemiah, son of Hahalya, and Ezra the scribe. Here, there are pious people from earlier times, as numerous as the sand of the sea, who cannot be counted and do not stop. They stand, with crowns upon their heads, clothed in garments of salvation and kindness. They are present in happiness and joy, elation and delight, enjoying the light of the Divine Presence.

While wandering Eden's paths, observing the virtues of the wise, I saw folks so filled with glory and splendor that the sun and moon dimmed because of their beauty. They were allowed to amble about the angelic realm. I knew not a one of them. I asked the man speaking to me about their tale. He said to me, "These are the righteous gentiles of the world who so triumphed in their knowledge and intellect that they ascended the rungs of the ladder of wisdom according to their capacities. They were not like their fathers, a wayward and defiant generation. Rather, they were intellectually curious about their Maker and Creator, who mercifully created them, the One who transformed them from nothingness to existence, and brought them to this world. They pondered the purpose for which they were created. When these righteous ones queried their fathers, and considered their responses, they realized that the answers were worthless. They spurned their former beliefs so as to openly scrutinize the faiths of their fellow men. When they examined all the faiths, they found that each one had dogmas to undergird its own foundation and to denounce fellow faiths. They did not pronounce, 'We shall be steadfast in our faith because we have received it transmitted from our fathers.' Rather, they chose elements from different confessions, true principles accepted by all wise people. These were the convictions to which they clung, turning astride from any universally denounced thing. They said, regarding the blessed Lord, 'We shudder and shake to name him, for each and every nation calls him by their own special name.' We say, 'His name shall be what it shall be.' We believe in the First Cause, authentic and giving life, who was, is, and will be. He created the world at the moment that his wisdom ordained it. The intensity of His light renders Him invisible to us. He neither tires nor does He become weary, and His wisdom cannot be fathomed. The one who is merciful toward His creations sustains them with the care of a shepherd tending to his flocks. He recalls us to Him at our end, and His glory shall gather us.'"

While ascending Eden's heights, we saw the most astounding sight—massive and monumental thrones. To me, these wonders of wonder made it impossible to turn one's eyes away. They surrounded one throne whose splendiferous light filled the earth, sparkling like a clear sapphire and as pure as the sky. A footstool stood at its base which was ample in width and it flashed with light. How I longed to sit upon that throne! I said, "Please, my lord! For whom is this glorified and charming throne, and for whom is the sculptured footstool?" He said to me, "By your life! This throne is intended for the most noble of shepherds, and it will wait for him. He is Judah, the lion's whelp, who overcame his brothers. The footstool, with its wings and flowers, is for the scribe, who shall remain at his feet. You shall sit upon it to be close to him." Upon hearing this, I remembered the greatness of Daniel, my brother, who led me on the way of truth and who smoothed my paths. Like a golden ornament for a sacred crown on my head, he befriended me when I fled. He is the life force of my body and the spirit of my soul.

The tale of his greatness, generosity, and character, his intellect, understanding, humility, and justice has filled the earth with praise for him. I said to my righthand man, "Please, my lord! Show me where my brother, Daniel, will dwell. What kind of house will you build for him? Where will be his repose?" He said to me, "Know that indeed his greatness has grown, and the earth has been filled with his praises. Only your greatness has impeded his arrival, for he bore the sins of many and interceded on behalf of sinners. Supreme Wisdom knew that without you he would neither settle nor be calm, so she positioned his tabernacle by your tabernacle. Even though your worth is beneath his, She knew that your company would delight him. He will be a Moses to your Joshua. Thus, all who will see your souls together, united, enmeshed, and inseparable, will say, 'Can two walk together without previously having met?'" Then, it is no wonder that I joyfully bloomed, knowing that my lot had been favorably cast, aware that my salvation is because of him. I said to the man, "By your life, my lord! Show me the glory of his throne where he shall repose, because I know that his height approaches the heavens, and he is as tall as the clouds." The man said to me, "Come with me and I will show you his joy and his honorable place." I followed him, right behind, until he brought me to the tent of Ohaliyav, son of Ahisamakh. Betzalel, son of Uri, the son of Hur, from the tribe of Judah, was there, together with all the princes of his tribe. Divine beings brought more than was necessary for the work to be done, while weaving charming and decorated canopies that shone like the splendor of the firmament.

They were adorned with every precious stone, and their beauty was like a sapphire. There were tables, lamps, thrones, and crowns for the pure souls. There, we saw a large ivory throne, encased in gold, whose very vision could animate someone or heal one's entire ailing body. Crown jewels glittered from it, and garments of blue, purple, and crimson yarns were strewn over it, sparkling like the luster of burnished bronze. These materials are the fairest from all the lands. At the top of the throne was a crown, which weighed as heavily as a talent of gold and precious stones. It is too precious to exchange for gold, nor can silver be paid out as its price. A voice calls out, "Proclaim that its profits go to those who abide before the Lord!" So the man speaking to me said, "Have you seen the crown and the lofty throne awaiting your brother, Daniel, who will claim it like a lioness and leap up like a lion? This is his repose forever more, and he will be stationed here because he listened to the words of the Lord." The world has no wiser man nor better craftsman, so I praised my Lord who brought him to rest and safe haven. I said, "Blessed is my Lord, unique among all others, who has not withheld his steadfast faithfulness from my master."

While ascending Eden's high heights, we saw a sight that made us curious. There, we noticed people who were wild animals in their lifetimes, harmful to the heavens and to fellow creatures alike. In their evil state, they died as war casualties do, with blood shed like water and their skin stinking like dung. Upon seeing them, here, sparkling like the splendor of the firmament, reaching heavenly heights as though their heads touched the clouds, I said in my heart, "Here, God has borne the sins of the multitude and interceded for the sinners." I asked the man speaking to me for an explanation of how these people merited such a prized status. He said to me, "These people sinned, committed iniquity, and engaged in crime. Because of their sins, they died prematurely, served by the bitterness of a cruel death. They died from being impaled, left in lions' dens, and in leopards' lairs. Altogether, they were forsaken to the birds of the sky and to avian predators. When they reached the bitter end, contemplating their evil deeds, they accepted their bitter demise with love, knowing that it came upon them as judgment and obligation. To them, death became more pleasant than life, as they envisioned a worse evil for themselves. For this reason, they are redeemed from a punishment more bitter than death. At their hour of death, their words and feelings of joy and excitement came from the opportunity to repay a bit of their debt in this corruptible world. They did not rage at their souls. Although their deaths were cruel and bitter, still they regarded them as a beautiful crown and a glorious diadem adorning their souls. Thus, they merited such commendable greatness on account of this deed."

From there we traveled on and saw a man dressed in sackcloth and rent garments, with dirt on his head. He was humming, hurting, and howling, and his lips were moving but his voice was silent. When he saw me, intent on approaching him, he wiped his tears away using his robes. Sighing deeply, he said to me, "My trusted friend! Come and be welcomed joyfully!" When I beheld his silhouette, I saw an incredible sight. This man, dressed in sackcloth and ashes, was the mightiest of shepherds whose reputation reached the highest heights. Such-and-such, the crown of the age, could be counted upon in any palace of wisdom. I said to him, "By my life, my lord! Why are you distressed? Why has your face fallen? What is this sackcloth wrapped around your waist?" He answered me, "My memories of a time when I was the happiest of all my townsmen leave me crestfallen. Oh, how I ran like a gazelle and fought bravely like a lion to fulfill the will of my Creator. With a mind sharper than all those who preceded me, I did not lack anything that my eyes asked of me. My family members placed me on a pedestal, having positioned me as their commander and chief. 'King!' they called me, and every person was blessed in my name. I claimed every choice piece of meat, both the shoulder and thigh. But, when I saw that all my family members were drawn to my handiwork, kneeling before me like desert-dwellers kneel and bowing like nations do, I regarded myself to be above the heaven of Araboth. My limbs waged war against Torah and wisdom, gathering themselves, customarily for war, with spears and knives.

"Thus, I was struck as though by a lion of the woods or a wolf of the desert. I said to my miserable heart: 'Let no one's wealth be comparable to mine, so I will make myself a palanquin of glory. Then, I will ascend to the lofty clouds and look like a god.' Thus, God's wrath went forth against me, and the plague of embarrassment began. I breached and exceeded the boundaries of pride, making a name for myself as one of the greatest of the land. My heart said, 'Abandon the enterprise of study, in which I was engaged, because it is utter futility! Buy yourself wealth and property that exceeds the value the treasuries of Egypt and Nubia!' Quickly, I rose and took all the collected wealth of my ancestors, as well as the silver and gold of the people around me, and I went to a faraway land to do business. But a voice called out, saying, 'Why do you go to Egypt? To drink the waters of the Shihor?' Marching ahead absently, God struck me with his hand, like a poor man thrusting his hand from the hole, setting a trap for my feet and hurling me backward. In the middle of my life, I died in a foreign land.

"What can I say? How can I justify myself? My sorrow is further magnified knowing that I overturned the fortunes of every person in my father's house. How did I, the offshoot of pious people, not think that all those produced by my family would die young? I should have been humble before God, not as a guilty being, but fearing his wrath with trembling and quivering limbs. I should have followed in the footsteps of those humble on earth, remaining in my home and standing through sorrow alongside my community. But, I was hurrying off to gather wealth, so the wheel of fortune turned on me, and I amassed none. Decimated, blinded, and infected by evil, I died. The matter that troubles me, that causes me to howl in turmoil, and to dissipate in misery is that I destroyed my land and killed my nation. My widow, who panicked when utter destruction occurred and her protection disappeared, ended her life with her own hands, casting her soul aside and abandoning her children as though they were not hers. It is no wonder my limbs bitterly groan, crying like a dying corpse, for I watched my dwelling being plundered and all its accoutrements disassembled. There is none to carry my tent, to display my textiles, because my sons, such-and-such and so-and-so, left me and are no more. Gone is the majesty of their number and noise. If only I had ancestral merit! If only the Lord's anger were incensed at me that it left me neither root nor branch. But now, where is the greatness of my righteous ancestors who were engraved on the tablet of the heart of time? Where is my father, Such-and such, a giant among giants? Where are our storehouses, plentiful and producing produce of all kinds? How have we become a target for the arrows of those near and far, exposed as one of the riffraff might expose himself. Woe to my iniquitous soul! I should have stripped off the coat of pride, blocked the burdensome bridle of lust, donned robes of fear and humility, and pleaded before my Creator to spare us the burning and the wrath. Instead, I multiplied my acquisitions, adding further to the Lord's wrath. Here I am, ashamed before my fathers, but at every instance that I remember the greatness, holiness, and diligence of my father, such-and-such, I recall and am terrified. My body is seized with shuddering. From ten measures of licentiousness that descended to the world, members of my household took nine as their fate, and only one remained for the world. With my arms pleading to the heavens, I pray that my son, such-and-such, should merit to learn and teach, to observe and to fulfill. Never should he wander from his worship, and may he keep his covenant and religion. Knowing that I loved him fiercely, and disciplined and educated him according to his capacities, I beg of you to encourage him in ethics and wisdom. For I know that you can do anything, and that nothing you propose is impossible for you." When I heard his words, my eyes shed tears. I said to him, "My lord! Let not the rumors frighten you. Before you now, I swear an oath of oaths that salvation has been planted by the Lord. Do not fear, do not tremble, for the thunder and the hail have ceased. So-and-so, your son, is faithful to holy ones and stands firmly with the Lord. You, crown of the age, the fairest of all the lands, go and untie the sackcloth from your waist. Dress yourself in priestly robes. By my life, I swear that if you do not place the pure crown on your head nor bedeck your robes with jewels of gold, I will never connect with your son so-and-so. My mouth will never converse with his." When he saw me struggling to comfort him, he did that which I did not even ask of him. He placed a royal crown on his head and bedecked his clothing with jewels. He said, "Blessed are you to the Lord, for you have comforted me. You have made me happy and joyful in place of my mourning. By my life! I will not fail you or forsake you, crown of days, for my success and all my desire is to see the honor which Sages will accord you." Then, the three of us wandered about the streets of Eden with all those standing behind us agape. A voice was heard even from afar, proclaiming: "Here comes Immanuel—it is time to laugh!"

When David heard that I arrived, he ran toward me, welcoming me in peace. Holding a harp and the lute, David's honor lit up the earth. He was accompanied by Asaf, Heiman, and Jeduthun, also holding harps and lutes, while the sons of Korah sounded their trumpets. David said to me, "Welcome in the name of my Lord! Are you the one who removes the decay from my pearls?" He hugged and kissed me, clung to me as a belt girds a man's waist. He said to me, "You have honored me with your interpretation of Psalms, and your comments revealed its exemplary greatness. You clarified its figures of speech that, until now, were unknown to man, like a virgin. By my life! After your soul is pleased with knowledge, I will truly honor you with my words and actions and I will do whatever you command."

David dispatched one of the assembled men to gather all the exegetes who had interpreted Psalms with their commentaries. All came at King David's command, led by David Kimḥi. Upon arrival, they bowed before King David, prostrating themselves seven times, and extended their greetings to him. David said to the exegetes assembled before him, "Each of you shall recite the psalm, 'God will arise, his enemies shall be scattered, his foes shall flee before him,' [Psalm 68] revealing its inner meaning and matters according to your reading." Then, each one arose and seized the opportunity to explain it this way or that way. David said, "While one exegete says: 'this is my interpretation,' another one says: 'this is my innovation,' but none of you bring comfort to my soul." David arose, kissed me on my forehead, and said, "This one is as delightful as a pouch of myrrh. He revealed the secret of this psalm so that no allusion or secret remains within its foundation or structure, from beginning to end." He commanded me to publicly recite my exegesis of the psalm, which I did. Neither did I hide any aspect of the psalm nor did I conceal anything. When the exegetes heard my interpretations, pondered their greatness, the exegetes were rendered mute. Then, David ordered the exegetes to honor me. They esteemed me and served me as though I was their king and their messiah.

While he was still speaking with me, Ezekiel, the prophet, appeared. Bellowing like a lion, he said, "I have invested tenfold in this commentator! Which man would cast me from this spot?" He said to me, "Blessed is my Lord who brought you here! Now, how are you? Are you well?" I answered, "Hello! Praise and gratitude be to God for bringing me to this lofty level, as a living person who sees that which no eye has seen." He said, "You truly honored me with your commentary on my book. Your expositions on the beginning and end of my book are a veritable cure for the disease of the commentators. Your interpretation of the chariot episode, extended like the staff of Moses, paved a way through a sea of doubt. All the springs burst out of their depths, and the children of Israel, that holy flock, crossed the waters of wisdom on dry land."

While he was still speaking with me, Jeremiah appeared, flanked by Elisha, to his left, and Elijah, to his right. Behind them stood Barukh ben Neriah. Jeremiah extended his hand to me and said, "Blessed is He who bestowed his honor upon you and who emanated his glory upon you. By my life! You are as precious to me as a crown on my head, as a seal on my heart and arm for the way you explained the verse 'Before I created you in the womb, I selected you; before you were born, I consecrated you' [Jeremiah 1:5] in your commentaries. Other contemporary exegetes failed to grasp its meaning, but you alone, uncovered its branches and roots, feeding the sweet nectar of its truths to the hungry."

While he was still speaking with me, Isaiah, the prophet, came and said to me, "Greetings, O exegete, who prophesied amongst the prophets. Your commentaries have earned you life in the world to come! My heart was overjoyed by your understanding of my book, ingesting its words, treading its wild paths, inhaling its secrets like the scent of perfume and myrrh. My words were nothing in the eyes of the commentators until you rose, and your explanations were pleasing to every eye. Thus, by my life, it is no surprise if we savor your love more than wine. I will be your advocate and savior, defeating anyone who challenges you in a court of law. You will repose in the courtyards of my home together with the purest souls. Your reputation will soar to the sky, and your stature will be as high as the clouds for bearing the sins of the collective and reaching the sinners. Your precious greatness became apparent to me in your exegesis of 'Why do you seek further beatings, that you continue to offend' [Isaiah 1:5] as I had intended it. Of all the sages and prophets before you, none have elucidated it."

While he was still speaking with me, King Solomon, may his name be remembered for good, appeared together with a chorus of prophets who authored scripture. When they recognized me from afar, they began laughing and blessing me in the Lord's name. They joyfully said, "Welcome, O you who bears understanding easily, like a carrier of sheaves. When you expounded our books, you revealed the golden apples that we had hidden in the vessels of our silver." I bowed before them with humility and courtesy, as proper, and I blessed them in the name of the Lord of hosts.

They took me up to heaven's high heights, and they brought me to the tent of Moses, the man of God. When I saw that his face glowed with radiance, my eyes began to fail. I said, "This must be the house of the Lord!" Then, Moses placed a veil over his face, and I appeared refreshed before him, not lacking anything desired by a person. Moses, the man of God, said to me, "Be praised, O you whose transgression is forgiven and whose sin is covered over! It has never been heard or seen before that a man like you, a sullied and polluted soul, can interpret the prophetic scriptures as clear as day. You have not earned eternal life through your own righteousness and decency, but only by virtue of your commentaries that explain concealed secrets. You will come to the grave at a ripe old age, having redeemed your soul from destruction and your lifeforce from the sword. In your exegesis of my book, the book of Job, you have breached the boundaries to create a reputation for yourself that rivals the reputations of the greatest of the land. You adorned yourself with glory like a bridegroom in your explanation of the secret of the Behemoth and Leviathan. Be praised in that you have merited knowledge of their secret, which no previous man has known."

Then Solomon said, "By my life! I am amazed at how you were able to tie together the verses of Proverbs and to write wondrous things on the 'Woman of Valor' narrative [Proverbs 31]. Your innovative reading of Song of Songs is a wonder of wonders that does not fail to satisfy anyone who sees it. On the verse 'O maidens of Zion, go forth and gaze upon King Solomon wearing the crown that his mother gave him on his wedding day, on his day of bliss' [Song of Songs 3:11], all the wise men of the age failed to glean my intention nor could they solve my riddle until you arose, increasing wisdom and honor, you exposed the glory of its secrets about the truth. Regarding Ecclesiastes, none of the exegetes of the ages saw any utility in it, and fools regarded its words as folly, until you came from the distant edge of the Carmel forest. Now they see its worth, its redemptive power, but only when it is too late."

While he was still speaking with me, the righteous Joseph, may he rest in peace, appeared. Like a groom emerging from his bridal canopy, Joseph wore a sizeable golden crown. When he approached the crowd, all happy and rejoicing, Joseph was followed by his eleven brothers, in the order of seniority, from eldest to youngest. Upon beholding the impressive company at Moses's tent, he bowed with humility and courtesy. He said, "Greetings to you, Moses, man of God, thriving like an olive tree in the house of the Lord. Peace unto you, Moses, who dwells in the highest dwelling of the one Above and abide in the protection of Shaddai. Peaceful greetings to the whole group ready to do justice for all." Moses said to him, "You are welcome with pleasure! Like the front of a holy crown of sanctity and testimony, he is exemplary in wisdom, humility, and piety. Peaceful greetings to you! How praiseworthy you are! Peaceful greetings to your brothers behind you!" Joseph turned around, seeing me, and said, "By my life! This man memorialized me favorably in his commentaries. It was as though he crowned my head with royalty when he judged me meritoriously with his words and wrote lengthy praise about me and my actions." He held out his arms and held me, saying, "Peaceful greetings to you, my heartfelt friend!" I answered, "May the armies of peace accompany you, O glorious man of piety! You are the one who clarifies hidden meanings and speaks noble things!" Joseph said to me, "By my life! It is you whom I have come now to see. It is your visage that I have been seeking because of the glorious things said about you. You prowl like a lioness and stalk like a lion. There is not one day on which we don't talk of you and of your tales. How we laugh at your riddles! Since the day Rabbi Elijah, your kinsman, came under the shade of our roof, he has regaled us with your poems and belles-lettres. Specifically, everyone recognizes your intellectual gravitas, expressed in your poems and rhymed prose, the fairest in all the lands. All poems other than yours, however, land like shattered fragments of limestone, unknown in the streets, mirages, works of mockery. Now, be strong, O beautiful lover, for you are a source of delight to us every day!"

While standing in that honorable place, we saw ten canopies with cloaks of blue and purple on the outside and refined gold on the inside. Many precious stones adorned them; their form was beautiful like a sapphire. There, one saw lofty thrones, as valuable as gold, framed with gold and studded with beryl. There were precious crowns whose splendor and beauty darkened the sunlight. I asked, "For whom are these precious canopies, thrones, and glorified crowns?"

Daniel, the precious man, said to me, "By your life! These are for the ten royal martyrs." I asked, "Where are they? Let us seek them out like seekers of the dawn." Daniel said, "They left this place with the angel, Michael, together with our holy master and Samuel. They are bowing and pleading before the Lord, my Lord, the God of Israel, praying on behalf of the surviving remnant to receive salvation. They saw the very bitter plight of Israel, and they will not rest until a spirit from above pours forth to hasten the redemptive end of days, and until He establishes and places Jerusalem renowned on Earth."

Daniel, the precious man, continued to speak to me, "Do you want to see the five honorable canopies reserved for your five friends who still live?" I answered, "I do wish that with my whole heart! If only you would show me their glory, splendor, greatness, and if you would identify them and their strengths, I would be comforted." He said to me, "Lift up your eyes and see, mark my word and understand the vision." I lifted my eyes and saw five awe-inspiring canopies, magnificent in form and condition, with crowns more splendid than gold or refined gold. He said to me, "These dignified canopies are the lot of the Lord's righteous servants who are inscribed on the tablet of the heart of time.

"The first canopy, in which joy and happiness are to be found, will fall by lot to so-and-so from Perugia. God has blessed his fortunes and favored his endeavors. He is imbued with perfection from head to toe, from side to side, and thus he is desirable before God. It is not hard to find praises of this man. The greatest among them is that he never told a lie. He is faithful both in action and in speech, a major advocate on behalf of public affairs. He sealed a deal with his eyes to never gaze at a virginal maiden, nor has profanity ever left his lips. He hated strife and fled from it, turning eastward when it was in the west. He never associated with wicked men, so divine honor shines upon him, enabling him to make roots, sprout, and blossom. He observed the commandment 'you shall not take vengeance or bear a grudge' [Deuteronomy 19:18], and is the first to volunteer in any place. His home is open with abundant generosity; he greets every person happily. Although he experienced some unfortunate events, too lengthy to recount here, he always says 'blessed be the name of the Lord.' He never raged about the circumstances of fate, and he suffered for the love of the trustworthy God. He built a dwelling as high as the heavens, and made his home a meeting place for the elders. His words are more delightful than gold and refined gold, and he would never mingle with dissenters. With him, the Lord struck a pact of friendship, and any man who thought himself equal in character was dreaming a dream. He is generous to the poor and nourishes them from his bounty. When faced with throngs of impoverished and destitute people, overwhelming as a squall, he reduced their neediness to a sprinkle. He relieves them with the rich fare of his house, and quenches their thirst with his refreshing streams. He dresses and covers the needy, like a cloak, but strips garments off the traitors. May the Lord bless all his possessions, both at home and in the field. From the heavens, may he receive healing and relief, and may his children be a blessing.

"The second canopy is for the honorable so-and-so, the army commander who merited eternal life when he stood in the breach on behalf of the Lord's nation. Considering his bravery, he is second only to the Hasmonean. He killed the two giants of Ariel, removing the disgrace from Israel. Among the three warriors, he made a name for himself with his noble steeds. When he raided for the Lord's war, he left impaled corpses as victims, whom his troops stripped. He decorates himself with the spolia of the Lord's enemies, instilling fear in his adversaries and confounding their plans. He pursued his enemies, overtook them, and he will not return until they are demolished. The Lord orders his angels to watch over him on all his paths, lest he even stub his toe on a stone, so that no ailment will approach his tent. Because his bravery is tempered by kindness, as his home is generously open, there is no breach in his house, no sortie, and no wailing. Liberation is there for those spent ones, and tired ones repose and find a resting place.

"There, all the desperate men recharge, finding food, drink, and company. His manner of speech is pleasant, and every traveler housed in the home is met with a welcoming presence. He hired women of his house to be perfumers, cooks, and bakers just to satisfy the thirst of the panting souls, so consumed by hunger that they pluck saltwort and wormwood. What can we say about his awe-inspiring wife? She is a nursemaid to all those abiding in the shelter of her shade. She has pity on the downtrodden and compassion toward the poor. She is both mother and nurse to every passerby. May the Lord reward her deeds amongst the pious women and prophetesses, and may her full reward come from My Lord of Hosts.

"The third canopy is for the noble rabbi, so-and-so, a man after your own heart. He favored you, blessed you, and magnified your name, at risk to his own life. He growled like a lion, pounced on his prey, so that the earth quaked from his wrath. He pushed back the adversaries of Judah and Benjamin, attacking from here and from there until his fierceness caused the sea of angst to stand still. He brought deliverance to Israel countless times; actions that pleased the Lord way more than a sacrificial cow. You would not believe it if it were told, but he removed idolatry from the earth, as well as anything contaminated by an unclean animal. Since he sought good things for his nation, God shall be with him, and grant him success on all his paths and endeavors. May he be more fertile and more numerous than his ancestors.

"The image of the fourth resembles a divine being who dared to ascend to the highest heights. The fourth awe-inspiring canopy is for him, prepared since the dawn of creation. He is the intellectual, so-and-so, son of such-and-such, who climbs the ladder's rungs, stretching out his hand to take fruit from the Tree of Life, and eating it to live forever. Honorable things are said about him, the one learned in scripture, Mishnah, and Targum. Lady Generosity cries out to him in the thronging, main thoroughfares, saying: 'He is a firstborn while the generous among the nations are the latecomers.' She calls him: 'The repairer of the communal breach, the reinforcer of the foundations of my house.' Since he made his home a Tent of Meeting for Torah instruction and moral instruction, his name was renowned and famed. Anyone who seeks the Lord can gather there, which I can attest as one who knows and witnesses. Thus, he shall be like the eternal stars alongside those who lead the masses to righteousness. He copied a bit from your commentaries, because of his love for them, and he sealed them on his heart. He will not be calm nor rest until he copies the remainder of them to ponder them and to understand their legacy. They are exemplars for him to see and imitate.

"The fifth canopy is for the intellectual rabbi, so-and-so from such-and-such city, whose own poetic display wiped out the memory of contemporary poets. The poems reached us and entertained us. His reputation grew as high as the heavens, and his throne was stationed above those of contemporaneous poets. Other poets throughout the world floundered in their attempts to compose poetry like his; they could not. Next to him, they are counted as nothingness, total zeroes. The fine quality of his musings and retorts, and the clarity of his language and ideas overwhelm all those who preceded him. Anyone whom he blesses—he shall be blessed; and anyone whom he curses—shall be cursed. Anyone whom he doesn't praise with his tongue—he is not truly praised.

"No one can compound a poem like him, for his poetry flickers like fire. His poetry is so lively and pleasant, whether in Hebrew, in the Christian tongue, or in Arabic, that no stranger could even come close. His hand is trained for battle, even when the armed are armed. With his sword, he accomplishes terrorizing feats and wonders of wonder with his spear that no eye can stop watching. He causes kings of all the nations to quake; barons of the earth are intimidated by his spear. With it, he performs wonders before their eyes. While waving his sword before them, he encircled Bethel, the Gilgal, Edom, and Assyria. Like a tiger lurking on a path, he encircled Egyptian territory and passed through Geshur. To behold his glory, charming maidens peeked over walls, while beautiful girls pranced before him. Yet, he keeps his integrity.

"Desired by nobles and kings, he was decorated by princes. He stands before kings, but he does not serve the benighted men. Nobles of the land fear the wrath of his verbal barbs, his written rebukes, and his dreaded leadership. He wrestled with both kings and bishops, but he prevailed. Their gates opened before him, and the palace was overrun. Upon seeing that all the nobles of the land blessed his name, he was a zealous defender of his land and had compassion on his nation. He stood in the breach against the treacherous. He risked his life, went to Provence, and appeared before the chieftain of Magdiel, where he defended Israel. He spun parables about the nobles of the land, railed against its respected people, held kings in derision, and mocked the princes. Seeking them out, he was like a merchant exchanging noble words for gold, silver, and clothing. He won fame among the nations. Wearing a crown of perfection, he fought a war for the Lord and his Torah at the gates, engaged with both the prophets of Ba'al and priests. His mind is so clever that it can diffuse such encounters. When others claim he owes them wheat, he cunningly responds that he owes them barley. With his delightful rhymed prose, he has demonstrated that Israel has full command of wisdom. Thus, he was allowed to access the angelic realm."

Following this, Daniel, the precious man, asked me, "Do you desire to see the dignified canopies reserved for the scholars of the world?" I answered, "By your life! I have longed to see them. Now, show me their glory!" He showed me the canopies, sparkling like sapphires, and adorned with every precious stone. It is exhausting to describe their splendor and the precious objects that surrounded their folds.[12] I said to him, "My lord! For whom are these precious objects I behold?"

He said to me, "Mark the word and understand the vision. These canopies are for the pious ones, the pride of this world, so-and-so, and such-and-such from Orvieto, who saw God's designs and appreciated his actions. They embody all the most precious attributes, and glorious things are said about them. But, mercy on the downtrodden merited them residence in this lofty spot, as they heard the cries of the downtrodden, not blocking them out. They pitied exiled refugees, not humiliating them, and they clothed the naked. Their charitable actions are wonders of wonder, and their helping hands accomplished astounding feats. Their homes are abundantly open,

---

12. The Hebrew word is *gevahot*, meaning mountains, but it is clear that Immanuel uses it for the rhyme. The shape of the canopy's folds resembles the mountains.

as are their hands, open to give charitably. Their welcoming smiles receive the poor with joy. O the multitudes of orphans they wed, the satisfaction they gave to widows. O the number of shackled prisoners they released! In leaner days, they still engaged in charity, satisfying thirsting souls. May they be blessed for caring for the lost, thus it is no wonder that they may enter the sanctuary of my Lord."

While standing in that lofty place, Daniel, the precious man said to me, "By your life! The Lord has given you a choice gift when he showed you wondrous things from the past and present. You observed the stations of the sacred and of the prophets who assemble in Eden, the divine garden, as well as the stations of the wicked, who sunk appallingly. With their souls among the lions, they pitifully moan. All this was revealed to you, by the Heavens, so that people on Earth should be aware of what is to come. And, thus, preserve all the things that you have witnessed in your mind, and inscribe them in a book for posterity. You shall keep it close to the ark so that future generations may know the words of this book. Now, while you still walk among the living, cry out and tell the people of your age all the things that your eyes beheld and that your ears heard. I, Daniel, who came forth to give you understanding as you began your pleas, surrender your soul to your divine Owner. By virtue of His kindness, He will overlook some of your iniquity. Now, whether you go left or right, may you reach the end where you shall rest. You will arise to claim your destiny at the end of days."

When he finished speaking, he disappeared, vanishing from my sight. I sought him but did not find him. In the eye of a storm, searching and hoping to find him, I awoke from my slumber. Remembering the things I had seen in a vision, I was so afraid, frightened, and terrified for my life that I awoke from my dream-filled sleep. With all my might, hurrying my hand to record the sights and sounds I witnessed, no detail was deleted or spared. May God, my joyful delight, my rock, my refuge, and my stronghold, who made me secure at my mother's breast and drew me from the stomach, be pleased with my prayer. May the hearts of the generous of God's people be nourished by my discourse, pouring forth like rain. May my words be impressed on their hearts, like on a tablet. May I not be compared to one who composes music for the dead or one who howls at the dead. Here I am, with my hands spread to the heavens, praying that, as long as there is life in me, I shall merit to learn and to teach, to observe, and to perform. At my end, may divine kindness be right beside me, sustaining me. May it give honor to the place where I shall be stationed, alongside those who lead the many to righteousness, forever and ever, like the stars.

NOTES

Introduction

1 Joseph Karo, *Shulḥan Arukh*, Oraḥ Hayyim (Warsaw: Wolf Press, 1875), 307:16.

2 I am indebted to Joshua Teplitsky for introducing me to Footprints, a database containing a wealth of information about Hebrew printed books. This information came from my search on the website at https://footprints.ccnmtl.columbia.edu/, accessed November 30, 2019.

3 *Maqamat* are collections of short, independent narratives written in ornamental rhymed prose with verse insertions that share a common plot-scheme and two constant protagonists: the narrator and the hero.

4 Rina Drory, "The Maqama," in *The Literature of Al-Andalus*, ed. Maria Rosa Menocal, Raymond P. Scheindlin, and Michael Sells (Cambridge: Cambridge University Press, 2000), 190–211.

5 Isabelle Levy, *Jewish Literary Eros: Between Poetry and Prose in the Medieval Mediterranean* (Bloomington: Indiana University Press, 2022).

6 Judah Al-Harizi, *Taḥkemoni*, ed. Y. Yahalom and N. Katsumata (Jerusalem: Ben Zvi Institute, 2010); Jacob ben Eleazar, *Sipure ahavah shel Yaʿaḳov ben Elʿazar*, ed. Y. David (Tel Aviv: Ramot/Tel-Aviv University, 1992/1993); Solomon Ibn Saqbel, "Ne'um Asher Ben Yehudah," in *Hebrew Poetry in Spain and Provence*, ed. H. Schirmann (Jerusalem: Mossad Bialik, 1954), 554–565.

7 *Shibuts* (integration) is a technique that incorporates a biblical or extrabiblical citation into a verse. According to Dan Pagis, the *shibuts* differs from a conventional biblical citation in that it cannot stand without the textual context. The other method for referencing scripture is the allusive technique known as *remez/remizah* (hints), which hints at a biblical character or event without directly citing the text. See Dan Pagis, *Hiddush u-Masoret be-Shirat ha-Hol ha-Ivrit: Sefarad ve-Italia* (Jerusalem: Keter, 1976), 75. Shari Lowin describes the use of *shibuts* and *remizah* in Sephardic love poetry in Lowin, *Arabic and Hebrew Love Poems in Al-Andalus* (New York: Routledge, 2014), 11–13.

8 Although Immanuel does not acknowledge any influence other than Al-Harizi on the structure of his anthology, Dante reworked his poetry into

a prosimetric setting in the *Vita Nuova*, a fourteenth-century anthology written in Italy.

9 H. Schwarzbaum, "The Prophet Elijah and R. Joshua b. Levi" [Hebrew], *Yeda-am* 7 (1960): 22–31. For the Talmudic accounts of Rabbi Joshua ben Levi, see BT Ketubot 77b and BT Berakhot 51a.

10 M. D. Cassuto draws parallels between Daniel and Cato of *Purgatory* in *Dante v'Immanuel ha-Romi* (Jerusalem: Mossad Bialik, 1965), 29.

11 Abraham Geiger, "Daniel Loves Immanuel of Rome," in *Otzar Nehmad*, 3 (Vienna: Y. Knepfelmakhers Bukhhandlung, 1856), 125; Hermann Vogelstein, *Rome*, trans. Moses Hadas (Philadelphia: Jewish Publication Society of America, 1940), 209. Cecil Roth identifies five people named Daniel in Immanuel's circle. He believes that Daniel was Judah Romano's brother and Immanuel's cousin; see Cecil Roth, "The Historical Background of Maḥberot Immanuel," in *Sefer Assaf*, ed. Moshe David Cassuto, Joseph Klausner, and Julius Gutmann (Jerusalem: Mossad Ha-Rav Kook, 1952), 453.

12 Rabbi Hayim Joseph David Azulai, *Shem Ha-Gedolim*, part 2 (Vienna: Romm Press, 1852), 22.

13 The popular commentaries exist in twelve extant manuscripts each. The commentary on Proverbs was published in Naples in 1487 and republished by David Goldstein in 1981 with a critical introduction, but the text itself was never subjected to critical analysis. Giovanni De Rossi, a Christian Hebraist, published excerpts from the commentary on Psalms in Parma in G. De Rossi, *R. Immanuelis Salomonis, Scholia in selecta loca Psalmorum* (Parma, 1806). Immanuel's commentary on Job is briefly discussed by Robert Eisen in *The Book of Job in Medieval Jewish Philosophy* (Oxford: Oxford University Press, 2004). Immanuel's Esther commentary is also briefly discussed by Barry Walfish in *Esther in Medieval Garb* (Albany: State University of New York Press, 1993), 128–129. The introduction to the commentary on Ruth was published by Murray Rosenthal in "The *Haqdamah* of Immanuel of Rome to the Book of Ruth," *Approaches to Judaism in Medieval Times* 2 (1985): 169–185. Immanuel acknowledges his commentaries to Job, Song of Songs, and Ecclesiastes in *Maḥberet* 1:341–342; the Five Scrolls (Esther, Lamentations, Ruth, Song of Songs, Ecclesiastes) and Psalms in *Maḥberet* 1:343. See also *Maḥberet* 28: 833–850, 872–909. I am indebted to James T. Robinson for sharing his transcription of Immanuel's commentary on Ecclesiastes with me.

14 Haim Kreisel, "Philosophical Interpretations of the Bible," in *The Cambridge History of Jewish Philosophy* (Cambridge: Cambridge University Press, 2009).

15 James T. Robinson, "Maimonides, Samuel Ibn Tibbon, and the Construction of a Jewish Tradition of Philosophy," in *Maimonides After 800 Years: Essays on Maimonides and His Influence* ed. Jay M. Harris (Cambridge, MA: Harvard University Center for Jewish Studies, 2007), 293.

16 James T. Robinson, "We Drink Only from the Master's Water: Maimonides and Maimonideanism in Southern France, 1200–1306," in *Studia Rosenthalia* 40 (2007–2008): 41.

17 Immanuel, *The Book of Proverbs with the Commentary by Immanuel of Rome, Naples ca. 1487*, ed. D. Goldstein (Jerusalem, Magnes Press, 1981), 1–2.

18 Immanuel, *Commentary on the Pentateuch*: Genesis 2:10, in Parma, Biblioteca Palatina, MS. Cod. Parm. 3220, fols. 229r–228v.

19 Immanuel, *Commentary on Genesis*, in Parma, Biblioteca Palatina, MS. Cod. Parm. 3220, fol. 108v.

20 Gregg Stern, "What Divided the Moderate Maimonidean Scholars of Southern France in 1305?" in *Be'erot Yitzhak: Studies in Memory of Isadore Twersky*, ed. Jay M. Harris (Cambridge, MA: Harvard University Press, 2005), 347–76.

21 Daniel Jeremy Silver, "Who Denounced the 'Moreh'?" *Jewish Quarterly Review* 57 (1967): 505–506.

22 Immanuel, *Commentary on Psalms*, Parma, Biblioteca Palatina, MS. Cod. Parm. 2843, fol. 44v; *The Book of Proverbs with the Commentary by Immanuel of Rome, Naples ca. 1487* 15:13, ed. David Goldstein, 58–61; *Commentary on Job* 40:15, in Parma, Biblioteca Palatina, MS. Cod. Parm. 2877, fol. 130r.

23 The commentary on the Pentateuch utilizes extensive unattributed citations from Rashi and Abraham Ibn Ezra, but only a small percentage of the comments are attributed. The commentary on Genesis was first published by Franco Michelini Tocci in *Il commento di Emanuele Romano al Capitolo I della Genesi* (Rome: Università di Roma, 1963). Tocci's commentary was heavily criticized, by both David Goldstein and Devorah Schechterman, for his reliance on a corrupt manuscript that resulted in an erroneous edition. David Goldstein's PhD dissertation offers a critical edition of the first ten chapters of Genesis; see his "The Commentary of Immanuel Ben Solomon of Rome on Chapters I–X of Genesis: Introduction, Hebrew Text, and Notes (Edited from Two Manuscripts)" (University of London, 1966); Devorah Schechterman's 1984 PhD dissertation, "The Philosophy of Immanuel of Rome in Light of His Commentary on the Book of Genesis" [Hebrew] (Hebrew University of Jerusalem, 1984) focuses on Immanuel's exegesis of Genesis using more reliable manuscripts. David Goldstein's critique of Tocci is found in David Goldstein, "Longevity, the Rainbow, and Immanuel of Rome," *Hebrew Union College Annual* 42 (1971): 243–244. See also Moritz Steinschneider, "Immanuel und Dante," *Hebraische Bibliographie* 11 (1871): 52.

24 Against Dov Jarden, who claimed that the commentary borrowed from Zeraḥiah of Barcelona's commentary on Proverbs, Aviezer Ravitzky doubted that Immanuel knew of Zeraḥiah, as his name is never mentioned in the *Maḥbarot*. Rather, per Ravitzky, both Zeraḥiah's and Immanuel's commentaries draw heavily from Maimonides' exegesis of Proverbs in the *Guide*. See Aviezer Ravitzky, "The Thought of R. Zeraḥiah b. Isaac b. Shealtiel Ḥen and the Maimonidean-Tibbonian Philosophy in the 13th Century" PhD diss. [Hebrew] (Hebrew University of Jerusalem, 1977), 113; Moses Ben Maimon, *The Guide of the Perplexed*, 2 vols. ed. S. Pines (Chicago: University of Chicago Press, 1963), III:22–23.

25 James Robinson calls Immanuel a "compiler more than original exegete" in Robinson, "From Digression to Compilation: Samuel Ibn Tibbon and Immanuel of Rome on Genesis 1:11, 1:14, and 1:20," *Zutot* 4 (2006): 79. Devorah Schechterman claims that Immanuel was knowledgeable of scholastic scribal modes in "The Philosophy of Immanuel of Rome," 93–115. Sarah Stroumsa demonstrates that medieval Judeo-Arabic authors were inconsistent in their methods of citation and attribution, depending on factors such as genre and ideological school. See Sarah Stroumsa, "Citation Tradition: On Explicit and Hidden Citation in Judeo-Arabic Philosophical Literature," in *Masoret Ve-Shinui Ba-Tarbut Ha-'Arvit-Ha-Yehudit Shel Yeme-Ha-Benayim: Divre Ha-Ve'idah Ha-Shishit* (Ramat Gan: Bar Ilan University Press, 2000), 167–78.

26 Raphael Menahem Leboff, "Biur Tzurot HaOtiot," *Siynay* 152 (2018): 49–91. "Ploni [Immanuel] wrote a book on the interpretation of the shapes of the letters and he likened the ones, tens, and hundreds to the divine ones, heavenly ones, and natural ones (sciences)," in Immanuel of Rome, *Maḥberoth Immanuel Haromi: Edited on the Basis of Early Manuscripts and Printed Editions with Introduction, Commentary, Source References, Appendices and Indices*, 2d ed., ed. Dov Jarden (Jerusalem: Mossad Bialik, 1957), 23 (lines 324–325), 202 (lines 174–199). Immanuel, *Commentary on Proverbs* 19:5 in Parma, Biblioteca Palatina, MS. Cod. Parm. 2965, fol. 101r; *Commentary on Psalms* 118, in Parma, Biblioteca Palatina, MS. Cod. Parm. 2844, fol. 36v.

27 See Immanuel's comment in Immanuel of Rome, *Maḥberoth*, ed. D. Jarden, 23 (lines 321–322); Parma, Biblioteca Palatina, MS. Cod. Parm. 2304; Parma, Biblioteca Palatina, MS. Cod. Parm. 2285; Wilhelm Bacher, "Immanuel b. Salomo's Eben Bochan," *Monatsschrift fur Geschichte und Wissenschaft des Judenthums* 34 (1885): 241–257; Kaufman, "Notizen I. Zu Immanuels Eben Bochan," *Monatsschrift fur Geschichte und Wissenschaft des Judenthums* 34 (1885): 335–336; Moshe Idel, "The Study Program of R. Yoḥanan Alemanno," *Tarbiz* 48, nos. 3/4 (1979): 304.

28 Immanuel's explanation of Abraham Ibn Ezra's comment on Exodus 33:21 exists in twelve manuscript copies.

29 Albert Russell Ascoli, *Dante and the Making of a Modern Author* (Cambridge: Cambridge University Press, 2008); Alastair Minnis, *Medieval Theory of Authorship* (Philadelphia: University of Pennsylvania Press, 2010).

30 Albert Russell Ascoli, "The Author in History," in *Dante and the Making of a Modern Author*, 3–64.

31 Ascoli, *Dante and the Making of a Modern Author*, 10.

32 Anna Pegoretti, "Early Reception Until 1481," in *The Cambridge Companion to Dante's "Commedia,"* ed. Zygmunt G. Barański and Simon Gilson (Cambridge: Cambridge University Press, 2018), 249. For a modern example of this heuristic practice, see Ascoli, *Dante and the Making of a Modern Author*, 11.

33 On palinodic/recantatory echoes in Dante's work, see Ascoli, *Dante and the Making of a Modern Author*, 274–300.

34 On Claude Lévi-Strauss's bricoleurs, see Matt Rogers, "Contextualizing Theories and Practices of Bricolage Research," *Qualitative Report* 17 (2012): 3. For more on bricolage in the medieval context, see Claire Sponsler, "In Transit: Theorizing Cultural Appropriation in Medieval Europe," *Journal of Medieval and Early Modern Studies* 32, no. 1 (2002): 17–40.

35 Immanuel, *Commentary on Ecclesiastes*, in Cincinnati, Hebrew Union College, MS. Acc. 167, fol. 43v.

36 Immanuel, *Commentary on Proverbs* 10:6–9, in Parma, Biblioteca Palatina, MS. Cod. Parm. 2966 fols. 29v–30r.

37 Moshe David Cassuto, *Dante v'Immanuel ha-Romi* (Jerusalem: Mossad Bialik, 1965).

38 Saul Tchernikovski, *Immanuel of Rome: A Monograph* (Berlin: Eshkol, 1925), 149.

39 For the lovers, see Dante Alighieri, *The Divine Comedy: Inferno*, ed. Robert Hollander and Jean Hollander (New York: Anchor Books, 2002), canto 5; David Fishelov, "From Dante's 'Inferno' to Immanuel's 'Tophet,'" *Bikkoret U'farshanut* 27 (1991): 19–42.

40 Dan Pagis, *Ḥidush u-masoret*, 271–273. For Jewish tours of the netherworld, see Martha Himmelfarb, *Tours of Hell: An Apocalyptic Form in Jewish and Christian Literature* (Philadelphia: University of Pennsylvania Press, 1983).

41 Roma, Biblioteca Casanatense, MS. 433; Fabian Alfie, "Immanuel of Rome, Alias Manoello Giudeo: The Poetics of Jewish Identity in Fourteenth-Century Italy," *Italica* 75, no. 3 (1998): 307–329.

42 Dvora Bregman, "On the Acceptance of the Sonnet in Hebrew Poetry," *Tarbiz* 56 (1986): 109–124.

43 Roma, Biblioteca Casanatense, MS. 433

44 Walfish, *Esther in Medieval Garb*, 231–233.

45 Fabian Alfie, "Immanuel of Rome, Alias Manoello Giudeo: The Poetics of Jewish Identity in Fourteenth-Century Italy," *Italica* 75, no. 3 (1998): 307–329; Umberto Cassuto, "L'Elemento Italiano Nelle 'Mechabberoth' Di Immanuele Romano," *Rivista Israelitica* 2 (1905): 29–38, 109–115, 156–163, 199–205, 235–244; Immanuel of Rome, *Maḥberoth*, ed. D. Jarden, 105–106.

46 The two Italian sonnets that mention the Guelphs and Ghibellines are "Io steso non mi conosco" and "Se san Pietro and san Paul." P. Jones, *The Italian City-State: From Commune to Signoria* (Oxford: Clarendon Press, 1997); Chris Wickham, *Sleepwalking into a New World: The Emergence of Italian City Communes in the Twelfth Century* (Princeton, NJ: Princeton University Press, 2015); J. Maire Vigueur, *Cavaliers et citoyens: Guerre, conflits et société dans l'Italie communale, XIIe–XIIIe siècles* (Paris: École des Hautes Études en Sciences Sociales, 2003); R. Krautheimer, *Rome: Profile of a City, 312–1308* (Princeton, NJ: Princeton University Press, 1980); E. Duprè Theseider, *Roma dal comune di popolo alla signoria Pontificia* (1252–1377) (Bologna: L. Cappelli, 1952).

47 J. Rollo-Koster, *Avignon and Its Papacy, 1309–1417: Popes, Institutions, and Society* (Lanham, MD: Rowman and Littlefield, 2015); J. Rollo-Koster,

Raiding Saint Peter: Empty Sees, Violence, and the Initiation of the Great Western Schism (1378) (Leiden: Brill, 2008).

48 Anna Esposito, *Un'altra Roma: Minoranze nazionali e comunità ebraiche tra Medioevo e Rinascimento* (Rome: Il Calamo, 1995).

49 Anna Esposito, "Gli Ebrei a Roma Nella Seconda Metà Del '400 Attraverso i Protocolli Del Notaio Giovanni Angelo Amati," in *Aspetti e Problemi Della Presenza Ebraica Nell'Italia Centro-Settentrionale: (Secoli XIV e XV); [Presentazione Di Sofia Boesch Gajano]* (Rome: Università di Roma, 1983), 29–125.

50 Luigi Rossi, "'Populus Firmanus Iterum Petit Hebreos': Fermo, Secoli XIV–XVI," in *La Presenza Ebraica Nelle Marche Secoli XIII–XX*, ed. Sergio Anselmi and Viviana Bonazzoli (Ancona: Quaderni monografici di Proposte e richerche, 1993).

51 There is only one complete copy of the *Maḥbarot* in MS. Paris 1286, as many editions only contain a few *maḥbarot* rather than all twenty-eight.

52 *Maḥberet Ha-Tofet V'Ha-Eden* was printed alone in Prague in 1613; in Frankfurt am Main in 1713; and in Berlin in 1922 by Eliezer Goldschmidt. Leib Mehokek printed *Tofet V'Ha-Eden* together with the *maḥberet* on old age (25) and the *maḥberet* on wine (26) in Berlin in 1796, and those three *maḥbarot* were printed again in Berlin in 1778; Isaac Ben Yaakov, *Otzar Ha-Sefarim* (Vilnius: Press of Widow & Sons Romm, 1857) 314, §895.

53 Moses Rieti, *Mikdash Me'at* (Vienna: J. Goldenthal, 1851), 106.

54 Immanuel Francis, *Metek Sefatayim* (Cracow: Fisher Press, 1892), 34.

55 Hezekiah David Bolaffio, *Ben Zekunim* (Leghorn: Sa'adon Press, 1793), 35.

56 Dvora Bregman, "On the Acceptance of the Sonnet in Hebrew Poetry," *Tarbiz* 56 (1986): 109–124; Dvora Bregman mentions this influence in *The Golden Way: The Hebrew Sonnet During the Renaissance and the Baroque*, trans. Ann Brener, Medieval and Renaissance Texts and Studies (Tempe: Arizona State University Press), 2–3.

57 J. Chotzner, "Immanuel Di Romi, A Thirteenth Century Hebrew Poet and Novelist," *Jewish Quarterly Review* 4 (1892): 75.

58 Chotzner, "Immanuel Di Romi," 74.

59 Cecil Roth, *The Jews in the World of the Renaissance* (Philadelphia: Jewish Publication Society of America, 1959), 95.

60 David Malkiel, "Eros as Medium: Rereading Immanuel of Rome's Scroll of Desire," in *Donne Nella Storia Degli Ebrei d'Italia*, ed. Cristina Galasso E Michele Luzzati (Florence: Giuntina, 2007), 35–59.

Chapter 1

Epigraphs: https://seforimblog.com/2009/10/wine-women-and-song-part-iii/, accessed July 5, 2018; Heinrich Graetz, *History of the Jews*, vol. 4 (Philadelphia: Jewish Publication Society of America, 1967), 63.

1 Parma, Biblioteca Palatina, MS. Cod. Parm. 3098 and 2961.

2 Shimon Bernfeld, "Rabbi Immanuel of Rome and His Maḥbarot," *Luach Ahiasaf* 4 (1896): 24. Guy Shaked, "Immanuel Romano: Una Nuova

Biografia," in *Maḥberet Prima* (Milan: Aquilegia, 2002), 167–168. Shaked's calculation is based on a comment that it had been 5,880 years since certain stars had been visible. The year AM 5880 is 1328 in the Christian calendar, leading Shaked to assume that *Maḥberet* 27 was composed that year.

3 Isaac Markus Jost, "Beitrag zur judischen Geschichte und Bibliographie," *Wissenschaftliche Zeitschrift für Jüdische Theologie* 1 (1835): 362–366.

4 Immanuel of Rome, *Maḥberoth*, ed. D. Jarden, 511.

5 Moritz Güdemann posited 1270–1330 as Immanuel's lifetime, exactly sixty years in length. See Moritz Güdemann and Abraham Shalom Friedberg, *Ha-Torah ṿeha-ḥayim bi-yeme ha-benayim be-Tsarfat ṿe-Ashkenaz*, vol. 2 (Tel Aviv: Makhon le-firsumin, 1968), 91. Heinrich Graetz suggested a birth year of 1265, while Shaul Tchernikovski assumed that *Maḥberet Ha-Tofet V'Ha-Eden* could have been written only following the publication of the *Commedia*, in 1322. Using Immanuel's self-professed age of sixty, Tchernikovski calculated 1260 as Immanuel's birth year. He also claims that the death of Immanuel's younger friend in the introduction to *Tofet V'Ha-Eden* referred to Dante's death in 1321. See Saul Tchernikovski, *Immanuel of Rome* (Berlin: Eshkol, 1925), 148–149. An undated Latin inscription in the flyleaf of Immanuel's commentary on Song of Songs notes that "Immanuel was born in the year 1241, and he was an eminent poet whose elegant compositions are extant," but the author of this note is unknown; the data likely come from the catalog of Christian scholar Johann Christian Wolf (d. 1739). See British Library, Harley MS. 5797, flyleaf 004r. Ilana Tahan, chief curator of Judaica at the British Library, informed me that the previous owners of the collection now called Harley are unknown. The collection was assembled by the earls of Harley in the early eighteenth century; Johann Christopher Wolf, *Bibliotheca Hebraea* (Hamburg: Chr. Liebezeit e.a., 1715). A current example of extracting biographical details from Immanuel's poetic corpus is found in Dario Internullo, *Ai Margini Dei Giganti: La Vita Intelletuale Dei Romani Nel Trecento (1305–1367)* (Rome: Viella, 2016), 217.

6 Shimon Bernfeld explained that *Sefer Tekhunah* referred to an abridgment of Ptolemy's *Almagest* by Abū Muḥammad Jābir ibn Aflaḥ, an eleventh-century Muslim astronomer from Seville. The book was translated into Hebrew twice, first by Jacob ben Makhir and then by Samuel ben Judah of Marseilles in 1336. Bernfeld read a line in the eighth *maḥberet* as a reference to this book and concluded that Immanuel lived past 1336. The Jarden edition, reflecting Paris BNF MS héb 1286, renders the word *Tevunah*. See Shimon Bernfeld, "Rabbi Immanuel of Rome and His Maḥbarot," *Luach Ahiasaf* 4 (1896): 23.

7 On the papal decree and whether it was executed, see Joseph Shatzmiller, "The Papal Monarchy as Viewed by Medieval Jews." In *Italia Judaica: Gli Ebrei Nello Stato Pontificio Fino Al Ghetto (1555)*. Rome: Ministero Per I Beni Culturali e Ambientali Ufficio Centrale Per I Beni Archivisti, 1998, 30–42.

8 Eleazar Birnbaum, "Maḥzor Roma: The Cluj Manuscript Dated 5159 A.M./ 1399 C.E. and the Public Fast in Rome in 1321 C.E.," *Jewish Quarterly Review* 76, no. 2 (1985): 59–95; Joseph Shatzmiller, "The Papal Monarchy as Viewed by Medieval Jews," 30–41.

9 Cecil Roth drew conclusions based on Immanuel's sixty years but also noticed the similarity to Dante's introduction. Cecil Roth, *The Jews in the World of the Renaissance* (Philadelphia: Jewish Publication Society of America, 1959), 100. See Dante Alighieri, *The Divine Comedy: Inferno*, canto I.

10 Immanuel, *Commentary on Song of Songs*, ed. Israel Ravitsky, in "R. Immanuel b. Shlomo: Commentary to the 'Song of Songs' Philosophical Division," Master's thesis, Hebrew University, 1970, 201–202, §86b.

11 Immanuel, *Commentary on Song of Songs*, ed. Ravitsky, 209, § 94a.

12 Yossef Schwartz, "Cultural Identity in Transmission: Language, Science, and the Medical Profession in Thirteenth-Century Italy," in *Entangled Histories: Knowledge, Authority, and Transmission in Thirteenth-Century Jewish Cultures*, ed. Elisheva Baumgarten, Ruth Mazo Karras, and Katelyn Mesler (Philadelphia: University of Pennsylvania Press, 2017), 181–203.

13 Dana W. Fishkin, "A Lifetime in Letters: New Evidence Concerning Immanuel of Rome's Timeline," *Jewish Quarterly Review* 112, no. 3 (2022): 406–433.

14 See Cecil Roth, "New Light on Dante's Circle," *Modern Language Review* 48, no. 1 (1953): 27.

15 Isabelle Levy, "Immanuel of Rome and Dante," in *Digital Dante* (New York: Columbia University Libraries, 2017), http://digitaldante.columbia.edu/history/immanuel-of-rome-and-dante-levy/, accessed May 9, 2018. A translation of Cino's lyrics is found in Cecil Roth, "New Light," 28, where Roth claims that Immanuel lost a close friend from Gubbio, while most others interpret it as Immanuel's wife. Cassuto insists that this was Immanuel's young non-Jewish lover described in the third *maḥberet*. M. D. Cassuto, *Dante v'Immanuel ha-Romi*, 12–13. Also see Immanuel of Rome, *Maḥberoth*, ed. D. Jarden, 17.

16 Cecil Roth, "The Historical Background of Maḥbarot Immanuel," in *Sefer Assaf*, ed. Moshe David Cassuto, Joseph Klausner, and Julius Gutmann (Jerusalem: Mossad ha-Rav Kook, 1952), 447.

17 Luca Carlo Rossi, "Una Ricomposta Tenzone (Autentica?) Fra Cina Da Pistoia e Bosone Da Gubbio," *Italia Medioevale e Umanistica* 31 (1988): 45–79.

18 Levy, "Immanuel of Rome and Dante."

19 Levy, "Immanuel of Rome and Dante."

20 Devorah Schechterman, "The Philosophy of Immanuel of Rome in Light of His Commentary on the Book of Genesis" (Jerusalem: Hebrew University, 1984), 3–11; Parma, Biblioteca Palatina, MS. Cod. Parm. 2445, fol. 147v. The recipes for ink are followed by *Edut Hashem Ne'emanah*, a medieval Hebrew polemical treatise that Daniel Jael attributes to Immanuel; he

corrects himself in a marginal note that reveals Solomon ben Moses to be the author. As Immanuel's father was Solomon ben Moses, Jael considers the possibility that Immanuel's father authored the polemical treatise.

21 Parma, Biblioteca Palatina, MS. Cod. Parm. 2445, fol. 142r.

22 Città del Vaticano, Biblioteca Apostolica Vaticana, MS. Ebr. 436, fol. 1.

23 Abraham b. Menahem Alatrino was a scribe who copied at least five extant manuscripts.

24 Matti Huss, "The Status of Fiction in the Hebrew Maqama: Judah Al-Harizi and Immanuel of Rome," *Tarbiz* 67, no. 3 (1998): 355.

25 Dvora Bregman, *The Golden Way: The Hebrew Sonnet During the Renaissance and the Baroque*, trans. Ann Brener, Medieval and Renaissance Texts and Studies (Tempe: Arizona State University Press, 2006).

26 Immanuel mentions his descent from the Kitim in Immanuel of Rome, *Maḥberoth*, ed. D. Jarden, 34 (line 591), and his citation of Jossipon appears in David Goldstein, "The Commentary of Immanuel Ben Solomon of Rome on Chapters I–X of Genesis: Introduction, Hebrew Text, Notes" (PhD diss., University of London, 1966), 194; Parma, Biblioteca Palatina, MS. Cod. Parm. 2304, fol. 70r and Parma, Biblioteca Palatina, MS. Cod. Parm. 2285, fol. 91r.

27 The sixth *maḥberet*, in which Immanuel affirms the greatness of Rome, presents Immanuel in a poetic duel with a Provençal poet; see Immanuel of Rome, *Maḥberoth*, ed. D. Jarden, 105–123.

28 Immanuel, *Commentary on Job*, in Parma, Biblioteca Palatina, MS. Cod. Parm. 2961.

29 Abraham Berliner identified this as Ceprano in *Geschichte der Juden in Rom von der ältesten Zeit bis zur Gegenwart (2050 Jahre)* vol. 2 (Frankfurt am Main: J. Kauffmann Press, 1893), 53–54; Moses Rieti, *Mikdash Me'at* (Vienna: J. Goldenthal, 1851), 106. See the special edition of *Prooftexts* devoted to Moses Rieti and *Mikdash Me'at*: *Prooftexts* 23, no. 1 (Winter 2003).

30 Città del Vaticano, Biblioteca Apostolica Vaticana, MS. Barb. Lat. 3953, 16th century; Immanuel Francis, "Metek Sefatayim," in *Hebraische Prosodie*, ed. Heinrich Brody (Kracow: Josef Fischer, 1892), 34.

31 Esposito, "Gli Ebrei a Roma Nella Seconda Metà Del '400 Attraverso i Protocolli Del Notaio Giovanni Angelo Amati," in *Aspetti e Problemi Della Presenza Ebraica Nell'Italia Centro-Settentrionale: (Secoli XIV e XV); [Presentazione Di Sofia Boesch Gajano]* (Rome: Università di Roma, 1983), 29–125.

32 Simona Foa, "Immanuel da Roma," in *Dizionario Biografico degli Italiani*, vol. 62 (2004); for a fuller treatment of the "Bisbidis" poem, see Isabelle Levy, "Immanuel of Rome's Bisbidis: An Italian Maqāma?" *Medieval Encounters* 27 (2021): 78–115.

33 Christopher Wickham, "The 'Feudal Revolution' and the Origins of the Italian City Communes," *Transactions of the Royal Historical Society* 24 (2014): 29–55.

34 David Abulafia, *Frederick II: A Medieval Emperor* (New York: Viking Press, 1988).

35 Città del Vaticano, Biblioteca Apostolica Vaticana, MS. Ebr. 300, fol. 17a.
36 Alfie, "Immanuel of Rome, Alias Manoello Giudeo," 317–318.
37 These rituals included a Jewish representative bowing before a new pope and handing him a Torah scroll, and taxes were demanded to finance the "Agonis e Testaccio" games. See Vogelstein, *Rome*, 181–182, 202, 218–219.
38 P. J. Jones, "Communes and Despots: The City State in Late-Medieval Italy," *Transactions of the Royal Historical Society* 15 (1965): 71–96.
39 Immanuel, *Commentary on Proverbs* 28:2–3, in *The Book of Proverbs*, ed. Goldstein, 167.
40 Immanuel of Rome, *Maḥberoth*, ed. D. Jarden, 149 (lines 227–228).
41 Shulamit Elizur, *Hebrew Poetry in Spain in the Middle Ages*, vol. 3 (Ramat Aviv: Open University of Israel, 2004), 264–265.
42 Immanuel of Rome, *Maḥberoth*, ed. D. Jarden, 74 (lines 65–68, and 315, lines 144–148). He recalls being treated well in Camerino and lauds his patron and the patron's wife in Immanuel of Rome, *Maḥberoth*, ed. D. Jarden, 327–331 (lines 404–508).
43 Dana Fishkin, "Letters of Loathing: Immanuel of Rome and Romance Epistolary," in *Medieval Jewish Romance*, ed. Caroline Gruenbaum and Annegret Oehme (Kalamazoo, MI: Arc Humanities Press, forthcoming).
44 Cicero, *De Inventione*, trans. H. M. Hubbell, Loeb Classical Library 386 (Cambridge, MA: Harvard University Press, 1949), 55.
45 Cicero, *De Inventione*, I, xix, 57.
46 Dov Jarden argued that the two introductions were alternate versions of the introduction to the *Maḥbarot.* Immanuel of Rome, *Maḥberoth*, ed. D. Jarden, 33; Huss, "The Status of Fiction in the Hebrew Maqama," 371.
47 Jefim Schirmann, "The Function of the Hebrew Poet in Medieval Spain," *Jewish Social Studies* 16 (1954): 240–244.
48 Fermo, Italy, Archivio di Stato, Cod. Dipl. MS. 829.
49 Cecil Roth, "The Historical Background of Maḥberot Immanuel," in *Sefer Assaph*, ed. Moshe David Cassuto, Joseph Klausner, and Julius Gutmann (Jerusalem: Mossad Ha-Rav Kook, 1952), 445.
50 Giuseppe Sermoneta, "La Dottrina dell'intelletto e La 'fede Filosofica' di Jehudah e Immanuel Romano," *Studi Medievali* 6, no. 2 (1965): 3–78. Devorah Schechterman sees symbolic significance in the *Sar*'s character, suggesting that he represents Immanuel's potential intellect that has actualized itself; Schechterman, "The Philosophy of Immanuel of Rome," 153. Dov Jarden acknowledges that, while the patron and the traveler express different voices, both were written by Immanuel; see in Immanuel of Rome, *Maḥberoth*, ed. D. Jarden, 33.
51 H. G. Enelow, "Review of *Immanuel of Rome* by Shaul Tchernikovski," *Jewish Quarterly Review* 16, no. 2 (1925): 209–212.
52 Huss, "The Place of Fiction," 351–378.
53 Immanuel of Rome, *Maḥberoth*, ed. D. Jarden, 5 (lines 51–54).
54 Immanuel of Rome, *Maḥberoth*, ed. D. Jarden, 3–6, 6–7.
55 Immanuel of Rome, *Maḥberoth*, ed. D. Jarden, 7 (lines 81–84).

56 Huss, "The Place of Fiction," 351–378.

57 *Commentary on Job*, in Parma Cod. Parm. MS. 2877, fols. 002a–b.

58 David Goldstein claims that mention of a commentary is not sufficient proof for dating, but rather that Immanuel simultaneously glossed many biblical books. Nevertheless, the sense from this preface is that the Proverbs gloss was substantial enough to draw financial support from a patron. See Immanuel, *Commentary on Proverbs*, ed. Goldstein, 10.

59 Immanuel of Rome, *Maḥberoth*, ed. D. Jarden, 6 (lines 72–73).

60 Immanuel of Rome, *Maḥberoth*, ed. D. Jarden, 7 (lines 93–94).

61 Parma, Biblioteca Palatina, MS. Cod. Parm. 2877, fol. 2b.

62 Immanuel includes a panegyric poem addressed to Menaḥem in *Maḥberet* 8. In Paris, Bibliotheque, National, MS. 1287, Cambridge, England, Cambridge University Library, Ms. Add. 402, and Parma, Biblioteca Palatina, MS. Cod. Parm. 2121, the addressee of the poem is Solomon. See Immanuel of Rome, *Maḥberoth*, ed. D. Jarden, 153 (line 322).

63 Immanuel of Rome, *Maḥberoth*, ed. D. Jarden, 5 (lines 284–285), 179 (lines 11–14), and 233 (lines 6–9).

64 Immanuel ends the third *maḥberet* saying that the affair forced him out of the patron's house for ten years. The fourth *maḥberet* opens after ten years of Immanuel's exile from the patron had passed, and he was welcomed back into his home. Jarden notes the literary character of the third *maḥberet* and argues that the spat between Immanuel and the patron constitutes the only realia in the story. Immanuel of Rome, *Maḥberoth*, ed. D. Jarden, 15.

65 Chotzner bases this view on Immanuel's description of an unfortunate financial incident where he acted as a creditor for a friend and lost all his money when the loan could not be repaid, in Chotzner, "Immanuel Di Romi," 68; Immanuel of Rome, *Maḥberoth*, ed. D. Jarden, 11 (lines 44–45).

66 Immanuel, *Commentary on Proverbs* 6:1–2, in Biblioteca Palatina, MS. Cod. Parm. 2966, fol. 19r.

67 Chotzner, "Immanuel Di Romi," 66. For a description of the biographical fallacy, see Roland Barthes, "The Death of the Author," in *Image, Music, Text* (London: Fontana Press, 1977), 142–148. The biographical fallacy is well described as "the explanation of a work is always sought in the man or woman who produced it, as if it were always in the end, through the more or less transparent allegory of the fiction, the voice of a single person, the author 'confiding' in us" (143). For a description of how fiction functions in Immanuel's *Maḥbarot*, see Huss, "The Status of Fiction in the Hebrew Maqama."

68 Moses Avigdor Shulvass, *The Jews in the World of the Renaissance* (Leiden: Brill, 1973), 29. Emphasis mine.

69 Shaked, "Immanuel Romano: Una Nuova Biografia," 166.

70 Michael A. Meyer, "Two Persistent Tensions Within Wissenschaft Des Judentums," *Modern Judaism* 24, no. 2 (2004): 105–119.

71 Leopold Zunz, "Rom A. 1270 bis 1330," in *Wissenschaftliche Zeitschrift für Jüdische Theologie* 4 (1839): 193–198. Heinrich Graetz called Immanuel an anomaly in *History of the Jews*, vol. 4 (Philadelphia: Jewish Publication

Society of America, 1967), 63; Michael A. Meyer, "The Emergence of Jewish Historiography: Motives and Motifs," *History and Theory* 27, no. 4, Beiheft 27: Essays in Jewish Historiography (December 1988): 162.

72 Enelow, "Review of Immanuel of Rome by Shaul Tchernikovski," 209. Israel Zangwill, a British playwright, and Martin Buber, an Austrian philosopher, strongly advocated for Jewish assimilation in the twentieth century.

73 Heinrich Graetz, *History of the Jews*, 64.

74 Heinrich Graetz, *History of the Jews*, 59.

75 Eva Hölter, "Dante's Long Road to the German Library: Literary Reception from Early Romanticism Until the Late Nineteenth Century," in *Dante in the Long Nineteenth Century: Nationality, Identity, and Appropriation*, ed. Aida Audeh, and Nick Havely (Oxford: Oxford University Press, 2012), 229.

76 Chotzner, "Immanuel Di Romi," 73.

77 Chotzner, "Immanuel Di Romi," 64.

78 Chotzner, "Immanuel Di Romi," 65.

79 Ida Grassi, "Il primo periodo della 'Giovane Italia' nel Granducato di Toscana (1831–1834)," *Rivista storica del Risorgimento italiano* 2 (1897): 904–947.

80 Sabato Morais and Samuel David Luzzato, *Italian Hebrew Literature* (New York: Hermon Press, 1926), 9.

81 Arthur Kiron, "Heralds of Duty: The Sephardic Italian Jewish Theological Seminary of Sabato Morais," *Jewish Quarterly Review* 105, no. 2 (2015): 215–218.

82 Asher Salah, "A Matter of Quotation: Dante and the Literary Identity of Jews in Italy," in *The Italia Judaica Jubilee Conference* (Leiden: Brill, 2012), 182.

83 Luzzatto calls Immanuel "amico di Dante" in *Appendice all'opera intitolata della letteratura italiana nella seconda meta del secolo XVIII di Camillo Ugoni*, 2d ed. (Brescia: Nicolò Bettoni, 1868), 16.

Chapter 2

Epigraphs: Immanuel of Rome, *Maḥberoth*, ed. D. Jarden, 217 (line 14); 159 (line 443).

1 Aviezer Ravitsky, "The Hypostasis of Supernal Wisdom in Jewish Philosophy of the Thirteenth Century," *Italia: Studi e Richerche Sulla Storia, La Cultura e La Letteratura Degli Ebrei D'Italia* 3 (1982): 10.

2 Israel Ta-Shma, "The Acceptance of Maimonides' Mishneh Torah in Italy," *Italia: Studi e Richerche Sulla Storia, La Cultura e La Letteratura Degli Ebrei D'Italia* 13/15 (2001): 79–90; Shulvass, *The Jews in the World of the Renaissance*, 312; Isaiah Sonne, "Sifrut Ha-Mussar V'HaPhilosophia B'Shirei Immanuel Ha-Romi" *Tarbiz* (1934): 326; Ravitsky, "The Hypostasis of Supernal Wisdom," 10.

3 Igor H. De Souza, *Rewriting Maimonides: Early Commentaries on the "The Guide of the Perplexed"* (Berlin: De Gruyter, 2018), 19–91; Moshe Idel,

"Maimonides' 'The Guide of the Perplexed' and the Kabbalah," *Jewish History* 18, nos. 2/3 (2004): 197–226; Giuseppe Sermoneta, *Un glossario filosofico ebraico-italiano del XIII del secolo* (Rome: Edizioni dell'Ateneo, 1969).

4 One example of this is found in Mahzor Roma, in Parma, Biblioteca Palatina, MS. Cod. Parm. 2888, fols. 79–110.

5 Robinson, "Maimonides, Samuel Ibn Tibbon, and the Construction of a Jewish Tradition of Philosophy"; Robinson, "We Drink Only from the Master's Water"; and Carlos Fraenkel, "From Maimonides to Samuel Ibn Tibbon: Interpreting Judaism as a Philosophical Religion," in *The Cultures of Maimonideanism* (Leiden: Brill, 2009), 177–211.

6 According to Tamar Rudavsky, "Maimonides had little regard for the intellectual acumen of the average person, and did not expect that the majority of individuals would be able to engage in sophisticated intellectual pursuits." See Tamar Rudavsky, *Jewish Philosophy in the Middle Ages: Science, Rationalism, and Religion* (Oxford: Oxford University Press, 2018), 78. Maimonides provides general rules for interpreting parables in the introduction to *The Guide of the Perplexed*. He distinguishes between two types of prophetic parable: one in which each word has significance, and the other in which the central concept of the allegory is important, but each word does not bear significance. See Maimonides, *The Guide of the Perplexed*, trans. S. Pines (Chicago: University of Chicago Press, 1963), 8–14. Scholars are divided over Maimonides' motivation for writing abstractly, with Leo Strauss and Alfred Ivry claiming that Maimonides obscured his philosophical convictions that were contrary to conventional rabbinic ideas to protect his reputation. See Alfred Ivry, *Maimonides' "The Guide of the Perplexed": A Philosophical Guide* (Chicago: University of Chicago Press, 2016); Leo Strauss, "How to Begin to Study *The Guide of the Perplexed*," in *The Guide of the Perplexed*, trans. S. Pines, xi–lvi; for an opposing view, see Hava Tirosh-Samuelson, *Happiness in Premodern Judaism: Virtue, Knowledge, and Well-Being* (Cincinnati, OH: Hebrew Union College Press, 2003).

7 Aviezer Ravitzky, "Samuel Ibn Tibbon and the Esoteric Character of the 'The Guide of the Perplexed,'" *Association for Jewish Studies Review* 6 (1981): 87–123. For a detailed description of Ibn Tibbon's impact, see Haim (Howard) Kreisel, "Moses Ibn Tibbon: Translator and Philosophical Exegete," in *Judaism as Philosophy: Studies in Maimonides and the Medieval Jewish Philosophers of Provence* (Brookline, MA: Academic Studies Press, 2015), 79–82.

8 For full bibliography on Samuel Ibn Tibbon, see Carlos Fraenkel, *From Maimonides to Samuel Ibn Tibbon: The Transformation of the Dalalat al-Hairin into the Moreh Nevukhim* [Hebrew] (Jerusalem: Hebrew University Magness Press, 2007); James T. Robinson, "The Ibn Tibbon Family," in *Beerot Yitzchak: Studies in Memory of Isadore Twersky* (Cambridge, MA: Harvard University Press, 2005), 193–225.

9 Moshe Halbertal, *Concealment and Revelation: Esotericism in Jewish Thought and Its Philosophical Implications*, trans. Jackie Feldman (Princeton, NJ: Princeton University Press, 2007), 110–111.

10 Samuel Ibn Tibbon, *Perush ha-Millot ha-Zarot*, appendix to *Maimonides, Moreh ha-Nevukhim*, ed. Y. Even-Shemuel (Jerusalem: Mossad ha-Rav Kook, 1987). The fourteenth-century scholar Moses ben Solomon of Salerno, a Jew patronized by the royal court, wrote a commentary on *The Guide of the Perplexed* as well as a Hebrew-Italian philosophical glossary. Moses was familiar with the *Guide*'s Hebrew and Latin translations, and he engaged a Christian scholar in his commentary to discuss difficult passages in the *Guide*. Rationalist Jewish scholarship entered Italy through the royal courts, flourishing alongside the Jewish community in southern Italy until the expulsion of the Jews from the region in the thirteenth and fourteenth centuries. Thus the focal center of scholarship shifted from the south to Rome and the north, where new Jewish communities were being formed. On Moses, see Giuseppe Sermoneta, *Un glossario filosofico ebraico-italiano del XIII del secolo* (Rome: Edizioni dell'Ateneo, 1969).

11 James T. Robinson, *Samuel Ibn Tibbon's Commentary on Ecclesiastes: The Book of the Soul of Man* (Tübingen: Mohr Siebeck, 2007); James T. Robinson, "From Digression to Compilation: Samuel Ibn Tibbon and Immanuel of Rome on Genesis 1:11, 1:14, and 1:20," *Zutot* 4 (2006): 81–97.

12 Jacob Anatoli, *Malmad ha-Talmidim* (Lyck: Mekize Nirdamim, 1866); Luciana Pepi, ed., *Il pungolo dei discepoli: Il sapere di un ebreo e Federico II* (Palermo: Officina di studi medievali: Fondazione Federico II, 2004); Halbertal, *Concealment and Revelation*, 115; Israel Bettan, "The Sermons of Jacob Anatoli," *Hebrew Union College Annual* 11 (1936): 391–424; Aviezer Ravitsky, "On the Sources of Immanuel's Proverbs Commentary" [Hebrew], *Qiryat Sefer* 56, no. 4 (1981): 735–738.

13 Mauro Zonta, *La Filosofia Antica Nel Medioevo Ebraico: Le Traduzioni Ebraiche Medievali Dei Testi Filosofici Antichi* (Brescia: Paideia, 2002), 180–188; Schwartz, "Cultural Identity in Transmission," 181–203.

14 See Lynn Thorndike, *Michael Scot* (London: Nelson, 1965). Dante places Scot in *Inferno*, canto XX, with the magicians. Martin Gordon, "The Rationalism of Jacob Anatoli," PhD diss. (Yeshiva University, 1974), 72, 108, 25.

15 Immanuel of Rome, *Maḥberoth*, ed. D. Jarden, 542.

16 James T. Robinson, "The 'Secret of the Heavens' and the 'Secret of Number': Immanuel of Rome's Mathematical Supercommentaries on Abraham Ibn Ezra in His Commentary on Qohelet 5:7 and 7:27," *Aleph* 21, no. 2 (2021): 279–308; Kreisel, "Moses Ibn Tibbon: Translator and Philosophical Exegete"; Immanuel's commentary on Song of Songs appears in Israel Ravitsky, "R. Immanuel b. Shlomo: Commentary to the 'Song of Songs' Philosophical Division" (Master's thesis, Hebrew University, 1970), 18.

17 For more detail on differences between Maimonidean biblical exegesis and that of the Ibn Tibbon family, see Kreisel, "Moses Ibn Tibbon: Translator and Philosophical Exegete," 82–83.

18 Yossef Schwartz, "Thirteenth Century Hebrew Psychological Discussion: The Role of Latin Sources in the Formation of Hebrew Aristotelianism,"

in *The Letter Before the Spirit: The Importance of Text Editions for the Study of the Reception of Aristotle* (Leiden: Brill, 2012), 192–193; Caterina Rigo, "Un'antologia Filosofica di Yehuda Ben Mosheh Romano," *Italia: Studi e Richerche Sulla Storia, La Cultura e La Letteratura Degli Ebrei D'Italia* 10 (1993): 73–104; Caterina Rigo, "The Be'urim on the Bible of R. Yehudah Romano: The Philosophical Method Which Comes Out of Them, Their Sources in the Jewish Philosophy and in the Christian Scholasticism," PhD diss. (Hebrew University, 1996), 53–60, 168–392; Caterina Rigo, "Human Substance and Eternal Life in the Philosophy of Rabbi Judah Romano," *Jerusalem Studies in Jewish Thought* 14 (1998): 181–222; Ravitsky, "The Thought of R. Zeraḥiah b. Isaac b. Shealtiel Ḥen."

19 Immanuel of Rome, *Maḥberoth*, ed. D. Jarden, 217–231; Moses Rieti, *Mikdash Me'at* (Vienna: J. Goldenthal, 1851).

20 Immanuel of Rome, *Maḥberoth*, ed. D. Jarden, 219 (lines 45–56).

21 Immanuel of Rome, *Maḥberoth*, ed. D. Jarden, 219 (lines 52–53).

22 Moshe Idel, *R. Menahem Recanati: The Kabbalist* (Tel-Aviv: Schocken Publishing House, 1998); Dana W. Fishkin, "A Lifetime in Letters: New Evidence Concerning Immanuel of Rome's Timeline," *Jewish Quarterly Review* 112, no. 3 (2022): 406–433. Caterina Rigo, "The Be'urim on the Bible of R. Yehudah Romano."

23 Sermoneta, "La dottrina dell'intelletto," 3–78.

24 Sermoneta, "La dottrina dell'intelletto," 38–42.

25 Immanuel of Rome, *Maḥberoth*, ed. D. Jarden, 23–25 (lines 317–370).

26 Fishkin, "A Lifetime in Letters."

27 Maimonides, *Guide* II:4–10, trans. S. Pines, 255–273.

28 Herbert Davidson, *Alfarabi, Avicenna, and Avveroes on Intellect: Their Cosmologies, Theories of Active Intellect, and Theories of Human Intellect* (Oxford: Oxford University Press, 1992), 128.

29 Parma, Biblioteca Palatina, MS. Cod. Parm. 2843, fols. 45r, 50r–53v; David Blumenthal, *Philosophic Mysticism: Studies in Rational Religion* (Ramat Gan: Bar Ilan University, 2006), 53–56.

30 Immanuel, *Commentary on Psalms*, in Parma, Biblioteca Palatina, MS. Cod. Parm. 2843, fols. 45r, 50r–53v; Blumenthal, *Philosophic Mysticism*, 53–56. David Blumenthal uses the word "Godself," which best conveys the human inability to know God.

31 He describes the actualization of the material intellect in *Commentary on Song of Songs*, in London, British Library, Harley MS. 5797, fol. 87r and fols. 89r–v, as well as in Immanuel, *Commentary on Proverbs*, in Parma, Biblioteca Palatina, MS. Cod. Parm. 2966, fol. 7r.

32 Rigo, "Human Substance and Eternal Life in the Philosophy of Rabbi Judah Romano," 181–222.

33 Immanuel, *Commentary on Genesis* 2:10, in Goldstein, "The Commentary of Immanuel Ben Solomon of Rome on Chapters I–X of Genesis," 60–61; Immanuel, *Maḥberoth*, ed. D. Jarden, 541 (line 713), 546 (line 756); Maimonides, *Mishneh Torah*, Hilkhot Teshuva 8:2.

34 Immanuel, *Commentary on Song of Songs*, in London, British Library, Harley MS. 5797, fol. 86r.

35 Maimonides, *Eight Chapters*, chapter 1, in *Ethical Writings of Maimonides*, ed. R. Weiss and C. Butterworth (New York: Dover Press, 1975), 61. Immanuel, *Commentary on Song of Songs* in London, British Library, Harley MS. 5797, fol. 113v; for Immanuel's identification of three faculties of imagination, cognition, and memory, see Immanuel, *Commentary on Proverbs 4:9*, in Parma, Biblioteca Palatina, MS. Cod. Parm. 2966, fol. 15r.

36 Immanuel develops the metaphor mentioned by Moses Ibn Tibbon in Immanuel, *Commentary on Song of Songs*, in London, British Library, Harley MS. 5797, fols. 115v–116r: "The fruit is covered by three layers: the bottom layer clings to the fruit and is thin, and the second layer is hard, and the third top layer is dirty and bitter. So too are the parts of the soul." Immanuel identifies the tripartite division of "degrees" as levels of actualization in *Commentary on Song of Songs*, in London, British Library, Harley MS. 5797, fol. 113v.

37 Immanuel, *Commentary on Song of Songs*, in London, British Library, Harley MS. 5797, fols. 81v–82r.

38 Immanuel, *Commentary on Genesis*, in Parma, Biblioteca Palatina, MS. Cod. Parm. 3220, in Goldstein, "The Commentary of Immanuel ben Solomon of Rome on Chapters I–X of Genesis," 100. Maimonides' interpretation of the biblical verse, "Let us make man in our image and our likeness" (Genesis 1:26), likens the rational faculty's capability to apprehend immaterial beings to God. See *Guide* II:6, trans. S. Pines, 263.

39 Immanuel, *Commentary on Song of Songs*, in London, British Library, Harley MS. 5797, fol. 115r. On the Intellect being above time, see Immanuel, *Commentary on Song of Songs*, in London, British Library, Harley MS. 5797, fol. 89v.

40 Aristotle, *De Anima* III:7, in *The Philosophy of Aristotle*, trans. J. Creed and A. Wardman (New York: Signet, 1963), 300.

41 Immanuel, *Commentary on Genesis*, in Parma, Biblioteca Palatina, MS. Cod. Parm. 3220, in Goldstein, "The Commentary of Immanuel ben Solomon of Rome on Chapters I–X of Genesis," 100. "He [King Solomon] said: 'The prettiest amongst the women, he called the human soul, he meant the material intellect that is the faculty of preparation in the soul, the prettiest of women because it has the most glorious and purest form of all the forms in the souls of living creatures. Or he hinted that the human soul is encased in pure and clear matter over the matter of all other inferior creatures.'" Immanuel, *Commentary on Song of Songs*, in London, British Library, Harley MS. 5797, fol. 81v.

42 Immanuel, *Commentary on Song of Songs*, in London, British Library, Harley MS. 5797, fol. 79r.

43 Immanuel, *Commentary on Ecclesiastes*, in Cincinnati, OH, Hebrew Union College Library, Ms. Acc. 167, fol. 57r.

44 Mitchell Dahood, S.J., "Psalm 68 (68:1–36)," in *Psalms II: 51–100: Introduction, Translation, and Notes* (New Haven, CT: Anchor Yale Bible, 1968),

130–152; Samuel Iwry, "Notes on Psalm 68," *Journal of Biblical Literature* 71 (1952): 161–165.

45 Dahood, "Psalm 68 (68:1–36)," 130–152, n.1.

46 Dahood, "Psalm 68 (68:1–36)," 134.

47 Immanuel of Rome, *Maḥberoth*, ed. D. Jarden, 546 (lines 835–844), 547 (lines 845–850).

48 שהעיד מחברו הוא נאמ׳ על דרך מליצת השיר על דרך שיר השירים שאין דבר מדבריו כפשוטו לכן יפליג מחבירו לזכור המכוון בדרך רמז רחוק מן המובן ממנו לפי פשוטו See Immanuel, *Commentary on Psalms*, in Parma, Biblioteca Palatina, MS. Cod. Parm. 2843, fol. 179r.

49 Immanuel, *Commentary on Psalms*, in Parma, Biblioteca Palatina, MS. Cod. Parm. 2843, fol. 179r.

50 Immanuel, *Commentary on Psalms*, in Parma, Biblioteca Palatina, MS. Cod. Parm. 2843, fol. 180r.

51 I am indebted to Rachel B. Katz for her help in translating this psalm and puzzling over its meanings with me.

52 Judah Romano, *Bi'ur on Kaddish and Kedusha* in Parma, Biblioteca Palatina, MS. Cod. Parm. 2759, fols. 19v–20r.
שער ארבעים ותשעה בביאור אחר על מאמ׳ ואמרו אמן יהי שמיה רבא והנמשך אחריו אולי המכוון בצוואה הזאת ההערה על הברכה האלוהית המתחייבת להגדלה לסיבת המציאות הנמצא בפועל ואם המשלי המציאות אי זה מציאות ביכלת האלהי המצאתו ונרמז המציאות בפועל בלעלם והמשלי המציאות כולם אם המשלי המציאות בפועל ואם המשלי המציאות ביכלת האלהי המצאתו בלעלמי עלמייא להיות נמצאים המשלים אלהיים לא מהמציאות הנמצא בפועל לבד כי אם מכל מציאות נמצא ביכלת האלהי וראוי לקרוא ההמשלים עלמי עלמייא להיותם מעון העולמות והמציאיות וקיומם ואמרי לסבת המציאות והעולם או לסבת עלמי עלמייא להיות זה הדרך אפשרי למין האנושי ר״ל הגעתו מהפעולה אל ההמשל ומההמשל אל נושאו ולא על תכונת ההתהפכות והבינהו.

53 Maimonides, *The Guide of the Perplexed* II.30, trans. S. Pines, 353: "Whenever it [scripture] mentions a thing among those that exist, having been produced in time and subsisting in durable, perpetual, and permanent fashion, it says with reference to it *that it was good*." Thank you to Rachel B. Katz for the reference.

54 Immanuel, *Commentary on Psalms* 68:9, in Parma, Biblioteca Palatina, MS. Cod. Parm. 2843, fol. 180v.

55 I thank Rachel B. Katz for reminding me that Maimonides identifies the Sabians as attributing generative powers to the astral bodies in *Guide* III:29. In his epistle to Can Grande della Scala, Dante notes that, despite the number of causes to generate something, God, as the primary cause, is the most powerful and direct creator of that entity. See Dante Alighieri, "Epistle to Can Grande," Testo critico della Societa' Dantesca Italiana, Edited by Ermenegildo Pistelli. Florence: Societa' Dantesca Italiana, 1960, §56, https://dante.princeton.edu/pdp/epistolae.html, accessed October 19, 2022. For more on the epistle, see Robert Hollander, *Dante's Epistle to Cangrande*,

Recentiores: Later Latin Texts and Contexts (Ann Arbor: University of Michigan Press, 1993).

56 Immanuel, *Commentary on Psalms* 68:14, in Parma, Biblioteca Palatina, MS. Cod. Parm. 2843, fol. 182v.

57 Immanuel, *Commentary on Psalms* 68:14, in Parma, Biblioteca Palatina, MS. Cod. Parm. 2843, fol. 182v.

58 Immanuel, *Commentary on Psalms* 68:14, in Parma, Biblioteca Palatina, MS. Cod. Parm. 2843, fol. 182v.

59 Immanuel, *Commentary on Psalms* 68:14, in Parma, Biblioteca Palatina, MS. Cod. Parm. 2843, fol. 183v.

60 Immanuel, *Commentary on Proverbs* 5:6, in Parma, Biblioteca Palatina, MS. Cod. Parm. 2966, fol. 17v.

61 See Maimonides, *Guide* III:27, trans. S. Pines, 510–511; Immanuel, *Commentary on Psalms* 68:14, in Parma, Biblioteca Palatina, MS. Cod. Parm. 2843, fol. 182v.

62 והמכוון בהם הוא כי הוכנו כחותיה והמצות אשר ניתנו לעם הקודש להשלים שתי מציאיות אשר בנו והם שלמות הגוף ושלמות הנפש והכנפי' המחופים בכסף הם משל לכחות אשר בנפש האדם כדי להגיע בהם אל שלמות הגוף אשר בהם תודע הנהגת הבית והמדינה. ואברותיה המכוסות בחרוץ ירקרק רמז לכחות השכלי' אשר באמצעותם תגיע הנפש אל שלמותה האחרון והוא השכלת המושכלות ולהאמין דעות אמיתיות ולפרוע חובות האלהים עליו.

Immanuel, *Commentary on Psalms* 68:14, in Parma, Biblioteca Palatina, MS. Cod. Parm. 2843, fol. 183v.

63 Maimonides, *Guide* III:27, trans. S. Pines, 510–512; Tirosh-Samuelson, *Happiness in Premodern Judaism*, 219.

64 Howard (Haim) Kreisel, "Reasons for the Commandments in Maimonides' *Guide of the Perplexed* and in Provencal Jewish Philosophy," in *Judaism as Philosophy: Studies in Maimonides and the Medieval Jewish Philosophers of Provence* (Boston: Academic Studies Press, 2015), 361–395.

65 Immanuel, *Commentary on Psalms* 68:14, in Parma, Biblioteca Palatina, MS. Cod. Parm. 2843, fol. 182v.

66 Immanuel, *Commentary on Proverbs* 31, in Parma, Biblioteca Palatina, MS. Cod. Parm. 2966, fol. 142v.

67 Immanuel, *Commentary on Psalms* 68:15, in Parma, Biblioteca Palatina, MS. Cod. Parm. 2843, fol. 184r.

68 Immanuel, *Commentary on Proverbs* 1:6–7, in Parma, Biblioteca Palatina, MS. Cod. Parm. 2966, fol. 3r; Maimonides, *Guide* I:34, trans. Pines, 75 and 77.

69 Immanuel, *Commentary on Proverbs* 1:6–7, in Parma, Biblioteca Palatina, MS. Cod. Parm. 2966, fol. 3r.

70 Immanuel, *Commentary on Song of Songs* 3:6, in London, British Library, Harley MS. 5795, fol. 94v.

71 In Immanuel, *Commentary on Proverbs* 29:3, in Parma, Biblioteca Palatina, MS. Cod. Parm. 2966, fol. 123r, he explains: "Keeps company with prostitutes—he meant one who does not direct his study to the divine sciences but rather is satisfied with the applied sciences that are called 'prostitutes'

because they entice a man's heart"; in *Guide* I:33–34, Maimonides' order is the study of logic, applied sciences, natural sciences, and divine sciences.

72 These are arithmetic (*ḥokhmat ha-mispar*), geometry (*ḥokhmat ha-tishboret*), music (*ḥokhmat ha-niggun*), the theory of weight (*ḥokhmat ha-mishkalot*), mensuration (*ḥokhmat ha-middot*), optics (*ḥokhmat ha-mabatim*), and astronomy (*ḥokhmat ha-tekhuna*). See also Harry Austryn Wolfson, "The Classification of Sciences in Mediaeval Jewish Philosophy," in *Hebrew Union College Jubilee Volume* (Cincinnati, OH: Hebrew Union College, 1925), 300. Immanuel enumerates these in his *Commentary on Proverbs* 1:6–7, in Parma, Biblioteca Palatina, MS. Cod. Parm. 2966, fol. 3r.

73 Immanuel, *Commentary on Song of Songs* 1:11, in London, British Library, Harley MS. 5797, fol. 84v.

74 Immanuel, *Commentary on Song of Songs*, 1:11, in London, British Library, Harley MS. 5797, fol. 84v.

75 Immanuel, *Commentary on Psalms* 68:21, in Parma, Biblioteca Palatina, MS. Cod. Parm. 2843, fol. 186r.

76 Immanuel, *Commentary on Psalms* 68:23–24, in Parma, Biblioteca Palatina, MS. Cod. Parm. 2843, fols. 187r–v.

77 Maimonides, *Guide*, III:54, trans. Pines, 635. Explicating Genesis, Maimonides interprets human creation in the image and likeness of God as, "because of the divine intellect conjoined with man, that it is said of the latter that he is in the image of God and in His likeness." See Maimonides, *Guide* I:1, trans. S. Pines, 23. He also claims: "His [An individual's] ultimate perfection is to become rational in actu, I mean to have an intellect in actu; this would consist in his knowing everything concerning all beings that it is within the capacity of man to know in accordance with his ultimate perfection." Maimonides, *Guide* III:27, trans. S. Pines, 511.

78 Maimonides, *Guide* III:51, trans. S. Pines, 623–624.

79 Maimonides, *Eight Chapters*, chapter 7, in *Ethical Writings of Maimonides*, trans. Weiss and Butterworth, 82–83; Alfred Ivry, "The Image of Moses in Maimonides' Thought," in *Maimonides After 800 Years: Essays on Maimonides and His Influence*, ed. Jay M. Harris (Cambridge, MA: Harvard University Press, 2007), 113–134.

80 Alfred Ivry claims that Maimonides offers conjunction as a remote ideal toward which people should strive. See Alfred Ivry, "Maimonides' Psychology," in *Maimonides and His Heritage*, ed. Idit Dobbs-Weinstein, Len Goodman, and James Allen (Albany: State University of New York Press, 2009), 56; Immanuel, *Commentary on Song of Songs* 1, in London, British Library, Harley MS. 5797, fol. 79r.

81 Immanuel, *Commentary on Song of Songs* 5:1 in London, British Library, Harley MS. 5797, fol. 101v.

82 Immanuel, *Commentary on Proverbs* 31, in Parma, Biblioteca Palatina, MS. Cod. Parm. 2966, fols. 137r–143r.

83 Immanuel, *Commentary on Proverbs* 3:6, in Parma, Biblioteca Palatina, MS. Cod. Parm. 2966, fols. 9v–10r.

84 Immanuel, *Commentary on Genesis*, in Goldstein, "The Commentary of Immanuel ben Solomon of Rome on Chapters I–X of Genesis," 50. Another example is Immanuel, *Commentary on Proverbs* 4:11, in *The Book of Proverbs*, ed. Goldstein, 24.

85 Hillel of Verona, *Sefer Tagmule Ha-Nefesh: Book of the Rewards of the Soul*, ed. Joseph Baruch Sermoneta (Jerusalem: Israel Academy of Sciences and Humanities, 1981), 167–168.

86 Exodus 33:20 and 33:23; Maimonides, *Mishneh Torah*, Sefer Ha-Madda, Hilkhot Yesode Ha-Torah 1:10.

87 Maimonides, *Guide* III:51, trans. S. Pines, 624.

88 Immanuel returns to this subject frequently in his gloss of Psalms. See Immanuel, *Commentary on Psalms* 17, in Parma, Biblioteca Palatina, MS. Cod. Parm. 2843, fol. 36v, where the Psalmist requests to be watched by God rather than be governed by the arbitrary laws of nature. Maimonides' comment about this is found in *Guide* III:18. For Samuel Ibn Tibbon, see Samuel ben Judah Ibn Tibbon, *Commentary on Ecclesiastes (The Book of the Soul of Man)*, ed. James T. Robinson (Jerusalem: World Union of Jewish Studies, 2016), 215–216.

89 Immanuel, *Commentary on Proverbs* 2:7, in Parma, Biblioteca Palatina, MS. Cod. Parm. 2966, fol. 7v; he also reiterates this message in *Commentary on Psalms* 1:6, in Parma, Biblioteca Palatina, MS. Cod. Parm. 2843, fol. 5v, and in *Commentary on Psalms* 39, in Parma, Biblioteca Palatina, MS. Cod. Parm. 2843, fol. 107r.

90 Eisen, *The Book of Job in Medieval Jewish Philosophy*, 105–108.

91 Immanuel, *Commentary on Job* 33, in Parma, Biblioteca Palatina, MS. Cod. Parm. 2877, fols. 99v–100v.

92 Immanuel, *Commentary on Job* 33, in Parma, Biblioteca Palatina, MS. Cod. Parm. 2877, fol. 100r.

93 Immanuel, *Commentary on Job* 33, in Parma, Biblioteca Palatina, MS. Cod. Parm. 2877, fol. 100r.

94 Immanuel of Rome, *Maḥberoth*, ed. D. Jarden, 82–89 (lines 835–844). This is explored in Isaiah Sonne, "The Influence of Ethical and Philosophic Literature on the Poetry of Immanuel of Rome" [Hebrew], *Tarbiz* 5 (1934): 324–340.

95 Immanuel of Rome, *Maḥberoth*, ed. D. Jarden, 259 (lines 302–304).

96 Immanuel of Rome, *Maḥberoth*, ed. D. Jarden, 477–479 (lines 24–193).

97 Richard C. Dales, *The Problem of the Rational Soul in the Thirteenth Century* (Leiden: E. J. Brill, 1995).

98 James Robinson, "Soul and Intellect," in *The Cambridge History of Jewish Philosophy* (Cambridge: Cambridge University Press, 2009), 524–558; Steven Harvey, "Shem Tov Ibn Falaquera's Deot Ha-Philosophim," in *The Medieval Hebrew Encyclopedias of Science and Philosophy: Proceedings of the Bar-Ilan University Conference* (Dordrecht: Springer, 2000), 211–247; Haim Kreisel, "Levi ben Avraham and His Encyclopedia of Philosophy and Judaism, Livyat Hen," in *Judaism as Philosophy: Studies in Maimonides and the Medieval Jewish Philosophers of Provence* (Boston: Academic Studies Press, 2015).

Chapter 3

Epigraph: Ruth Morse, *Truth and Convention in the Middle Ages* (Cambridge: Cambridge University Press, 1991), 19.

1 Maimonides, "Eight Chapters," chapter 5, in *Ethical Writings of Maimonides*, ed. Weiss and Butterworth, 75–78.

2 Maimonides, "Eight Chapters," chapter 4, in *Ethical Writings of Maimonides*, ed. Weiss and Butterworth, 67–74.

3 Maimonides, "Eight Chapters," chapter 7, in *Ethical Writings of Maimonides*, ed. Weiss and Butterworth, 80–83.

4 Maimonides, *Guide* III:54, trans. S. Pines, 635.

5 Maimonides, *Guide* III:51, trans. S. Pines, 622; Guide III:54, trans. S. Pines, 635.

6 Maimonides, *Guide* II:23, trans. S. Pines, 321; Maimonides, *Guide* III:51, trans. S. Pines, 627.

7 Immanuel cites *Hilkhot De'ot* II:1 and II:2 in Immanuel, *Commentary on Proverbs* 3, in Parma, Biblioteca Palatina, MS. Cod. Parm. 2966, fols. 14r–v.

8 See Immanuel, *Commentary on Proverbs* 14:4, in Parma, Biblioteca Palatina, MS. Cod. Parm. 2966, fols. 47r–v.

9 Immanuel, *Commentary on Proverbs*, in Parma, Biblioteca Palatina, MS. Cod. Parm. 2966, fols. 47r–v.

10 Immanuel, *Commentary on Song of Songs*, in Milan, Ambrosian Library, Ms. Y 44 Sup., fol. 115v; Ravitsky, "R. Immanuel b. Shlomo: Commentary to the 'Song of Songs' Philosophical Division," 228–229.

11 According to Aristotle, the nutritive soul and the rational soul are the other two components.

12 Immanuel, *Commentary on Proverbs* 12:10, in Parma, Biblioteca Palatina, MS. Cod. Parm. 2966, fol. 40r.

13 Ram Ben Shalom, "The First Jewish Work on the Seven Deadly Sins and the Four Virtues," *Mediaeval Studies* 75 (2013): 205–270.

14 Yeḥiel ben Yequtiel Anav, *Ma'alot Ha-Middot* (Warsaw: Widow Levin-Epstein, 1887), 3; Gavriel Yitshak Ravenna, "Ma'alot Ha-Middot: Its Character and Purposes," in *A Wise-hearted Woman: In Memoriam of Dr. Sara Fraenkel*, ed. Bracha Yaniv (Jerusalem: Art Plus, 2010), 25–52.

15 Benjamin b. Abraham Anav, *Masa Gei Hizayon* (Riva di Trento, 1560; rpt., Lemberg: M. Wolff, 1859).

16 Jonathan P. Decter, "Em Kol Hai: Virtues and Vices in Benjamin Ben Anav of Rome's Masa Gei Hizayon," in *Ot LeTova: Essays in Honor of Professor Tova Rosen*, ed. Eli Yassif, Haviva Ishay, and Uriah Kfir (Be'er Sheva: Ben Gurion University Press, 2012), 54–70; Colum Hourihane, ed. *Virtue and Vice: The Personifications in the Index of Christian Art* (Princeton, NJ: Princeton University Press, 2000); Lina Bolzoni, *The Web of Images: Vernacular Preaching from Its Origins to St. Bernardino of Siena* (Aldershot: Ashgate, 2004).

17 Benjamin b. Abraham Anav, *Sh'arei Etz Hayim*, in Cincinnati, OH, Hebrew Union College Library, MS. 317, fols. 4v–8v.

18 Isaiah Sonne, "The Influence of Ethical and Philosophic Literature on the Poetry of Immanuel of Rome" [Hebrew], *Tarbiz* 5 (1934): 324–340; Joseph Dan, *Sifrut Ha-Musar ve-Ha Derush* (Jerusalem: Keter, 1975), 51.

19 Immanuel of Rome, *Maḥberoth*, ed. D. Jarden, 86 (lines 337–338).

20 Immanuel of Rome, *Maḥberoth*, ed. D. Jarden, 87 (lines 360–361).

21 Immanuel of Rome, *Maḥberoth*, ed. D. Jarden, 89–90 (lines 413–415).

22 Immanuel of Rome, *Maḥberoth*, ed. D. Jarden, 89–90 (lines 413–415); On the echo-poem, see Bregman, *The Golden Way*, 152, 213.

23 The poem is found in Immanuel of Rome, *Maḥberoth*, ed. D. Jarden, 90–94.

24 Rome, Bibliotheca Casanatense MS. 2916, fols. 197v–198v. In an electronic communication, Professor Malachi Beit-Arie identified the poem's handwriting to be from around the year 1300.

25 Hartwig Hirschfeld, "Immanuel of Rome and Other Poets on the Jewish Creed," *Jewish Quarterly Review*, n.s. 5, no. 4 (1915): 529–542; Hanna Kasher and Uri Melamed, "The Emergence of the Piyyut Yigdal Elohim Hay," in *ha-Tefilah be-Yiśra'el: hebeṭim ḥadashim* [Jewish Prayer: New Perspectives], ed. Uri Ehrlich (Be'er Sheva: Ben Gurion University Press, 2016), 155–171; Avraham Melamed, "Maimonides' Thirteen Principles: From Elite to Popular Culture," in *The Cultures of Maimonideanism: New Approaches to the History of Jewish Thought* (Leiden: Brill, 2009), 171–190.

26 Immanuel of Rome, *Maḥberoth*, ed. D. Jarden, 90 (lines 434; 436).

27 Immanuel of Rome, *Maḥberoth*, ed. D. Jarden, 93 (lines 481–487).

28 Immanuel of Rome, *Maḥberoth*, ed. D. Jarden, 144 (lines 122–128).

29 Immanuel of Rome, *Maḥberoth*, ed. D. Jarden, 142 (lines 81–84).

30 Baḥya Ibn Pakuda, "Duties of the Heart," chapter on Abstinence, 7:12.

31 Immanuel calls Baḥya "the divine sage" in his *Commentary on Proverbs* 16:3, in *The Book of Proverbs*, ed. Goldstein, 93.

32 Immanuel of Rome, *Commentary on Song of Songs 2:7*, in London, British Library, Harley MS. 5797, fol. 87v.

33 Immanuel of Rome, *Maḥberoth*, ed. D. Jarden, 333 (line 16).

34 Immanuel cites unattributed lines from Solomon Ibn Gabirol's *Mivḥar ha-Peninim*, Ibn Hasdai's *Ben Ha-Melekh V'Ha-Nazir*, Hunayn Ibn Ishaq's *Musrei Ha-Filosofim*, *S'arei Ha-musar*, *Mishlei Shu'alim*, *Sefer Sha'ashuim*.

35 Munich, Bayerische Staastbibliotek, MS. Cod. Hebr. 327.

36 Jones, "Communes and Despots," 71–96.

37 Rossi, "'Populus Firmanus Iterum Petit Hebreos'"; Ariel Toaff, *The Jews in Umbria, Volume 1 (1245–1435): Documentary History of the Jews in Italy* (Leiden: E. J. Brill, 1993), xi–xii; Daniel Waley, *The Papal State in the Thirteenth Century* (London: Macmillan Press), 1961.

38 A prime example of this kind of cooperation is found in a document from Ascoli-Piceno, published in Giuseppe Fabiani, *Gli Ebrei e il Monte di Pietá in Ascoli* (Ascoli-Piceno: Società Tipolithografica Editrice, 1942), 169–172; Leon Poliakov, *Jewish Bankers and the Holy See: From the Thirteenth to the*

Seventeenth Century, trans. Miriam Kochan (London: Routledge and Kegan Paul, 1977), 53–54.

39 Immanuel, *Commentary on Proverbs* 28:2, in Parma, Biblioteca Palatina, MS. Cod. Parm. 2966, fols. 117v–118r.

40 Immanuel, *Commentary on Proverbs* 28:2. On the transition to singular rule, see Trevor Dean, "The Rise of the Signori," in *Italy in the Central Middle Ages, 1000–1300* (Oxford: Oxford University Press, 2004), 104–124.

41 Augustine Thompson, *Revival Preachers and Politics in Thirteenth-Century Italy* (Eugene, OR: Wipf and Stock, 2010), 8.

42 Glenn Kumhera, *The Benefits of Peace: Private Peacemaking in Late Medieval Italy* (Leiden: Brill, 2017), 19–20.

43 Kumhera, *The Benefits of Peace*, 20–58; Katherine Jansen, *Peace and Penance in Late Medieval Italy* (Princeton, NJ: Princeton University Press, 2020); James A. Palmer, *The Virtues of Economy: Governance, Power, and Piety in Late Medieval Rome* (Ithaca, NY: Cornell University Press, 2019).

44 Immanuel, *Commentary on Proverbs* 6, in Parma, Biblioteca Palatina, MS. Cod. Parm. 2966, fol. 22v.

45 Immanuel, *Commentary on Proverbs* 6, in Parma, Biblioteca Palatina, MS. Cod. Parm. 2966, fol. 22v.

46 Lucio Tomei, "Genesi e primi sviluppi del Comune nella Marca meridionale: Le vicende del Comune di Fermo dalle origini alla fine del periodo svevo (1268)," in *Società e cultura nella Marca meridionale tra alto e basso Medioevo: Atti del 4. Seminario di studi per personale direttivo e docente della scuola: Cupra Marittima, 27–31 ottobre 1992* (Grottamare: MediaPrint 2000, 1995), 160–162.

47 Thompson, *Revival Preachers and Politics in Thirteenth-Century Italy*, 9.

48 Lester K. Little, "Pride Goes Before Avarice: Social Change and the Vices in Latin Christendom," *American Historical Review* 76, no. 1 (1971): 16–49; Carlo Delcorno, "Medieval Preaching in Italy (1200–1500)," in *The Sermon*, ed. Beverly Mayne Kienzle (Turnhout: Brepols, 2000), 449–560. Daniel Lesnick, *Preaching in Medieval Florence: The Social World of Franciscan and Dominican Spirituality* (Athens: University of Georgia Press, 1989), 101.

49 Carol Lansing, "Gender and Civic Authority: Sexual Control in a Medieval Italian Town," *Journal of Social History* 31, no. 1 (1997): 33–59.

50 Thompson, *Revival Preachers and Politics in Thirteenth-Century Italy*, 136–156.

51 Bernadette Paton, *Preaching Friars and the Civic Ethos: Siena, 1380–1480* (London: Centre for Medieval Studies, Queen Mary and Westfield College, University of London, 1992); Lesnick, *Preaching in Medieval Florence*.

52 Lesnick, *Preaching in Medieval Florence*, 96–102, 136–146.

53 Humbert of Romans, *Treatise on Preaching* (*De eruditione praedictorum*), trans. Dominican students of the Province of St. Joseph; ed. Walter M. Conlon (Westminster, Maryland: Newman Press, 1951).

54 Barbara Rosenwein and Lester Little, "Social Meaning in the Monastic and Mendicant Spiritualties," *Past and Present* 63 (1974): 22.

55 Thompson, *Revival Preachers and Politics in Thirteenth-Century Italy*, 179–189.

56 Lesnick, *Preaching in Medieval Florence*, 108–111; M. S. Kempshall, *The Common Good in Late Medieval Political Thought* (Oxford: Oxford University Press, 1999), 317–338.

57 Kempshall, *The Common Good in Late Medieval Political Thought*, 26–75. "Public utility and the common good are better and more worthy than the individual good and than one's own benefit; true and natural reason teaches that man must love God, the common good and the benefit of the people more than his own good or his own benefit" (Giles of Rome, *De regimine principum*, I.iii.3, in Grace Allen, "Vernacular Encounters with Aristotle's *Politics* in Italy, 1260–1600," PhD diss. [University of London, 2015], 52).

58 Immanuel of Rome, *Maḥberoth*, ed. D. Jarden, 23–24.

59 London, Montefiore, MS. 504; St. Petersburg, MS. Guenzburg 133, fols. 159r–160v; London, Montefiore, MS. 485, fols. 24v–25v; Parma, Biblioteca Palatina, MS. Cod. Parm. 2844, fol. 180v; Milan, Biblioteca Ambrosiana, Cod. P13 Sup.; Firenze, MS. Plut. I, 26, fols. 122v–127r; Cambridge, MS. Add. 539.

60 Caterina Rigo, "The Be'urim on the Bible of R. Yehudah Romano: The Philosophical Method Which Comes out of Them, Their Sources in the Jewish Philosophy and in the Christian Scholasticism," PhD diss. (Jerusalem: Hebrew University, 1996).

61 Immanuel, *Commentary on Proverbs* 29:27, in Parma, Biblioteca Palatina, MS. Cod. Parm. 2966, fol. 24v.

62 Immanuel, *Commentary on Genesis*, in Goldstein, "The Commentary of Immanuel ben Solomon of Rome on Chapters I–X of Genesis," 123.

63 Maimonides, *Guide*, I:1, trans. S. Pines, 12–13.

64 Numbers 19:2.

65 Mishnah Avot 3:5.

66 Immanuel, *Commentary on Song of Songs* 4:1, in London, British Library, MS. Harley 5797, fol. 98r.

67 London, Montefiore Library, MS. 485, fols. 24v–25v.

68 London, Montefiore Library, MS. 485, fols. 24v–25v.

69 Kasher and Melamed, "The Emergence of the Piyyut Yigdal Elohim Hay."

70 Immanuel of Rome, *Maḥberoth*, ed. D. Jarden, 24 (line 338).

71 Immanuel, *Commentary on Psalms* 1, in Parma, Biblioteca Palatina, MS. Cod. Parm. 2843, fol. 5r.

72 Isaac Heinemann, *Reasons for the Commandments in Jewish Thought: From the Bible to the Renaissance*, trans. Leonard Levin (Boston: Academic Studies Press, 2008).

73 Kreisel, "Reasons for the Commandments in Maimonides' *Guide of the Perplexed* and in Provencal Jewish Philosophy," 361–395.

74 Immanuel, *Commentary on Song of Songs*, in London, British Library, MS. Harley 5797, fol. 80v; Maimonides, *Mishneh Torah*, Hilkhot De'ot, 1:4.

75 Immanuel, *Commentary on Song of Songs*, in London, British Library, MS. Harley 5797, fol. 80v.

76 Immanuel, *Commentary on Song of Songs* 4:5, in London, British Library, MS. Harley 5797, fol. 98r.

77 Immanuel, *Commentary on Song of Songs* 2:5, in London, British Library, MS. Harley 5797, fol. 87v.

78 Immanuel, *Commentary on Song of Songs* 1:1, in London, British Library, MS. Harley 5797, fol. 79v.

79 Immanuel, *Commentary on Song of Songs* 2:5, in London, British Library, MS. Harley 5797, fol. 87v.

80 Immanuel, *Commentary on Song of Songs* 1:10, in London, British Library, MS. Harley 5797, fol. 83v.

81 Immanuel, *Commentary on Song of Songs* 6:10, in London, British Library, MS. Harley 5797, fol. 113r; Immanuel, *Commentary on Song of Songs* 3, in London, British Library, MS. Harley 5797, fol. 95v; Immanuel, *Commentary on Song of Songs* 2:14, in London, British Library, MS. Harley 5797, fol. 91r; Immanuel, *Commentary on Song of Songs* 1:9, in London, British Library, MS. Harley 5797, fol. 83v.

82 Immanuel, *Commentary on Song of Songs* 1:10, in London, British Library, MS. Harley 5797, fol. 83v.

83 Immanuel, *Commentary on Song of Songs* 1:10, in London, British Library, MS. Harley 5797, fol. 83v.

84 Immanuel, *Commentary on Psalms*, in Parma, Biblioteca Palatina, MS. Cod. Parm. 2843, fol. 52r.

85 Immanuel, *Commentary on Psalms*, in Parma, Biblioteca Palatina, MS. Cod. Parm. 2843, fol. 52v.

86 Giuseppe Sermoneta, “Le Correnti Del Pensiero Ebraico Nell’Italia Medievale,” *Italia Judaica* 1 (1983): 280.

87 Immanuel, *Commentary on Psalms*, in Parma, Biblioteca Palatina, MS. Cod. Parm. 2843, fol. 53r.

88 Immanuel, *Commentary on Psalms*, in Parma, Biblioteca Palatina, MS. Cod. Parm. 2843, fol. 54r.

89 Immanuel, *Commentary on Psalms*, in Parma, Biblioteca Palatina, MS. Cod. Parm. 2843, fols. 53v, 54v.

90 Immanuel, *Commentary on Psalms* 19:8, in Parma, Biblioteca Palatina, MS. Cod. Parm. 2843, fol. 54v.

91 Immanuel, *Commentary on Proverbs* 29:18, in Parma, Biblioteca Palatina, MS. Cod. Parm. 2966, fols. 125r–v.

92 Ravitsky, “R. Immanuel b. Shlomo: Commentary to the ‘Song of Songs,’” 181.

93 London, Montefiore Library, MS. 485, fols. 24v–25v.

94 Robinson, “Maimonides, Samuel Ibn Tibbon, and the Construction of a Jewish Tradition of Philosophy,” 291–306.

95 London, Montefiore Library, MS. 485, fols. 24v–25v.

96 Hillel of Verona, *Sefer Tagmule Ha-Nefesh: Book of the Rewards of the Soul*, 81.

97 Immanuel, *Commentary on Song of Songs* 6:10, in London, British Library, MS. Harley 5797, fols. 112v–113r.

Chapter 4

1 Himmelfarb, *Tours of Hell*; Dov Weiss, "Jews, Gentiles, and Gehinnom in Rabbinic Literature," in *Studies in Rabbinic Narratives*, vol. 1, ed. Jeffrey Rubenstein (Providence, RI: Brown Judaic Studies, 2021), 337–375.

2 Alan F. Segal, *Life After Death* (New York: Doubleday, 2004), 248–281.

3 Maimonides, *Mishneh Torah*, Hilkhot Teshuva 8:I–III.

4 The Talmud names seven levels of heaven, identified through biblical verses in BT Hagigah 12b.

5 In BT Berakhot 17a, Rab states that the righteous sit enthroned, with crowns on their heads, enjoying the radiance of the Shekhina; Midrash "Eleh Ezkerah" envisions the martyrs of the second-century Hadrianic persecution in a heavenly academy, seated on golden thrones while learning Torah from Rabbi Aqiba. See Midrash "Eleh Ezkerah," in Adolph Jellinek, *Beit HaMidrash* (Jerusalem: Wahrmann, 1967), 2:64–72.

6 BT Berakhot 28b, Midrash Tanhuma, Leviticus, 8.

7 Immanuel, *Commentary on Proverbs* 2:7, in Parma, Biblioteca Palatina, MS. Cod. Parm. 2966, fol. 7r.

8 Fishelov, "From Dante's 'Inferno' to Immanuel's 'Tofet,'" 19–42.

9 Immanuel, *Commentary on Proverbs* 30:25, in Parma, Biblioteca Palatina, MS. Cod. Parm. 2966, fols. 134v–135r.

10 Immanuel of Rome, *Maḥberoth*, ed. D. Jarden, 533 (lines 525–530).

11 Job 17:6.

12 Immanuel, *Commentary on Job*, in Parma, Biblioteca Palatina, MS. Cod. Parm. 2877, fol. 57v.

13 George Corbett, *Dante's Christian Ethics: Purgatory and Its Moral Contexts* (Cambridge: Cambridge University Press, 2020).

14 Immanuel, *Commentary on Genesis* 2:8, in Parma, Biblioteca Palatina, MS. Cod. Parm. 3220, fol. 231v; Goldstein, "The Commentary of Immanuel Ben Solomon of Rome on Chapters I–X of Genesis," 48.

15 Goldstein, "The Commentary of Immanuel Ben Solomon of Rome on Chapters I–X of Genesis," 60.

16 Immanuel, *Commentary on Psalms* 36:9, in Parma, Biblioteca Palatina, MS. Cod. Parm. 2843, fol. 96v.

17 Immanuel, *Commentary on Genesis* 2:10, in Parma, Biblioteca Palatina, MS. Cod. Parm. 3220, fols. 229r–228v.

18 Immanuel, *Commentary on Genesis*, in Parma, Biblioteca Palatina, MS. Cod. Parm. 3220, fol. 108v.

19 Stern, "What Divided the Moderate Maimonidean Scholars?" 347–376.

20 Silver, "Who Denounced the 'Moreh'?" 505–506.

21 Immanuel, *Commentary on Psalms*, in Parma, Biblioteca Palatina, MS. Cod. Parm. 2843, fol. 44v; *Commentary on Job* 40:15, in Parma, Biblioteca Palatina, MS. Cod. Parm. 2877, fol. 130r.

22 BT *Berakhot* 17a.

23 Maimonides, *Mishneh Torah*, Hilkhot Teshuva 8:II.

24 Immanuel, *Commentary on Proverbs* 3:32, in Parma, Biblioteca Palatina, MS. Cod. Parm. 2966, fol. 14v; Immanuel, *Commentary on Song of Songs* 3:11, London, British Library, MS. Harley 5797, fol. 96r.

25 Immanuel, *Comment on Proverbs* 4:9, in Parma, Biblioteca Palatina, MS. Cod. Parm. 2966, fol. 15r.

26 Immanuel of Rome, *Maḥberoth*, ed. D. Jarden, 546 (line 828).

27 Immanuel mentions the crown of pride in Immanuel of Rome, *Maḥberoth*, ed. D. Jarden, 537 (line 607).

28 Immanuel of Rome, *Maḥberoth*, ed. D. Jarden, 537 (line 630).

29 *Bamidbar Rabbah* 2:13; BT *Hagigah*, 12a; Saadia Gaon, *Book of Beliefs and Opinions* 6:3.

30 Immanuel of Rome, *Maḥberoth*, ed. D. Jarden, 539 (lines 663–664).

31 Immanuel, *Commentary on Song of Songs*, in London, British Library, Harley MS. 5797, fol. 95r.

32 Immanuel, *Commentary on Psalms* 118:27, in Parma, Biblioteca Palatina, MS. Cod. Parm. 2844, fol. 59v.

33 James T. Robinson, "On or Above the Ladder? Maimonidean and Anti-Maimonidean Readings of Jacob's Ladder," in *Interpreting Maimonides: Critical Essays*, ed. C. Manekin and D. Davies (Cambridge: Cambridge University Press, 2018), 85–98; Samuel Ibn Tibbon, *Ma'amar Yikavu Ha-Mayim* (Pressburg: M. Bisliches, 1837), 54.

34 Immanuel, *Commentary on Proverbs* 4:3 in Parma, Biblioteca Palatina, MS. Cod. Parm. 2966, fol. 15r.

35 Immanuel of Rome, *Maḥberoth*, ed. D. Jarden, 310 (lines 22–23).

36 Immanuel, *Comment on Proverbs* 30:26, in Parma, Biblioteca Palatina, MS. Cod. Parm. 2966, fols. 134v–135r; Immanuel, *Comment on Proverbs* 12:26, in Parma, Biblioteca Palatina, MS. Cod. Parm. 2966, fol. 43r.

37 Immanuel, *Comment on Proverbs* 31:29, in Parma, Biblioteca Palatina, MS. Cod. Parm. 2966, fol. 142v.

38 Immanuel, *Commentary on Song of Songs*, in London, British Library, Harley MS. 5797, fol. 94r.

39 Immanuel, *Comment on Proverbs* 15:24 in Parma, Biblioteca Palatina, MS. Cod. Parm. 2966, fol. 56r.

40 Immanuel of Rome, *Maḥberoth*, ed. D. Jarden, 539 (line 661).

41 Immanuel of Rome, *Maḥberoth*, ed. D. Jarden, 513 (lines 45–46); Dante Alighieri, *The Divine Comedy: Inferno*, canto III.

42 Ezekiel 37:11; for Talmudic debates over whether the passage refers to individual resurrection or national restoration, see the *baraita* in b. Sanhedrin 92b.

43 Immanuel, *Commentary on Proverbs* 15:11, in Parma, Biblioteca Palatina, MS. Cod. Parm. 2966, fol. 54v. The emphasis is mine.

44 Teodolinda Barolini, "*Inferno* 4: The Cultural Other," in *Commento Baroliniano*, Digital Dante (New York: Columbia University Libraries, 2018), https://digitaldante.columbia.edu/dante/divine-comedy/inferno/inferno-4/7, accessed on June 2, 2019.

45 Maimonides explored Galen's critiques of Moses in his *Medical Aphorisms*; see Gerrit Bos, *Maimonides, Medical Aphorisms, Hebrew Translation by R. Zeraḥyah Ben Isaac Ben She'altiel Ḥen* (Boston: Brill, 2020), 263–268. Two translations of Maimonides' *Medical Aphorisms* (*Pirke Moshe*) into Hebrew were completed in Rome during the final decades of the thirteenth century by Zeraḥiah Ḥen and Nathan Ha-Me'ati.

46 Davidson, *Alfarabi, Avicenna, and Averroes on Intellect*, 81. Immanuel probably knew of Avicenna's theories through Samuel Ibn Tibbon's *Ma'amar Yikavu Ha-Mayim*; see Gad Freudenthal, "(AL-)Chemical Foundations for Cosmological Ideas: Ibn Sînâ on the Geology of an Eternal World," in *Physics, Cosmology and Astronomy, 1300–1700: Tension and Accommodation* (Dordrecht: Kluwer Academic Publishers, 1991), 47–73. Hillel of Verona, *Tagmule Ha-Nefesh*, 90–93.

47 Expounding Proverbs 26:13, Immanuel argues that the metaphysical theories of Plato and Aristotle should not be ignored because they stem from a gentile source. Immanuel, *Commentary on Proverbs* 26:13 in Parma, Biblioteca Palatina, MS. Cod. Parm. 2966, fol. 110r.

48 Immanuel of Rome, *Maḥberoth*, ed. D. Jarden, 515 (lines 106–108).

49 The association of women and immodesty also has established antecedents in early medieval tours of hell, but as most of these tours were transmitted in Syriac, Greek, or Latin, it is unlikely that Immanuel knew of them. Moses Gaster, "Hebrew Visions of Hell and Paradise," in *Studies and Texts in Folklore, Magic, Mediaeval Romance, Hebrew Apocrypha and Samaritan Archaeology*, vol. 1, ed. Moses Gaster (London: Maggs, 1925–28), 125–141.

50 For links between contrapasso and Jewish forms of punishment, see Emanuel Menachem Artom, "Precedenti biblici e talmudici del 'contrapasso,'" in *Dante e la Bibbia*, ed. G. Barblan (Florence: Olschki, 1988): 55–62.

51 Immanuel of Rome, *Maḥberoth*, ed. D. Jarden, 515 (lines 107–108).

52 Immanuel of Rome, *Maḥberoth*, ed. D. Jarden, 515 (lines 104–105).

53 Immanuel of Rome, *Maḥberoth*, ed. D. Jarden, 515 (line 105).

54 Dante, *The Divine Comedy: Inferno*, canto V.

55 Immanuel, *Commentary on Psalms* 68, in Parma, Biblioteca Palatina, MS. Cod. Parm. 2834, fol. 177r.

56 Immanuel, *Commentary on Psalms* 68, in Parma, Biblioteca Palatina, MS. Cod. Parm. 2834, fol. 177v.

57 Immanuel of Rome, *Maḥberoth*, ed. D. Jarden, 554 (lines 1025–1027).

58 Baḥya Ibn Pakuda, "Duties of the Heart," Fourth Treatise on Trust 4:103.

59 Immanuel, *Commentary on Proverbs* 24:20, in Parma, Biblioteca Palatina, MS. Cod. Parm. 2966, fol. 98v.

60 Malachi Beit-Arie, *Hebrew Codicology: Historical and Comparative Typology of Hebrew Medieval Codices* (Jerusalem: Israel Academy of Sciences and Humanities, 1981), 138–140.

61 Immanuel, *Commentary on Proverbs* 11:18, in Parma, Biblioteca Palatina, MS. Cod. Parm. 2966, fol. 36r.

62 Immanuel of Rome, *Maḥberoth*, ed. D. Jarden, 538 (lines 627–630).

63 Immanuel of Rome, *Maḥberoth*, ed. D. Jarden, 538 (lines 640–645).
64 Pegoretti, "Early Reception Until 1481," 249–250.
65 Salah, "A Matter of Quotation," 167–197.

Chapter 5

1 Maimonides, *Guide* III:27, trans. S. Pines, 510–511.
2 Maimonides, *Guide* III:27, trans. S. Pines, 510.
3 Avraham Melamed, *The Philosopher-King in Medieval and Renaissance Jewish Political Thought* (Albany: SUNY Press, 2003).
4 Maimonides, *Guide* III:27, trans. S. Pines, 510.
5 Maimonides, *Guide* III:27, trans. S. Pines, 510.
6 Immanuel of Rome, *Maḥberoth*, ed. D. Jarden, 524 (line 298).
7 BT Kiddushin 30b.
8 Immanuel of Rome, *Maḥberoth*, ed. D. Jarden, 524 (lines 305–306); Immanuel, *Commentary on Exodus*, in Parma, Biblioteca Palatina, MS. Cod. Parm. 3221, fol. 95b.
9 This term, of biblical origin (I Samuel 25:29), was interpreted by Tannaitic sages as a reference to eternal life.
10 Immanuel, *Commentary on Proverbs* 20:20, in Parma, Biblioteca Palatina, MS. Cod. Parm. 2966, fols. 78v–79r.
11 Mark Johnston, "The Treatment of Speech in Medieval Ethical and Courtesy Literature," *Rhetorica: A Journal of the History of Rhetoric* 4, no. 1 (1986): 21–49.
12 Immanuel of Rome, *Maḥberoth*, ed. D. Jarden, 524 (line 302).
13 BT Niddah, 30b.
14 Immanuel, *Commentary on Proverbs* 10:18, in Parma, Biblioteca Palatina, MS. Cod. Parm. 2966, fols. 31r–32r.
15 Immanuel of Rome, *Maḥberoth*, ed. D. Jarden, 517 (lines 136–137).
16 Immanuel of Rome, *Maḥberoth*, ed. D. Jarden, 517–518 (lines 154–156).
17 The description of the windows is in I Kings 6:4, and BT Menahot 86b explains that, contrary to typical windows meant to beckon light from the outside into the structure, the windows narrowed toward the top to radiate light to the areas surrounding the Temple.
18 Immanuel of Rome, *Maḥberoth*, ed. D. Jarden, 518–519 (lines 176–180).
19 Immanuel of Rome, *Maḥberoth*, ed. D. Jarden, 517 (lines 145–146).
20 The biblical verse in Isaiah refers to blessings of fertility and bounty bestowed on the land, and this suggests that the woman was likely pregnant. This is also hinted by the fact that he must watch his wife engage in a purification ritual that Jewish law links to marital relations between spouses and procreation.
21 Immanuel, *Commentary on Psalms*, in Parma, Biblioteca Palatina, MS. Cod. Parm. 2844, fol. 1r.
22 Immanuel, *Commentary on Proverbs* 21:13 in Parma, Biblioteca Palatina, MS. Cod. Parm. 2966, fol. 82v.

23 Yedidya Dinari, "The Impurity Customs of the Menstruant Woman: Sources and Developments" [Hebrew], *Tarbiz* 49 (1989): 302–324; Tirzah Meacham (leBeit Yoreh), "An Abbreviated History of the Development of the Jewish Menstrual Laws," in *Women and Water: Menstruation in Jewish Life and Law*, ed. R. Wasserfall (Waltham, MA: Brandeis University Press, 1999), 82–100.

24 Shulamit Ben Shaya, "The Laws of Nidda in the Halakhic Works of France from the School of Rashi Until the Semak," PhD diss. (Bar Ilan University, 2016); Elliot Horowitz, "Between Cleanliness and Godliness: Aspects of Jewish Bathing in Medieval and Early Modern Times," in *Tov Elem: Memory, Community and Gender in Medieval and Early Modern Jewish Societies*, ed. Elisheva Baumgarten, Amnon Raz-Krakotzkin, and Roni Weinstein (Jerusalem: Hebrew University Press, 2011), 29–54.

25 Shaye J. D. Cohen, "Purity, Piety, and Polemic: Medieval Rabbinic Denunciations of 'Incorrect' Purification Practices," in *Women and Water: Menstruation in Jewish Life and Law*, ed. R. Wasserfall (Waltham, MA: Brandeis University Press, 1999), 82–100.

26 Immanuel of Rome, *Maḥberoth*, ed. D. Jarden, 532 (lines 495–496).

27 Immanuel of Rome, *Maḥberoth*, ed. D. Jarden, 532 (lines 500–501).

28 Immanuel, *Commentary on Proverbs* 14:25, in Parma, Biblioteca Palatina, MS. Cod. Parm. 2966, fols. 51r–v.

29 Immanuel of Rome, *Maḥberoth*, ed. D. Jarden, 532 (line 495) 469–475.

30 Leviticus 5:19–21.

31 Immanuel of Rome, *Maḥberoth*, ed. D. Jarden, 532 (line 496–497).

32 These categories are discussed in Leviticus 4 and Numbers 15.

33 Mishnah Avot 4:2 recounts "*Aveirah gorreret aveirah*."

34 There were varying views on the significance of animal sacrifice in the Middle Ages. While Maimonides explains that sacrifices were designed to wean the Israelites away from their surrounding pagan practices, Nahmanides adamantly disagrees. He explains that the animal is a substitute for the sinner, inspiring the sinner's repentance and good behavior. See Nahmanides on Leviticus 1:9.

35 BT Megillah 14b.

36 Immanuel, *Commentary on Exodus*, in Parma, Biblioteca Palatina, MS. Cod. Parm. 3221, fol. 94r.

37 Thomas Aquinas, *Summa Contra Gentiles*, part 3, chapter 122.

38 Immanuel, *Commentary on Genesis*, in Parma, Biblioteca Palatina, MS. Cod. Parm. 3220, fols. 56–54.

39 Immanuel, *Commentary on Genesis*, in Parma, Biblioteca Palatina, MS. Cod. Parm. 3220, fols. 56–54.

40 Immanuel, *Commentary on Genesis*, in Parma, Biblioteca Palatina, MS. Cod. Parm. 3220, fols. 56–54.

41 Immanuel of Rome, *Maḥberoth*, ed. D. Jarden, 545 (lines 795–796).

42 Immanuel of Rome, *Maḥberoth*, ed. D. Jarden, 545 (lines 806–808).

43 Immanuel of Rome, *Maḥberoth*, ed. D. Jarden, 546 (lines 819–821).

44 Immanuel of Rome, *Maḥberoth*, ed. D. Jarden, 546 (lines 821–822).
45 Immanuel, *Commentary on Proverbs* 11:24, in Parma, Biblioteca Palatina, MS. Cod. Parm. 2966, fol. 36v.
46 Immanuel, *Commentary on Proverbs* 11:24, in Parma, Biblioteca Palatina, MS. Cod. Parm. 2966, fol. 36v.
47 Immanuel of Rome, *Maḥberoth*, ed. D. Jarden, 546 (lines 826–827).
48 BT Bava Batra 75a.
49 Immanuel, *Commentary on Psalms* 68:21, in Parma, Biblioteca Palatina, MS. Cod. Parm. 2843, fol. 176r. He reiterates this point in his comment on Psalm 36:9 found in Parma, Biblioteca Palatina, MS. Cod. Parm. 2843, fol. 96v; Immanuel, *Commentary on Psalms* 118, in Parma, Biblioteca Palatina, MS. Cod. Parm. 2844, fols. 31v–32r. Whether these friends were ever named in an earlier iteration of the poem is unknowable, but their importance lies in their virtuous acts and in their order of appearance, which expresses a classificatory hierarchy of honorable behaviors; Roth, "The Historical Background of Maḥberot Immanuel," 449.
50 Immanuel of Rome, *Maḥberoth*, ed. D. Jarden, 550 (lines 935–936).
51 Immanuel of Rome, *Maḥberoth*, ed. D. Jarden, 550 (lines 937–939).
52 Immanuel of Rome, *Maḥberoth*, ed. D. Jarden, 551 (line 944).
53 Immanuel of Rome, *Maḥberoth*, ed. D. Jarden, 551 (line 956).
54 Immanuel of Rome, *Maḥberoth*, ed. D. Jarden, 551 (lines 948–949).
55 Immanuel of Rome, *Maḥberoth*, ed. D. Jarden, 551 (lines 961–962).
56 Immanuel of Rome, *Maḥberoth*, ed. D. Jarden, 552 (lines 965–966).
57 Immanuel, *Commentary on Proverbs* 8:36, in Parma, Biblioteca Palatina, MS. Cod. Parm. 2966, fol. 27v.
58 Immanuel, *Commentary on Proverbs* 11:30, in Parma, Biblioteca Palatina, MS. Cod. Parm. 2966, fol. 37v.
59 Immanuel of Rome, *Maḥberoth*, ed. D. Jarden, 552 (line 969).
60 Immanuel of Rome, *Maḥberoth*, ed. D. Jarden, 552 (lines 970–971).
61 Immanuel of Rome, *Maḥberoth*, ed. D. Jarden, 552 (lines 973–974).
62 Immanuel of Rome, *Maḥberoth*, ed. D. Jarden, 552 (lines 981–982); this common trope, deployed by medieval Hebrew poets, is exemplified in Judah Al-Harizi's *Taḥkemoni*, chapter 40.
63 Immanuel of Rome, *Maḥberoth*, ed. D. Jarden, 552 (lines 992–993).
64 Cecil Roth, "The Historical Background of Maḥberot Immanuel," 447–448; Shatzmiller, "The Papal Monarchy as Viewed by Medieval Jews," 30–41.
65 Immanuel of Rome, *Maḥberoth*, ed. D. Jarden, 553 (lines 999–1000).
66 Immanuel of Rome, *Maḥberoth*, ed. D. Jarden, 553 (line 1007).
67 Immanuel, *Commentary on Proverbs* 19:22, in Parma, Biblioteca Palatina, MS. Cod. Parm. 2849, fol. 60r.
68 Immanuel of Rome, *Maḥberoth*, ed. D. Jarden, 531 (lines 465–466).
69 Immanuel of Rome, *Maḥberoth*, ed. D. Jarden, 531 (lines 469–475).
70 Immanuel of Rome, *Maḥberoth*, ed. D. Jarden, 531 (lines 467–468).
71 Immanuel of Rome, *Maḥberoth*, ed. D. Jarden, 531 (lines 479–480).

72 These were ten sages who were killed in antiquity, although there are variant lists of their names. Ra'anan Boustan (Abusch), "From Martyr to Mystic: *The Story of the Ten Martyrs, Hekhalot Rabbati*, and the Making of Merkavah Mysticism," PhD diss. (Princeton, 2004); Shmuel Shepkaru, "From After Death to Afterlife: Martyrdom and Its Recompense," *Association for Jewish Studies Review* 24, no. 1 (1999): 1–44.
73 Immanuel of Rome, *Maḥberoth*, ed. D. Jarden, 531 (lines 483–485).
74 Immanuel of Rome, *Maḥberoth*, ed. D. Jarden, 531 (lines 483–485).
75 Immanuel of Rome, *Maḥberoth*, ed. D. Jarden, 531 (line 457).
76 Jeffrey Woolf, "Saints in Tophet: Immanuel of Rome on the Suicides of Ashkenaz" [Hebrew], *Peamim* 133–134 (2012): 11–25.
77 Immanuel of Rome, *Maḥberoth*, ed. D. Jarden, 524 (line 315).
78 Immanuel of Rome, *Maḥberoth*, ed. D. Jarden, 525 (lines 318–320).
79 Immanuel, *Commentary on Proverbs* 28:9, in Parma, Biblioteca Palatina, MS. Cod. Parm. 2966, fol. 119r.
80 Immanuel of Rome, *Maḥberoth*, ed. D. Jarden, 525 (line 330).
81 Immanuel, *Commentary on Psalms* 73:6, in Parma, Biblioteca Palatina, MS. Cod. Parm. 2843, fol. 202r.
82 Immanuel, *Commentary on Proverbs* 28:5, in Parma, Biblioteca Palatina, MS. Cod. Parm. 2966, fol. 120r.
83 Immanuel of Rome, *Maḥberoth*, ed. D. Jarden, 529–530 (lines 434–437).
84 Immanuel of Rome, *Maḥberoth*, ed. D. Jarden, 527 (lines 385–386).
85 Mishnah Ta'anit 2:1; BT Ta'anit 16a; Tosefta Hagigah 1:4; BT Hullin 24b.
86 Leo Landman, *The Cantor: An Historic Perspective* (New York: Yeshiva University Press, 1972), 128–130.
87 Immanuel of Rome, *Maḥberoth*, ed. D. Jarden, 528 (lines 392–394).
88 Immanuel of Rome, *Maḥberoth*, ed. D. Jarden, 528 (lines 401–402).
89 Immanuel of Rome, *Maḥberoth*, ed. D. Jarden, 534 (lines 543–544).
90 Immanuel, *Commentary on Proverbs* 16:8, in Parma, Biblioteca Palatina, MS. Cod. Parm. 2966, fol. 58v.
91 Maimonides, *Guide* III:27, trans. S. Pines, 510.
92 Immanuel, *Commentary on Proverbs* 18:20–23, in Parma, Biblioteca Palatina, MS. Cod. Parm. 2966, fols. 68r–v; Immanuel, *Commentary on Proverbs* 28:2, in Parma, Biblioteca Palatina, MS. Cod. Parm. 2966, fols. 117v–118r.
93 Immanuel of Rome, *Maḥberoth*, ed. D. Jarden, 527 (lines 380–382).
94 Immanuel of Rome, *Maḥberoth*, ed. D. Jarden, 527 (lines 372–373).
95 Immanuel of Rome, *Maḥberoth*, ed. D. Jarden, 526 (lines 363–364).
96 Immanuel, *Commentary on Proverbs* 27:22, in Parma, Biblioteca Palatina, MS. Cod. Parm. 2966, fol. 116v.
97 Immanuel of Rome, *Maḥberoth*, ed. D. Jarden, 526 (line 357).
98 1 Kings 17:1.
99 Aaron Freimann, "Jewish Scribes in Medieval Italy," in *Alexander Marx Jubilee Volume on the Occasion of His Seventieth Birthday* (New York: Jewish Theological Seminary of America, 1950), 231–342.

100 Hermann Vogelstein and Paul Rieger, *Geschichte der Juden in Rom*, vol. 1 (Berlin: Mayer & Müller, 1896), 332.
101 Immanuel of Rome, *Maḥberoth*, ed. D. Jarden, 527 (lines 365–367).
102 Immanuel of Rome, *Maḥberoth*, ed. D. Jarden, 527 (lines 369–370).
103 Immanuel of Rome, *Maḥberoth*, ed. D. Jarden, 536 (lines 600–603).
104 For Dante's Neutrals, see Dante Alighieri, *The Divine Comedy: Inferno* III.
105 Immanuel of Rome, *Maḥberoth*, ed. D. Jarden, 544 (lines 772–775).
106 Immanuel, *Commentary on Ecclesiastes* 7:17, in Cincinnati, Hebrew Union College, MS. Acc. 167, fols. 62v–63r.
107 Immanuel, *Commentary on Psalms* 112:10, in Parma, Biblioteca Palatina, MS. Cod. Parm. 2844, fol. 21r.
108 Immanuel, *Commentary on Ecclesiastes* 7:17, in Cincinnati, Hebrew Union College, MS. Acc. 167, fols. 62v–63r.
109 Maimonides, *Guide* III:27, trans. S. Pines, 510.

Chapter 6

1 Maimonides, *Guide* III:27, trans. S. Pines, 510–511.
2 Maimonides, *Guide* III:8, trans. S. Pines, 434–435.
3 Numbers, 12:4–16; Miriam is identified as the wife of Caleb and mother of Hur in BT *Sotah* 11b and in *Exodus Rabbah* 1:17.
4 Immanuel, *Commentary on Proverbs* 12:25, in Parma, Biblioteca Palatina, MS. Cod. Parm. 2966, fols. 42v–43r.; BT Berakhot 5a.
5 Midrash Mishle 31:10.
6 Leviticus 5:23; Maimonides, *Mishneh Torah*, Hilkhot She'elah U'Fikadon. The same language appears in Baḥya Ibn Pakuda's "Duties of the Heart." He says: "A person should think of himself as if a king had placed a deposit in his charge but did not fix a definite date when it should be returned. The king told him to expect his visit at any time and that he should not leave for another place but always be at hand when the king would seek him. Would it be right on the part of the depositary to live outside the royal residence as long as he had the deposit in his possession? Another analogous representation that has been made is as follows: one should represent to himself that he is like a debtor with no fixed time for repayment of the debt, expecting every moment to be called upon for repayment." Immanuel used the same terminology referring both to *pikadon* (deposit) and *hov* (debt) in this passage. See Baḥya Ibn Pakuda, "Duties of the Heart," trans. Moses Hyamson (New York: Feldheim, 1925), 232–234.
7 B. Rosh Hashana 17a; "Tractate Gehinnom," in A. Jellinek, *Beit HaMidrash* (Jerusalem: Wahrmann, 1967), I:147–149.
8 Immanuel of Rome, *Maḥberoth*, ed. D. Jarden, 526 (line 344).
9 M. Sanhedrin 3:3 invalidates gamblers as Jewish witnesses. A full treatment of gambling in Jewish history is Leo Landman, "Jewish Attitudes Toward Gambling," *Jewish Quarterly Review* 57 (1967): 1–21, and Leo Landman, "Jewish Attitudes Toward Gambling II," *Jewish Quarterly Review* 58, no. 1 (1967): 34–62.

10 Immanuel of Rome, *Maḥberoth*, ed. D. Jarden, 516 (lines 113–114).
11 Paton, *Preaching Friars and the Civic Ethos*, 314–316.
12 Immanuel, *Commentary on Proverbs* 30:4, in Parma, Biblioteca Palatina, MS. Cod. Parm. 2966, fol. 127v.
13 Immanuel of Rome, *Maḥberoth*, ed. D. Jarden, 519 (lines 196–197).
14 Immanuel of Rome, *Maḥberoth*, ed. D. Jarden, 519 (lines 197–198); Howard Kreisel, "The Practical Intellect in the Philosophy of Maimonides," *Hebrew Union College Annual* 59 (1988): 189–215.
15 Maimonides, *Guide* I:2, trans. S. Pines, 24–26; Maimonides, *Treatise on Logic*, chapter 8.
16 Michael Monbeck, *The Meaning of Blindness: Attitudes Toward Blindness and Blind People* (Bloomington: Indiana University Press, 1973), 48–53.
17 Immanuel of Rome, *Maḥberoth*, ed. D. Jarden, 528 (lines 409–411).
18 Immanuel of Rome, *Maḥberoth*, ed. D. Jarden, 529 (lines 416–419). This line is an unattributed citation from Samuel Ibn Tibbon's *Commentary on Ecclesiastes*; see Samuel ben Judah Ibn Tibbon, *Commentary on Ecclesiastes (The Book of the Soul of Man)*, ed. James T. Robinson (Jerusalem: World Union of Jewish Studies, 2016), 217.
19 See Immanuel, *Commentary on Proverbs* 8:35, in Parma, Biblioteca Palatina, MS. Cod. Parm. 2966, fol. 27v.
20 Immanuel, *Commentary on Proverbs* 10:4, in Parma, Biblioteca Palatina, MS. Cod. Parm. 2966, fol. 29v.
21 Dana W. Fishkin, "The Sting of Satire: The Jesus Figure in Immanuel of Rome's Hell," *Prooftexts: A Journal of Jewish Literary History* 36 (2018): 357–384.
22 Immanuel, *Commentary on Proverbs* 2:20, in Parma, Biblioteca Palatina, MS. Cod. Parm. 2966, fols. 8r–v.
23 Immanuel of Rome, *Maḥberoth*, ed. D. Jarden, 534 (lines 532–534).
24 Immanuel of Rome, *Maḥberoth*, ed. D. Jarden, 521 (lines 234–235).
25 Immanuel of Rome, *Maḥberoth*, ed. D. Jarden, 521 (lines 237–238).
26 Immanuel of Rome, *Maḥberoth*, ed. D. Jarden, 521 (line 247).
27 Immanuel of Rome, *Maḥberoth*, ed. D. Jarden, 522 (lines 255–263).
28 Maimonides, *Mishneh Torah*, Hilkhot Avadim, 3:14; *Sefer Ha-Hinukh* 482:1.
29 Rashi and Ibn Ezra on Ecclesiastes 11:1; Avot De-Rabbi Natan 3:9.
30 Immanuel, *Commentary on Ecclesiastes*, in Cincinnati, OH, Hebrew Union College Library, Ms. Acc. 167. fol. 93v.
31 Maimonides, *Mishneh Torah*, Hilkhot Loveh U'Malveh, 1:1.
32 Immanuel of Rome, *Maḥberoth*, ed. D. Jarden, 522 (line 255).
33 Immanuel of Rome, *Maḥberoth*, ed. D. Jarden, 522 (line 266).
34 Immanuel of Rome, *Maḥberoth*, ed. D. Jarden, 522 (lines 269–271).
35 Maimonides, *Guide*, Introduction. On the ladder, see S. Klein Braslavy, "Maimonides' Interpretations of Jacob's Dream About the Ladder" [Hebrew], *Bar-Ilan Year Book* 22–23 (1988): 329–349.
36 James T. Robinson, "On or Above the Ladder?" 85–98; Yehuda Halper, "The Road to Hell Is Paved with Good Philosophers: The Ladder of Knowledge in

Immanuel of Rome's *Hell and Heaven*," in *The Popularization of Philosophy in Medieval Islam, Judaism, and Christianity*, ed. Marieke Abram, Steven Harvey, and Lukas Muehlethaler (Turnhout: Brepols, 2022), 351–362.

37 Immanuel, *Commentary on Psalms* 15, in Parma, Biblioteca Palatina, MS. Cod. Parm 2843, fol. 34v.

38 Immanuel of Rome, *Maḥberoth*, ed. D. Jarden, 523 (lines 274–275).

39 Andrew L. Gluck, "The King in His Palace: Ibn Gabirol and Maimonides," *Jewish Quarterly Review* 91, nos. 3/4 (2001): 337–357.

40 Maimonides, *Guide* III:51, trans. S. Pines, 620.

41 Immanuel of Rome, *Maḥberoth*, ed. D. Jarden, 523 (lines 279–282).

42 Immanuel of Rome, *Maḥberoth*, ed. D. Jarden, 219 (lines 51–52).

43 David Goldstein appended Judah's comments on Proverbs from the British library manuscript edition of Immanuel's gloss (MS. Add. 11567) to his own edition of Immanuel's Proverbs commentary. See Immanuel, *Commentary on the Book of Proverbs*, ed. Goldstein, 14, 21–30.

44 The claim that they are family is based on Immanuel's own admission in the twelfth *maḥberet*, where Immanuel says, "He is my brother, my crown, bone of my bones, and flesh of my flesh." See Immanuel of Rome, *Maḥberoth*, ed. D. Jarden, 217 (line 14). It is also referenced by Moses Rieti in Moses Rieti, *Mikdash Me'at* (Vienna: J. Goldenthal, 1851), 105.

45 Maimonides, *Commentary on the Mishnah*, Introduction to Perek Helek, Eighth Principle.

46 Immanuel of Rome, *Maḥberoth*, ed. D. Jarden, 543 (lines 745–749).

47 Immanuel of Rome, *Maḥberoth*, ed. D. Jarden, 543 (lines 749–750).

48 Immanuel of Rome, *Maḥberoth*, ed. D. Jarden, 523 (lines 292–293).

49 Immanuel of Rome, *Maḥberoth*, ed. D. Jarden, 542 (line 718); this vignette is analyzed in Halper, "The Road to Hell Is Paved with Good Philosophers," 357–358.

50 Dante, *Divine Comedy, Inferno*, canto IV.

51 Immanuel, *Commentary on Proverbs* 26:13, in Parma, Biblioteca Palatina, MS. Cod. Parm. 2966, fols. 110r–v.

52 Maimonides, *Mishneh Torah*, Hilkhot Melakhim 8:11. The formulation appears in a first century *Tosefta*, in which two Palestinian rabbis disagree about the probability of salvation for a non-Jew. Rabbi Joshua's opinion that gentiles do have a share in the world to come, codified by Maimonides, was expanded to refer to those who observed the seven Noahide laws. Motivation for one's observance of commandments serves Maimonides as a distinguishing factor between classes of gentiles, as "righteous gentiles" observe the Noahide commandments because they were divinely ordained, while the "gentile sages" are motivated by rational considerations.

53 Immanuel of Rome, *Maḥberoth*, ed. D. Jarden, 542 (line 721).

54 Immanuel of Rome, *Maḥberoth*, ed. D. Jarden, 542 (lines 726–731).

55 Immanuel of Rome, *Maḥberoth*, ed. D. Jarden, 542 (719–720).

56 Richard C. Dales, *Medieval Discussions of the Eternity of the World* (Leiden: E. J. Brill, 1990).

57 Immanuel, *Commentary on Psalms* 111, in Parma, Biblioteca Palatina, MS. Cod. Parm. 2844, fol. 17r.
58 Immanuel of Rome, *Maḥberoth*, ed. D. Jarden, 546 (line 832).
59 Immanuel of Rome, *Maḥberoth*, ed. D. Jarden, 546 (lines 833–834).
60 See 1 Chronicles 6:16, 2 Chronicles 25:1; BT *Baba Batra* 14b describes the composite authorship of the book of Psalms. David includes the compositions of ten authors, including the three characters here and the three sons of Korah.
61 Immanuel, *Commentary on Proverbs* 26:13, in Parma, Biblioteca Palatina, MS. Cod. Parm. 2966, fol. 110r. Immanuel repeats the comment and elaborates on it in his exegesis of Genesis 4:17–24, in D. Goldstein, "The Commentary of Immanuel," 116–117; Amnon Shiloah, "A Passage from Immanuel Ha-Romi on the Science of Music," *Italia: Studi e Richerche Sulla Storia, La Cultura e La Letteratura Degli Ebrei D'Italia* 10 (1993): 9–18.
62 Immanuel of Rome, *Maḥberoth*, ed. D. Jarden, 548 (line 835).
63 Immanuel, *Commentary on Psalms* 118, in Parma, Biblioteca Palatina, MS. Cod. Parm. 2844, fols. 28r–32v.
64 Immanuel of Rome, *Maḥberoth*, ed. D. Jarden, 546 (lines 835–836).
65 Immanuel, *Commentary on Psalms* 119:59, in Parma, Biblioteca Palatina, MS. Cod. Parm. 2844, fol. 42v.
66 Immanuel, *Commentary on Song of Songs* in London, British Library, MS. Harley 5797, fol. 83v.
67 Immanuel of Rome, *Maḥberoth*, ed. D. Jarden, 547 (line 856); Meira Polliack, "Ezekiel 1 and Its Role in Subsequent Jewish Mystical Thought and Tradition," *European Judaism: A Journal for the New Europe* 32, no. 1 (1999): 70–78; Robert A. Harris, "The Reception of Ezekiel Among Twelfth-Century Northern French Rabbinic Exegetes," in *After Ezekiel: Essays on the Reception of a Difficult Prophet*, ed. Andrew Mein and Paul M. Joyce (New York: Clark International, 2011), 71–88.
68 Immanuel of Rome, *Maḥberoth*, ed. D. Jarden, 547 (lines 855–858).
69 Immanuel compares Solomon's composition of the book of Proverbs to the drawing of water from a well, linking the water to the wisdom of Proverbs, in the introduction to his gloss on Proverbs. Immanuel, *Commentary on Proverbs* 11:24, in Parma, Biblioteca Palatina, MS. Cod. Parm. 2697, fol. 1r.
70 Ivry, "The Image of Moses in Maimonides' Thought."
71 Immanuel of Rome, *Maḥberoth*, ed. D. Jarden, 547 (lines 862–863).
72 BT *Hagigah* 14b; Tosefta *Hagigah* 2:3–4; JT *Hagigah* 2:1, 77b; Jeffrey Rubenstein, "Elisha ben Abuya: Torah and the Sinful Sage," in *Journal of Jewish Thought and Philosophy* 7, no. 2 (1997): 139–225. Yehuda Liebes, *The Sin of Elisha* (Jerusalem: Hebrew University Press, 1990).
73 Immanuel, *Commentary on Proverbs* 22:2, in Parma, Biblioteca Palatina, MS. Cod. Parm. 2966, fol. 86v.
74 Parma, Biblioteca Palatina, MS. Cod. Parm. 3128, fols. 229v–283r.

75 Parma, Biblioteca Palatina, MS. Cod. Parm. 2961, fol. 141v.
76 Maimonides, *Guide* II:32, trans. Pines, 362.
77 Immanuel of Rome, *Maḥberoth*, ed. D. Jarden, 547 (lines 864–865).
78 See Parma, Biblioteca Palatina, MS. Cod. Parm. 3128, fols. 142v–226v.
79 Immanuel of Rome, *Maḥberoth*, ed. D. Jarden, 547 (line 865).
80 Immanuel of Rome, *Maḥberot Immanuel*, ed. D. Jarden, 548 (line 883). The attribution of Mosaic authorship of the book of Job is found in the Talmud, BT *Baba Batra* 14b, and it was the prevailing opinion of the time.
81 Eisen, *The Book of Job in Medieval Jewish Philosophy*, 105–107.
82 Immanuel, *Commentary on Job*, in Parma, Biblioteca Palatina, MS. Cod. Parm. 2877, fol. 130r.
83 The digression is found in Parma, Biblioteca Palatina, MS. Cod. Parm. 2877, fols. 130r–135r.
84 While there are a few lines from Samuel Ibn Tibbon's *Ma'amar Yikavu Ha-Mayim* and *Commentary on Ecclesiastes*, this reading of Job 40 and its correlation to Genesis, Isaiah, and Ezekiel is entirely original.
85 Immanuel of Rome, *Maḥberoth*, ed. D. Jarden, 548 (lines 886–887).
86 Immanuel of Rome, *Maḥberoth*, ed. D. Jarden, 548 (lines 887–889).
87 Immanuel, *Commentary on Song of Songs*, in London, British Library, Harley MS. 5797, fol. 96r.
88 Immanuel of Rome, *Maḥberoth*, ed. D. Jarden, 548 (line 890).
89 Fishkin, "A Lifetime in Letters: New Evidence Concerning Immanuel of Rome's Timeline."
90 Immanuel of Rome, *Maḥberoth*, ed. D. Jarden, 549 (lines 900–901).
91 Immanuel, *Commentary on Genesis* 37, in Parma, Biblioteca Palatina, MS. Cod. Parm. 3220, fol. 64v. On the following folio, fol. 65r, Immanuel continues his praise of Joseph's morality, especially in light of his youth.
92 Giuseppe Sermoneta, "Prophecy in the Writings of R. Yehuda Romano," in *Studies in Medieval Jewish History and Literature*, vol. 2, ed. Isadore Twersky (Cambridge, MA: Harvard University Press, 1984), 337–374.
93 Robinson, *Samuel Ibn Tibbon's Commentary on Ecclesiastes*, 172.
94 Immanuel, *Commentary on Proverbs* 31:16, in Parma, Biblioteca Palatina, MS. Cod. Parm. 2966, fol. 139r.
95 Immanuel, *Commentary on Proverbs* 10:6–9, in Parma, Biblioteca Palatina, MS. Cod. Parm. 2966, fols. 29v–30r.
96 Immanuel, *Commentary on Psalms* 119:173, in Parma, Biblioteca Palatina, MS. Cod. Parm. 2844, fol. 60v.
97 Immanuel, *Commentary on Psalms* 126:2, in Parma, Biblioteca Palatina, MS. Cod. Parm. 2844, fol. 71v.
98 Immanuel of Rome, *Maḥberoth*, ed. D. Jarden, 553–554 (lines 1011–1015).
99 Immanuel of Rome, *Maḥberoth*, ed. D. Jarden, 554 (line 1027).
100 Immanuel of Rome, *Maḥberoth*, ed. D. Jarden, 548 (lines 880–883).
101 Immanuel of Rome, *Maḥberoth*, ed. D. Jarden, 538 (lines 626–629).

Conclusion

1 Immanuel, *Commentary on Psalms* 113, in Parma, Biblioteca Palatina, MS. Cod. Parm. 2844, fols. 21r–22v.
2 Immanuel of Rome, *Maḥberoth*, ed. D. Jarden, 5 (lines 51–54).
3 Immanuel of Rome, *Maḥberoth*, ed. D. Jarden, 4 (lines 32, 35–36).
4 Immanuel of Rome, *Maḥberoth*, ed. D. Jarden, 5 (line 55).
5 Immanuel of Rome, *Maḥberoth*, ed. D. Jarden, 553 (lines 1011–1012).
6 Immanuel, *Commentary on Proverbs* 10:5, in Parma, Biblioteca Palatina, MS. Cod. Parm. 2966, fol. 30r.
7 Immanuel, *Commentary on Proverbs* 31:16, in Parma, Biblioteca Palatina, MS. Cod. Parm. 3240, fol. 170r.
8 Immanuel, *Commentary on Proverbs* 15:14, Parma, Biblioteca Palatina, MS. Cod. Parm. 2966, fols. 54v–55r.
9 Immanuel of Rome, *Maḥberoth*, ed. D. Jarden, 538 (lines 629–637).
10 Immanuel of Rome, *Maḥberoth*, ed. D. Jarden, 538 (lines 641–643).
11 Giovanni Carsaniga, "Literary Realism in Italy: Verga, Capuana, and Verismo," in *The Cambridge Companion to the Italian Novel*, ed. Peter E. Bondanella and Andrea Ciccarelli (New York: Cambridge University Press, 2003), 62.

BIBLIOGRAPHY

Primary Sources

Immanuel's Works (Manuscript)

'Even Boḥan, in Parma, Biblioteca Palatina, MS. Cod. Parm. 2285.

'Even Boḥan, in Parma, Biblioteca Palatina, MS. Cod. Parm. 2304.

"Amor non lesse mai l'avemaria," in Rome Biblioteca Casanatense, MS. 433, fol. 131v.

"Bisbidis di Manoello giudeo a magnificentia di messer Cane de la Scala," in Rome, Biblioteca Casanatense, MS. 433, fols. 132r–133v.

Bi'ur Tzurot Ha-Otiyot, in British Library, London, England Add. 27173.

Biurim, in Florence, Italy, Laurentian Library, Ms. Plut.I.26.

Commentary on Ecclesiastes, in Cincinnati, Hebrew Union College, MS. Acc. 167.

Commentary on Job, in Parma, Biblioteca Palatina, MS. Cod. Parm. 2877.

Commentary on Job, in Parma, Biblioteca Palatina, MS. Cod. Parm. 3098.

Commentary on the Pentateuch, in Parma, Biblioteca Palatina, MS. Cod. Parm. 3220–3224.

Commentary on Prophets, in Parma, Biblioteca Palatina, MS. Cod. Parm. 3128.

Commentary on Proverbs, in Bavarian State Library, Munich, Germany Cod. hebr. 25.

Commentary on Proverbs, in Città del Vaticano, Biblioteca Apostolica Vaticana, MS. Ebr. 230.

Commentary on Proverbs, in Hamburg, Germany, Hamburg State and University Library Carl von Ossietzky, MS. Levy 10.

Commentary on Proverbs, in London, British Library, MS. Add. 11567.

Commentary on Proverbs, in Paris, National Library of France, MS. Hebr. 234.

Commentary on Proverbs, in Parma, Biblioteca Palatina, MS. Cod. Parm. 2037.

Commentary on Proverbs, in Parma, Biblioteca Palatina, MS. Cod. Parm. 2531.

Commentary on Proverbs, in Parma, Biblioteca Palatina, MS. Cod. Parm. 2697.

Commentary on Proverbs, in Parma, Biblioteca Palatina, MS. Cod. Parm. 2846.

Commentary on Proverbs, in Parma, Biblioteca Palatina, MS. Cod. Parm. 2848.

Commentary on Proverbs, in Parma, Biblioteca Palatina, MS. Cod. Parm. 2849.

Commentary on Proverbs, in Parma, Biblioteca Palatina, MS. Cod. Parm. 2961.

Commentary on Proverbs, in Parma, Biblioteca Palatina, MS. Cod. Parm. 2965.

Commentary on Proverbs, in Parma, Biblioteca Palatina, MS. Cod. Parm. 2966.
Commentary on Proverbs, in Parma, Biblioteca Palatina, MS. Cod. Parm. 3097.
Commentary on Proverbs, in Parma, Biblioteca Palatina, MS. Cod. Parm. 3240.
Commentary on Proverbs and *Song of Songs*, in Cincinnati, Hebrew Union College, MS. Acc. 167.
Commentary on Proverbs and *Song of Songs*, in National Central Library of Rome, Rome, Italy Ms. Or. 72.
Commentary on Psalms, Esther, Ruth, and Lamentations, in Parma, Biblioteca Palatina, MS. Cod. Parm. 2843, 2844.
Commentary on Song of Songs, in Bavarian State Library, Munich, Germany Cod.hebr. 25.
Commentary on Song of Songs, in Cambridge, England, Cambridge University Library, Ms. Add. 383, 1.
Commentary on Song of Songs, in Città del Vaticano, Biblioteca Apostolica Vaticana, MS. Ebr. 85.
Commentary on Song of Songs, in Hamburg, Germany, Hamburg State and University Library Carl von Ossietzky, MS. Levy 9.
Commentary on Song of Songs, in London, British Library, Harley MS. 5797.
Commentary on Song of Songs, in Milan, Italy, Ambrosian Library, Ms. Y 44 Sup.
Commentary on Song of Songs, in Oxford, England, Bodleian Libraries, University of Oxford, Ms. Mich. 455.
Commentary on Song of Songs, in Parma, Biblioteca Palatina, MS. Cod. Parm. 2215.
Commentary on Song of Songs, in State Library of Berlin, Berlin, Germany Ms. Or. Qu. 646.
Commentary on Song of Songs and *Job*, in Paris, National Library of France, MS. Hebr. 235.
Drashot, in London, Montefiore Library, MS. 485.
"*Eftaḥ be-khinor*" ("I shall begin with a lyre"), in Rome, Bibliotheca Casanatense, MS. 2916, fols. 197v–198v.
Likkutei Derushim, in Parma, Biblioteca Palatina, MS. Cod. Parm. 2486.
Likkutim, in Parma, Biblioteca Palatina, MS. Cod. Parm. 2445.
Likkutim, in Parma, Biblioteca Palatina, MS. Cod. Parm. 3025.
Likkutim, in Zurich, Switzerland, Zürich Central Library, Ms. Heid. 107.
Maḥberot Immanuel, in British Library, London, England MS. Or. 1002.
Maḥberot Immanuel, in Cambridge, England, Cambridge University Library, Ms. Add. 402.
Maḥberot Immanuel, in London, England, London School of Jewish Studies Library, Ms. 13.
Maḥberot Immanuel, in Paris, National Library of France, MS. Hebr. 1286.
Maḥberot Immanuel, in Paris, National Library of France, MS. Hebr. 1287.
Maḥberot Immanuel, in Parma, Biblioteca Palatina, MS. Cod. Parm. 647.
Maḥberot Immanuel, in Parma, Biblioteca Palatina, MS. Cod. Parm. 2121.
Maḥberot Immanuel, in Parma, Biblioteca Palatina, MS. Cod. Parm. 2445.

Maḥberot Immanuel, in Parma, Biblioteca Palatina, MS. Cod. Parm. 3526.
Maḥberot Immanuel, in Roma, Biblioteca Casanatense, MS. 167.
"Risposta di Manoello a Messer Bosone" in Rome, Biblioteca Casanatense, MS. 433, fols. 131r–v.
"Tenzone with Bosone da Gubbio," in Città del Vaticano, Biblioteca Apostolica Vaticana, MS. Barb. Lat. 3953, fol. 128r.
"The Sixth Maḥberet," in Parma, Biblioteca Palatina, MS. Cod. Parm. 2306.

Additional Manuscript Sources

Anav, Benjamin b. Abraham. *Sh'arei Etz Hayim*, in Cincinnati, OH, Hebrew Union College Library, MS. 317.
"Contract," Fermo, Italy, Archivio di Stato, Cod. Dipl. MS. 829.
"Immanuel's Family Tree," in Parma, Biblioteca Palatina, MS. Cod. Parm. 2445.
Mahzor Roma, in Parma, Biblioteca Palatina, MS. Cod. Parm. 2888.
"Notes on the Flagellants in Italy in 1260," in Città del Vaticano, Biblioteca Apostolica Vaticana, MS. Ebr. 300, fols. 17v–18r.
Philosophical Miscellany, in Munich, Bayerische Staatsbibliotek, MS. Cod. Hebr. 327.
Prophets (With Deed of Sale), in Città del Vaticano, Biblioteca Apostolica Vaticana, MS. Ebr. 436.

Printed Sources

De Rossi, G. *R. Immanuelis Salomonis, Scholia in selecta loca Psalmorum*. Parma: Ex Imperiali Typographeo, 1806.
Immanuel of Rome. *The Book of Proverbs with the Commentary by Immanuel of Rome, Naples ca. 1487.* Edited by D. Goldstein. Jerusalem, Magnes Press, 1981.
———. *Maḥberoth Immanuel Haromi: Edited on the Basis of Early Manuscripts and Printed Editions with Introduction, Commentary, Source References, Appendices and Indices*. 2d ed. Edited by Dov Jarden. Jerusalem: Mossad Bialik, 1957.
Ravitsky, Israel. "R. Immanuel b. Shlomo: Commentary to the 'Song of Songs' Philosophical Division." Master's thesis, Hebrew University, 1970.
Tocci, Franco Michelini. *Il commento di Emanuele Romano al Capitolo I della Genesi*. Rome, Università di Roma, 1963.

Additional Primary Printed Sources

Al Harizi, Judah. *Taḥkemoni*. Edited by Y. Yahalom and N. Katsumata. Jerusalem: Ben Zvi Institute, 2010.
Alighieri, Dante. *The Divine Comedy: Inferno*. Edited by Robert Hollander and Jean Hollander. New York: Anchor Books, 2002.
———. "Epistle to Can Grande," Testo critico della Societa' Dantesca Italiana. Edited by Ermenegildo Pistelli. Florence: Societa' Dantesca Italiana, 1960,

§56, https://dante.princeton.edu/pdp/epistolae.html, accessed October 19, 2022.

Anatoli, Jacob. *Malmad ha-Talmidim*. Lyck: Mekize Nirdamim, 1866.

Anav, Benjamin b. Abraham. *Masa Gei Hizayon*. Riva di Trento, 1560; reprinted, Lemberg: M. Wolf, 1859.

Anav, Yeḥiel ben Yequtiel. *Ma'alot Ha-Middot*. Warsaw: Widow Levin-Epstein, 1887.

Aquinas, Thomas. *Summa Contra Gentiles*. Torino: Casa Editrice Marietti, 1934.

Aristotle. "*De Anima*." In *The Philosophy of Aristotle*, trans. J. Creed and A. Wardman. New York: Signet, 1963.

Azulai, Rabbi Hayim Joseph David. *Shem Ha-Gedolim*, part 2. Vilna: Y. R. Rom, 1852.

Ben Eleazar, Jacob. *Sipure ahavah shel Ya'aḳov ben El'azar*. Edited by Y. David. Tel Aviv: Ramot/Tel Aviv University, 1992/1993.

Ben Maimon, Moses. *Ethical Writings of Maimonides*. Translated by R. Weiss and C. Butterworth. New York: New York University Press, 1975.

Ben Maimon, Moses. *The Guide of the Perplexed*, 2 vols. Edited by S. Pines. Chicago: University of Chicago Press, 1963.

———. *Mishneh Torah: Hu Ha-Yad Ha-Ḥazaḳah*. Jerusalem: Mossad ha-Rav Kook, 1962.

Ben Yaakov, Isaac. *Otzar Ha-Sefarim*. Vilnius: Press of Widow & Sons Romm, 1857.

Bolaffio, Hezekiah David. *Ben Zekunim*. Leghorn: Sa'adon Press, 1793.

Francis, Immanuel. *Metek Sefatayim*. Cracow: Fisher Press, 1892.

Hillel ben Samuel. "First letter to Maestro Gaio." In *Hemdah Genuzah*, ed. Zebi Hirsch Edelmann. Königsberg: Gruber & Euphrat, 1856, 21a–22b.

Hillel of Verona. *Sefer Tagmule Ha-Nefesh: Book of the Rewards of the Soul*. Edited by Joseph Baruch Sermoneta. Jerusalem: Israel Academy of Sciences and Humanities, 1981.

———. *Vom Vollendung der Seele [Sefer tagmule ha-nefesh]*. Translated and introduced by Yossef Schwartz. Freiburg: Herder Verlag, 2009.

Humbert of Romans. *Treatise on Preaching* (*De eruditione praedictorum*). Translated by Dominican students of the Province of St. Joseph, and ed. Walter M. Conlon. Westminster, MD: Newman Press, 1951.

Ibn Pakuda, Baḥya. "Duties of the Heart" *(Hovot Ha-Levavot)*. Translated by Moses Hyamson. New York: Feldheim, 1925.

Ibn Saqbel, Solomon. "Ne'um Asher Ben Yehudah." In *Hebrew Poetry in Spain and Provence*, ed. H. Schirmann Jerusalem: Mossad Bialik, 1954, 554–565.

Ibn Tibbon, Samuel. *Commentary on Ecclesiastes (The Book of the Soul of Man)*. Edited by James T. Robinson. Jerusalem: World Union of Jewish Studies, 2016.

———. *Ma'amar Yikavu Ha-Mayim*. Pressburg: M. Bisliches, 1837.

———. *Perush ha-Millot ha-Zarot*. In *Maimonides, Moreh ha-Nevukhim* (appendix). Edited by Y. Even-Shemuel. Jerusalem: Mossad ha-Rav Kook, 1987.

Jellinek, Adolph. *Beit HaMidrash*. Jerusalem: Wahrmann, 1967.

Karo, Joseph. *Shulḥan Arukh*. Warsaw: Wolf Press, 1875.

Rieti, Moses. *Sefer Mikdash Me'at.* Vienna: J. Goldenthal, 1851.

Saadia Gaon. *Book of Beliefs and Opinions.* Translated by Samuel Rosenblatt. New Haven, CT: Yale University Press, 1989.

Sefer Jossipon. Edited by David Flusser. Jerusalem: Bialik Institute, 1978.

Tractate Gehinnom. In *Beit HaMidrash*, ed. A. Jellinek. Jerusalem: Wahrmann, 1967.

Secondary Sources

Abulafia, David. *Frederick II: A Medieval Emperor.* Oxford: Oxford University Press, 1988.

Adler, Joseph. "Immanuel of Rome." *Midstream* 48, no. 2 (2002): 16–19.

Alfie, Fabian. "Immanuel of Rome, Alias Manoello Giudeo: The Poetics of Jewish Identity in Fourteenth-Century Italy." *Italica* 75, no. 3 (1998): 307–329.

Allen, Grace. "Vernacular Encounters with Aristotle's *Politics* in Italy, 1260–1600." PhD diss., University of London, 2015.

Artman-Partock, Tali. "No (Jewish) Women in Hell." In *Language, Gender and Law in the Judaeo-Islamic Milieu*, ed. Zvi Stampfer and Amir Ashur. Leiden: Brill, 2020, 110–139.

Artom, Emanuel Menachem. "Precedenti biblici e talmudici del 'contrapasso.'" In *Dante e la Bibbia*, ed. G. Barblan. Florence: Olschki, 1988, 55–62.

Ascoli, Albert Russell. *Dante and the Making of a Modern Author.* Cambridge: Cambridge University Press, 2008.

Bacher, Wilhem. "Immanuel b. Salomo's Eben Bochan." *Monatsschrift fur Geschichte und Wissenschaft des Judenthums* 34 (1885): 241–257.

Barolini, Teodolinda. "*Inferno* 4: The Cultural Other." In *Commento Baroliniano*, Digital Dante. New York: Columbia University Libraries, 2018. https://digitaldante.columbia.edu/dante/divine-comedy/inferno/inferno-4/7.

Barthes, Roland. *Image, Music, Text.* London: Fontana Press, 1977.

Battistoni, Giorgio. *L'Inferno e il paradiso.* Florence: Giuntina, 2000.

Beit-Arie, Malachi. *Hebrew Codicology: Historical and Comparative Typology of Hebrew Medieval Codices.* Jerusalem: Israel Academy of Sciences and Humanities, 1981.

Ben Shalom, Ram. "The First Jewish Work on the Seven Deadly Sins and the Four Virtues." *Mediaeval Studies* 75 (2013): 205–270.

Ben Shaya, Shulamit. "The Laws of Nidda in the Halakhic Works of France from the School of Rashi Until the Semak." PhD diss., Bar Ilan University, 2016.

Berliner, Abraham. *Geschichte der Juden in Rom von der ältesten Zeit bis zur Gegenwart (2050 Jahre)*, vol. 2. Frankfurt am Main: J. Kauffmann Press, 1893.

Bernfeld, Shimon. "Rabbi Immanuel of Rome and His Maḥbarot." *Luach Ahiasaf* 4 (1896): 19–43.

Bettan, Israel. "The Sermons of Jacob Anatoli." *Hebrew Union College Annual* 11 (1936): 391–424.

Birnbaum, Eleazar. "Maḥzor Roma: The Cluj Manuscript Dated 5159 A.M./1399 C.E. and the Public Fast in Rome in 1321 C.E.," *Jewish Quarterly Review* 76, no. 2 (1985): 59–95.

Blumenthal, David. *Philosophic Mysticism: Studies in Rational Religion*. Ramat Gan: Bar Ilan University, 2006.

Bolzoni, Lina. *The Web of Images: Vernacular Preaching from Its Origins to St. Bernardino of Siena*. Aldershot: Ashgate, 2004.

Bos, Gerrit. *Maimonides, Medical Aphorisms, Hebrew Translation by R. Zeraḥyah Ben Isaac Ben She'altiel Ḥen*. Boston: Brill, 2020.

Boustan (Abusch), Ra'anan. "From Martyr to Mystic: 'The Story of the Ten Martyrs,' 'Hekhalot Rabbati,' and the Making of the 'Merkavah Mysticism.'" PhD diss., Princeton University, 2004.

Bregman, Dvora. *The Golden Way: The Hebrew Sonnet During the Renaissance and the Baroque*, trans. Ann Brener. Medieval and Renaissance Texts and Studies. Tempe: Arizona State University Press, 2006.

———. "On the Acceptance of the Sonnet in Hebrew Poetry." *Tarbiz* 56 (1986): 109–124.

Brener, Ann. "The Scroll of Love by Immanuel of Rome: A Hebrew Parody of Dante's Vita Nuova." *Prooftexts: A Journal of Jewish Literary History* 32, no. 2 (2012): 149–175.

———. "Stealing Wisdom: A Story of Books (and Book-Thieves) from Immanuel of Rome's Mahbarot." *Prooftexts* 28, no. 1 (2008): 1–27.

Cantor, Bernard. "Essay on Immanuel of Rome." Master's thesis, Hebrew Union College, Cincinnati, 1916.

Carsaniga, Giovanni. "Literary Realism in Italy: Verga, Capuana, and *Verismo*." In *The Cambridge Companion to the Italian Novel*, ed. Peter E. Bondanella and Andrea Ciccarelli. New York: Cambridge University Press, 2003, 61–74.

Cassuto, M. D. *Dante v'Immanuel ha-Romi*. Jerusalem: Mossad Bialik, 1965.

Cassuto, Umberto. "L'Elemento Italiano Nelle 'Mechabberoth' Di Immanuele Romano." *Rivista Israelitica* 2 (1905): 29–38, 109–115, 156–163, 199–205, 235–244.

Cassuto, Umberto, and Angel Sáenz-Badillos. "Immanuel (ben Solomon) of Rome." *Encyclopedia Judaica*, 2d ed., vol. 9, ed. Michael Berenbaum and Fred Skolnik. Detroit: Macmillan Reference USA, 2007, 740–741.

Chotzner, J. "Immanuel Di Romi, A Thirteenth Century Hebrew Poet and Novelist." *Jewish Quarterly Review* 4 (1892): 64–89.

Cohen, Shaye J. D. "Purity, Piety, and Polemic: Medieval Rabbinic Denunciations of 'Incorrect' Purification Practices." In *Women and Water: Menstruation in Jewish Life and Law*, ed. Rahel Wasserfall. Hanover, NH: Brandeis University Press, 1999, 82–100.

Corbett, George. *Dante's Christian Ethics: Purgatory and Its Moral Contexts*. Cambridge: Cambridge University Press, 2020.

Dahood, Mitchell, S. J. "Psalm 68 (68:1–36)." In *Psalms II: 51–100: Introduction, Translation, and Notes*. New Haven, CT: Anchor Yale Bible, 1968, 130–152.

Dales, Richard C. *Medieval Discussions of the Eternity of the World*. Leiden: E. J. Brill, 1990.

———. *The Problem of the Rational Soul in the Thirteenth Century*. Leiden: E. J. Brill, 1995.

Dan, Joseph. *Sifrut Ha-Musar ve-Ha Derush* [Hebrew Ethical and Homiletical Literature]. Jerusalem: Keter, 1975.

Davidson, Herbert. *Alfarabi, Avicenna, and Avveroes on Intellect: Their Cosmologies, Theories of Active Intellect, and Theories of Human Intellect.* Oxford: Oxford University Press, 1992.

De Souza, Igor H. *Rewriting Maimonides: Early Commentaries on the "The Guide of the Perplexed."* Berlin: De Gruyter, 2018.

Dean, Trevor. "The Rise of the Signori." In *Italy in the Central Middle Ages, 1000–1300*, ed. David Abulafia. Oxford: Oxford University Press, 2004, 104–124.

Debenedetti, Santorre. "I sonetti volgari di Immanuele Romano." *Studi filologici*. Milan: fol. Angeli, 1986, 9–19.

Decter, Jonathan P. *Dominion Built of Praise: Panegyric and Legitimacy Among Jews in the Medieval Mediterranean*. Philadelphia: University of Pennsylvania Press, 2018.

———. "Em Kol Hai: Virtues and Vices in Benjamin Ben Anav of Rome's Masa Gei Hizayon." In *Ot LeTova: Essays in Honor of Professor Tova Rosen*, ed. Eli Yassif, Haviva Ishay, and Uriah Kfir. Be'er Sheva: Ben Gurion University Press, 2012, 54–70.

Delcorno, Carlo. "Medieval Preaching in Italy (1200–1500)." In *The Sermon*, ed. Beverly Mayne Kienzle. Turnhout: Brepols, 2000, 449–560.

Dinari, Yedidya. "The Impurity Customs of the Menstruant Woman: Sources and Developments" [Hebrew]. *Tarbiz* 49 (1989): 302–324.

Drory, Rina. "The Maqama." In *The Literature of Al-Andalus*, ed. Maria Rosa Menocal, Raymond P. Scheindlin, and Michael Sells. Cambridge: Cambridge University Press, 2000, 190–211.

Eisen, Robert. *The Book of Job in Medieval Jewish Philosophy*. Oxford: Oxford University Press, 2004.

Elbaum, Jacob. "Women Who Entered Alive to Paradise" [Hebrew]. *Machanaim* 98 (1965): 129–131.

Elizur, Shulamit. *Hebrew Poetry in Spain in the Middle Ages*, vol. 3. Ramat Aviv: Open University of Israel, 2004.

Enelow, H. G. "Review of *Immanuel of Rome* by Shaul Tchernikovski." *Jewish Quarterly Review* 16, no. 2 (1925): 209–212.

Esposito, Anna. "Gli Ebrei a Roma Nella Seconda Metà Del '400 Attraverso i Protocolli Del Notaio Giovanni Angelo Amati." In *Aspetti e Problemi Della Presenza Ebraica Nell'Italia Centro-Settentrionale: (Secoli XIV e XV); [Presentazione Di Sofia Boesch Gajano]*. Rome: Università di Roma, 1983, 29–125.

———. *Un'altra Roma: Minoranze nazionali e comunità ebraiche tra Medioevo e Rinascimento*. Rome: Il Calamo, 1995, 31–125.

Fabiani, Giuseppe. *Gli Ebrei e il Monte di Pietá in Ascoli.* Ascoli-Piceno: Società Tipolithografica Editrice, 1942.

Fishelov, David. "From Dante's 'Inferno' to Immanuel's 'Tophet.'" *Bikkoret U'farshanut* 27 (1991): 19–42.

Fishkin, Dana W. "Letters of Loathing: Immanuel of Rome and Romance Epistolary." In *Medieval Jewish Romance*, ed. Caroline Gruenbaum and Annegret Oehme. Kalamazoo, MI: Arc Humanities Press, forthcoming.

———. "A Lifetime in Letters: New Evidence Concerning Immanuel of Rome's Timeline." *Jewish Quarterly Review* 112, no. 3 (2022): 406–433.

———. "The Sting of Satire: The Jesus Figure in Immanuel of Rome's Hell," *Prooftexts: A Journal of Jewish Literary History* 36 (2018): 357–384.

Foa, Simona. "Immanuel da Roma." In *Dizionario Biografico degli Italiani* 62 (2004), https://www.treccani.it/enciclopedia/immanuel-da-roma_%28Dizionario-Biografico%29/.

Fraenkel, Carlos. *From Maimonides to Samuel Ibn Tibbon: The Transformation of the Dalalat al-Hairin into the Moreh Nevukhim* [Hebrew]. Jerusalem: Hebrew University Magness Press, 2007.

———. "From Maimonides to Samuel Ibn Tibbon: Interpreting Judaism as a Philosophical Religion." In *The Cultures of Maimonideanism*, ed. James T. Robinson. Leiden: Brill, 2009, 177–211.

Freimann Aaron. "Jewish Scribes in Medieval Italy." In *Alexander Marx Jubilee Volume on the Occasion of His Seventieth Birthday.* New York: Jewish Theological Seminary of America, 1950, 231–342.

Freudenthal, Gad. "(AL-)Chemical Foundations for Cosmological Ideas: Ibn Sînâ on the Geology of an Eternal World, 1968." In *Physics, Cosmology and Astronomy, 1300–1700: Tension and Accommodation*, ed. Sabetai Unguru. Dordrecht: Kluwer Academic Publishers, 1991, 47–73.

———. "Maimonides' Philosophy of Science." In *The Cambridge Companion to Maimonides*, ed. Kenneth Seeskin. Cambridge: Cambridge University Press, 2005, 134–166.

Gaster, Moses. "Hebrew Visions of Hell and Paradise." In *Studies and Texts in Folklore, Magic, Mediaeval Romance, Hebrew Apocrypha and Samaritan Archaeology*, vol. 1, ed. Moses Gaster. London: Maggs, 1925–1928, 125–141.

Geiger, Abraham. "Daniel Loves Immanuel of Rome." In *Otzar Nehmad*, 3. Vienna: Y. Knepfelmakhers Bukhhandlung, 1856, 121–128.

Genot-Bismuth, Jacqueline. "La révolution prosodique d'Immanuel de Rome: Signification de l'introduction du sonnet." *Israel Oriental Studies* 11 (1991): 161–186.

Gluck, Andrew L. "The King in His Palace: Ibn Gabirol and Maimonides." *Jewish Quarterly Review* 91, nos. 3/4 (2001): 337–357.

Goldstein, David. "The Commentary of Immanuel Ben Solomon of Rome on Chapters I–X of Genesis: Introduction, Hebrew Text, Notes." PhD diss., University of London, 1966.

———. "Longevity, the Rainbow, and Immanuel of Rome." *Hebrew Union College Annual* 42 (1971): 243–244.

Gollancz, Hermann. *Tophet and Eden in Imitation of Dante's Inferno and Paradiso.* London: University of London Press, 1921.

Gordon, Martin. "The Rationalism of Jacob Anatoli." PhD diss., Yeshiva University, 1974.

Graetz, Heinrich. *History of the Jews*, vol. 4. Philadelphia: Jewish Publication Society of America, 1967.

Grassi, Ida. "Il primo periodo della 'Giovane Italia' nel Granducato di Toscana (1831–1834)." *Rivista storica del Risorgimento italiano* 2 (Turin, 1897): 904–947.

Güdemann, Moritz, and Abraham Shalom Friedberg. *Ha-Torah yeha-ḥayim bi-yeme ha-benayim be-Tsarfat ye-Ashkenaz*, vol. 2. Tel Aviv: Makhon le-firsumin, 1968.

Halbertal, Moshe. *Concealment and Revelation: Esotericism in Jewish Thought and Its Philosophical Implications*, trans. Jackie Feldman. Princeton, NJ: Princeton University Press, 2007.

Halper, Yehuda. "The Road to Hell Is Paved with Good Philosophers: The Ladder of Knowledge in Immanuel of Rome's *Hell and Heaven*." In *The Popularization of Philosophy in Medieval Islam, Judaism, and Christianity*, ed. Marieke Abram, Steven Harvey, and Lukas Muehlethaler. Turnhout: Brepols, 2022, 351–362.

Harris, Robert A. "The Reception of Ezekiel Among Twelfth-Century Northern French Rabbinic Exegetes." In *After Ezekiel: Essays on the Reception of a Difficult Prophet*, ed. Andrew Mein and Paul M. Joyce. New York: Clark International, 2011, 71–88.

Harvey, Steven. "Shem Tov Ibn Falaquera's Deot Ha-Philosophim." In *The Medieval Hebrew Encyclopedias of Science and Philosophy: Proceedings of the Bar-Ilan University Conference*, ed. Steven Harvey. Dordrecht: Springer, 2000, 211–247.

Havely, Nick. *Dante and the Franciscans: Poverty and the Papacy in the "Commedia."* Cambridge: Cambridge University Press, 2004.

Heinemann, Isaac. *Reasons for the Commandments in Jewish Thought: From the Bible to the Renaissance*, trans. Leonard Levin. Brookline, MA: Academic Studies Press, 2008.

Himmelfarb, Martha. *Tours of Hell: An Apocalyptic Form in Jewish and Christian Literature*. Philadelphia: University of Pennsylvania Press, 1983.

Hirschfeld, Hartwig. "Immanuel of Rome and Other Poets on the Jewish Creed." *Jewish Quarterly Review*, n.s. 5, no. 4 (1915): 529–542.

Hollander, Robert. *Dante's Epistle to Cangrande.* Recentiores: Later Latin Texts and Contexts. Ann Arbor: University of Michigan Press, 1993.

Hölter, Eva. "Dante's Long Road to the German Library: Literary Reception from Early Romanticism Until the Late Nineteenth Century." In *Dante in the Long Nineteenth Century: Nationality, Identity, and Appropriation*, ed. Aida Audeh and Nick Havely. Oxford: Oxford University Press, 2012, 225–247.

Horowitz, Elliot. "Between Cleanliness and Godliness: Aspects of Jewish Bathing in Medieval and Early Modern Times." In *Tov Elem: Memory, Community and Gender in Medieval and Early Modern Jewish Societies*, ed. Elisheva Baumgarten, Amnon Raz-Krakotzkin, and Roni Weinstein. Jerusalem: Hebrew University Press, 2011, 29–54.

Hourihane, Colum, ed. *Virtue and Vice: The Personifications in the Index of Christian Art*. Princeton, NJ: Princeton University Press, 2000.

Huss, Matti. "The Status of Fiction in the Hebrew Maqama: Judah Al-Harizi and Immanuel of Rome." *Tarbiz* 67, no. 3 (1998): 351–378.

Idel, Moshe. "Maimonides' 'The Guide of the Perplexed' and the Kabbalah." *Jewish History* 18, nos. 2/3 (2004): 197–226.

———. *R. Menahem Recanati: The Kabbalist*. Tel Aviv: Schocken Publishing House, 1998.

———. "The Study Program of R. Yoḥanan Alemanno." *Tarbiz* 48, nos. 3/4 (1979): 303–330.

Internullo, Dario. *Ai Margini Dei Giganti: La Vita Intelletuale Dei Romani Nel Trecento (1305–1367)*. Rome: Viella, 2016.

Ivry, Alfred. "The Image of Moses in Maimonides' Thought." In *Maimonides After 800 Years: Essays on Maimonides and His Influence*, ed. Jay M. Harris. Cambridge, MA: Harvard University Press, 2007, 113–134.

———. *Maimonides' "The Guide of the Perplexed": A Philosophical Guide*. Chicago: University of Chicago Press, 2016.

———. "Maimonides' Psychology." In *Maimonides and His Heritage*, ed. Idit Dobbs-Weinstein, Len Goodman, and James Allen. Albany: State University of New York Press, 2009, 51–60.

Iwry, Samuel. "Notes on Psalm 68." *Journal of Biblical Literature* 71 (1952): 161–165.

Jansen, Katherine. *Peace and Penance in Late Medieval Italy*. Princeton, NJ: Princeton University Press, 2020.

Johnston, Mark. "The Treatment of Speech in Medieval Ethical and Courtesy Literature." *Rhetorica: A Journal of the History of Rhetoric* 4, no. 1 (1986): 21–49.

Jones, P. J. "Communes and Despots: The City State in Late-Medieval Italy." *Transactions of the Royal Historical Society* 15 (1965): 71–96.

———. *The Italian City-State: From Commune to Signoria*. Oxford: Clarendon Press, 1997.

Jost, Isaac Markus. "Beitrag zur judischen Geschichte und Bibliographie" [A contribution to Jewish history and Bibliography]. *Wissenschaftliche Zeitschrift für Jüdische Theologie* 1 (1835): 362–366.

Kasher, Hanna, and Uri Melamed. "The Emergence of the Piyyut Yigdal Elohim Hay." In *ha-Tefilah be-Yiśra'el: hebeṭim ḥadashim* [Jewish Prayer: New Perspectives], ed. Uri Ehrlich. Beer Sheva: Ben Gurion University Press, 2016, 155–171.

Kaufmann, David. "Notizen I. Zu Immanuels Eben Bochan." *Monatsschrift fur Geschichte und Wissenschaft des Judenthums* 34 (1885): 335–336.

Kempshall, M. S. *The Common Good in Late Medieval Political Thought*. Oxford: Oxford University Press, 1999.

Kfir, Uriah. *A Matter of Geography: A New Perspective on Medieval Hebrew Poetry*. Leiden: Brill, 2018.

Kiron, Arthur. "Heralds of Duty: The Sephardic Italian Jewish Theological Seminary of Sabato Morais." *Jewish Quarterly Review* 105, no. 2 (2015): 206–249.

Klein Braslavy, Sarah. "Maimonides' Interpretations of Jacob's Dream About the Ladder" [Hebrew], *Bar-Ilan Year Book* 22–23 (1988): 329–349.

Krautheimer, Robert. *Rome: Profile of a City, 312–1308*. Princeton, NJ: Princeton University Press, 1980.

Kreisel, Haim (Howard). *Judaism as Philosophy: Studies in Maimonides and the Medieval Jewish Philosophers of Provence*. Boston: Academic Studies Press, 2015.

———. "Philosophical Interpretations of the Bible." In *The Cambridge History of Jewish Philosophy*, ed. Steven Nadler and T. M. Rudavsky. Cambridge: Cambridge University Press, 2009, 88–120.

———. "The Practical Intellect in the Philosophy of Maimonides." *Hebrew Union College Annual* 59 (1988): 189–215.

Kumhera, Glenn. *The Benefits of Peace: Private Peacemaking in Late Medieval Italy*. Brill, 2017.

Landman, Leo. *The Cantor: An Historic Perspective*. New York: Yeshiva University Press, 1972.

———. "Jewish Attitudes Toward Gambling." *Jewish Quarterly Review* 57 (1967): 1–21.

———. "Jewish Attitudes Toward Gambling II." *Jewish Quarterly Review* 58, no. 1 (1967): 34–62.

Lansing, Carol. "Gender and Civic Authority: Sexual Control in a Medieval Italian Town." *Journal of Social History* 31, no. 1 (1997): 33–59.

Leboff, Raphael Menahem. "Biur Tzurot HaOtiot" [Hebrew]. *Siynay* 152 (2018): 49–91.

Lesnick, Daniel. *Preaching in Medieval Florence: The Social World of Franciscan and Dominican Spirituality*. Athens: University of Georgia Press, 1989.

Levy, Isabelle. "Immanuel of Rome and Dante." In *Digital Dante*. New York: Columbia University Libraries, 2017. http://digitaldante.columbia.edu/history/immanuel-of-rome-and-dante-levy/.

———. "Immanuel of Rome's Bisbidis: An Italian Maqāma?" *Medieval Encounters* 27 (2021): 78–115.

———. *Jewish Literary Eros: Between Poetry and Prose in the Medieval Mediterranean*. Bloomington: Indiana University Press, 2022.

Liebes, Yehuda. *The Sin of Elisha*. Jerusalem: Hebrew University Press, 1990.

Little, Lester K. "Pride Goes Before Avarice: Social Change and the Vices in Latin Christendom." *American Historical Review* 76, no. 1 (1971): 16–49.

Lowin, Shari. *Arabic and Hebrew Love Poems in Al-Andalus*. New York: Routledge, 2014.

Luzzatto, Samuel David. *Appendice all'opera intitolata della letteratura italiana nella seconda meta del secolo XVIII di Camillo Ugoni.* 2d ed. Brescia: Nicolò Bettoni, 1868.

Malkiel, David. "Eros as Medium: Rereading Immanuel of Rome's Scroll of Desire." In *Donne Nella Storia Degli Ebrei d'Italia*, ed. Cristina Galasso and Michele Luzzati. Florence: Giuntina, 2007, 35–59.

———. "The Inheritance Tale in Immanuel of Rome's 'Mahbarot.'" *Prooftexts* 16, no. 2 (1996): 169–173.

Meacham (leBeit Yoreh), Tirzah. "An Abbreviated History of the Development of the Jewish Menstrual Laws." In *Women and Water: Menstruation in Jewish Life and Law*, ed. Rahel Wasserfall. Waltham, MA: Brandeis University Press, 2015, 22–39.

Melamed, Avraham. "Maimonides' Thirteen Principles: From Elite to Popular Culture." In *The Cultures of Maimonideanism: New Approaches to the History of Jewish Thought*, ed. James T. Robinson. Leiden: Brill, 2009, 171–190.

———. *The Philosopher-King in Medieval and Renaissance Jewish Political Thought.* Albany: SUNY Press, 2003.

Meyer, Michael A. "The Emergence of Jewish Historiography: Motives and Motifs." *History and Theory* 27, no. 4 (1988): 160–175.

———. "Two Persistent Tensions Within Wissenschaft Des Judentums." *Modern Judaism* 24, no. 2 (2004): 105–119.

Minnis, Alastair. *From Eden to Eternity: Creations of Paradise in the Later Middle Ages.* Philadelphia: University of Pennsylvania Press, 2015.

———. *Medieval Theory of Authorship.* Philadelphia: University of Pennsylvania Press, 2010.

Modona, Leonello. *Vita e opere di Immanuele Romano: Studio postumo del prof. Leonello Modona.* Florence: R. Bemporad and figlio, 1904.

Monbeck, Michael. *The Meaning of Blindness: Attitudes Toward Blindness and Blind People.* Bloomington: Indiana University Press, 1973.

Morais, Sabato, and Samuel David Luzzato. *Italian Hebrew Literature.* New York: Hermon Press, 1926.

Pagis, Dan. *Hiddush u-Masoret be-Shirat ha-Hol ha-Ivrit: Sefarad ve-Italia.* Jerusalem: Keter, 1976.

Palmer, James A. *The Virtues of Economy: Governance, Power, and Piety in Late Medieval Rome.* Ithaca, NY: Cornell University Press, 2019.

Paton, Bernadette. *Preaching Friars and the Civic Ethos: Siena, 1380–1480.* London: Centre for Medieval Studies, Queen Mary and Westfield College, University of London, 1992.

Pegoretti, Anna. "Early Reception Until 1481." In *The Cambridge Companion to Dante's "Commedia,"* ed. Zygmunt G. Barański and Simon Gilson. Cambridge: Cambridge University Press, 2018.

Pepi, Luciana, ed. *Il pungolo dei discepoli: Il sapere di un ebreo e Federico II.* Palermo: Officina di studi medievali: Fondazione Federico II, 2004.

Perry, Micha. "Jewish Heaven, Christian Hell: Rabbi Joshua Ben Levi's Vision of the Afterlife." *Journal of Medieval History* 43, no. 2 (2017): 212–227.

Poliakov, Leon. *Jewish Bankers and the Holy See: From the Thirteenth to the Seventeenth Century*. Translated by Miriam Kochan. London: Routledge and Kegan Paul, 1977.

Polliack, Meira. "Ezekiel 1 and Its Role in Subsequent Jewish Mystical Thought and Tradition." *European Judaism: A Journal for the New Europe* 32, no. 1 (1999): 70–78.

Rand, Michael. *Studies in the Medieval Hebrew Tradition of the Ḥarīrīan and Ḥarizian Maqama. Maḥberot Eitan ha-Ezraḥi*. Leiden: Brill, 2021, 94–134.

Rathaus, Ariel. "Poetiche della Scuola Ebraico-Italiana." *La Rassegna Mensile di Israel*, terza serie, 60/1–2 (1994): 189–226.

Ravenna, Gavriel Yitshak. "*Ma'alot Ha-Middot:* Its Character and Purposes." In *A Wise-hearted Woman: In Memoriam of Dr. Sara Fraenkel*, ed. Bracha Yaniv. Jerusalem: Art Plus, 2010, 25–52.

Ravitzky, Aviezer. "The Hypostasis of Supernal Wisdom in Jewish Philosophy of the Thirteenth Century." *Italia* 3 (1982): 7–38.

———. "On the Sources of Immanuel's Proverbs Commentary" [Hebrew]. *Qiryat Sefer* 56, no. 4 (1981): 735–738.

———. "Samuel Ibn Tibbon and the Esoteric Character of the 'The Guide of the Perplexed.' " *Association for Jewish Studies Review* 6 (1981): 87–123.

———. "The Thought of R. Zeraḥiah b. Isaac b. Shealtiel Ḥen and the Maimonidean-Tibbonian Philosophy in the 13th Century." PhD diss., Hebrew University, 1977.

Ravitsky, Israel. "R. Immanuel b. Shlomo: Commentary to the 'Song of Songs' Philosophical Division." Master's thesis, Hebrew University, 1970.

Rigo, Caterina. "The Be'urim on the Bible of R. Yehudah Romano: The Philosophical Method Which Comes Out of Them, Their Sources in the Jewish Philosophy and in the Christian Scholasticism." PhD diss., Hebrew University, 1996.

———. "Human Substance and Eternal Life in the Philosophy of Rabbi Judah Romano." *Jerusalem Studies in Jewish Thought* 14 (1998): 181–222.

———. "Un'antologia Filosofica di Yehuda Ben Mosheh Romano." *Italia* 10 (1993): 73–104.

Robinson, James T. "From Digression to Compilation: Samuel Ibn Tibbon and Immanuel of Rome on Genesis 1:11, 1:14, and 1:20." *Zutot* 4 (2006): 81–97.

———. "The Ibn Tibbon Family." In *Beerot Yitzchak: Studies in Memory of Isadore Twersky*, ed. Jay M. Harris. Cambridge, MA: Harvard University Press, 2005, 193–225.

———. "Maimonides, Samuel Ibn Tibbon, and the Construction of a Jewish Tradition of Philosophy." In *Maimonides After 800 Years: Essays on Maimonides and His Influence*, ed. Jay M. Harris. Cambridge, MA: Harvard University Center for Jewish Studies, 2007, 291–308.

———. "On or Above the Ladder? Maimonidean and Anti-Maimonidean Readings of Jacob's Ladder." In *Interpreting Maimonides: Critical Essays*, ed. C. Manekin and D. Davies. Cambridge: Cambridge University Press, 2018, 85–98.

———. *Samuel Ibn Tibbon's Commentary on Ecclesiastes: The Book of the Soul of Man*. Tübingen: Mohr Siebeck, 2007.

———. "The 'Secret of the Heavens' and the 'Secret of Number': Immanuel of Rome's Mathematical Supercommentaries on Abraham Ibn Ezra in His Commentary on Qohelet 5:7 and 7:27." *Aleph* 21, no. 2 (2021): 279–308.

———. "Soul and Intellect." In *The Cambridge History of Jewish Philosophy*, 524–58. Cambridge: Cambridge University Press, 2009.

———. "We Drink Only from the Master's Water: Maimonides and Maimonideanism in Southern France, 1200–1306." In *Studia Rosenthalia* 40 (2007–2008): 27–60.

Rogers, Matt. "Contextualizing Theories and Practices of Bricolage Research." *Qualitative Report* 17 (2012): 1–17.

Rollo-Koster, J. *Avignon and Its Papacy, 1309–1417: Popes, Institutions, and Society*. Lanham, MD: Rowman and Littlefield, 2015.

———. *Raiding Saint Peter: Empty Sees, Violence, and the Initiation of the Great Western Schism (1378)*. Leiden: Brill, 2008.

Rosen, Tova. "Metaphysics, Intertextuality and Gender in the Seventeenth Maḥberet of Immanuel Ha-Romi." In *Intertextuality in Literature and Culture: A Volume in Honor of Prof. Ziva Ben Porat*, ed. Michael Gluzman and Orly Lubin. Tel Aviv: Ha-Kibbutz Ha-Meukhad, 2012, 339–352.

Rosenthal, Murray. "The *Haqdamah* of Immanuel of Rome to the Book of Ruth." *Approaches to Judaism in Medieval Times* 2 (1985): 169–185.

Rosenwein, Barbara, and Lester Little. "Social Meaning in the Monastic and Mendicant Spiritualities." *Past and Present* 63 (1974): 4–32.

Rossi, Luca Carlo. "Una Ricomposta Tenzone (Autentica?) Fra Cina Da Pistoia e Bosone Da Gubbio." *Italia Medioevale e Umanistica* 31 (1988): 45–79.

Rossi, Luigi. "'Populus Firmanus Iterum Petit Hebreos': Fermo, Secoli XIV–XVI." In *La Presenza Ebraica Nelle Marche Secoli XIII–XX*, ed. Sergio Anselmi and Viviana Bonazzoli. Ancona: Quaderni monografici di Proposte e richerche, 1993, 53–83.

Roth, Cecil. "The Historical Background of Maḥberot Immanuel." In *Sefer Assaf*, ed. Moshe David Cassuto, Joseph Klausner, and Julius Gutmann. Jerusalem: Mossad Ha-Rav Kook, 1952, 444–458.

———. *The Jews in the World of the Renaissance*. Philadelphia: Jewish Publication Society of America, 1959.

———. "Lo sfondo storico della poesia di Immanuel Romano." *La Rassegna Mensile di Israel* 17, no. 10 (1951): 424–446.

———. "New Light on Dante's Circle." *Modern Language Review* 48, no. 1 (1953): 26–32.

Rubenstein, Jeffrey. "Elisha ben Abuya: Torah and the Sinful Sage." *Journal of Jewish Thought and Philosophy* 7, no. 2 (1997): 139–225.

Rudavsky, Tamar. *Jewish Philosophy in the Middle Ages: Science, Rationalism, and Religion*. Oxford: Oxford University Press, 2018.

Salah, Asher. "A Matter of Quotation: Dante and the Literary Identity of Jews in Italy." In *The Italia Judaica Jubilee Conference*, ed. Shlomo Simonsohn and Joseph Shatzmiller. Leiden: Brill, 2012, 167–197.

Schechterman, Devorah. "The Doctrine of Original Sin in Jewish Philosophy of the Thirteenth and Fourteenth Centuries." *Daat: A Journal of Jewish Philosophy and Kabbalah* 20 (1988): 65–90.

———. "The Philosophy of Immanuel of Rome in Light of His Commentary on the Book of Genesis" [Hebrew]. PhD diss., Hebrew University of Jerusalem, 1984.

Schirmann, Jefim. "The Function of the Hebrew Poet in Medieval Spain." *Jewish Social Studies* 16 (1954): 240–244.

Schwartz, Yossef. "Cultural Identity in Transmission: Language, Science, and the Medical Profession in Thirteenth-Century Italy." In *Entangled Histories: Knowledge, Authority, and Transmission in Thirteenth-Century Jewish Cultures*, ed. Elisheva Baumgarten, Ruth Mazo Karras, and Katelyn Mesler. Philadelphia: University of Pennsylvania Press, 2017, 181–203.

———. "Imagined Classrooms? Revisiting Hillel of Verona's Autobiographical Records." In *Schüler Und Meister*, ed. Andreas Speer and Thomas Jeschke. Berlin: W. de Gruyter, 2016, 483–502.

———. "Thirteenth Century Hebrew Psychological Discussion: The Role of Latin Sources in the Formation of Hebrew Aristotelianism." In *The Letter Before the Spirit: The Importance of Text Editions for the Study of the Reception of Aristotle*, ed. Aafke M.I. van Oppenraay and Resianne Fontaine. Leiden: Brill, 2012, 173–194.

Schwarzbaum, H. "The Prophet Elijah and R. Joshua b. Levi" [Hebrew]. *Yedaam* 7 (1960): 22–31.

Segal, Alan fol. *Life After Death*. New York: Doubleday, 2004.

Sermoneta, Giuseppe. "La Dottrina dell'intelletto e La 'fede Filosofica' di Jehudah e Immanuel Romano." *Studi Medievali* 6, no. 2 (1965): 3–78.

———. "Le Correnti Del Pensiero Ebraico Nell'Italia Medievale." *Italia Judaica* 1 (1983): 273–285.

———. "Prophecy in the Writings of R. Yehuda Romano." In *Studies in Medieval Jewish History and Literature*, vol. 21, ed. Isadore Twersky. Cambridge, MA: Harvard University Press, 1984, 337–374.

———. *Un glossario filosofico ebraico-italiano del XIII del secolo*. Rome: Edizioni dell'Ateneo, 1969.

Shaked, Guy. "Immanuel Romano: Una Nuova Biografia." In *Maḥberet Prima*. Milan: Aquilegia, 2002, 163–178.

Shatzmiller, Joseph. "The Papal Monarchy as Viewed by Medieval Jews." In *Italia Judaica: Gli Ebrei Nello Stato Pontificio Fino Al Ghetto (1555)*. Rome: Ministero Per I Beni Culturali e Ambientali Ufficio Centrale Per I Beni Archivisti, 1998, 30–42.

Shepkaru, Shmuel. "From After Death to Afterlife: Martyrdom and Its Recompense." *Association for Jewish Studies Review* 24, no. 1 (1999): 1–44.

Shiloah, Amnon. "A Passage from Immanuel Ha-Romi on the Science of Music." *Italia: Studi e Richerche Sulla Storia, La Cultura e La Letteratura Degli Ebrei D'Italia* 10 (1993): 9–18.

Shulvass, Moses Avigdor. *The Jews in the World of the Renaissance.* Translated by Elvin I. Kose. Leiden: Brill, 1973.

Silver, Daniel Jeremy. "Who Denounced the 'Moreh'?" *Jewish Quarterly Review* 57 (1967): 498–514.

Sonne, Isaiah. "The Influence of Ethical and Philosophic Literature on the Poetry of Immanuel of Rome." *Tarbiz* (1934): 324–340.

Sponsler, Claire. "In Transit: Theorizing Cultural Appropriation in Medieval Europe." *Journal of Medieval and Early Modern Studies* 32, no. 1 (2002): 17–40.

Steinschneider, Moritz. "Immanuel und Dante." *Hebraische Bibliographie* 11 (1871): 52–55.

———. *Introduction to Maḥbarot Immanuel.* Lemberg: Michael Wolff, 1870.

Stern, Gregg. "What Divided the Moderate Maimonidean Scholars of Southern France in 1305?" In *Be'erot Yitzhak: Studies in Memory of Isadore Twersky*, ed. Jay M. Harris. Cambridge, MA: Harvard University Press, 2005, 347–376.

Strauss, Leo. "How to Begin to Study *The Guide of the Perplexed.*" In *The Guide of the Perplexed*, trans. Shlomo Pines. Chicago: University of Chicago Press, 1963, xi–lvi.

Stroumsa, Sarah. "Citation Tradition: On Explicit and Hidden Citation in Judeo-Arabic Philosophical Literature." In *Masoret Ve-Shinui Ba-Tarbut Ha-'Arvit-Ha-Yehudit Shel Yeme-Ha-Benayim: Divre Ha-Ve'idah Ha-Shishit.* Ramat Gan: Bar Ilan University Press, 2000, 167–178.

Ta-Shma, Israel. "The Acceptance of Maimonides' Mishneh Torah in Italy." *Italia: Studi e Richerche Sulla Storia, La Cultura e La Letteratura Degli Ebrei D'Italia* 13/15 (2001): 79–90.

Tchernikovski, Saul. *Immanuel of Rome: A Monograph.* Berlin: Eshkol, 1925.

Theseider, E. Duprè. *Roma dal comune di popolo alla signoria pontificia.* Bologna: L. Cappelli, 1952.

Thompson, Augustine. *Revival Preachers and Politics in Thirteenth-Century Italy.* Eugene, OR: Wipf and Stock, 2010.

Thorndike, Lynn. *Michael Scot.* London: Nelson, 1965.

Tirosh-Samuelson, Hava. *Happiness in Premodern Judaism: Virtue, Knowledge, and Well-Being.* Cincinnati, OH: Hebrew Union College Press, 2003.

Toaff, Ariel. *The Jews in Umbria, Volume 1 (1245–1435): A Documentary History of the Jews in Italy.* Leiden: E. J. Brill, 1993.

Tocci, Franco Michelini. *Il commento di Emanuele Romano al Capitolo I della Genesi.* Rome: Centro di studi semitici, Istituto di studi del Vicino Oriente, 1963.

Tomei, Lucio. "Genesi e primi sviluppi del Comune nella Marca meridionale: Le vicende del Comune di Fermo dalle origini alla fine del periodo svevo (1268)." In *Società e cultura nella Marca meridionale tra alto e basso Medioevo: Atti del 4. Seminario di studi per personale direttivo e docente della scuola: Cupra Marittima, 27–31 ottobre 1992*. Grottamare: MediaPrint 2000, 1995.

Van Bekkum, Wout Jac. "The Emperor of Poets." *Studies in Hebrew Literature and Jewish Culture Presented to Albert van der Heide on the Occasion of His Sixty-Fifth Birthday*. Dordrecht: Springer, 2007, 203–212.

Vigueur, J. Maire, *Cavaliers et citoyens: Guerre, conflits et société dans l'Italie communale, XIIe–XIIIe siècles*. Paris: École des Hautes Études en Sciences Sociales, 2003.

Vogelstein, Hermann. *Rome*. Translated by Moses Hadas. Philadelphia: Jewish Publication Society of America, 1940.

Vogelstein, Hermann, and Paul Rieger, *Geschichte der Juden in Rom*. 2 vols. Berlin: Mayer & Müller, 1896.

Waley, Daniel. *The Papal State in the Thirteenth Century*. London: Macmillan Press, 1961.

Walfish, Barry. *Esther in Medieval Garb*. Albany: State University of New York Press, 1993.

Weiss, Dov. "Jews, Gentiles, and Gehinnom in Rabbinic Literature." In *Studies in Rabbinic Narratives*, vol. 1, ed. Jeffrey Rubenstein. Providence, RI: Brown University Press, 2021, 337–375.

Wickham, Christopher. "The 'Feudal Revolution' and the Origins of the Italian City Communes." *Transactions of the Royal Historical Society* 24 (2014): 29–55.

———. *Sleepwalking into a New World: The Emergence of Italian City Communes in the Twelfth Century*. Princeton, NJ: Princeton University Press, 2015.

Wolf, Johann Christopher. *Bibliotheca Hebraea*, vol. 1. Hamburg: Chr. Liebezeit e.a., 1715.

Wolfson, Harry Austryn. "The Classification of Sciences in Mediaeval Jewish Philosophy." In *Hebrew Union College Jubilee Volume (1875–1925)*. Cincinnati, OH: Hebrew Union College, 1925, 263–315.

Woolf, Jeffrey. "Saints in Tophet: Immanuel of Rome on the Suicides of Ashkenaz" [Hebrew]. *Peamim* 133–134 (2012): 11–25.

Zonta, Mauro. *La Filosofia Antica Nel Medioevo Ebraico: Le Traduzioni Ebraiche Medievali Dei Testi Filosofici Antichi*. Brescia: Paideia, 2002.

Zunz, Leopold. "Rom A. 1270 bis 1330." In *Wissenschaftliche Zeitschrift für Jüdische Theologie* 4 (1839): 193–198.

INDEX

Abulafia, Abraham, 40
adultery, civic disorder and, 111–12
afterlife, the, 2, 15–16, 74, 118, 127, 148; Christian vision of, 87; Jewish beliefs about, 85–86; light and radiance associated with, 92–95; Maimonidean tradition and, 40; Maimonides on crowns of blessed souls, 91–92; *maskilim* (intellectuals, knowers) and, 81; medieval theological debates about, 39; red heifer homily and, 75; retribution in, 66; Scholastic tradition and, 40; Torah commandments and, 79
agent (active) intellect, 3, 5, 31, 45, 46, 71; conjunction with, 151, 152; knowledge granted to human intellect by, 115; lack of virtue as obstacle to conjunction with, 77; love as symbol of conjunction with, 66; spiritual Eden as, 90; union of human intellect with, 60, 90, 148
Alatrino, Menaḥem ben Samuel, 25, 217n23
Albert the Great (Albertus Magnus), 43, 45, 70
Alemanno, Yoḥanan, 8
Al-Farabi, 97, 167
Al-Harizi, Judah, 3, 4, 30, 156, 209n8
allegory, 6, 34, 89, 101, 144–45, 157; in biblical commentaries, 7, 62, 80, 97, 115; favored by medieval rationalists, 42; four Edenic rivers of Genesis, 90–91, 94; heresy as sexual deviance, 134–35; in Immanuel's commentary on Psalms, 46–47, 48; parables and, 221n6; in red heifer homily, 72
allusion (*remez*), 48
Almagest (Ptolemy), 42, 215n6
Anatoli, Jacob, 42, 75
Anav, Benjamin b. Abraham, 62–63, 66, 81
Anav, Yeḥiel b. Yequtiel, 62, 66, 81
angels, 45, 49, 53, 143; in Dante's *Inferno*, 97; emanation into soul of man, 51; human–divine relationship and, 56; Jacob's ladder and, 94; punishment of sinners and, 111, 113; *Tofet*'s angels of death, 165, 183, 186
apostasy, 135
Aqiba, Rabbi, 145, 234n5
Arabic language, 41, 43, 62, 118, 206
argument (*argumentum*), 30, 33
Aristotelian philosophy/psychology, 3, 39–40, 42–45
Aristotle, 29, 39, 167; on actualization of mind, 45; concept of golden mean, 60; *De Anima*, 43; *Ethics*, 70; Immanuel's opinion of, 97, 236n47; *Liber de causis* attributed to, 43, 56; on three parts of the soul, 62, 229n11
Asaf (Levite musician), 143
ascetics (*perushim*), 61
auctoritates (authoritative texts), 9
authorship, 9, 25, 152, 244n60, 245n80
Averroes, 39, 42, 43
Avicenna (Ibn Sina), 43, 45, 52, 86, 97, 167
Avignon papacy, 12
Azulai, Hayyim Joseph David, 6

Baḥya Ibn Pakuda, 56, 62, 65, 76, 241n6
Barukh ben Neriah, 146, 177, 201
Behemoth (biblical creature), 147, 202
Beit-El family, 125
Benedict XI, Pope, 12
Ben Ha-Melekh V'Ha-Nazir (Ibn Hasdai), 66
Ben Zekunim (Bolaffio), 13
Bernardino da Siena, 131
Bernfeld, Shimon, 215n6
Be'urim (Judah Romano), 71, 150
biblical commentaries: of Recanati, 44; of Samuel Ibn Tibbon, 41, 55, 150; of Solomon ibn Gabirol, 66

biblical commentaries (*continued*), of Immanuel, 1, 2, 15, 99–101, 103; Aristotelian tradition and, 3, 39–40; I Chronicles, 95; Daniel, 5, 10, 75, 86, 99–100, 118; Deuteronomy, 66, 136, 175; earliest extant manuscript of, 22; Ecclesiastes, 6, 41, 126, 136, 137, 148, 175, 176, 202; Esther, 6, 12, 34, 108, 210n13; Exodus, 8, 105, 111–12, 131, 192, 212n28; Ezekiel, 95–96, 145; Hosea, 98; interplay with narrative poem, 88; Isaiah, 108, 120, 127, 191–92, 237n20; Jeremiah, 109, 132; Job, 31–32, 55–56, 71, 89, 117, 147, 202; I Kings, 237n17; Lamentations, 6, 136; Leviticus, 111; Maimonidean and Scholastic influences in, 42; Numbers, 15, 72, 73; philosophical exegesis and, 5–8; poetry and, 44, 57, 99, 127; prophecy and, 150–52; Ruth, 6, 210n13; I Samuel, 111; views on perfection in, 128. *See also* Genesis, Immanuel's commentaries on; Proverbs, Immanuel's commentary on; Psalms, Immanuel's commentaries on; Song of Songs, Immanuel's commentary on
Blumenthal, David, 223n30
Boccaccio, Giovanni, 12, 14, 15, 25
body, the, 24, 52, 53, 60, 73, 103, 143; binary of body and soul, 16, 34, 104, 142; death of, 46; duties of, 62; interdependence with soul, 50; perfection of, 50, 51, 104, 108, 113, 119, 151; physical punishment of sinning body, 106, 113; rational soul and, 45; red heifer homily and, 72; reunified with soul at resurrection, 78; soul imprisoned by, 56
Bolaffio, Hezekiah David, 13
Bosone da Gubbio, 12, 24–25
Bregman, Dvora, 14, 25, 214n56
Buber, Martin, 35, 220n72

Cangrande della Scala, 27, 225n55
Cassuto, M. D., 11, 216n15
celestial spheres, 49, 78, 88
Chotzner, Joseph, 14
Christians/Christianity, 2, 11, 37, 71, 100; Aristotle condemned in 1270s, 142; Christian theology, 42; intellectual elites, 57; mendicant preachers, 59, 60, 69–70; moralistic literature, 63; penitential movements, 2; polemics with Christian clergy, 119; rite of private confession, 119; Scholastics, 3, 42, 43, 54
Cicero, 30
Cino da Pistoia, 24–25, 216n15
Clement V, Pope, 12
Colonna family, 12
commandments, rationalization of, 76–81
Commentary on Kaddish and Kedushah (Judah Romano), 48–49
Commento di Emanuele Romano al Capitolo I della Genesi, Il (Tocci, 1963), 211n23
communal wellbeing, 16, 116, 123, 127, 128, 142; defined by Aristotle, 70; individual good inextricably linked to, 151; righteous individuals and, 104, 119. *See also* social order, maintenance of
Congregation Mikveh Israel (Philadelphia), 36
conjunction, 53–56, 57, 71, 97, 227n80; with agent intellect, 151, 152; teacher as agent intellect, 115; Tree of Life and, 118
Consolation for the Tribulations of Israel (Usque), 23
cosmos, three realms of, 57, 71

D'Ancona, Alessandro, 36
Daniel (biblical), 5
Daniel (guide figure), 4–5, 30, 87, 89, 96, 210n11; on the blind elders, 132, 172; on bonfire of rebellious souls, 165; on canopies for the righteous, 204–8; on cascading sin, 110, 111, 113; Immanuel charged with recording experiences of his journey, 152, 156, 208; introduction of, 164; possible throne in *Eden* for, 140, 196–97; praise for Immanuel's exegesis, 101, 118, 159–60, 190–92; redeemed by Immanuel's commentaries, 100; on repentant sinners, 126–27; on suicides, 179
Daniel b. Judah Ha-Dayan, 75
Daniel of Gubbio, 30
Dante Alighieri, 2, 4, 37, 126, 209–10n8; Cangrande della Scala as patron of, 27; death of (1321), 215n5; German Romantics' view of, 35–36; on God as primary cause, 225n55; Immanuel of Rome associated with, 10–12, 24–25; midlife status of, 23; sonnets of, 25–26. See also *Divine Comedy*
David, King, 15, 46, 47, 57, 111, 143–45, 200
De Anima (Aristotle), 43
Decameron (Boccaccio), 12
De eruditione praedictorum (Humbert of Romans), 70
Derashot (Immanuel's homilies), 8, 71–72
De Rossi, Giovanni, 210n13
didacticism, 2, 3, 5, 8
Divine Comedy (Dante), 2, 13, 27, 81, 88, 151; commentary tradition of, 9; German Romantics' view of, 35–36; Immanuel's awareness of, 22, 25; non-Christians barred from heaven, 141; *Paradiso*, 88, 100; *Purgatorio*, 88, 96, 100; reception in

Jewish circles, 97, 102. See also *Inferno*; *Maḥberet Ha-Tofet V'Ha-Eden*, influence of *Divine Comedy*
Doeg the Edomite, 125, 166, 180
Dominican order, 69, 70
Dominicus Gundissalinus, 43
dream visions, 56, 87
"Duties of the Heart" (Baḥya), 56, 62, 63, 65–66, 76, 241n6

Eden. See heaven (*Eden*)
Edut Hashem Ne'emanah (Solomon ben Moses), 216–17n20
Eftaḥ be-khinor ["I shall begin with a lyre"] (Maimonides), 64–65, 75, 157–58
Eight Chapters (Maimonides' commentary on *Pirkei Avot*), 41, 60, 61, 66; goal of human perfection and, 72; golden mean doctrine in, 76
Elijah (biblical prophet), 4, 145, 177
Elisha (biblical prophet), 145, 146, 177
Elisha ben Abuya, 145
eschatology, 16
ethics, 2, 5, 9, 59, 103, 114, 184, 199; in homiletical works, 159; human perfection and, 15; Jewish ethical works in Italy, 62–67; knowledge acquisition and, 58; Maimonidean tradition, 60–62; mendicant preachers and, 59
Ethics (Aristotle), 70
Even Boḥan (Immanuel of Rome), 8
Ezekiel (biblical prophet), 143, 145, 147, 149, 201
ezer elohi (divine aide), 150, 151, 158

fables, 30
Fermo, city of, 12–13, 26, 69
First Cause, God as, 3, 44, 49, 57, 141, 195, 225n55
Footprints database, 209n2
Francis, Immanuel, 13, 26
Franciscan order, 67, 69, 131, 159
Frederick II Hohenstaufen, 27, 28, 42

Galen, 96, 126, 167, 189, 236n45
gambling, 16, 131–32, 142, 242n9
Genesis, Immanuel's commentaries on, 7, 26, 45, 111, 211n23, 224n38; four Edenic rivers of, 90–91, 94, 147; Judah and Tamar affair, 112, 113, 194
Ghibellines. *See* Guelphs and Ghibellines
Giles of Rome, 70, 232n57
Goldschmidt, Eliezer, 214n52
Goldstein, David, 210n13, 211n23, 219n58, 243n43
Graetz, Heinrich, 21, 215n5
Greco-Arabic tradition, 39, 43, 86
Gubbio, town of, 26, 215n15
Guelphs and Ghibellines, 12, 27, 28, 213n46
Guide of the Perplexed, The (Maimonides), 6, 40–41, 97, 112, 211n24; communal order and, 104; ethics in, 61; Hebrew and Latin translations of, 221n10; Immanuel's biblical commentaries and, 50, 225n53; mysticism and, 44; on prophets, 146; rationalistic interpretation in, 93; on symbol of Jacob's ladder, 138

Hadrianic martyrs, 116, 120, 234n5, 240n72
halakhah, 40, 104, 109
Hayy ben Meqiz (Ibn Ezra), 86
heaven (*Eden*), 15, 16, 42, 43, 48, 128, 192–95; agent (active) intellect in, 45; biblical authors in, 142–49, 153–54, 200–204; biblical commentaries of Immanuel and, 9, 44, 46; as "bosom of Abraham," 65; canopies for righteous figures, 116–19, 143, 204–8; distinct regions of, 87; English translation of journey through, 192–208; grieving father character, 114–15, 197–200; guided tour of, 1, 4, 30; "highest heights" (*Ma'alot Ha-Eden*) of, 46, 126, 139, 143, 147, 152, 195, 197, 202, 206; Immanuel's choice of term, 89–90; Immanuel's place in, 13, 17; Jewish beliefs about, 85–86; ladder metaphor and, 93; literary persona of Immanuel in, 57; Maimonidean tradition and, 94–95; as physical space, 103, 127; rabbinic ideas about, 89; repentant sinners in, 126–27; righteous gentiles in, 141–42; thrones of Daniel and Judah, 139–41, 195–97. See also *Maḥberet Ha-Tofet V'Ha-Eden*
Hebrew language, 2, 8, 30, 37, 118, 206; grammars, 1, 8; Maimonides' works translated into, 41; sonnet form translated into, 12; writing about the soul in, 39
Heiman (Levite musician), 143, 194, 200
hell (*Tofet*), 10, 11, 74, 89, 128; abusive son character, 105–6, 177; adultery and murder as cascading sins, 110–13, 185–86; blind elders, 132–33, 172; corrupt communal leaders, 122–23, 153, 181; distinct regions of, 87, 123; doubting martyrs, 120–21, 185; Efratim, 129–31, 183–84; English translation of journey through, 164–92; false prophets, 125–26, 188–89; gamblers and suicides in, 131–32, 179; Ḥiel the Bethelite, 123–26, 179–81;

hell (*Tofet*) (*continued*) hypocritical cantors, 121–22, 177–78; hypocritical communal leaders, 122–23, 183; Immanuel's choice of term, 89–90; Jesus figure in, 134–36, 172–74; mental sinners, 120, 184–85; miserly brothers from Maresha, 136–39, 141, 174–77; as physical space, 103, 127; recasting of battle of Armaggedon, 99; *Sha'ar Shaleḥet* ("gate of dispersal") at entrance, 95; *shovavim* ("wicked ones"), 133–34, 182; tale of miser from Ancona, 107–9, 117, 170–72; voyeurs stalking ritual baths, 109, 182–83. See also *Maḥberet Ha-Tofet V'Ha-Eden*
heresy, 134–35
Hillel of Verona, 24, 43, 54–55, 57, 80
Hippocrates, 96, 126, 167, 189
History of the Jews (Graetz), 21
Holy Roman Empire, 27
homiletical literature, 69–70
Humbert of Romans, 70
Hunayn Ibn Ishaq, 66
Huss, Matti, 31
hypocrisy, Immanuel's condemnation of, 104, 119–27

Ibn Ezra, Abraham, 8, 42, 75, 137, 211n23, 212n28; *Hayy ben Meqiz*, 86; Psalm 68 praised by, 144
Ibn Gabirol, Solomon, 138, 230n34
Ibn Hasdai, 66
Ibn Saqbel, Solomon, 3
Ibn Tibbon, Judah, 62
Ibn Tibbon, Moses, 8, 15, 41–42, 77, 148
Ibn Tibbon, Samuel, 8, 41, 55, 58; *Commentary on Ecclesiastes*, 242n18, 245n84; *Ma'amar Yikavu Ha-Mayim*, 93, 245n84
Immanuel ben Solomon, 25
Immanuel of Rome: adaptation of Christian works with Jewish tradition, 81–82; as author and authority, 9–10, 89, 155–58; citing of own commentaries, 9, 16–17; Dante associated with, 1, 10–12, 24–25; ethics in, 15; Hebrew grammatical works, 8, 26; homiletical collection (*derashot*), 8, 71–72; hybridity of, 102; on immortality, 46; intertextual methodology of, 2, 5, 16, 17; Italian historical context and, 12–13; Italian sonnets of, 12, 26, 213n46; love poetry of, 1, 13–14; Maimonideanism in, 43–46; Maimonidean tradition and, 7, 16, 116; as *maskil* (intellectual), 10, 152; philosophical exegesis of, 5–8, 37; plagiaristic citation methods of, 8, 43–44, 71, 212n25; range of works by, 1; sonnet form translated into Hebrew by, 12; teaching role of, 135; theory of conjunction, 53–56, 78
Immanuel of Rome, biography / personal life of, 4, 14–15, 21–22, 161; dates of life and death, 22–26, 36, 215n5, 216n9; exile from Rome, 33–34, 219n64; location of residence, 26–27; loss of friend or lover, 24, 30, 64, 140, 216n15; scholars' imagining of, 35–37
"Immanuel studies," 35
immortality, 2, 103, 147; of Adam, 45; authorship and, 152, 154, 157; body–soul binary and, 50; knowledge/wisdom and, 46, 94; perdurance (immortality of the soul), 61; prayer for immortality at end of *Maḥberet Ha-Tofet V'Ha-Eden*, 99–101; rational intellect and, 129; Tree of Life as symbol of, 115, 118
Inferno (Dante), 88, 95, 100; Limbo (first circle of hell), 96, 97, 141; sins of lust in second circle, 97; story of Francesca and Paolo, 11, 98. See also *Divine Comedy*
Innocent IV, Pope, 27
intellect, 23, 86; hierarchy of providence and, 55; material, 46, 223n31, 224n41; separate intellects, 44–45, 52, 78; universal, 43. *See also* agent (active) intellect
Isaac ben Menaḥem, 31–32
Isaiah (biblical prophet), 143, 146, 147, 149, 178, 191, 193
Islamic world, 39
Israelites, 46, 73, 172
Italian language, 10, 37, 118
Italian peninsula, 16, 21, 57; communal government in, 28, 68, 69, 70; idealization of late medieval Italy, 35; Jewish presence in, 2, 39; locations associated with Immanuel, 26; Maimonidean tradition in, 40–43; mendicant orders in, 69–70; nationalism of Risorgimento, 36; Neoplatonic philosophy in, 3; political turmoil and violence in, 12, 27–29, 67–69; rationalist Jewish scholarship in, 222n10
Ivry, Alfred, 221n6, 227n80

Jacob ben Eleazar, 3
Jacob ben Makhir, 215n6
Jacob's ladder, 94, 138
Jael, Daniel, 25, 216–17n20
Jarden, Dov, 211n24, 218n50
Jedutun (Levite musician), 143
Jeremiah (biblical prophet), 143, 145, 146, 149, 177, 193, 194
Jewish studies, academic, 35
Jewish Theological Seminary (New York), 36

Jews, 71, 80; Ashkenazic, 40; French, 41; German, 11, 36; intellectual elites, 57
Jews, Italian, 2, 37, 41, 149; ethics among, 62–67; migration out of Rome, 12–13; papacy and, 27–28, 218n37
Joseph (biblical), 143, 148–49
Joshua (biblical), 125, 140, 177, 193, 202–3
Joshua ben Levi, Rabbi, 4
Jossipon, 26, 217n26
Judah Romano, 43–44, 48, 76, 77, 152, 210n11; *Be'urim*, 71, 150; canopy reserved for, 118; commentaries on Proverbs, 139, 243n43; *Commentary on Kaddish and Kedushah*, 48–49; familial relationship with Immanuel, 139, 140, 243n44; as the "lion," 15; prophecy and, 149; throne in *Eden* for, 139–40, 195–96; on Torah commandments and conjunction, 78; translations of Scholastic philosophy, 57
Judaism, 35, 119; conversion to, 157; netherworld journey genre and, 11

kabbalism, 44, 71, 80
Karo, Rabbi Joseph, 1, 13, 160
Kimḥi, Rabbi David, 15, 46, 47–48, 144, 145, 147, 149, 200
king's palace, image of, 138, 139, 177
Kitim (Noahide tribe), Immanuel's descent from, 26, 217n26
knowledge acquisition, 46, 58, 132, 157; agent intellect and, 115; health of body and soul in relation to, 60; immortality and, 94; ladder metaphor and, 93

language, 5, 6
Latin language, 9, 10, 12, 39, 43
Leviathan (biblical monster), 147, 202
Liber de Anima (Dominicus Gundissalinus), 43
Liber de causis, 43, 56
Liber Sextus Naturalium (Avicenna), 43
literary persona, of Immanuel, 17, 95, 116, 128, 136; biblical authors and, 142–43; Daniel as guide figure and, 5, 100; established as authoritative messenger, 2, 81; Mosaic role of, 139, 147, 149, 152; punishment of sinners and, 124; quest for knowledge and, 151; unnamed patron as foil to, 31
love poetry, 1, 13–14
Luzzato, Samuel David, 36

Ma'alot Ha-Middot (Yeḥiel b. Yequtiel Anav, ca. 1287), 62
Ma'amar Yikavu Ha-Mayim (Samuel Ibn Tibbon), 93, 245n84
maḥberet [pl. *maḥbarot*] (mixed prose and verse), 3, 4, 5; biblical interpretation and, 106; as didactic text, 16; interplay with exegetical works, 85, 142; on teaching, 10
Maḥberet Ha-Tofet V'Ha-Eden (Immanuel of Rome), 2, 8, 17, 40, 140, 151, 165; as allegorical tale, 157; body–soul binary in, 50; on communal order and individual sin, 105, 119; conjunction theory and, 54; Daniel as prophetic guide figure in, 4–5; dating of, 23, 215n5; on divine reward and punishment, 53; as dream vision, 56; English translation of, 163–208; historicist readings disconnected from, 116; Immanuel's stage of life and, 23–24; on individual and communal good, 71; Jewish literary predecessors of, 85–87; literary structure of, 87–89; *maskil* concept in, 80–81; as morality tale, 103; philosophical commentaries and, 104, 129; philosophical underpinnings of, 103; printing history of, 13, 214n52; Psalm 68 exegesis in, 15; social context and ethical imperative of, 59; as social critique, 159–60. *See also* heaven (*Eden*); hell (*Tofet*)
Maḥberet Ha-Tofet V'Ha-Eden, influence of *Divine Comedy*, 10–12, 16, 85, 87, 88–89, 101–2; adulterous women as doves, 97–99, 168; biblical commentaries and, 158, 161; bonfire of the rebellious, 96–97, 165–67; differences between the two works, 160; gate image and, 95–96; journey's end with prayer for immortality, 99–101; reference to the stars, 99–100, 208; as source of language and imagery, 94
Maḥberet Ha-Tofet V'Ha-Eden, terminology in, 89–91; adulterous women, 97–99; bonfire of the rebellious, 96–97; crowns, 91–92; gate, 95–96; ladder (Jacob's ladder), 93–95; light and radiance, 92–93
Maḥberot Immanuel [Immanuel's Compositions] (Immanuel of Rome), 2, 8, 15; biographical elements in, 21, 33–35, 64; dating of, 22–23; ethical context and, 64–66; Fermo setting of, 12–13; influence of different literary cultures in, 31; Italian literary forms/themes in, 12; Purim feaset in, 13, 26, 33; realism of, 25, 26; reception history of, 13–17, 214nn51–52; regional locales mentioned in, 67; reputational concerns of Immanuel and, 155–56; on role of poet and patron, 29–33, 64, 218n42; as "secular" poetry, 1; structure and influences of, 3–4, 155, 157; two introductions, 15, 30, 31, 32–33, 218n46; verisimilitude in, 12, 13, 16, 26, 136, 142, 160; *Wissenschaft*-era scholars and, 36

Maḥzor Roma (holiday prayerbook for Roman rite), 23
Maimonidean tradition, 5, 7, 89, 94; allegorical lexicon of, 6; binary of body and soul, 16; ethics, 60–62; exegetical methodology of Judah Romano and, 150; Immanuel and, 7, 16, 43–46, 155; in Italy, 40–43; "perfection of the body" and, 113; "welfare of the soul," 129
Maimonides, 6, 8, 52, 57–58, 62, 142, 211n24, 228n88; on afterlife as purely spiritual realm, 86; on animal sacrifices, 238n34; on biblical Moses, 139; on communal order and knowledge, 103–4; creation scheme of, 48; on divine will and prophecy, 146; as the "eagle," 15; *Eftaḥ be-khinor* (thirteen principles of faith), 64–65, 75; esoteric-exoteric paradigm of, 77–78; on fitness of communal leaders, 123; focus on perfection, 151; on hearing the truth, 141; on immortality of the soul, 45–46; king's palace symbol and, 138; on levels of perfection, 53–54, 227n77; *Medical Aphorisms*, 236n45; on parables, 221n6; paradigm of parabolic narrative, 73; on purpose of human existence, 129; rationalist orientation of, 39, 93; on "righteous gentiles" and "gentile sages," 141, 243n52; on separate intellects, 44–45; social contract and, 104–19. See also *Guide of the Perplexed, The*; *Mishneh Torah*
Malmad ha-Talmidim ["The Students' Goad"] (Anatoli), 42
maqama genre, 3, 209n3
Marche region (Le Marche), 12, 13, 27, 28, 29; Roman Jewish businessmen in, 67; tale of miserly brothers from Maresha, 136–39
marriage, defense of, 112–13
Masa Gei Hizayon (Benjamin b. Abraham Anav), 62–63
maskilim (intellectuals, knowers), 80, 94; biblical commentaries and, 100; canopies for, 117, 118; Immanuel as *maskil*, 10, 152
mathematics, 52, 227n72
Mazzini, Giuseppe, 36
Medical Aphorisms [*Pirke Moshe*] (Maimonides), 236n45
Mehokek, Leib, 214n52
metaphysics, 40, 52
Metatron (angel), 8
Metek Sefatayim (Francis), 13
Michael, archangel, 116, 192, 203
midrashic literature, 86, 92
Mikdash Me'at (Rieti), 13
Miriam (biblical), 130, 177
Mishnah, 125, 131, 194, 206; Mishnah Avot, 137, 146
Mishneh Torah (Maimonides), 40, 44, 137; on crowns of blessed souls, 91–92; Hilkhot De'ot, 61, 76
Mivḥar Ha-Peninim (Ibn Gabirol), 66, 230n34
Morais, Sabato, 36
Morse, Ruth, 59
Moses (biblical), 54, 60, 96, 176, 203, 236n45; authorship of book of Job attributed to, 147, 202, 245n80; Immanuel's persona linked to, 139, 147, 149, 152, 156; initiation scenes in Exodus, 156; relationship with Joshua, 140
Moses ben Solomon of Salerno, 222n10
musicians, 143
Musrei Ha-Filosofim (Hunayn Ibn Ishaq), 66

Nahmanides, 66, 67, 238n34
Neoplatonic philosophy, 3, 42, 43; intelligibles in the divine being, 49; Judah Romano and, 48; *Liber de causis* and, 56
Neum Asher Ben Yehudah (Ibn Saqbel), 3
Noahide laws, 243n52

omniscient narrative mode, 121
oratory, 29–30
Orsini family, 12
Orvieto, town of, 26, 67, 119, 207

Pagis, Dan, 209n7
papacy, 12, 27–28
parables, 1, 6, 80, 90, 221n6
patronage, 29–33
penitence/penance/repentance, 17, 56, 59, 89, 161; Franciscan order and, 67; spiritual guides and, 159
Pentateuch, 6, 42, 211n23
perfection, human, 15, 72, 77, 151; of the body, 50, 51, 104, 108, 113; ethics and, 58, 61; moral perfection as rare possibility, 60; Torah commandments and, 128
perfection, intellectual, 55, 100; actions in relation to, 77; communal order and, 123, 158; failure to achieve, 62, 138, 160; immortality of the soul and, 46; Maimoidean ethics and, 60, 103–4, 151; material hindrances to, 23; physical perfection distinguished from, 50, 153; supremacy of, 160
Perugia, city of, 26
Perugian benefactor, canopy in Eden for, 116–17, 204–5

Petrarch, 25
philosophical commentaries, 6, 73, 102, 104, 109
Pietro Alighieri, 9
pikadon (deposit), 130, 242n6
Pirkei Avot (Mishnaic tractate), 41, 60, 71
Plato, 96, 167, 236n47
Platonic philosophy, 48
poetry: Hebrew, 2, 14, 27; Italian, 1, 11; Provençal, 12, 26
prophecy, 71, 150–52, 154, 189
prostitution, 112, 177
Provençal language, 118
Provence, 39, 57
Proverbs, Immanuel's commentary on, 5–6, 32, 51, 66, 132, 210n13, 211n24, 219n58; on abuse of parents, 105; on adulterous women, 97; on afterlife and agent intellect, 148; on allegory, 158; "beast" as animal soul (*nefesh behemit*), 62; on biblical commentary and knowledge acquisition, 157; on cascading actions, 110; on cautious approach to acquiring knowledge, 145, 192; on communal government, 28; on crowns of the righteous, 92; earliest extant dated copy of, 71; on generosity and bestowing of knowledge, 115; goal of perfection and, 72; on good governance, 123; on hypocrisy, 119, 121, 122; on immortality of the righteous, 150–51; on intrinsic value of wisdom, 134; on Judah Romano, 139; on lending of money, 34; *maḥberet* affinities with, 135; punitive afterlife in hell, 95; reference to Ḥiel the Bethelite, 124–25; on sin and punishment, 108–9, 130; social disorder and violence in Italy and, 68–69; on speech acts, 106; tale of ant and fool, 88; on true nature of the soul, 86; Woman of Valor (*Eshet Ḥayil*) passages, 54, 147, 150, 202
Psalm 68, Immanuel's commentary on, 15, 40, 46–53; body-soul binary and, 50–51; on canopies for the righteous, 116, 239n49; divine creation of universe in, 49; emanation (verse 15), 51–52; Israel's victory at Armageddon, 98–99; King David and, 144–45; uniqueness of God (verse 19), 52–53
Psalms, Immanuel's commentaries on, 5, 44, 76, 78–79, 92, 228n88; on Adam's expulsion from Eden, 132–33; dove symbol, 98; eternity of the world as false supposition, 142; on *ezer elohi* (divine aide), 151; on hypocrisy, 121–22; King David and, 143–44, 200; on ladder of wisdom, 138; on luminescence of the righteous, 93; meat-in-cauldron image, 99; on rage of wicked souls, 127; on sin and punishment, 108, 155
Ptolemy, 42, 215n6

rabbinic tradition, 86, 87, 105, 160
Rashi, 42, 75, 137, 211n23
rationalism, 44, 81, 142, 153
Ravitzky, Aviezer, 211n24
realism, 5, 65, 153; Boccaccio and, 15, 25; eschatological, 16; in interplay of *maḥberet* and commentaries, 129; in medieval Romance works, 31
Recanati, Menaḥem, 44
red heifer ceremony (*parah adumah*), homily on, 8, 15, 60, 72, 73–76, 146, 159
remez/remizah (hints) technique, 209n7
Remigio de' Girolami, 70
rhetoric, 29–30
Rieti, Moses, 13, 26
Risorgimento, 36
Robert of Anjou, King, 22
Robinson, James, 211n25
Romance literature, as influence on Immanuel, 31, 151, 161
Rome, city of, 26, 29; expulsion of Jews (1320s), 119; migration of Jews out of, 12–13, 27; papacy and, 12, 28
Roth, Cecil, 14, 210n11, 216n9
Rudavsky, Tamar, 221n6

Saadia Gaon, 93
saints, 16, 87, 127, 128
Samuel ben Judah, 215n6
Sar [*Ha-Sar*] (The Nobleman), 3, 30, 33, 156, 218n50
Schechterman, Devorah, 211n23, 218n50
Schmeltzer, Lipa, 21
Scholasticism, 3, 40, 42, 43, 54, 57; Hebrew translations of Scholastic texts, 59; homiletical sermons and, 69–70
Scot, Michael, 42
Sefer Ha-Meshalim (Jacob ben Eleazar), 3
Sefer Taḥkemoni (Al-Harizi), 156
Sefer Tekhunah, 23, 215n6
semiotics, 6
Sermoneta, Giuseppe, 44
sexual deviance, 134, 135
Sha'ar Ha-Gemul (Nahmanides), 66
Sh'arei Etz Hayim (Benjamin b. Abraham Anav), 63
shibuts (integration) technique, 3, 209n7
Shoshan Emek Ayumah prayer, 121, 178

Shulḥan Arukh (Karo, 1565), 1, 2, 13
Shulvass, Moses, 34
Sicily, Kingdom of, 27
sin, 2, 5, 66, 81, 103, 125; cascading, 110–13; civic/communal disorder and, 69, 70, 106, 108–13, 128; interplay of physical and spiritual sins, 134–35; *Maḥberet Ha-Tofet V'Ha-Eden* as reflection on, 56, 159; mental, 120, 122; punishment of, 15, 74, 98, 130; red heifer rite as allegory of, 72; transgressions of the mind as, 129
sirventese lyrical form, 12
Soave, Moses, 36
social order, maintenance of, 16, 104, 115, 127, 153; individual and communal good, 70–71, 142; observance of the commandments and, 128; sin extending beyond family to, 106, 110. *See also* communal wellbeing
Solomon, King, 143, 145, 147–48, 182, 192, 201–2, 245n69
Solomon ben Moses, 163, 217n20
Song of Songs, Immanuel's commentary on, 6, 23, 42, 45, 202, 215n5, 223n31, 224n36; allegorical readings, 76–77, 80, 144–45; commandments and, 77; on crowns of the righteous, 92; gloss on nut garden, 61; King Solomon and, 148; ladder of wisdom, 94; on love as symbol of conjunction, 66; on luminescence of the righteous, 93; on study of applied and divine sciences, 52, 226–27n71
soul, 50, 56, 75, 224n41; debates over nature of, 57; immortality of, 43, 46, 60, 61, 93, 127; impure, 73; rational intellect and, 129; red heifer as symbol of, 73; reincarnation of, 97; souls of celestial spheres, 78; three parts of, 45; unknowable true nature of, 86, 142
Spain, 39
Steinschneider, Moritz, 7
Strauss, Leo, 221n6
Stroumsa, Sarah, 211n25
suicide, 16, 131, 142
Summa Contra Gentiles (Aquinas), 112

Tabernacle, 107, 140
Tagmule Ha-Nefesh [On the Recompense of the Soul] (Hillel of Verona), 43, 54–55, 80
Tahan, Ilana, 215n5
Taḥkemoni (Al-Harizi), 3, 4, 30
Tale of Hell and Heaven. See *Maḥberet Ha-Tofet V'Ha-Eden*
Talmud, 35, 80, 97; abuse of parents condemned in, 105; Menahot, 237n17; on salvation in afterlife, 86, 234nn4–5; tale of Rabbie Meir and Bruriah, 130
Targums (Aramaic translations of the Bible), 6, 86, 206
Tchernikovski, Shaul, 215n5
Tempier, Etienne, 57
Thomas Aquinas, 43, 45, 70, 112, 113
three realms (celestial, supernal, earthly), 57, 71
Three Treatises on the Intellect (Averroes), 43
Tibbonide school, 41–42, 60, 79, 103, 129
Tikkun Middot Ha-nefesh (Ibn Gabirol), 66
Tocci, Franco Michelini, 211n23
Tofet. *See* hell (*Tofet*)
Torah, 42, 46, 51, 58, 64, 74, 148, 158; commandments of, 76–81, 128; conjunction and, 78; granted at Mount Sinai, 144; Immanuel's biblical commentaries and, 100–101, 191; shunned in favor of physical pleasure, 134; Torah study for material purposes, 133–34, 173, 182
Torah study, 41
Tosefta, 243n52
Tree of Life, 94, 115, 118, 206
Truth and Convention in the Middle Ages (Morse), 59

Umbria, 12, 13, 26; Franciscan movement in, 67; mendicant preachers in, 59; as part of papal state, 28; as region of importance to Immanuel, 27, 29
"unicity theory," 43
Usque, Samuel, 23

Virgil, 10, 88, 141
virtue, individual and communal, 70–71, 232n57

Walfish, Barry, 210n13
wine from days of creation, homily on, 8, 15, 71, 80, 159
Wissenschaft des Judentums movement, 35, 36
Wolf, Johann Christian, 215n5

Yigdal Elohim ḥai ["Exalted be the living God"] (hymn), 65, 75
Yom Kippur, 121, 122, 178, 183
Yom Kippur oration, 76

Zangwill, Israel, 35, 220n72
Zeraḥiah Ḥen of Barcelona, 24, 40, 211n24
Zunz, Leopold, 7

www.ingramcontent.com/pod-product-compliance
Lightning Source LLC
Chambersburg PA
CBHW021349300426
44114CB00012B/1138
9780814350355